William A. (William Addison) Phillips

Labor, Land and Law

A Search for the Missing Wealth of the Working Poor

William A. (William Addison) Phillips

Labor, Land and Law
A Search for the Missing Wealth of the Working Poor

ISBN/EAN: 9783744666343

Printed in Europe, USA, Canada, Australia, Japan

Cover: Foto ©Suzi / pixelio.de

More available books at **www.hansebooks.com**

LABOR, LAND AND LAW

A SEARCH FOR THE MISSING WEALTH

OF THE WORKING POOR

BY

WILLIAM A. PHILLIPS

MEMBER COMMITTEE ON PUBLIC LANDS, FORTY-THIRD CONGRESS, AND ON BANKING AND CURRENCY, FORTY-FIFTH CONGRESS

NEW YORK
CHARLES SCRIBNER'S SONS
1886

TO

MY DEAR WIFE

ANNA B. S. PHILLIPS

WHO HAS VERY MATERIALLY ASSISTED IN

THE PREPARATION OF THIS WORK, IT

IS AFFECTIONATELY INSCRIBED

BY THE AUTHOR

AUTHOR'S NOTE.

SINCE this work was first undertaken questions involving the rights of workingmen and the forms of landholding have steadily grown in general interest. For the better study of these subjects the facts herewith submitted have been collated. Care has been taken to present in as readable shape as possible, a large part of what is known of the various kinds of land tenure among men. The effects of the different forms of landholding on the industrial interests, have been traced, and, also, the origin and growth of many of those individual and family rights which have left their marks on our social system. Slavery, vassalage, serfdom, and the various modes of employing and remunerating or robbing labor have been placed before the reader, and the change from master workman to capitalist employer, the organization of capital, the formation and growth of guilds, trades unions and labor societies, considered.

A long experience amidst the wonderful developments of the Western states, and the privilege of having taken part in the public discussion and consideration of great economic questions, while they have furnished an interesting field for observation and study, have also tended to modify previous opinions and mould the views which are here presented. The works of many other writers on the subject have been referred to and discussed. The purpose being to throw all possible light on the subject, their books have been analysed in all frankness. It is the hope of the writer that the references to them may not be considered unfair or uncourteous.

WASHINGTON, D. C., *December*, 1885.

CONTENTS.

CHAPTER VII.

THE LAND SYSTEM OF MODERN EUROPE.

CHAPTER VIII.

THE LAND SYSTEM OF THE BRITISH EMPIRE.

CHAPTER IX.

THE ABORIGINAL AMERICAN SYSTEM OF LAND TENURE.

CHAPTER X.

ERA OF EUROPEAN DISCOVERY AND SETTLEMENT IN AMERICA—RIGHT OF DISCOVERY—RIGHT OF CONQUEST.

CHAPTER XI.

HISTORY OF THE LAND POLITY OF THE UNITED STATES.

CHAPTER XIII.

SHADOWS OF THE COMING AMERICAN ARISTOCRACY.

CHAPTER XIV.

REMEDIES.

LABOR, LAND AND LAW.

INTRODUCTORY CHAPTER.

Raising the wind—The relations of law to labor and land—Distribution of created wealth and ownership of accumulated property—Natural and commercial price of labor—Contracts as a basis for society, versus the doctrine of right and wrong—Inventors only enjoy limited rights—Chattel titles to land a monopoly—Titles based on discovery, conquest or first use—Causes of inequality between rich and poor—Organized capital and corporations—Gambling in stocks and breadstuffs—Slavery and land monopoly twin robbers of labor—Prof. Sumner—Walker—Henry George.

It is related that a certain Eastern potentate fell into the impecunious condition, common to many of his predecessors, and all of his successors, and set his wits to work to devise a remedy. A farmer of imposts who had often aided him, in this dilemma came to his rescue. He offered him sixty thousand tomans for all the winds that should ever blow over Cashmere. The monarch at first affected to be staggered at the proposition. He was unable to find anything in precedents to warrant it, but, although a believer in the doctrine that whatever is, is right, he was forced to admit that a monarch may introduce useful innovations. Of course, it was assumed that he was the supreme owner and disposer of all things in his dominions, not only for his own brief, erratic span of life, but for all time, and so he came to the conclusion that as everything in the world had been sold which could be sold, there was no good reason why the winds, unstable though they might be, should be exempted if a purchaser could be found. After a proper amount of preliminary haggling a sale was made and the transaction legalized by all that signatures, seals and parchment could do for it.

Before the public had fairly got over laughing at the absurdity of this novel bargain, the owner of the wind issued a proclamation forbidding all persons in Cashmere from using his wind to turn their windmills, winnow their corn, propel their vessels or employ it in any other manner, until they had first entered into agreements with him and obtained leases for the various localities, covenanting to pay certain amounts for the privilege. Then the laughing turned to lamentation. The monarch met the torrent of petitions and complaints by affecting to deplore the circumstance. He could not, of course, foresee all that had occurred, but his sacred word was involved. Rulers of that type are usually very particular about their sacred word. Driven to desperation, the inhabitants contributed the amount that had been paid for the wind and tendered it to their sovereign so that this unheard of transaction could be cancelled.

The matter was not to be so easily arranged. The owner of the winds of Cashmere would not think of such a thing. He had acquired a vested right in them. Since it had become purchasable the wind had greatly risen, in price at least. Wind stocks were on an upward market. The owner insisted that his title was good. He did not claim it merely by his right of discovery of the commercial value of the wind, or that he had been the first to preempt this privilege, but he had fairly bought it from the representative of government, and declared that his title was begirt, and founded on all that was sacred in law or the theory of eminent domain and supreme authority. It would be altogether unfair to ask him to surrender this valuable privilege for anything less than what it might bring him in case he should be allowed to keep it. The proposition of the people was merely a bald scheme of robbery. It was subversive of all property rights; was socialistic, agrarian and revolutionary; and to force him to accept of a price so inadequate would strike a fatal blow at the best interests of society and undermine the whole fabric on which the rights of property rested.

This reasoning was, of course, entirely conclusive to the monarch, who was undoubtedly the confederate of the farmer of imposts, but, as human endurance can only be stretched to certain limits, it was agreed between them that a fair price for the wind, at that date, would be ten times what was originally paid for it. This amount was finally raised by a long-suffering people, who merely exacted a promise from the commercial monarch that he would never sell the wind again, but permit it in God's providence to blow over them free and unrestricted as of yore.

I have introduced this incident with the hope of throwing some light on the preliminary question—What is property? The public mind has become a good deal confused about the meaning of the term, and questions of *meum* and *tuum* embarrassed by doubtful words and more doubtful doctrines of political economy. Originally the word "property" referred to the quality of a thing, but as it is with its modern meaning we have to do, we find Webster's definition of it to be "The exclusive right of possessing, enjoying and disposing of a thing, ownership;" and adds from Shakespeare, "To take as one's own—to appropriate." Assuming that property is the exclusive right (or power) to possess, enjoy or dispose of a thing, the question occurs as to what things are justly subject to individual interest and will. Are the winds of the air, the waters of the deep or the surface of the earth, things from which one man can justly exclude all others, or which he has any right to speculate in or buy and sell? Can anything properly be treated as property but that which is produced by individual labor, effort or genius? It is now getting to be pretty generally conceded, according to the morals, religion and law of the highest types of modern civilization, that a man has a right to the proceeds of his own labor. It must not be forgotten that this is by no means universal among mankind, and that little more than twenty years have elapsed since, in our own country, a portion of the population, nearly ten per cent. of it in fact, and they of the producing classes, had no right to the proceeds of their own labor, did not even own their own persons, and that local law placed the ownership of the proceeds of their labor in the hands of a privileged and aristocratic class. When, therefore, we come to consider the question of property, we are forced to consider another element besides natural resources and human labor, and that is law. Property does not so much consist in what a man may have in his hands at the time, as in that which is respected as property by the community in which he lives: that which law will protect him in; that which the law declares to be his, and to the extent, and in the manner, and for the purposes for which the law declares it to be his, and subject to its changes and limitations. In estimating the foundation of property or wealth, according to the present accepted maxims of society, we of necessity include the three great elements of *labor, land* and *law.*

There are but two titles to property of any kind: law or force. The old free-booting maxim of "They may take who have the power, and they may keep who can," or the bulwarks established by organized and enlightened law: power, or the highest human sense of justice. A strong brute tears from the grasp of a weak one the food it is eating, and the latter relinquishes it with a whine. The eagle seizes from the fish hawk the trout the latter has piratically taken from the deep, and thus the robber from the robber rends the prey. In the dusky pool the big fish eat the little ones. In barbarous society the strong oppress the weak, but there never was a condition of human society so barbarous that a sense of justice did not remain to protest against wrong. Human nature, as light and opportunity is given, seeks protection in organized society.

We can rejoice, therefore, that at the present stage in the progress of our country, the legitimate fruit of a man's labor is recognized as his exclusive property. It is his, not only as an abstract proposition of right, but as a proposition entitled to the protection of law. It does not militate against this doctrine that he may, occasionally, be cheated out of a part of it. He is no longer the victim of despotic violence, and intelligent, progressive law is rapidly entering every field where chicanery is endeavoring to do the work once done by violence.

What are the products of human labor? The value of a day's labor is what it can under ordinary circumstances produce. Some men can produce more in a day than others. Skilled labor is worth more than unskilled labor, because you have to add to the value of each day of such labor the time and expense of educating and preparing the workman for his work. All of these circumstances enter into the commercial value of a man's labor, but do not destroy the principle that a man has a right to what his labor fairly produces. In order to work effectively, especially in dense and civilized society, laborers need to have certain privileges, and to use certain appliances which may or may not be the laborer's own. The laborer is thus forced to earn not only as much as will furnish him with food and clothing, but enough to pay for the use of the appliances, machinery or improvements he uses. Accumulated capital thus becomes a sharer in what is produced by labor, and if the distribution is perfectly fair, society can exist and flourish. It is just here the wrongs of modern society begin. If the streets were hemmed in with palaces and filled with gold, men and women would suffer and starve for the food and clothing of each year, unless some one worked to produce it. Labor alone produces. Capital at best is inert and can only facilitate. Why should it distribute the proceeds? The capital accumulated yesterday is not so much entitled to the consideration of society as the living, toiling, suffering producing labor of to-day. Capital is entitled to a share of the profits, but before they can be properly distributed, a sufficient amount to provide for the laborer and his family, according to the conditions of the society in which he lives, must be deducted. The theory of one school of political economists is that labor must use capital and appliances before it can produce. Instead of labor hiring capital or appliances, as a matter of fact capital and appliances hire labor. They do more: they fix the price. Capital, moreover, is restive under any interference with its bargains. It insists that the law of supply and demand is the only thing that should regulate the price of labor. This is the fundamental basis of modern theories of political economy. It is the law of selfishness organized. There may be a certain degree of conscience or consideration on the part of an employer mixed with it, but these are purely accidental or unnecessary elements. If a man with capital or able to be in active business only wants five laborers and is offered ten, it is his privilege to haggle with them, and reduce the price from one dollar to fifty cents; and, on the other hand, if two capitalists, or men in business, each need ten laborers and only ten are offered, they are to bid against each other and raise the price, say from fifty cents to one dollar. When not interfered with by an outside power, or law of organized society, this is the law of supply and demand pure and simple. It will be observed, however, that capital, acting intelligently under this law of self interest, never bids the price of labor much above what it can profitably employ it at. On the other hand, it is always the selfish interest of capital to get labor as cheap as it can, and thus enhance its profits. The operation of this rule must and does work to the disadvantage of the laborer. It is the operation of this unrestricted law of selfishness that constantly tends in highly civilized societies to make the rich grow richer and the poor poorer.

In a rude or barbarous condition of society the personal rights of property are easily defined. The hunter finds and kills a wild animal. Assuming that all things in nature are the property of man, he claims it by right of first discovery, and he and his family eat it, and clothe themselves with its skin. He discovers fruits, roots and nuts, which others have not found. He catches and spears fish. Even he must have capital. He makes and accumulates bows, arrows, knives, spears, fishing tackle, a boat, and finally the hut or skin tent that shelters him. This home, rude although it may be, he considers his own. If he is able, he defends it against all comers. Even barbarous society recognizes his right to it. He probably does not make it an article of merchandise. He certainly does not attempt to sell every foot of earth on which it may have stood: that he claims merely by an occupancy-right. His right over it ceases when he migrates. In this primitive condition of society, we do not find that the possessor of the rude capital we have described obtains the services of some young man, or wanderer without such capital, to use his tools, and hunt and fish for both while he slumbers indolently in his abode. According to the law of supply and demand he could do this; and if it was done in barbarous society, we would soon have a lower depth of degradation than even barbarism presents to us, and a privileged class, contributing but little to the public interests. Barbarous society does not admit of this, and is, therefore, not burdened by a large non-productive class.

Artificial society is something altogether different. Its conditions force us to ask if the law of organized selfishness is the only possible producer of civilization and luxury? There are not lacking those who tell us that wealth, prosperity and a high degree of civilization can only be produced under the rule "every one for himself and the Evil One take the hindmost." That emulation to produce its highest fruits must be stimulated by the hope of making profit out of the ignorant, inexperienced, poverty-stricken and unwary, and that law must not be permitted to interfere with the sanctities of a bargain, no matter how unfair.

Highly civilized and densely populated communities can only exist where there are great accumulations of what men call property. It is a singular and sad circumstance, moreover, that where we find the greatest wealth, we also find the most fearful poverty. In our modern civilized society, property, when created by human labor, runs into ruts. Those who do the hardest work, with few exceptions, get the smallest portion of its proceeds, and gradually settle to the bottom. Those who, by the aid of capital, manage and direct labor, live better and are more apt to get rich than those who merely labor. Capital, through usury, increases its gains out of all proportion to the benefits it confers upon society. When a young man in a great city or densely populated community gets old enough to work, if he has not the capital to develop his own labor, he must accept what the man who has, or controls capital, is willing to give him. The political economist cries: "Would you compel an employer to give more for labor than he can buy it for?"

> "The real value of a thing
> Is just as much as it will bring."

In answering such questions intelligently, we must take a broader view, and carefully examine the modes of distribution and production, and the assumption by capital of the power to fix its profits and the wages of labor. Philosophers, moralists and lawgivers all tell us that the greatest happiness and prosperity of all the component parts of society is a condition demanded by a just public policy. It is not in accordance with public policy that property when created should drift into enormous, princely fortunes on one hand, creating pauperism on the other. The laboring producers are entitled to a full share of the blessings they create, and any cause of unequal distribution of proceeds is wrong, and such operations may be properly inquired into. When we find the officers of a great corporation, such as a railway company, sitting down to fix expenses and salaries, determining that they can only pay a laboring man one dollar per day, or three hundred dollars a year; skilled laborers and mechanics six hundred; engineers and conductors ten or twelve hundred, and so forth, we may consider it a reasonable and prudent management of the great corporate interests intrusted to them. If, however, they also vote the president ten or twelve thousand dollars a year, the general superintendent eight or ten thousand, and each of the board, for certain duties, real and imaginary, similar amounts, it might strike an impartial observer as hardly a fair distribution of what the enterprise produces. When we also find that the capital invested has been duplicated or triplicated by watered stock; that mortgages have been placed on such properties without adding anything to their real or productive value; that these great interests have been distorted and perverted, in order to make real or fictitious fortunes for a few men; when we further see, as a result of these proceedings, ruin threatening the enterprise, and the laborers and employees so ground by reduced pay for their labor that they cannot properly maintain their families,—those who have thus mismanaged should be required to give a better reason for their oppressive orders than a desire to pay heavier dividends on such inflated capital, or greater salaries to the managers.

The law of supply and demand as a measure of values is only true in certain conditions, and subject to certain limitations. When we find a condition of society in which nine-tenths of the people subsist by hiring their labor, and when we find these laborers or producers of the wealth of society, instead of growing richer as society grows richer, aggregating capital as the wealth of the community they live in increases, constantly growing *relatively* poorer as compared with those who own and represent the capital engaged,—the causes which lead to this public calamity are also subject matter for legitimate inquiry. It has been said that there is no necessary antagonism between labor and capital. They supplement each other. All partnerships, to endure, must be perfectly fair, and of mutual benefit. Capital, if employed, should increase the laborer's wealth. If it does not do this, he is better without it. In order to preserve society prosperous and continuous, the laborer must be preserved. All society is interested to prevent the accumulation of enormous fortunes out of the wealth produced by the exertions of workers for wages. Following great fortunes we inevitably find the poorly clad, poorly fed, poorly housed, poorly educated, children of the laboring classes. In an era of great development they are poorly developed. In an era of great luxury they have few luxuries. The very grandeur of the civilization they are helping to build becomes a mockery to them. It really makes them poorer to see the evidences of wealth all around them, yet out of their reach. The wide differences of such a society may be said to inflict a species of moral degradation on them. Living in poorly ventilated houses or hovels, how can it benefit them to look at the palaces of the rich? When, in addition to these inequalities, we see an increasing pauperism developed, we are startled, and must become convinced that there are fundamental wrongs existing, and that these diseases must find a remedy before there can be a healthy condition of the body politic.

Ricardo, in his writings on wages, says: "The natural price of labor is that price which is necessary to enable the laborers, one with another, to subsist and to perpetuate their race without either increase or diminution." He also says: "The market price of labor is the price which is really paid for it, from the natural operation of the proportion of the supply to the demand." And again: "It is when the market price of labor exceeds its natural price that the condition of the laborer is flourishing and happy, that he has it in his power to command a greater proportion of the necessaries and enjoyments of life, and, therefore, to rear a healthy and numerous family." And again: "When the market price of labor is below its natural price, the condition of the laborer is most wretched."

The foregoing views will be found almost in the same language in Adam Smith's "Wealth of Nations." He is the founder of the peculiar theories that have been put in circulation under the name of "Political Economy." Ricardo gave to these theories their extreme but logical sequence. According to him it is not the interest of laborers that their numbers increase, and thus weaken the demand for them. Malthus is chiefly distinguished for suggestions in the same direction. If this was logically true it would be for the interest of laborers to produce as little property as possible. If the laborer, by reducing the hours of labor from ten to five, can enhance the value of what he produces so as to get as much for it, why work ten? The folly of this proposition would be best shown if all laborers in a country adopted the same rule. There would be just half as much produced, and consequently just half as much to distribute. While there may be over-production in a few fancy or unusual articles, it may be safely assumed that there is never over-production of the necessaries of life so long as any considerable class is deprived of them. The evil, therefore, does not lie in over-production but in unfair distribution. Under our mercantile system there is no such thing as the natural price of a day's labor. Neither can the value of a laborer's day's work be measured by what it requires to feed and clothe a laborer and his family, because it may take a dollar or ten dollars to do that. A system of political economy that suggests that the true interests of a laborer are best promoted by having two children rather than four, is as monstrous as that doctrine of the survival of the fittest which in China takes supposed sickly children and drowns them in the canal. A true political economy is that which secures the greatest prosperity and happiness of the industrious classes, giving them a proper share of the fruits of their labor, thus enabling them to purchase a larger number of manufactured articles.

Prof. Sumner, the political economist of one of our first universities, and a fair representative of the class which endeavors to preserve the doctrines of Ricardo and Malthus, against the innovations of modern thought and ancient morals, in his recent work "What social classes owe each other," assumes that they owe nothing but "civility." His doctrine is that the basis of modern civilized society is "Contracts" or bargains, and that capital alone produces civilization. On page 59 of the work referred to, he says that man, as a brute in the state of nature, has nothing, and merely exerts himself to appropriate the productions of nature. Civilization makes a change. On page 60 he tells us that this change is wrought "by capital." As change has produced the "capital" it is difficult to see how capital could have produced the "change." Brute man had, of course, nothing when he started. What made him start? On the same page in which the Professor says capital wrought the change he naively says: "It is wonderful that primitive man could have started." If the Professor's theory is correct it would have been altogether impossible. The desire to overestimate the power and productiveness of capital leads this school of philosophers into many strange doctrines. On page 61 he says: "From the first step man made above the brute, the thing that made his civilization possible was capital." On page 63, however, he inadvertently wanders into another theory and says: "It is in the middle range, with enough social pressure to make energy needful and not enough social pressure to produce despair, that the most progress has been made." Besides capital, it would seem that the Professor has stumbled on such a thing as "energy." Is it not possible that in tracing the causes that may have led a barbarous man to be something better, richer and more learned than he was, we may discover the mainsprings of human aspiration, energy and desire? Energy, even according to the Professor, is not stimulated by "capital," but by the want of it. What produces and has always produced capital is labor. Political economists need not waste their time trying to demonstrate that a bag of dollars placed in a barrel can be hatched into two bags. What they should consider is how best to stimulate labor to the greatest productiveness consistent with the health and moral culture of the laborer. Buckle, on the second page of his first volume of the "History of Civilization," says: "The unequal distribution of wealth is the fertile source of social disturbances."

Can we escape the dominion of moral law? Is it possible to found a healthy, prosperous and continuous society on contracts? It is the end of modern enlightened law that all customs, mercantile systems and schemes of finance must be founded on fair dealing. Formerly gambling debts could be collected. Hard and dishonest bargains when they passed into written obligations claimed sanctity and observance. According to our modern system a man goes into court and pleads want of consideration. It is not enough that a matter between men is a bargain: it must be a just bargain. From this it is a short step in jurisprudence to sit in judgment on all distributions and exchanges. Do you say this is intermeddling? If so, it is only intermeddling with wrong. Is no one interested in a transaction or bargain except the two who enter into it? Yes, the state as much as the individual, is vitally interested in seeing that bargains are founded on the doctrine of perfect equivalents. Modern law even goes beyond this. It asserts, and the assertion is maintained, that the inventor of a valuable machine is not entitled to the exclusive benefits flowing from it. The public have certain rights therein. If the inventor had an absolute right, he and his descendants ought to be secured in a patent for all time. Society does not permit this. It says that the inventor of a useful machine, or the author of a book, shall have a share in its profits for a limited number of years, when the product of his genius and labor shall become public property. It will not do to say that this is a peculiar case, and that the author or inventor accepts a limited interest in his property, in consideration for the protection he gets during the limited period. The protection he gets is the protection of law, which, if necessary, he has to vindicate in the courts. So, also, has society and nations the task of protecting all property. Civilized society has to bear the expensive system of legislatures, executive officers, courts, sheriffs, policemen; nor can it be shown that communities and nations have not as deep an interest in accumulated property as the individual claimant or owner thereof.

When capital has grown to be in excess of the moderate competence which industry and thrift can fairly produce, it is a just subject for the heaviest burdens of the state; and this not only because it is most able to bear them, but because there is good reason to believe that great fortunes have been accumulated by a system of distribution of the proceeds of labor unfair to the laborers. There is nothing communistic or agrarian in such propositions. While the case of the helplessly poor is one of the legitimate burdens of society, and one which should be borne kindly and humanely, largely from accumulated capital, and while no property should be recognized as such save what has been honestly earned, no good can ever be accomplished by a leveling process between the poor and the justly rich. Such a step would destroy that enterprise which is the very life of society. If, according to Professor Sumner "Energy" lies at the foundation of prosperity, we must take care that its back be not broken. This is the rock on which many social reformers split. To preserve that independent, hopeful spirit which makes a man work, economise and struggle for the comfort of himself and family is one of the vital principles of true political economy. After all, it only means that a man shall be protected in his honest earnings. It does not mean that the lazy shall fare as well as the industrious. A sound form of society will repudiate non-producing classes, whether they be lazy paupers or sturdy capitalists who draw the lion's share of the annual outputs of human labor by ingenious financial devices. You can find in society, we will say, twenty men; one of them is a capitalist, and nineteen who are workers for wages under him. He is successful. He expends for himself and family, we will say, eleven thousand a year. He lives in an elegant house. He and his family "dress in purple and fine linen and fare sumptuously every day." He drives in a carriage and his children are educated in the best colleges. Under the law of supply and demand, he pays his wage workers, we will say, an average of six hundred dollars a year each. He, of course, manages the concern. He expends for himself almost as much as he gives his nineteen workers for wages. If he is very rapacious, and wishes still further to accumulate, he screws them down until they can hardly keep soul and body together. It is true, they can seek out a new employer who is probably like the old one, or, by close economy, may haply save enough to become employers themselves. Should this law of bargains govern society, it would destroy the weak, and repudiate every doctrine of religion and morals. The essential conditions of a thriving and permanent community are that labor shall command and secure the highest rate, and capital be procured at the lowest rate of interest. The most eminent of the Rothschilds declared that a business that continuously paid three per cent. for its capital would inevitably fail. There is, therefore, a just and honest limit to the earnings of accumulated wealth, and it has been maintained that only such capital as exists in the shape of productive machinery or improvements is entitled to any share in what is produced.

Of all the systems of human oppression, none have been more fertile of mischief and wrong than landed aristocracy: individual claims to portions of the earth's surface, to the exclusion of the rights of others. To "have and to hold" means that other men and women shall *not* have and hold. Land holding is the monopoly of what Aristotle styled "the bounty of nature." When a man buys a section of six hundred and forty acres, a mile square, of the earth's surface, and has it conveyed to him, his heirs and assigns forever, it is not a piece of property he can put in his pocket or tie behind his saddle. In law we call it "real property" in contradistinction to "personal property." Is it property at all? It is really an agreement between this owner, or pretended owner, and some other power or person to defend him in his attempt to exclude all the rest of the human race from using it, except in his interest. It is really a mortgage, not on this particular piece of the earth, but upon all the men and women who may happen to be born upon the earth, with the necessity of raising and eating bread. This so-called property is simply *law* for the benefit of the few against the many. There is not any other thing recognized by society as property so absolutely dependent on public recognition and defense as titles to land. Some king or government claimed to have the right to grant land or certain uses of it. Whether that grant was a lease, a holding under the feudal system, a sale for a certain period, or on certain conditions, or pretended to be an absolute sale of it as a mere chattel, the essence of it was military or political power.

This brings us to the next view of the subject. What is known as a government or a nation is not merely a thing of geographical limits; it is a combination of men, a body politic. It is, however, almost inseparable from geographical limits. You can scarcely imagine a nation without a country. Our maps and our histories divide the earth's surface into certain distinctly marked tracts and divisions. For convenience, on our modern maps they are colored differently. Each portion is recognized as belonging to the nation named; we will say France or Germany, or Mexico, or the United States. Why?

Every one recognizes the portion in question to belong to the nation it represents. How do they get or maintain this title? Occupancy, violence and power are the sole bulwarks of these possessions. Nine-tenths of the wars among mankind have been about the boundaries of these subdivisions. Do the British own their islands because they speak English? Did those who speak French naturally inherit the region of earth between the Rhine and the Bay of Biscay? Is the Spanish language the patent to the peninsula? No! These divisions are not created by differences of language, but differences of language are created by these divisions. Separate men into distinct nations, with a different polity and segregated interests, and they soon cease to understand each other's forms of speech. Language, that wonderful garment of thought, is subject to hidden laws of fashion, and is the most mutable of all things.

This political or governmental assertion of title to land is a proper matter to inquire into. It rests on the sword. It must not be forgotten, however, that this is merely an assertion of one nation as against another. Each nation claims the right to maintain the integrity of its territory. Into the minds of its people this lesson is instilled as the highest sense of duty, and affectionately called patriotism. Countries have been over-run and conquered many times in history. In barbarous periods a wandering horde crossed a frontier, and, if successful, butchered the inhabitants ruthlessly, and left their bodies to fertilize the soil that now belonged to the conquerors. Fortresses were built, armies mustered and disciplined, navies created; all these to defend the country and consecrate a portion of the earth to the Hun or the Sclav, the Goth or the Latin race. Without for a moment assuming that all countries thus shaped, or governments thus created, were justly or properly founded, or that their present existence is for the benefit of the race, it is, nevertheless, necessary, as they do exist, to consider them. The world as constituted is not Utopia. We do not know whether the world would be better and men happier if all dwellers on the earth were one people, but they are not. The supposed hostile interests and prejudices between nations have been the occasion of great wrong and misery upon the earth. An armed mob, called an army, wins a victory in the enemy's country, and through this accident claims the right to rob the helpless tillers of the soil. Theoretically, governments are the essence of law, but this government is mere brute force. I take it for granted that it is the business of civilization to devise remedies for this evil. All men are interested in the establishment of justice and equity, protection and order, against mere violence. International law is ill-defined and crude; but when the honest judgment of combinations of nations acquire power and can dictate to physical strength, something will be gained. We have, to some extent, established the rights of the man as against the state, and we can hope for a more intelligent mode of determining the rights of nations toward each other. The divine right of kings over the lives and property of their subjects is pretty well exploded among civilized nations. Let us hope that the divine right of violence and fraud can also be brought to an end. Let us remember that much of what we call *rights* to-day, grew out of force and usurpation. When men and societies who have and claim such privileges rest them solely on violence, we can understand them. They are likely to maintain them just so long as no one else has the power or the spirit to resist them. This age, however, presents new problems. We have inherited the fruits of violence and fraud, and are endeavoring to reconcile them to the doctrines of enlightened law.

Let us accept the situation that a government asserts its rights to a land or country. Against this stands the broad axiomatic truth that the earth is the equal heritage of all men. In the United States we have practically asserted the broadest right. Not only our native population, but emigrants from all countries have been invited to equal participation in the soil. Whether this has been done wisely in all things will be considered hereafter. Narrowed down to the state or nation, this organized government neither has nor should have any power to dispose of the soil save upon terms, now and forever, for the benefit of all men alike. The government of the United States has been founded on the doctrine of the perfect equality of the rights of all men. "Governments derive their just power from the consent of the governed." Laws for the benefit of the few against the many are in violation of its fundamental principles. If we start with the doctrine that everything must be subservient to the best interests of all, the maxim we have quoted must be maintained and all else treated as usurpation and resisted. The government of the United States is merely an aggregated body of men, bound together on the understanding that all shall be perfectly equal before the law, with equal justice, equal privileges, equal power. We get the best inspiration of law from divine laws, and they are distilled to us through the highest and purest human conscience. Recognizing the necessity of power to give effect to human law, we accept that power as the attribute of the majority, and therefore recognize that nothing is law, or can have the sanctity thereof, save the will of the people legitimately expressed.

The function of the majority is to determine what is best for all. Where it has not done this it has violated the compact on which all came together, and the mistakes must be corrected. The right or power of the state over land should be to see that it is used for the equal benefit of all. To give a monopoly of land to a few is to give the bread and meat of the people to a few. The state never had any right to do that. In making the attempt it exceeded its powers. The unjust systems that have grown up under it call for reform. By the state we mean a government, and by a government we must understand a government of to-day. The government of to-day has no right to govern the people fifty or a hundred years hence. Admitting their right of determining for the generation or the year they represent, the kind of usufruct title, lease or sale of the earth's surface that may exist, they certainly have no right to dispose of it against all future generations. On what conceivable plea of power can they create mischievous and unequal systems that shall harass generations after the bodies of these short-sighted rulers are dust? Because they represent the people to-day, how shall they pretend to despotize over the people of all time, and in their own interest lay a mortgage on the bones and sinews of millions yet unborn?

When the "right of discovery" and the "right of conquest," as doctrines, begin to be subject to a very heavy strain, the advocate for this property created by fraud or force pleads the statute of limitations. When reminded that lapse of time cannot sanctify a wrong, he further pleads the law of "use and wont." Again he urges that the public interest demands that there shall be a limit to all human controversies. If the doctrine "whatever is, is right," cannot be fully recognized, he insists that at all events sudden changes in the existing status of society are dangerous; that interference with long-settled property interests is unsafe and agrarian; and that all property holders, from the owner of an acre to a principality, should make common cause against those who would inquire into their title to what they are now holding.

Let it not be urged that the condition of laboring people gives no occasion for intelligent inquiry and reform. We present to the world a nation increasing in riches faster than any other nation, and, at the same time, the laborers whose toil produces this wealth, if not growing poorer, are relatively sinking as a class. We have multiplied innumerable labor-saving machines, and yet the workingmen and women of the country labor as hard as their ancestors did. Our unexampled prosperity is followed by a steadily increasing poorer class, while vagrancy and crime also increase. Our country presents a comparatively boundless empire, of almost virgin soil, and yet we see the singular anomaly of a rapidly increasing class of tenants and renters. Instead of a thriving yeomanry, there is a tendency to farming by the wholesale, on speculation or by joint stock companies. Before we have fairly passed the squatting era, and while there are still unoccupied homesteads to be taken, the evils of the system of land tenure we have permitted confront us. We are certainly laying the foundation of a landed aristocracy. We have allowed our timbered regions to be devastated and destroyed, until the condition thus produced affects the productiveness of some of our agricultural regions, and the comfort of many of our people. We present a startling picture of speculation in lands and lots by those who add nothing to their improvement, and fortunes are made without labor by the increase of population and the efforts of those who do not benefit by it. Speculation, and the fact that land has been made a chattel, enhances the valuation of lands and lots so as to put them beyond the reach of those who are poor or even those in moderate circumstances. An acre of land produces no more wheat or corn when it is valued at one hundred dollars than it did when it was valued at ten, and yet this has a tendency to increase the tax called rent to the producer. A house and lot valued at five hundred dollars offers as great comfort or conveniences as when the same house is valued at five thousand, and yet it costs the man who occupies it much more. This price, caused by speculation, is not conducive to the public interest. It is true it enables a few to acquire great fortunes without giving the public an equivalent. The condition of affairs arising from these speculative values, so far as they are created by an increase of population, raise prices without corresponding public benefit, the public do not share what they thus create, and, on the contrary, it actually increases their burdens. Not the least evil of this system is that it disturbs that fair distribution of the wealth produced by industry, and founds aristocratic classes, raised above the necessity of labor.

Men do not properly estimate the evil of an increasing non-producing class. In England, a certain school of political economists said the non-producing classes were a blessing, because they furnished a market for the surplus production arising from the labor of the poor. The larger the non-producing class in any country, in proportion to the laborers, the harder must the laborers work, and the more poorly must they be paid. If wealth maintained the power of keeping up its profits until fifty per cent. of the population lived upon it, the other fifty per cent. would have to work to keep them. If, then, the end of civilization is to increase wealth to such an extent that we are to have a large aristocratic class, we must, of necessity, have a large class of poor laborers. If the laborers should get a much larger proportion of what their labor produces than they now do, they would have better houses, be better clothed and fed, be better educated, have more books and more time to read them; *but then* we would not have so many palaces, or so many magnificent, luxurious households. Is the elegant architecture of our civilization the best evidence of its greatness and power? If this is all that it can produce, is it worth the price? Above all, how long can it last? We may shut our eyes and exclaim, "After me, the deluge." It remains to be seen whether a written constitution will prove a sufficient shield for the rights of the people. An aristocracy is even more abhorrent than a king, and aristocracies are usually created by great wealth, and fostered by unequal privileges. The foundations of American aristocracy are already laid, and this has partly arisen from carelessness about the true foundation of a free republic. It seems, unhappily, to be the ambition of too many men to place their families at once above want and work. The public interests are lost sight of in the scramble. While age may justly have accumulated moderate wealth, and live in comfort or even luxury, there is no reason why youth should be exempted from toil by the curse of a competence. Hereditary wealthy families are not in harmony with American ideas. A just public policy should tend to scatter and redistribute wealth. The only thing that renders this inequality of condition endurable, is the hope entertained by most poor men that they and theirs will happily rise above the calamities that affect so many others in the community. When all unoccupied land is taken, and a dense population confronts us, the lines of society will grow more inflexible, and the disparity of condition will be greater and more clearly defined. Such changed conditions are rapidly approaching, and will produce one of three things: The destruction of the representative power and freedom of the people; peaceful remedies wisely taken in time which will secure perfect equality of rights, or the overthrow of the aristocracy by violence and anarchy.

Our progressive and scheming civilization has developed new forms of speculation and new organizations to give power to capital. Corporations have already become more formidable than the government. Law has clothed them with artificial power without placing proper restriction on its selfish and unjust exercise. There is not adequate security against the frauds they perpetrate. Aggregated capital is managed by boards of directors or trustees whose first business is to advance their own individual interests, and then, so far as consistent with it, the interests of the stockholders. Every dollar of actual cash contributed by stockholders to build railroads, telegraphs or other public enterprises, under great corporations, is apt to be represented on its books, certificates of stock and in the public markets by what are called its stocks, to twice, thrice or even ten times its true value. Capital thus manages and demands that it shall be multiplied, and that this fictitious wealth shall make equal charge out of the profits of an enterprise created by labor and a small amount of capital. Contracts are given for construction, by directors to their partners and confederates for more than the construction costs, and thus the public and the innocent stockholders are cheated. Mortgages are sometimes placed on these properties and much of the money thus raised expended extravagantly in bonuses, salaries and pretended dividends as profits. While there may be a few well-conducted corporations and companies, the corporate system as it exists, in the main, is a hive of gigantic swindling, into which absolute fair dealing and equity among men does not enter. It is indeed amazing that the intelligence of this nineteenth century should have permitted such a system of unequal distribution and fraud to have been created; and, seeing the system operate, that law, which ought to be the safeguard of perfect equity, should for any length of time permit it to continue.

Then we have gambling in corn. Meat and bread put up to be the football of stock-jobbers. Of all gambling this is the most iniquitous. It is bad enough that shrewd operators are thus allowed to fleece inexperienced dupes, but that these two between them should be permitted to put up and down the price of the bread and meat of sixty millions of people is perfectly monstrous. It is useless to say that they merely speculate in the natural rise of these articles. This unnatural speculation cannot get into successful operation until the bulk of what is produced in the current year goes into the hands of middle men. Then combinations are formed to force up and down prices. This system is fed by trickery and misrepresentation as gross as the trickery by which a jockey ever palmed off a blind horse on an innocent customer. Foreign markets and the condition of the coming crops have a little to do with prices, but for all the artificial changes in the price of the food of the people, the gamblers in what are called "options," "puts" and "calls" are responsible. Of course, there is a legitimate business in buying, storing and disposing of surplus bread and meat, but there is scarcely a business requiring in greater degree the safeguards of law, and from which all gambling and artificial speculation should be so thoroughly banished. If what is sometimes termed "free competition" means that the more cunning and adroit shall profit by unfair bargains with the illiterate or unsophisticated, enlightened law must make an end of all such phases of "free competition."

There have been two favorite modes of robbing laborers. First, by the slavery which seized his person, and by threats and violence which compelled him to work for the tyrant who claimed to be his master. Second, by seizing the surface of the earth from which human sustenance must be drawn, and, on the plea of exclusive ownership, compelling the cultivator to give half of what he produced from the earth to another. Political economists have preached about the "Doctrine of rent," and, accepting the claim of ownership as an inevitable fact, have proceeded to demonstrate that rent was the difference between good land and poor land, when every one knows that rent could not exist but for monopoly. The doctrine that the surface of the earth can be made a chattel independent of its use is a modern conception, and of evil tendency, and our American land tenures are the result of a chapter of accidents. We inherited all the bad parts of the English system, and launched on a career of speculation in which we were reckless of human rights.

The writer is not insensible to the embarrassments that a highly refined and artificial condition of society throw around these questions. He is aware that many of the most splendid of ancient empires have been founded on robbery, piracy, slavery and murder. The palaces of kings cannot always hide the hovels of the laboring poor. Great modern cities seem to afford a better field to able, unscrupulous and adroit managers, than to quiet, honest mediocrity, or even to quiet, honest ability. There bargains rule. At the very threshold of reform, we are met with the assertion of "vested rights" which are probably only vested wrongs. I am loath to believe that if you strip enterprise and energy of every element of dishonesty, men will lapse into barbarism. It may be styled agrarianism, when a reformer of abuses endeavors to set bolts and bars against the unjust exactions by which the accumulated capital of yesterday seeks to place its foot on the necks of the laborers of to-day.

There will be just inequalities in the condition of men so long as there are differences among them as to industry and thrift. The accumulation of enormous fortunes is always a calamity, and often a crime. It is doubtful if the unfair transactions that lie at the base of colossal wealth are as great misfortunes as the wielding of such a giant power by an unscrupulous person. Some men might be compared to magnets, having the power to draw to them gold from every avenue of society. We are too much in the habit of admiring this accomplishment. It is high time that we had a code of morals that would cease to hold it up to emulation. In founding the government of the United States, great strides were made in the progress of civil liberty. The principles then enunciated must not be permitted to become mere "glittering generalities." It took nearly a century to abolish slavery in a free country, and aristocracy and inequalities founded on injustice have not yet found their remedies.

I shall discuss the remedies in the proper place. There is much to admire in the ideas of Mr. Henry George, but making the government the landlord is a proposition it will be well to carefully consider. Those who own the land rule the country. Government is not an abstract theory but an organization of men who may closely follow or conspire against its principles. Frequent elections and oft-renewed responsibility are checks, yet there may be danger in giving even to those who happen to administer our free government the power to decide the length and character of land tenures, or, what is of more significance, to provide an enormous revenue, which would flow in as rent to fill the treasury, no matter what the wish of the people may be in each year as to taxation or expenditure. Of course, it will be said that this rent is only another form of tax, but it is not an annually assessed tax; on the contrary, it would be a steadily growing revenue, which the national landlord might soon assume to be his own property. It is possible that in this way the government would become stronger than the people. The rulers, moreover, who would demand the rent would, at the same time, have the power to distribute, divide and fix tenure to the national inheritance.

Instead of the assumption that the land belongs to the nation or government, let it be asserted that the land belongs to the people. Fundamental and specific law should secure and consecrate it for the use or benefit of all the people, to be redistributed as the changes in society occur, and instead of the details of tenure being managed by the general government, they should be under local supervision as near as possible to the people. The old town organizations offer the primitive model.

Mr. Francis Walker, in his "Land and its Rent," follows the theory that rent is created by the difference between rich and poor land. The necessity of ownership by somebody is assumed. His general conclusions, in the work referred to, are that it is the interest of all classes to have an agricultural system that will yield the largest production of wealth. This does not reach or touch the question as to whom it properly belongs.

The system of agriculture that would produce the largest amount at the smallest possible cost would be a wholesale farming that would abolish small farmers. Instead of the independent yeoman, cultivating his land and living in his house as the head of his establishment, we would have the agricultural community in three classes: the landlord, the farmer, or overseer, and laborers. In the same way and on the same principle, an enormous dry goods house swallows up in its growth and progress a thousand of the small establishments of independent traders. By this wholesale process the men become dependent salesmen and clerks, workers for wages. In this way goods may be sold cheaper and the power of capital is augmented, but the independence and comfort of the individual is reduced. We propose, therefore, to inquire whether the happiness and comfort of the great mass of the people is not the first consideration, and all others subordinate to it. Mr. E. H. G. Clark, in a recent essay, "Man's Birthright," thinks that he has found the philosopher's stone, that is to correct the errors of Mr. George, in a two per cent. annual tax, which he believes will confiscate the entire property in fifty years and be a "patent made easy" year of jubilee. He does not inform us who is to pay the tax, or show us that it will not be the man who rents and cultivates the land, or the man who buys the corn, rather than the man who is the landlord and claims to have title to the soil. If Mr. Clark would take the ground that the rent should be paid in lieu of taxes, to support public burdens, he would approximate to Mr. George's platform. A two per cent. tax on fixed values is what we have in many states now.

In approaching a subject of such magnitude with the becoming diffidence imposed by its perplexities, I shall, as succinctly as possible, glean from history the salient points that throw light on the establishment of existing land systems. Men have often a slavish disposition to respect precedents without stopping to scrutinize the circumstances on which they were founded, or to remember that for much of what is good in modern society we are indebted to innovation. Systems and principles must be considered in so far as they affect governments and men. In an age when it is announced that bargains or contracts should alone govern society, and that men owe each other nothing but politeness, let us not altogether forget, that the brotherhood of the race and equity and religion are a fundamental basis for society. Cool, calculating, selfishness may be deemed the best balance wheel of society, but experience shows us that it brings communities into a condition when organized benevolence or revolution are indispensable.

CHAPTER I.

THE POLITICAL AND SOCIAL SYSTEM OF ANCIENT ISRAEL.

"THE LAND SHALL NOT BE SOLD FOREVER, FOR THE LAND IS MINE; FOR YE ARE STRANGERS AND SOJOURNERS WITH ME."—LEV. XXV. 23.

Scope of the Hebrew laws—The patriarchate the primitive government of the Semitic races—Laws framed to regulate land tenure before land was possessed—Available area of Judea—Distinction between property in the country and in walled cities—Land nationalization rejected—Family tenure of land—The year of jubilee—Usurpations of the monarchy—Tithes and taxes—The peculiar and advantageous features of Jewish polity.

IF we are to discard the study of abstract propositions and recondite theories, as foundation for social economics and law, and gather data from the records of human experience and history, no finer study presents itself than the wonderful polity of the ancient Jewish nation. Accepting their own record, and studying the early portions from the five books of Moses, we have facts differing from those of all other human history. Other nations, like them, have begun by being nomads and wanderers. Other nations, like them, have had a government of popular acceptance followed by a monarchy, with all its despotisms, splendor and mishaps. Perhaps no other nation ever before had a government without a country, and a complete code of law before they had courts or recognized earthly executive authority. Human history affords us no similar accepted code. It was a strange compound of simplicity and minute intermeddling. Their religious duties and ceremonials were set forth with a wonderful perspicuity. The food they should eat was prescribed. Habits of cleanliness were systematized into law. Their laws of marriage were rigid. The laws of hospitality, even, were defined, and law dictated the duties of charity. Of course, there is much in the books of the law adapted to only such a people and such a time, but the great essentials are the highest conception of purity and equity. In regard to those regulations which refer to food, the cultivation of the soil, cleanliness and other things which are now considered as of little importance, or not properly within the scope of governmental powers, the result proves that in neglecting them we have not gained, and that the books of Leviticus and Deuteronomy might still be read to great advantage.

The ten commandments we have carefully preserved, but while the books of the Mosaic law remain in the Old Testament, they are practically considered as abrogated. Neither does there appear to be a full realization of all that the ten commandments involve. The fourth commandment, for instance, enjoins the observance of the Sabbath. While the portion of the commandment enjoining rest is often caviled at, many seem to overlook altogether the binding force of the other portion of the command: "Six days shalt thou labor." Among the ancient Jews the law of labor was as imperative as the day of rest. The Jewish economy furnished neither opportunity for nor toleration of a non-producing class. All men were compelled to work.

The patriarchal system did not originate with the Jews; they inherited it. This primitive form of aristocracy was, and still is, common to Arabia, and, indeed, to all that region, the Sheik (elder) being the head. Abraham, Isaac and Jacob were each the chief and ruler of a great household. The elder or head assumed a regal authority, exercising even the power of life and death. Seventy souls of the family of Jacob entered Egypt. They maintained a distinct identity, but were invited guests and friends, one of their number being a chief ruler under Pharaoh. They were assigned a locality in the land of Goshen. For four hundred and thirty years this germ of the Jewish nation grew, and when they went forth from Egypt they had an army of six hundred thousand men. It is estimated that this gave a population of two millions and a half. Of the form of local government they maintained in Egypt, we have very meagre accounts, yet each tribe kept its genealogies and distinct political existence, the number of fighting men of each tribe being stated. The law had not been given, or the five books of Moses written, but they were a people bound together by blood, religious customs, and cemented into a nationality by their hopes and traditions. Had the Jews followed the usual course of emigrants to foreign countries, and merged in the population of Egypt, becoming part of it by absorption, they would not have been the victims of hatred and jealousy. They were a distinct people, not mingling with their neighbors. They rejected the religious belief of the Egyptian. They acquired no foothold as owners of the land; in fact, all of the valuable land in Egypt was then held by the priests, the sovereign and the army. The common people of Egypt were renters under one of these three. Egypt had at that time one of the best developed forms of ancient civilization. It has been said that it was in Egypt that these shepherd patriarchs acquired a knowledge of written language, of the arts and sciences, of public works and manufactures. They acquired a knowledge of slavery through the hardest of all lessons, a bitter experience. We are simply told that another king arose who knew not Joseph. Old services and the hospitality evoked by them were forgotten. In point of fact, a new dynasty had arisen, and Hebrew and Egyptian alike were under the power of the conquerors. The religion of Egypt had not changed. Its land system, always bad, had not improved. So far as the Egyptian people were concerned it was merely a change from one tyrant to another. With the Israelites it was worse. Always isolated, and subject to the jealousies of the people, they were now stripped of the friendship or favoritism of the rulers. They had, indeed, a chequered experience of the power and barbaric splendor of Egypt. They had seen a king of Egypt use the surplus revenue, or wealth of his kingdom, to buy all the corn in the years of plenty, and had also seen him with that corn buy the title to a large portion of the land of Egypt. As they refused to become a homogeneous portion of the Egyptian people, it was morally certain that they must strive for ascendency or sink to the bottom, and, as they continued to multiply, equally certain that a disruption had to come sooner or later. Fugitives from slavery, without a polity or a country, the Jewish nation crystallized in the wilderness. Forty years wandering inured them to privation and gave them nerve. The generation that had trembled at the commands of its Egyptian taskmasters passed away. They had not forgotten that Abraham, while a wanderer upon the face of the earth, had purchased in Canaan, of Ephron, the Hittite, for four hundred shekels of silver, the field and cave of Macpelah, and that the Lord had promised to give them a country flowing with milk and honey.

It is certainly an interesting study to contemplate the code of law and ethics in the books of Exodus, Leviticus and Deuteronomy. Here we have the most thorough system of legislation for land before they possessed land, and the order of crops and the seventh or fallow year, in which the land was to rest and recuperate, prescribed before they had sown a seed. Then followed after the seven times seven, the year of jubilee, when all the land that had been alienated, mortgaged or sold, should go back to the original family to whom it belonged. The land should not be sold forever, only and excepting a house with its lot within a walled city. That was a chattel.* Within one year from the date of its sale it could be redeemed. The houses in villages and cities not walled were "counted as the fields of the country," and went back to the original family in the day of jubilee. Even the temporary sales were rigidly

* Lev. xxv. 30.

regulated. There was little room for speculative prices. According to the fruits they would produce for the years of cultivation between the period of sale and the year of jubilee, the price was to be computed. At any time the person so selling was permitted, if able, to redeem, or redeem through a friend, by paying for the years that were to intervene before the year of jubilee. At that time, without pay, the transaction was at end. The law which authorized six years for crops and one year for fallow and rest, prevented the land from being scourged and rendered barren by temporary occupants. In the year of jubilee, captives taken in war and all servants and debtors were set free. Even the servants, who at the expiration of their six years of service voluntarily relinquished liberty, and had their ears bored through with an awl, went out in the year of jubilee.* The land law of the Jews, we are told, was somewhat famous among ancient nations, and several of them attempted to copy it.† The permission to sell for limited periods was not considered an alienation of land such as we permit. Diodorus Siculus informs us that it was not lawful for the Jews to sell their own inheritance. This law of the Hebrews prevented the rich from absorbing the lands, and for this reason the Jews were never cursed with a landed aristocracy. The rulers neither owned nor controlled the land, and were, therefore, unable to draw great revenues from it to support armies, by which the rights of the people could be overthrown. When military service was required, the family supplied the soldiers with needed food from home. They had the spoil of the enemy, but a hireling soldiery was unknown, at least in her earlier history. Slavery existed, as it existed in every nation at that time, but in Israel the slaves were protected by law; were treated as part of the household, and the year of jubilee fixed the limit of bondage. The Israelites had learned more than the arts and sciences during their experience in Egypt.

* Jennings' Antiquities of the Jews, page 468. † Ibid.

A careful study of the ancient Jewish polity will show that the lands were kept as the equal possession of all the people of each generation. It was impossible it could aggregate in large tracts in a few hands. The term of alienation may be said to have been limited to a period that on an average would cover the generation that so disposed of it, and was merely a limited privilege to secure payment of debts. An increase of population would diminish the amount of the estate that would revert to each of the descendants, and vice versa. Their whole system was carefully founded on the idea that as population increased the redistributions and reduction of amounts held for use should keep pace with it.

It has been estimated, at a moderate computation, that the land to be divided among the Israelites in the time of Joshua, on both sides of the Jordan, that is, of available land, was at least twenty-five millions of acres. One estimate of the number of acres to each head of a family is about forty-two.* The lowest estimate of the number of acres to each family was twenty-two. In addition to this there was the pasture lands in the mountains and the oasis of the desert. It has also been computed that, as population increased, if it should be necessary to reduce this to six acres to each family, it could support an agricultural population of four millions of families, or twenty millions of people, besides those in the cities who might be engaged in other pursuits.†

It will thus be seen that the outlines of the Jewish land policy were: *First,* a division for each tribe. *Second,* a division for each family in each tribe. *Third,* while temporary alienations were permitted on a clearly defined basis, once in each fifty years it went back, with all its belongings, to the descendants of the family originally owning it, and, of course, had to be subdivided according to the number of interested

* Wine's Commentaries on the Laws of the Ancient Hebrews, page 388.

† Ibid., page 391.

families. *Fourth,* the land was not permitted to be exhausted, but must have a fallow or rest once in seven years, no matter who occupied it. *Fifth,* that while all improvements and farms in the field, and in villages, were thus held for the use of each succeeding generation and could not be alienated from them, the piece of ground on which a house stood in a walled city was held to be a chattel, which, if sold, could not, after the lapse of one year, be redeemed. This was, no doubt, on the theory that the lots in a walled city could produce nothing; that they were only the foundation for the buildings that covered them, and probably because the population of these cities constantly fluctuated. These were the peculiar features of the Jewish land laws. In the laws of inheritance, all the succeeding generations were considered. "To many thou shalt give the more inheritance, and to few thou shalt give the less inheritance. To every one shalt his inheritance be given according to those that were numbered of him." * Sons and daughters had their share, but if a woman married out of her tribe she lost her share of the tribal inheritance of land.†

In many respects, this Jewish polity differed from that of ancient nations. With most of these the land was claimed by the sovereign. The cultivators were tenants and paid rent or tribute to the government, and with them this was one of the main sources from which revenue was derived. The Jewish monarchs were not recognized as having any title or claim to the land. One of the serious offences committed by the kings being the attempt to appropriate the land of other men, as witness the case of Ahab, who took the vineyard of Naboth the Jezreelite. In fact, the Jewish plan of government was essentially democratic or popular.‡ The will of the people was the highest law, consistent with the fact that it

* Num. xxvi. 54.

† Num. xxxvi. 7, 9.

‡ Von Ranke's Universal History, page 49.

recognized the will of the Deity as the source of all law. Even the question of worship was submitted to them. "If God be God, serve him, and if Baal, serve him." It was indeed a theocracy, but a theocracy that recognized no man as the vicegerent of God. Popular assemblies settled the most important questions, and the doctrine of equal, popular rights lay at the foundation of their religion and morals.

The early days of the Jewish nation, before the monarchy, were the days of its simplicity and power. It then existed according to the spirit and tenor of its laws. A throne was offered to Gideon, but he patriotically rejected it, and said: "Jehovah shall rule over you." Their religion was the worship of the unseen God, and a repudiation of all idols. Of the whole nation it was said: "And ye shall be unto me a kingdom of priests."* The law as given originally by Moses will be found much simpler and purer than a good deal that was engrafted on it. The penalty of stealing a man and making a slave of him was death. A species of slavery to extinguish debt was allowed, but these slaves were not permitted to be oppressed, and, as has been said, slavery had its limit. False weights and measures were an abomination. A laborer was not to be defrauded, but what was due him was to be paid ere the sun went down. Usury was forbidden, and, although they subsequently exacted usury from the heathen, it had originally little color of law.† A stranger sojourning with them was to be treated as one born among them. They were not permitted to oppress strangers. In their buying and selling they were enjoined "not to defraud one another." They were not to glean their fields and vineyards bare; a part was to be left for the poor,—and on all rested the obligations of hospitality in its broadest extent.

On this government of the people a species of monarchy was engrafted. It was an accident, and worse than an acci-

* Ex. xix. 6.

† Ex. xxii. 25, 26.

dent. Samuel warned the people of their folly when they demanded a king, and they had abundant reason to repent of it. The reign of the first monarch, Saul, was disastrous, its decadence dating almost from its beginning. The Jewish government was a theocracy; grave questions were referred to the Lord, and answers obtained by the priests from the Urim and Thummim. Saul undertook to consult the Lord himself, and from that moment Samuel took issue with him. Had Samuel failed to do this, there would have been no check upon an ambitious ruler. Although the sceptre had departed from Saul's house, he remained on the throne until his death, when the Jewish kingdom was rent in twain. David at first only established his authority over Judah and Benjamin, and Ishbosheth, Saul's son, had an uncertain kingly authority over the other ten tribes. Ishbosheth proved to be neither a statesman nor a politician, and soon quarrelled with his men of might. David was a good politician and adroit ruler. He cemented the tribe of Benjamin to Judah, and to the fortunes of his house by removing the capitol to Jerusalem in the country of Benjamin. The capitol played no small part in the polity of the Jewish government. Every man was required to go up thither at least once a year. There many of the tithes were received. The whole system eventually built up much wealth and power about Jerusalem. This power, and the religion centreing there, were the anchors of the Jewish state.

As has been said the government of Israel, whether of judges or monarchs, did not claim the land. It belonged to the people, and to the people alike of each succeeding generation. The government and the church were supported by tithes. One-tenth of all the increase was assessed under the Levitical law, whether of fruits, grain or herds. Tithes have been denounced as the most iniquitous of all taxes. It is not the purpose of this chapter to argue that question, but to state the facts.

This one-tenth of the annual production supported the

church with its priests and ceremonies, and a system of education the most general, and, for that reason, the best of the ancient world. Other nations, like the Greeks, had schools of a very high order where a few great men were taught. Tithes also maintained the complete judicial system, and preserved the public records which were carefully and jealously kept. Indeed, the whole government machinery was maintained by tithes. It is proper to add that there was a poll tax. It was levied the first time when the Jews were numbered in the wilderness, and was "appointed for the service of the tabernacle of the congregation." * It was at first, and in all the earlier and better portions of Jewish history, an exigency tax.† Originally, it amounted to half a shekel, but in the later period of the Jewish history, when it became annual, and in the Roman days it was about one-fourth of a shekel, equal to about twenty-five or thirty cents. Josephus informs us that Vespasian directed the same tax to be paid, but into the Roman instead of the Jewish treasury. How often the kings levied taxes, and what they consisted of, is not very well known, but the record shows that the people groaned under their exactions.

Let us compare the tithes with our own taxes. With us, land is taxed to the owner. It is safe to say that land does not produce much more, over and above the seed and the necessary expense, than from ten to twenty per cent. of its fixed value. If ten per cent. of this latter was taken for tax it would be from one to two dollars per acre. If we average our taxes for all purposes, they are not much less, and it must be borne in mind that we place a tax on the land at a fixed valuation, whether there is a crop or not.

We must remember that the tithes were not necessarily the property of the Jewish sovereign, but were really or nominally controlled by the church. The Jewish monarchy was

* Ex. xxx. 12.

† Lowman's Civil Government of the Hebrews, page 96.

weak. Property in the soil is the natural foundation for power, because everybody is dependent on it. The Jewish king had nothing to do with that. So far as he was able, he became a part of the theocracy. He had in that way some control over the tithes. David, as has been said, was an astute politician. His reign was chiefly distinguished by efforts to build up the monarchy. By caution and forbearance he was finally enabled to stretch his authority over all the twelve tribes. These tribes were, however, independent states. The kingly authority was exercised very gently upon them. On all important questions they held their own councils. David did not attempt to concentrate the great wealth and power at Jerusalem, which his son, after him, succeeded in doing. By conquests over his neighbors he extended the boundaries of most of the tribes. He was thus able to add to their landed inheritance, and to enrich them with the spoils of their enemies.

His son Solomon became the head of the theocracy as well as king. He commenced the great temple by voluntary contributions. In his reign the Jewish empire extended from the Mediterranean to the great river (Euphrates). With the exception of a few cities and limited territories of the Phœnicians, it touched Egypt at the south, and reached almost to the gates of Damascus. His father David had succeeded in taking Damascus, one of the most important of his conquests, for it lay at the threshold of overland commerce between the great empires of the East and West.* During the early part of Solomon's reign this was lost. He, however, erected fortified places on the great commercial roads in order to control them, and made alliances with Pharaoh, of Egypt, and the Phœnician kings of Tyre. In cementing his power, his father, King David, had organized an independent military force, instead of depending on the armies furnished by the

* Von Ranke's Universal History, page 48.

tribes. At the muster of all the tribes, in David's reign, the valiant men who drew the sword were one million three hundred thousand. The Gibborum was a separate force, and was the army of the king. With this he placed garrisons in the cities. Thus a military aristocracy began to grow up in his reign, which was continued and increased during that of Solomon, becoming very objectionable to the tribes. This, and the burdens laid upon the people to maintain such a system were fertile causes of the future evils that befell the kingdom. The reign of Solomon was not so much a period of conquest as had been that of his father. He cemented his power, but in building the temple and the palaces of ivory his reign became one of splendor and luxury, and these began to sap the life of the people. The seeds of dissolution were sown, and when the son of Solomon ascended the throne of his father, the ten states of the Jewish empire made demands before they would acknowledge him. "All Israel came to Shechem to make him king." It was really an election. As a preliminary, they demanded: "Make thou the grievous service of thy father, and his heavy yoke that he put on us, lighter, and we will serve thee." Not being a statesman, this he refused to do. Even in the days of Solomon, a prophet had marked out a man of another tribe and house as his successor. Jeroboam, of the tribe of Ephraim, had assisted King Solomon in securing compulsory service for his great buildings. While so engaged, he betrayed ambitious schemes, and fled into Egypt to escape the wrath of Solomon. In Egypt he married a princess, the sister of the then Pharaoh, and she aided him in his designs. When the ten tribes revolted, exclaiming, "What portion have we in David, neither have we inheritance in the son of Jesse," then the Jewish empire was forever rent in twain, and the conspirator, Jeroboam, now appeared as the king of the ten tribes. Rehoboam at first intended, at the head of an army, to subdue them, but was admonished by a prophet to desist, which was evidently judicious advice.

The two ambitious ruling tribes were Ephraim and Judah. Usually, all the kings were chosen from one or the other of these tribes. Joshua was of the tribe of Manasseh.* Gideon was of the tribe of Manasseh, as was Deborah. Ephraim and Manasseh were the two tribes who trace their origin to Joseph and his Egyptian wife.† The Jewish law was stringent in forbidding marriages with other nations for the avowed reason that it might lead to idolatry. It is difficult to say just how strictly this rule was observed. Moses had an Ethiopian wife.‡ Benjamin, the full brother of Joseph by Rachel, and the tribe which sprang from him, furnished the first King of Israel, Saul. Strangely enough, and although David overthrew the house of Saul, by his arts as a statesman he converted the tribe of Benjamin, until Judah and Benjamin were fast allies. It is not surprising that jealousies grew up between the ambitious rulers of the great tribes of Judah and Ephraim. Before the monarchy each of these states was comparatively independent, consulting upon, and to a great extent determining their own affairs. The Levites, to whom was assigned the administration of the law and religious ordinances, were *not* permitted to own land. Certain cities were set apart for their residences and the immediate suburbs for their cattle. They were thus stripped of the means of consolidating their power, and, practically, had little more than a sufficient income. The wisdom of David for a time checked the jealousies among the tribes, but his descendants, in their pride and aristocracy, forgot his maxims. The great tribe of Ephraim was the fitting rival of Judah when an opposition wanted a head. Jeroboam, jealous of the power of Jerusalem, borrowed the idolatry of the Philistines. When Ephraim revolted, the Jewish monarchy

* Von Ranke's Universal History, page 34. † Ibid., page 37.

‡ Num. xii. 1.

had not sufficient power to check it. Had there been a great army, well secured revenues, and a powerful king, the ten tribes and the rights of their people might have been trampled under foot. The army of the king could not cope with the army of the tribes. The constitution of the Jewish nation, its ideas, principles and law, had nothing in common with monarchy or absolutism. Until its polity was utterly overthrown an enduring monarchy could not be placed upon it. It is, also, well to remember that a great population had grown up in Israel. It has been estimated that at that time, it was as dense as it is in England or Bengal at the present day. Then, and shortly after the disruption, the mountains of Judea were terraced, even to a greater extent than they now are in China.

Jewish history should, properly, be divided into three periods. From Abraham to Moses there elapsed upwards of four hundred years of the patriarchal state, in which the germs of the nation grew. From Moses to the monarchy nearly four hundred years passed away. That was the golden era of the Jewish nation. Its judges and rulers were of popular acceptance. During that four hundred years their peculiar political system was built. Its law was written. Her land system founded on an idea based not only on the rights of all but the rights of each generation. The errors in the system were the barnacles placed there by those who could never have founded such a polity. Then came the five hundred years of wretched monarchy. Schism, disunion, disruption, bad rulers, and attempts to degrade the people and change the principles of the government. Its degenerate fragments were swallowed up by conquest when its wealth and its corruption rendered it a rich prize and an easy prey. The attempt to rebuild and remodel was but a partial success. It struggled along weak internally and the victim of conquest after conquest; on the advent of the Christian era, it was finally rent in fragments; and the people who had been taught by law the evils of usury went forth wanderers and usurers on the face of the earth.

Examining it carefully, it was a wonderful polity, that system of the ancient Jewish nation. It took cognizance of the fact, that a healthy body could only be enjoyed by eating healthy food. Surrounded by nations debased by horrid and obscene crimes, diseased bodies and all manner of uncleanliness, they were taught that cleanliness was next to godliness. Their law pointed out the dangers of usury. Their land belonged to the people, to all the people, and equally to the people of all time. Much in their legal system appears to us now to be barbarous. Tried by the standard of a highly refined age, it doubtless was harsh and perhaps cruel. The laws of a nation can never be safely placed far ahead of the people they are to govern. Idealists lay down theoretical principles. Statesmen adapt the machinery of government to the people and elevate the standard of law, only as fast as they can be lifted. Visionaries chide delay, and visionaries in their place are useful. In studying the Jewish laws, we are, therefore, to study not the few acute or startling points, but the circumstances and condition of the people. We have to study, moreover, the nations by whom they were surrounded, and their besetting sins. We must look, also, to the tendencies of their government. Its underlying principles of purity, morality, equality and justice. Modern men, with all their genius and literature, inheriting the wisdom and wealth of antiquity, may smile at some of the Jewish laws and pronounce them not adapted to the present times; when they have done so, they should read and ponder over the wonderful history and law of the ancient Jewish people. If they can rise above their own prejudices, they will possess a better conception of human nature, government and law. The modern man may boast of the grandeur of his own civilization, he will also feel that in our progress we have forgotten many things, a knowledge of which is necessary for a well-organized and permanent state.

The Jewish nation has passed away, but its history and law have, to a partial extent, become a part of our civilization.

Though scattered, the Hebrews have still an identity. They have left their mark on nearly every later nation, for Christianity sprang from Judaism, and still reveres the old Bible, and accepts much of its law. Ten tribes of ancient Israel have been lost. Like their fathers, they once more became wanderers, not to a promised land, but away from the faith and polity of Israel. Imaginative historians endeavor to trace them in Arabia, India, Siam, China, or even among the aborigines of America. These vain speculations merely show that the great fragments of Israel, wherever they are, have practically passed into oblivion. The ideas on which the Hebrew nation was built are older than the theories and doctrines on which the foundations of Greece and Rome lay, but they have survived both.

Israel has not a country; her people have ceased to make their annual pilgrimages to Jerusalem, and the smoke of her altars does not now ascend to heaven, but there is a wonderful vitality in what is left of her principles. The Year of Jubilee is but a tradition; no longer does the trumpet's sound declare a home for homeless wanderers, or rescue the unfortunate from the grasping hand of avarice. Cleanliness, from being a statute, has passed into the dominion of taste. The law regulating food is confronted by the independent assertion of a man's right to poison his body, and sow in his system the seeds of disease if he chooses. If usury is a crime, the boundaries of that enormity have been lost in a fog thrown around them by political economists, and the laws against it do not seem to be remembered even in Lombard street or Amsterdam. In spite of all this decadence there is enough of the old ideas left to crystallize a Hebrew element at once distinct, and yet certainly potent, in every great modern nation.

CHAPTER II.

SYSTEMS OF LAND AND LABOR IN ANCIENT EMPIRES.

Similarity of populations on the Nile and Euphrates—Landlords and rent in Egypt—All below the privileged army and priesthood had to work—Only one occupation allowed—Every citizen's home and business registered, in Ancient Egypt—Legislation against borrowing money—In Chaldea and Babylon the king and his satraps the sole tyrants—The king as landlord—Persian political economy—Laborers should not be robbed beyond the point when they would cease to produce—Carthage a combination or corporation for merchandising, piracy and slave dealing—Carthage called a republic, but drifted into three classes, slaves, a mercenary army and an aristocracy—Theory and practice of government in Greece—Land laws of Lycurgus—Gold and silver banished—Constant struggle between the aristocrats and laboring people of Greece—Solon and Athens—Debt on land and slaves abolished—Legal value of silver coin increased by law—Timocracy, or man's rights measured by his property—Greece, eaten up by landed and other aristocrats surrenders to tyrants—Rome a robbers' den—Reduction of the aristocracy and rise of the republic—Division of land among the people—Seven acres enough—Land assigned on two year terms—Gradual absorption of land and money by the equestrian order—Slaves take the place of free laborers—Death of Tibèrius Gracchus—Overthrow of the republic—Citizens subsidized—Swallowed up by despotism and immorality.

THE recorded pages of ancient history are a very barren field in which to glean a knowledge of the condition of the people. Of wars, conquerors, kings and emperors, there is a surfeit. We read of great temples and palaces; of mighty pyramids, towers, walls, artificial lakes and canals, but are rarely informed whether they were built by an enslaved people, or by captives of war dragged from other countries to perform the menial tasks of the conquerors. We are apt to measure the greatness of ancient nations by the monuments erected upon human suffering and degradation. Herodotus estimates that it required over one hundred thousand laborers for thirty years to build the great pyramid.

The most ancient seats of learning, wealth and power, of which we have record, are the Chaldean, Babylonian and the Egyptian. The empires on the Euphrates in many respects resembled the empires on the Nile. Both were extremely fertile regions. In both the agricultural systems depended on irrigation. Both were almost surrounded by deserts. The valley of the lower Nile is shut in by hills which approach within fifteen miles of the river.* Babylon was the daughter of Chaldea.† The civilization of Egypt and Chaldea were identical.‡ Their modes of agriculture, religion, manners and customs, and, to some extent, their architecture were similar. In each slavery existed, and while laborers were also hired, the condition of the laboring classes was at once abject and unhappy. Rawlinson, one of the best authorities, informs us that the lands in Egypt were held by three parties. The king, or monarch, had one-third, the priests one-third, and the army, which was largely the executive arm of the government, one-third. About one-fifth of the produce was exacted as rent or tribute. The enormous labor of creating and maintaining the canals and lakes for irrigation, was done, under the supervision of the army, largely by slaves. To equalize and extend the period of the irrigation from the Nile, and prevent disastrous floods, a lake (Mœris) three hundred feet deep was dug; into this a great portion of the floods could be drained to prevent an overflow. When the river fell below the point at which it could easily furnish water for the canals, the water was drawn from the lake for irrigation. § A shower of rain scarcely ever falls in Egypt.

If representative governments did not exist in Asia, it

* Rawlinson's Ancient Monarchies, vol. i., page 51.

† Ibid., page 47. ‡ Ibid., page 57.

§ Rollin's Ancient History, vol. i., page 127.

would be difficult to trace anything like them in Egypt. Nearly all these Oriental governments were theocracies. The priesthood represented the law, supposed to be divine law. In most of them the priests claimed to have some method of communicating with the gods. It was so in Egypt, and in Babylon, and in Greece the utterances of the Delphic oracle had great acceptance. There is a wonderful similarity in these governments in that respect. In Egypt the priesthood was a distinct and privileged class, and ranked next to the king; they were not allowed to practice polygamy, although the rest of the people were. The priest's share of the available land was free from taxation or tribute.* In addition to their sacred functions, they promulgated the only law known. The king had to enter the temple each morning to worship, when it was customary for the priests to advise him what course to pursue. Even the food of the king, which was plain, was prescribed by law.

Next to the priesthood stood the army. In the days of their power the army, under continual pay, consisted of four hundred thousand men. This army constituted the third estate or privileged class, and to enter it was considered an honor. Each soldier was allowed for the purpose of subsisting himself and family, irrigated land equal to "half a French acre," free from all rent, tax or tribute: also, five pounds of bread, two pounds of meat and a quart of wine daily.† The standing army was, of course, a sufficient menace against all revolt or rebellion.

The monarch who had an army subject to his authority, had also the revenue of rent, tax or tribute from at least the third of all the irrigated lands. Nor was this his only source of revenue. He levied imposts on commerce, and several branches of trade. A percentage of certain fisheries brought

* Rawlinson's Ancient History, vol. i., page 143.

† Rollin's Ancient History, vol. i., page 151.

revenue. Public works were chiefly created and maintained by slave labor, the slaves being largely aliens, captives of war, or persons purchased from the Phœnicians, Greeks, or the semi-barbarous people in central Africa.

As the monarch, the priests and the army owned the land, they thus held the real substance of power: the remainder of the people were divided into three classes in the following order of rank: shepherds, husbandmen and artificers, or artizans.* Each man had his place of business assigned by law, and no one was permitted to have two separate occupations or professions; nor could he make a change in his business very easily. This was done really or ostensibly to allow a fair field to each occupation. No man was allowed to be a useless idler in the state. Every man had to enter his name and business in a register. If he gave a false statement he was put to death.

Under the law, people were allowed a reasonable liberty in their individual business, provided they did not attempt to interfere with the authority of the government. It was the boast of the early Egyptian rulers that murder was almost invariably punished, and the murder of a slave was as much a violation of the law as the murder of a freeman. No slave or foreigner was admitted to the immediate service of the prince,† and thus one of the chief avenues to advancement was shut against them.

Egypt was styled the granary of the world. Its chief grain products were wheat, barley and rye. It also produced flax and cotton.‡ Cotton was first introduced into upper Egypt in very early times. It was used to a considerable extent in manufacturing clothing for the people. The fine cotton goods of Egypt were greatly prized in Greece. Except the date palms and the sycamore, Egypt had no lofty trees. Herodotus

* Rollin's Ancient History, vol. i., page 153. † Ibid., page 139.

‡ Heren's Ancient Nations of Africa, vol. ii., page 349.

informs us, that "when the river is full and the plains are become a sea, there springs up in the water great quantities of lilies, called lotus by the Egyptians." These the inhabitants gather and from what is contained in them make a kind of bread. The root is also made into food. Herodotus says, that the use of the wine press was unknown in Egypt, although wine was allowed to be used by the priests and the people were permitted to drink it at festivals. We have seen that the military order also consumed it. Wine was largely imported from Greece, and was also obtained through the Phœnicians. The "father of history" informs us, that the common people of Egypt, at other times than festivals, "drank a kind of beer made from barley." It is proper to state, however, that vineyards were not altogether unknown in Egypt. Among other productions spoken of by Herodotus was the byblus, which is produced in shallow water. From it the papyrus or paper, cordage and other articles of merchandise was made. It was, in addition, prepared into food and its stalk chewed for its juice.

Breeding of cattle, swine, horses, asses, mules, camels and goats, constituted the second great producing interest next to agriculture. As the Egyptians worshiped the sacred bull, and as rams as well as serpents were in their pantheon, we might have been led to expect that the Egyptians, like the people of India, would not have made food of cattle or sheep, and that this would have affected their production. It does not appear to have been the case, however. Horses were reared for war and were chiefly used by the military order and the aristocracy; they were likewise largely used for exportation.* Cattle were produced for labor as well as food. Large flocks of sheep were reared for the wool and were used for food. The period of cultivation was a very brief one in Egypt, the crops following immediately after the flood.

* Heren's Ancient Nations of Africa, vol. ii., page 356.

Plowing could hardly be said to be needed, although plowing and stirring the soil to considerable extent was done. The great object was to have the crops in at once on the fresh deposit, when the water abated, so that they could mature before the earth thoroughly dried out. Irrigating, where it was practicable, was carried on by canals and ditches, and water for the purpose was also pumped from the river. Indeed, the more we are enabled to learn of the Egyptians, the more we are forced to admit that they were not deficient in the arts of production. They even hatched eggs in ovens. Egypt had as colonies a great many cities and communities in Europe, Asia and Africa. It was almost as famous as Tyre, for dyes and cloths, and had quite a trade in gold, ivory and slaves, with the interior of Africa.

Egypt, at one time, had stringent laws against usury, or, more correctly, against borrowing money. The legislation of Egypt against borrowing money, while it was done ostensibly in the interests of the people, was also a policy against the cumulative power of capital in money. The rulers already held the other sources of wealth and did not intend to have any rivals. This legislation against the productive power of money was not peculiar to Egypt, for many of the more enlightened of the ancient nations did the same thing. The tendency of the poor and needy to pay usurious rates of interest is at least as old as Egypt, and when the money of a country has added to its other forces the power of addition and multiplication, in adroit hands, it will soon draw to itself all the wealth that there is in any country. The Egyptian law was designed to prevent such a result. In Egypt, moreover, borrowing had some additional drawbacks. He who ran into debt in the middle portion of Egyptian history, was very apt to run into slavery. At the usual rate of interest it would not have taken very many generations to reduce the whole of the industrious population to a condition of servitude.

Heren informs us that the later Egyptian governments

regulated loans, fixed the rate of interest, and partially permitted a creditor to indemnify himself for a debt when he could do it from other property besides the person of his debtor. The general policy of Egypt was to prevent the aggregation of capital by usury. During a portion of her history, the citizens of Egypt proper were not allowed to be enslaved for debt.

The manufactures of Egypt were as important and probably as highly developed as those of any nation. Heren says that two or three thousand years ago their weaving was brought to as great or even greater perfection than ours at present. The same authority tells us that their dyes were splendid. They had a great business in fabrics of wool, flax, cotton, gold thread and other material. The Egyptian earthenware was of very fine quality. They were also skillful workers in metals, gold, silver, bronze and brass. After the waste and destruction of three thousand years her architecture presents the most imposing monuments of human power and skill.

While the area of Egypt was limited, its food-producing power was great, thus creating large populations: for this reason we find the government had a fixed and continuous policy of encouraging emigration.* They sent colonies to all parts of the world, carrying their laws, customs and boasted politeness with them. Homer tells us that the Ethiopians were divided from the rising to the setting of the sun. This appeared to have been more for the purpose of disposing of their surplus population than with a policy of possessing colonies and retaining them. For many centuries there was the closest relations between the cities of Egypt, Phœnicia, Asia Minor and Greece. To Egypt the scholars of Greece and other countries resorted to finish their education and acquire information as to her arts and literature.

* Rollin's Ancient History, Vol. i., page 151.

Many changes occurred in the history of Egypt. The Ethiopians conquered Egypt and held it for several generations. After that there were many changes in the rulers and yet no fundamental changes in the constitution of its government. Caste ruled in Egypt. The military, the priesthood and the monarch held the wealth as well as the power of Egypt in their grasp. So long as these three agreed the people had no power to resist them.

Heren informs us that Psammetichus overthrew and finally forced the military caste of the Egyptians to emigrate to Ethiopia. He and his successors stripped them of their lands, and the later rulers depended nearly altogether on mercenary soldiers, chiefly from other countries. To sustain them, heavier exactions were made from the people. In order to keep the turbulent spirits of this unpatriotic army employed, and to offer them the inducement of plunder, indispensable for such soldiers, foreign conquests were attempted, chiefly in Asia, and these were not always successful. Weakened, robbed and dispirited, it is no wonder that Egypt succumbed to the Persian conqueror. It is significant of the indifference of the people, that he was able in one battle and a siege of ten days, to decide the fate of the whole country. Cambyses lost an army of seventy thousand men, endeavoring to penetrate the upper Nile, destroyed by the inhospitable deserts rather than hostilities. From this period forward the history of Egypt is one of wars, conquests, and political vicissitudes, in which the people suffer from one set of kingly robbers after another, Darius, Xerxes, Ochus, Alexander. Then for nearly three hundred years Egyptian history is again elevated by the dynasty of the Ptolemys and then came Cæsar, Anthony and the Romans, and for more than three hundred years it was a Roman province: its wealth was drained to benefit an alien nation. Then came the conquest of the Persians once more, and then of the Saracen and Turk. In the midst of all these, Egypt, the cradle of human civilization and power, has sunk so low that no people are now as wretched, spiritless or poverty-stricken, and this notwithstanding the country possesses the finest natural resources.

The valleys of the Tigris and Euphrates were richer than even the Nile. Herodotus tells us that no country in the world is so fertile, and that the blade of wheat is often four fingers in width. Babylon, Nineveh and all their ruling cities were dens of plunder. The monarch owned the land and demanded heavy tribute from it. The system of irrigation was in charge of the king and his subordinates, while the wretched agriculturist was ground to death between the exactions of the monarch and his horde of petty princes, deputies and tax collectors. Herodotus tells us of one governor who derived from his province two bushels of silver each day in tribute, and who had a stud of sixteen thousand mares. Hosts of slaves captured in war were employed to perform the most menial tasks, but the condition of the poor native laborer was hardly any better. He was generally so severely burdened by regular taxes and special tribute for war purposes, that it was almost impossible for him to retain a bare subsistence. If he made more he was obliged to conceal it, or expose himself to petty banditti, or further exaction from deputies of royal robbers.

The worst governments known to men have been governments of deputies. A royal ruler may have an occasional gleam of greatness about him, and even his position invites from him some exercise of magnanimity, but a deputy has all the vices of his master added to his own. No portion of the globe has been so governed by deputies as the various Asiatic countries. These ancient deputies, local governors and petty satraps, to some extent resemble the directors of our modern railroads, whose first business is to get rich themselves, and finally, to extract from their employees all they can for the benefit of the corporation. An Eastern potentate rarely made any inquiries of his deputy so long as he sent forward a liberal amount of tribute.

The gods of the Assyrians were gods of war. War and conquest ran through their whole dominion. They adopted a somewhat novel policy intended to open a field of enterprise to the ambitious at home, and maintain a subordinate population in the seats of empire. As fast as they, by force of arms, subjugated states, they sent all the inhabitants thereof who might be troublesome to them, as slaves, to the country of the conqueror, and colonized the countries taken with numbers of their own people, who thus became the local rulers of the conquered provinces.* The vanquished people were subject to tribute. Phœnicia and Israel fell before them. They carried their arms with great atrocity into Armenia and the other northern provinces, and in case of revolt or refusal to pay tribute, flayed the insurgents alive. They conquered a portion of Media and built fortresses in that country. Egypt paid tribute. Damascus became an outpost for their troops, and while Arabia did not entirely succumb, it was subject to their influence. Indeed, Assyria is the first great conquering power we encounter in the history of the world. It united the Semetic races for the first time of which we have record.† In all its annals of blood and violence it would be vain to seek for statutes maintaining human rights, a religion founded on justice, or a people whose interests were ever considered. An empire resting on an aristocracy of soldiers, and maintained by tribute and slavery, is all that can be discovered.

The founding of a new Persian empire, about 230 A.D., under Artaxerxes, was of significant importance in this, that it re-established an authority strong enough to cope with the Romans, if not to drive them from Asia, and substituted the rule of the Aryan Persians for that of the ruder Scyths of the North. Five hundred years had elapsed between the old Persian empire and this revival. In the meantime, Jew, Christian, Greek and pagan had spread their forms of worship,

* Von Rankes Universal History, page 81. † Ibid.

and, to a more limited extent, their forms of society. Artaxerxes, as soon as his authority was placed on a secure footing, re-established the religion of the Mâgi, and the doctrines of Zoroaster. In a brief space the places of worship of all the other religions were closed, and, although the Zoroastrian doctrines were not supposed to be persecuting, Artaxerxes, at least, was proscriptive. It is said in the Zendavesta that there were twin deities, the spirits of good and evil, Ormuzd, the creator, and Ahriman, the destroyer, and that their battle is fought in a being called Time. All created things are regarded as designed for the struggle against evil. The doctrine that the good deity only permits evil was not held by the Persians. Their code of morals taught that he is a wise man who brings his offering to the altar, and a good man who has a well-ordered household, and produces the greatest quantity of corn, fodder, and fruit-bearing trees. In the sacred books little is said of monarchy.

One of Artaxerxes' maxims was that "The king should never use the sword when the cane would answer," * which merely indicated the gradations in despotism. He also held that it was the true policy of the government to make the people feel absolute security.† This was a very good maxim, but how far it was possible, under a satrapy in which the local ruler was kept in his place by forwarding a certain annual tribute, is not so clear. Another of his celebrated opinions was: "There can be no power without an army, no army without money, no money without agriculture, and no agriculture without justice." ‡ This, doubtless, sounds well. What is meant I suppose by "no agriculture without justice," is that the exactions of the rulers must never reach a point at which the agriculturist would cease producing. This suggests the cause of the ruin of nearly all these governments.

* Rawlinson's 7th Monarchy, vol. i., page 67.

† Ibid., page 61.

‡ Ibid.

To temper rapacity with moderation may not require much "justice," but some brains. We are further told by the same eminent authority we have quoted, that "heavy tributes were laid on the land." * In point of fact these monarchs claimed to own all the land, not only of their native country, but the countries they conquered. They were the mighty potentates who could decide on what conditions men should live upon the earth.

No great constitutional government was formed in Asia with a complete code of law, much less a republic. The towns and communities had their rule and customs, and none of the empires we have described charged themselves with the faithful execution of what we consider the legitimate functions of government. They conquered, plundered and exacted tribute. The wars were merely between those who claimed this privilege.

One of the most wonderful forms of society that ever existed in ancient or modern times was what is styled the Phœnician. Herodotus tells us that "the Phœnicians emigrated from the Red Sea to the Mediterranean, and having made their settlements, applied themselves to merchandise." There was an ancient Tyre on the Red Sea, and also a place of that name on the Persian Gulf. In the time of the Carthaginians there was also a Tyre on the Mediterranean in the west. They seem, in their migration, to have had a habit, like the people of these United States, of reproducing and multiplying the old names. Heren informs us that all the nations who traded on the Mediterranean were at the same time pirates, and it was their particular business to kidnap men from the coasts.† The inlets on the coastline between Egypt and Greece gave shelter to a thriving and industrious nation of traders and seamen.‡

* Rawlinson's 7th Monarchy, vol. i., page 112.

† Heren's Ancient Nations of Africa, vol. ii., page 369.

‡ Von Ranke's Universal History, page 60.

The communities of the Phœnicians might be styled independent cities. Tyre adopted a constitutional monarchy in the days of Solomon. There never was a Phœnician empire. They remembered and maintained their own kinship, and aided each other, and refused to take part in military operations against any branch of their own people. As they freely intermarried with all the people where they planted colonies, their identity was maintained by the distinct religious and commercial ideas that animated them. Labor was performed by slaves. Their armies were largely of mercenaries hired from all nations. They excelled in the arts and manufactures. Their ships carried raw material from every nation, and carried back rich manufactures. Their religion was a mixture of Babylonian idolatry and Parseeism, and closely resembled types found in the Arabian peninsula before the time of Mahomet. Its purpose was to blind and overawe the masses rather than teach pure morality. They worshiped in "high places." Baal and Astarte were among their divinities. The sun was an object of adoration, as the eye of God, and the summer solstice was their great festival. Their rites were cruel and unclean. Human sacrifices stained their altars, and oxen, horses and other animals were also sacrificed. They passed their children through the fire to Moloch by placing them in the arms of the frightful metal deity, Baal, that dropped them in the furnace. Immorality also disgraced their forms of worship.

Gold, however, was the chief god they worshiped. For it their ships sailed beyond the pillars of Hercules and down the African coast, where they procured gold dust, not from the desert sands, which are never golden; but they obtained it together with slaves and ivory from the interior and the great mountainous districts in Africa, which were, and are still supposed to be rich in gold. They visited Gaul (France), Britain, Hibernia, and Scandinavia. From Britain they procured tin, and from the mountains of Greece and Asia Minor, copper, and lead and tin also from Spain. Their bronzes and brass ornaments were the admiration of nations. They procured the murex principally from the coasts of Greece, and from them produced their most famous dyes. Their looms wove the finest fabrics. Wool they chiefly obtained from Greece and Arabia. They manufactured and had a commerce in amber, and it is believed they traded in the Baltic and thus obtained it. It would not be surprising if they had visited what is now China, and it is also believed that they visited the western as well as the eastern coast of the Americas.

The Phœnicians were a strange nation of commercial adventurers. They have been styled the Jews of ancient times, but differ from them very widely in many particulars. Their ships sailed to "the uttermost parts of the earth." The rowers and other laborers were slaves; the fighting force, mercenaries from all countries, organized and governed by Phœnicians. In their voyages to many of the countries they visited they were very secretive. None were permitted to have knowledge of their more important maritime secrets, save societies or associations bound by obligations of secrecy. From this has arisen the idea that the masonic order originated with them.

The purpose of their secrecy was to prevent other nations from finding out their sources of trade. Their vessels watched those ships which attempted to pass the straits of Gibraltar or pillars of Hercules. Besides hand-to-hand conflicts when vessels were driven together, trained slingers from the Balearic islands, and bowmen, waged this naval warfare. The most important manœuvre in these early naval engagements was to run each other down. The Phœnicians acquired great skill in making large and strong vessels for this purpose, and they had them manned with numerous sweeps worked by a great body of rowers, in order to turn rapidly and be driven with great force upon the enemy. To this they chiefly owed their supremacy on the sea.

While their traditional policy was to place the world under tribute by trade, and to plant colonies to aid them in that purpose, we do not often find them overrunning great landed territories that could be taken from them by more powerful nations, and laid under tribute. Their stations were trading stations, often limited in extent and many of them abandoned on the appearance of serious opposition. With the Egyptians they tried to cultivate alliance, but as the dwellers on the Nile were also a commercial people, they were continually embroiled in wars with them. The Phœnicians were masters of the Mediterranean before the Greeks became a maritime power; as the Greek colonies pushed out into Sicily and Asia Minor the wars between the Greeks and Phœnicians began. When Xerxes the Persian invaded Greece he without much difficulty effected an alliance with the Phœnicians and Carthaginians, both of whom furnished ships. When Alexander invaded Asia he had not forgotten the share Tyre had in the former wars and laid siege to it. Nebuchadnezzar had taken and destroyed the old Tyre on the mainland and the inhabitants never rebuilt it but took shelter on the island where the city was four miles in circumference. There with their fleets they supposed they were impregnable. The siege by Alexander lasted eight months. Tyre fell in the year 332 B.C. It maintained some little importance afterward but never regained its power. Before the last calamity and during its various troubles, many of its citizens fled to Carthage and other colonies, and carried with them much wealth.

Carthage had the most remarkable history of any people of the Phœnician stock. The founders of Carthage in making the settlement purchased from the native inhabitants a tract of ground for the use of the city, and as they were a commercial people they agreed that the greater part of the price should be an annual tribute. As soon as they became strong enough they went to war with their creditors and thus cancelled the obligation. They did more; in a very short time that region of Africa styled Libya was placed under tribute.* A part of Libya was susceptible of cultivation. Whether the inhabitants were originally agriculturists or became so under the influence of Carthage is not very clear. They produced not only grain in considerable quantities, but other articles. To keep these native tribes in subjection, they placed colonies of their own people among them, who intermarried with them, and these people were known as Carthaginian-Libyans. To the east, west and south of them were nomadic tribes. The nomads were not only in their pay as mercenaries, but as common carriers, regular caravans to the valley of the Nile and Central Africa being established. From the foundation of Carthage to its overthrow, about seven hundred years elapsed. It always pretended to be a republic. It was the boast of Carthaginians that for five hundred years there was no considerable sedition to disturb, or tyrant to oppress their people.† They selected three different authorities, which were supposed to balance each other, or act as counterpoises. They had a senate, two supreme magistrates, called suffetas, and popular assemblies for deliberation. As Carthage grew, the tribunal of one hundred was added. The suffetas were chosen each year. The senate was composed of old, distinguished, and, finally, of rich persons, for a man had to be possessed of a certain amount of property before he was eligible.‡ While it has been alleged that no office could be obtained except by election, it is pretty certain that the wealthy classes filled nearly all positions of power. As no salaries were paid, they were really the only persons who could maintain the degree of state required.

Carthage derived her revenue from customs on all articles exported or imported; from tribute and from mines which she worked by slave labor, in all countries where she could

* Heren's Ancient Nations of Africa, vol. i., page 31.

† Rollin's Ancient History, vol. i., page 191. ‡ Ibid., page 193.

find them. In times of great necessity, her tribute amounted to half the production.* Aristotle points out what he calls the defects in the government of Carthage—"First, that it permitted a man to have more than one occupation; second, that a certain estate or amount of wealth was required to render a man eligible for the higher offices; and, thirdly, that they used money to carry elections." While the assemblages of the people were supposed to be the highest tribunal, everything tended to aristocracy. They were a purely and highly commercial people. Everything was bought and sold in Carthage. The adventurers of her own and every other country were paid to fight her battles. The great, wealthy families supplied the generals, although they were supposed to be elected. The families of Hanno and the Barcas furnished the most notable, among the latter, Hannibal, Hamilcar and Asdrubal. Almost half of Africa and Europe were, at different times, in the pay of Carthage.† Tribes of Gauls, at an early period, fought in her armies. The small force of Carthaginians constituted the most splendid corps. Next to these were the Spanish and Celtic troops. Italy furnished several tribes, and even Greece. The Balearic slingers could hurl stones with sufficient force to break shield and buckler. One of her most formidable forces was the Arab cavalry, who, in their rapid wheeling and fierce charges, often decided the fate of battle. Ten thousand of these nomadic cavalry were in their service at one time. Their armies must have produced a curious effect in the field, and Polybius says the Carthaginians purposely composed their armies of people of different languages so that they could not conspire together against them. It must, however, have been a difficult force to handle. We are told that these troops were largely armed with spear and knife, until after the battle of Thrasymene,

* Heren's Ancient Nations, vol. i., page 149.

† Heren's Ancient Nations of Africa, vol. i., page 250.

when Hannibal exchanged them for the Roman arms. In the Roman war with Regulus, the Carthaginian fleet was composed of three hundred and fifty vessels and one hundred and sixty thousand men, including mercenary soldiers and slave rowers.*

In this strange organization we find an empire almost without a country: an aggregation of men, with money as the motive power: great wars fought without patriotism, and whole nations enslaved and purchased by an ingenious, active, unscrupulous and selfish race. A few great families were very wealthy. The city was a citadel for spoils. There was absolutely nothing in their economy upon which a happy, prosperous working class could permanently thrive. Her commerce was selfish, secret, exacting. Her morals were low, and uttered no protest against hopeless slavery, piracy, slave-dealing, or conquest for aggrandisement. Her religion inspired cruelty and melancholy. When it was cheaper to bribe the councils of her enemies than to fight them, they did not hesitate to do so, and during her struggle with Rome, Jugurtha turned his back on the imperial city, and said, "There is a city for sale if you can only find a purchaser."

Their history instructs us that an aristocracy of wealth may become as dangerous as a landed aristocracy. The liberality of the rich chiefly consisted in deporting the poorer classes to some of their many colonies, where they would enable the rulers to extend their spider's web, and would not remain to foment disturbances at home. Some of the ancient, moralizing philosophers tell us that when the people permitted the senate largely to rule, it governed well, as the senators were wise persons of acknowledged character, who had a *deep* interest in the state. Polybius informs us that when the people attempted, or did take the rule in their own hands, they were led by factions and demagogues, until this resulted

* Heren's Ancient Nations of Africa, vol. i., page 247.

in the overthrow of Carthage. The truth is that it was impossible to govern this central den of pirates, robbers and thieves, by a government of the people, unless on principles of equal distribution.

Greece affords us the most elaborate and benignant theories of government and the most sorrowful aggregate of statistics. On endeavoring to obtain data we are met by another difficulty; it is extremely hard to sift out legend and mythical figures from plain reliable facts. Most of the old Greek worthies were, if we are to believe them, descended from the gods. Their gods, moreover, were much too numerous to afford a very elevated grade of deity. If we estimate these fanciful personages, their ways, works and belongings, including all the satyrs and other monsters by whom they were surrounded, they do not afford us a very high opinion of the morals of a people who could invent and look up to such a pantheon.

Greece, unlike Egypt and Babylon, had no great river with its rich grain products, and thus was not naturally adapted for a despotism. It was mountainous. Most of it was chiefly valuable for raising flocks and herds, and while it possessed some fine valleys, no inconsiderable portion of it was naturally very poor. This wonderful cluster of mountains, islands, bays, deep gulfs and peninsulas, seemed to mark the region as the home of shepherds and fishermen, or the commercial marts for Asia, Africa and Europe. There is little reason to doubt the fact that Greece, in remote periods, had been the theatre on which horde after horde had settled and ship-load after ship-load found a haven from the horrors of war or the pressure of tyranny. It was the boast of the Hellenes that they were descended from the gods, and the people of Attica, Ionians, claimed to be autochthones. From all that can be gathered, the tribes or race styled Pelasgi, seemed to have occupied all lower Greece and most of the islands, when they were intruded upon by the Ionians and Dorians. One or two irruptions came from the north, from or beyond Thrace, and seemed to be a martial people driven from their homes by some political convulsion. It is also equally certain that the Phœnicians had stations and trade on these shores and continued to have them until the commercial and political rivalry, incident to the growth and progress of the Greeks, drove them elsewhere. The first money used in Greece was Phœnician money.* Even before the time that the Phœnicians had passed from the Persian Gulf and the Red Sea to the Mediterranean, or at least, before they had risen to be a great maritime power, Thothmes III. of Egypt, had conquered Cyprus and Crete, and many islands and parts of Greece, and founded colonies there.† It is not a little singular, that one of the early cities founded in Greece, Thebes, should be named after the capital of Egypt.

Herodotus relates that the Phœnicians who came with Cadmus to *Thebes*, introduced letters along with other branches of knowledge to the Greeks. He also informs us that the Ionian books were made of Egyptian papyrus. It is sufficient for the purpose of this work, to show that the elements out of which intellectual Greece grew were of mixed origin, and that some of the most enlightened of ancient nations contributed toward it.

The Lakedæmonians long maintained their contempt for literature and the arts. The ambition of the citizen was to be trained in athletic exercises and inured to hardship and war. Slaves were obtained to perform their menial labor. In early times, according to Herodotus, the Spartans were the most lawless of all the Greeks, and foreigners were afraid to approach them. Their early history is one of turbulent disorder and incessant war. Some time between 820 and 996 before Christ, it is related that a prince or philosopher named Lycurgus, after having visited foreign seats of learning, undertook to restore order and give a constitution to Lakedæmonia.‡ As a

* Von Ranke's Universal History, page 128.

† Rawlinson's Ancient Egypt, vol. ii., page 255.

‡ Grote's Greece, vol. i., page 464.

preliminary, he consulted the Delphic oracle in Bœtia, probably to give an appearance of religious authority to what he intended to do. We learn, that even in that early period, nearly every city in Greece had an aristocratic and a democratic or plebeian class. The avaricious and grasping spirit of a few had reduced the masses to great poverty, which they, as a martial people, were no longer inclined to endure. As Lycurgus belonged to the privileged orders it is more than probable that his attempts were tolerated by the rich in order to prevent worse mischief. Before his time the land had been monopolized until the masses of the people had no land. He induced the people to ordain that the land should belong to the commonwealth, and succeeded in procuring a new distribution of it, founded on the idea that each citizen of the state was entitled to a share sufficient to produce a maintenance.* Observing the aggressive power of money, he adopted the novel expedient of banishing it from the state. Whatever we may think of some of his measures, he was, undoubtedly, conscious of the dangerous tendencies of accumulated capital in money. Plutarch, in his sketch upon Lycurgus, says, that in banishing gold and silver from the community he substituted stamped iron, which had little or no value in itself, and therefore could not be exchanged for foreign luxuries. To correct the abuses of luxury and the enervating effect of refinement, indolence and excess, laws were framed to provide plain diet, plain garments, and induce simple habits and self denial. The children at a certain age were the property of and under care of the state, and their training was rigid. The system was to make them warriors rather than peaceful citizens. The form of government he adopted, whatever it might pretend to be, was certainly anything but democratic. It was a close, unscrupulous, well-obeyed oligarchy.† The senate was a body

* Rollin's Ancient History, vol. i., page 332.

† Grote's Greece, vol. i., page 474.

of twenty-eight "ancient men" appointed for life. They had two kings, who also sat in the Agora and took part in its deliberations, thus making it a body of thirty persons.* In addition to these senators, and to give this oligarchy a popular aspect, Sparta had periodic assemblages of the people, in the open air, between the river Knakion and the bridge. No discussion was permitted in these assemblies. No amendments could be offered. They simply voted on the propositions sent them by the aristocratic senate. Such was the constitution of Lycurgus. It is only surprising that he should have been permitted to carry out such reforms as he instituted. Nothing but the desperate condition to which society was reduced rendered it possible.

Among the struggling Grecian states the great rival of Sparta was Athens. Its institutions, simple at first, soon drifted into disorder. Athens almost from the beginning until the time of Solon was in the hands of an oligarchy. A few great families controlled her concerns. They had done so in a manner to threaten the very existence of the state. The rich and most productive land, the plains and valleys were monopolized by them. The masses were driven to the poor land in the mountains. Commerce and sea-faring were one great source of Athenian wealth. This also fell into a few hands. The real estate held by the poorer classes was mortgaged, the common mode being to set up a pillar with the amount of the debt and to whom due engraved on it. Under a law general in all that region a man who ran in debt could be sold as a slave,—sold to labor in his own country, or sold to a foreigner. Sometimes to escape from debt a man would sell his children. Families were thus torn and scattered. As the citizens of Attica were not totally spiritless, it is scarcely wonderful that they were ready to end this intolerable state of affairs at any cost. To facilitate the matter the

* Grote's Greece, vol. i., page 468.

leading aristocratic families fell out among themselves.* In this condition of affairs Solon appeared. He had been elected archon 594 before Christ. The archons had succeeded the kings and were at first hereditary and then appointed for ten years and finally every year: at that time there were nine of them having varying functions. Their duties were executive and judicial. The chief archon had the power of life and death. The archons had to be selected from families that had been free for three generations. Solon belonged to one of the first aristocratic families, an ancestor, Codrus, being one of the most eminent archons. It is said that his father had wasted much of his substance in prodigality, which caused Solon in his earlier years to devote himself to commerce, and in this way he visited many parts of Greece and Asia. It seems that about the time of his election as archon, the long-continued suffering and debasement of the poor, the injustice of the rich, the corruption of the ruling powers and the attendant evils had reached a point when the laws could not be administered. The mutiny of the poor Thetes and uneasiness of the middle classes made all parties willing to confer extraordinary authority on Solon.

His first great act was the abolition of slavery, so far as the citizens of Athens and Attica were concerned.† This, however, did not include the abolition of alien slavery. Not only did he prohibit the enslavement of citizens for the future, but all who had been enslaved were declared free. His next step modified the cruel law of Draco, which inflicted death for any offense. The death penalty was now only to be inflicted in cases of homicide, or treason against the state.‡ The next step of Solon was to cancel at once all debts in which the debtor had borrowed on his person or his lands. It swept off all the numerous mortgages on the lands in

* Von Ranke's Universal History, page 138.

† Ibid., page 141.

‡ Plutarch's Lives, vol. i., page 135.

Attica, leaving them free.* These, however, were not the only debts in the state. Those who were a little better off than the poorest were still in debt; and, as the first measure of relief, the Seisachtheia, rendered the middle class less able to meet their creditors, as a measure of general relief for the debtor class, he increased the legal value of the silver coin, making what was worth seventy-three drachms worth one hundred.† It appears, however, that the Greeks, in common with other nations, had the two standards of gold and silver. Gold had flowed into Greece until it was worth, *as the standards stood,* considerably less than silver.‡ In our day, when the more rapid production of silver has reduced its commercial value *relatively below gold,* there is a demand from the moneyed interests of the country that the silver standard be changed, by purchasing and putting into the coinage a sufficient quantity of silver to bring it up to the present price of the gold standard. Solon's remedy was just the other way, I presume on the theory that, if in a time of public distress it was necessary to disturb the standard, it was better to do it in the interest of the debtor, rather than the creditor class. In these measures of relief, Solon did not provide a distribution of the land, which the popular, or democratic party expected. The poor railed against Solon for not doing so, and the rich railed against him for the loss of their money. The most careless observation of the work of Solon will show that he was no democrat, but merely sought to effect in that crisis a compromise between the aristocracy and the people. An amazing circumstance is recorded which exhibits the state of society. Three friends in whom he had confidence saw him while engaged on his laws, and learned from him that he had concluded not to touch the land question, but confine his relief measures to the abolition of citizen slavery and debt.

* Grote's Greece, vol. i., page 582. † Ibid., page 583.

‡ Von Ranke's Universal History, page 142.

Profiting by the information thus obtained, they borrowed largely, and with the money purchased lands. By this sharp performance they were, when Solon's laws were promulgated, absolved from their debt, and owners of the land. The sufferers were not slow to charge Solon with the transaction. The lawmaker, to remove the suspicion this affair occasioned, discharged his debtors to the extent of five talents.* Solon was willing to continue the magistracy in the hands of the rich men, but resolved to take the people, in some shape, into the other parts of the government. He constituted the areopagus of those who had been archons for one year. He, as an archon, became a member of this new body. The people, Solon divided into four classes. First, those whose annual income was equal to five hundred medimni of corn, or upwards. Five hundred medimni of corn is nearly seven hundred bushels. One medimni of corn, at that time, was equal to one drachma in money. Those whose income equalled from three to five hundred drachma composed the second class. Those who had between two and three hundred, the third class. The fourth class, by far the most numerous, was composed of those persons who did not possess land that could yield two hundred medimni. The first class was alone eligible to the archonship, and to all commands. The second class were called the knights, or horsemen of the state, as being able to keep a horse and perform military service in that capacity. The third class, called the Zeugitae, formed the heavy-armed infantry, and were bound to serve the state, each with his full panoply. Each of these three classes were entered in the public schedule as possessing taxable property, but this tax diminished according to the scale of the income, being a graduated income tax. The first class was rated at twelve times the size of his income, the second at ten and the third at five. The fourth, and largest class, was

* Plutarch's Lives, vol. i., page 140.

not considered to have taxable incomes, and were styled Thetes. Many in the fourth class who had incomes from one to two hundred drachmas were not exactly poor, and the term Thete, as ultimately applied to a poor citizen without property, did not properly belong to them. Aristotle called this a Timocracy, in which a man's rights, duties, functions, honors and responsibilities were measured according to his property. To show the relative values it has been stated that a sheep was worth a drachma, the price of a bushel and a third of grain, and an ox five drachmas. It is almost impossible to get even an approximate estimate of the wages of a poor landless Thete. He worked at the harvest and at odd jobs; traveled over the country to pick up work where he could, and, it is stated, was generally very glad to get work for his board and clothes. The new legislative body, the council of four hundred, determined all questions submitted to them. As the fourth estate could hold no office, they had merely a voice in selecting from among the other classes. Under this system the middle classes were intended to be a counterpoise or balance against the aristocratic classes. With this government all the citizens were forced to be contented. Solon enacted other laws regulating inheritance or bequests. Land could not be devised to any but the legal heirs, and personal property only in certain cases. He enacted laws regulating marriage and expenditures at weddings, funerals, etc. He had a singular law disfranchising all who remained neutral during a revolution or disturbance. He attempted to regulate exports by providing that nothing should be exported except oil. Attica, however, was largely a commercial community, and it does not appear that this law was, to any extent, enforced. He had, also, statutes regulating trades, and forbidding emigrants from entering the state, except useful artisans, who renounced their old state and came to be permanent citizens.

It does not appear that the special enactments of Solon

survived very long, except laws relating to slavery and the punishment of crimes. The aristocracy, as matters quieted down, had great advantages from possessing the best part of the country, and they soon had the state as full of intrigues as ever. Solon gave the people some power, but he left them too weak to cope with a rich oligarchy.

Perhaps the oldest and happiest form of government is a city or town with its surrounding country, independent in itself, and controlling its own interests. With a free government within, and secure against the invasion of outside tyrants, possessing political organizations designed solely for the public welfare, we can conceive that such a state offers the highest field for human development. Greece affords the world a precedent for part of this picture. She did not lack theories of government, but in the turbulent beginnings of each state the seeds of inequality were planted, chiefly by permitting the lands to drift into the hands of a privileged class. The Persian invasion unified Greece. The states had been, to some extent, held together by the Olympic, Pythian and other games, and the Delphic oracle. While the common danger aroused patriotic feeling against the Persian, and all shared in the historic glory of Marathon, Salamis and Plataea, it unfortunately encouraged the martial spirit. The aristocrats of Athens, when the battle of Plataea was still pending, contemplated treason to their country, and the overthrow of the growing democracy by Persian rule.*

The Peloponnesian war was not only a war against the growth of Athens, but of aristocracy against the growing democracy of the capital of Attica. With the triumph of the oligarchs came the change. The conquest of Greece by the Macedonian king was only rendered possible because the people everywhere had been placed under the feet of aristocrats. Then followed the Roman conquests and the steady decline of the Grecian people.

* Timayenis Greece, page 97.

Her artists had filled Greece with splendid monuments. Her philosophers and historians filled the world with their ideas, and gave history its first clear, intelligent record. The science of government was profoundly studied. Plato's ideal republic still allures, and the speculations of the adroit, shrewd Aristotle, still interest. It is reported by Plutarch, that when Solon was planning his reforms and new constitution for Athens, he was laughed at by Anardin, who asked him if he supposed he could "restrain the covetousness and avarice of his countrymen by written laws, since these were but spider's webs that might catch the poor and weak, but were easily broken by the mighty and rich." Every convulsion which at its close left the aristocrats in possession of their privileges was followed by their slowly regaining political power. The other cause of Grecian decay was slavery. Only in a few cities and states of Greece were the citizens exempt from being made slaves, and in them all, at least one third of the population were alien slaves. These were of every race and color. The aristocrats worked their estates with slaves. Among these slaves were mechanics and artisans. It was no wonder that the poor Thetes, poor citizens without land, were in more wretched plight than even the slaves. All the philosophy of her schoolmen could not rise above such a condition of society. Their literature, science and art, only illuminated its ghastly horrors.

There was an ancient city and state near the city of Rome, from which it is said Rome, in its youth, derived a knowledge of letters, the arts, architecture, weights, measures and surveying. The Etruscans, if not of Phœnician origin, resembled the Phœnicians so closely in the arts they possessed, their manufactures, their city by the sea, and their general habits and characteristics, that they at least copied after them. They were merchants, manufacturers, sailors, pirates and slave dealers. Their city was of massive architecture. They employed mercenary soldiers, and appear to have been an independent state or city of aristocrats. All the menial or disagreeable labor was performed by slaves. Other nations warred on the land, they warred and plundered on the sea, and where the prisoners they took were not ransomed by their friends, they were treated with terrible and merciless cruelty. The government of the Etruscans was an oligarchy with hardly a redeeming trait. The lucumones were at once civil rulers, military rulers, landed proprietors and priests.* The government was maintained by, and for, class interests, and the condition of the people was helpless, depressed and wretched. There was no separation of the functions of government. The same men were law-makers, judges, governors; they imposed and collected taxes, and commanded her armies and navies.

It was from this people, that the men who founded Rome claimed to have learned nearly all they knew of civilization. In its original state, Rome was but a small castle on the summit of the Palatine Hill. The founder, to give it strength and a distinct nationality, hoisted a standard, which indicated that it was a common asylum for criminals, debtors or murderers from all countries. Before the death of the founder, these outlaws had covered with their habitations the Palatine, Capitoline, Aventine and Esquiline hills, with Mounts Coelius and Quirinalis.

After a turbulent history, in which Rome and the provinces she was continually acquiring steadily increased in plunder and population, the people began to obtain a higher conception of government. It may be imagined that a monarchy beginning with an election, and liable to end in assassination, whenever the ruler grew unpopular, was not without its safeguards: but, as is always the case with such governments, Rome went steadily from bad to worse. The Tarquins seemed, in spite of elections, to be quietly settling themselves upon the throne, when the vicious conduct of one of them led

*George Rawlinson's Early Civilization, page 128.

to the abolition of royalty, and the banishment of the family. It is probable that too much importance has been given in history to the rape of Lucretia, as that was merely the last straw that broke the camel's back. The theory on which the Roman colony was founded was the equal rights of all its citizens. When provinces were conquered, the lands were to be divided, and, first, a portion given to those who had none, as it was assumed that each citizen must have within his own possession the means of subsistence. The remainder of the land acquired was to be equally divided among all the citizens. Proper steps were not taken to permanently secure such a distribution, and as everything was subject to the commercial test, it was not long before a landed and moneyed aristocracy was built up. Ferguson, in his Roman Republic, informs us that under the early monarchy the people were divided into patricians and plebeians. It was intended that the official positions and dignities should only be conferred on the patricians, and the patricians were, in fact, those who had a certain amount of property. We therefore need not be at all surprised when the above accomplished historian informs us, that on the overthrow of the monarchy the government of Rome was entirely aristocratic. The patricians had absorbed the greater portion of the land and other wealth. They had reduced many of the citizens to peonage through debt. They held all the offices, and there was no distinction in the legislative, executive and judicial functions. They levied and expended taxes, commanded armies, and officered them by virtue of their position and wealth.

It may well be supposed that the expulsion of the Tarquins was an easy task, compared with that of building a free republic on such a foundation. The Romans, however, were not destitute of courage and vigor, and their first effort was to separate the functions of government, and create offices to be filled by the people. They sent commissioners to Greece to study the laws adopted there; in fact, Rome borrowed her religion and law largely from Greece. The patricians were, of course, alarmed at all these proceedings. They did not hesitate to denounce them as mere agrarian violence. They were, indeed, too prudent to call in question the power of the people, as the highest authority in the state, but they did their best to foment jealousies among their opponents. They adroitly hired claqueers to hoot and deride the popular champions, and finally the senate, on the pretext that the state was menaced by enemies from without and turbulence within, appointed a dictator. Having consolidated this power sufficiently, as they thought, the patricians again commenced oppressing the poorer citizens, reducing many of them to slavery under the pretext that they were in debt to their patrons. They continued their tyrannical practices until the mass of the laboring people left the capital and camped on the sacred hill. For months this continued, and business may be said to have been suspended. It was a very famous strike. The patricians vainly invited them to return to their homes and their labor, but they replied that free men own no country where they are not permitted to enjoy their freedom. While the patricians had retainers sufficient to guard the approaches to fortified Rome, they suffered for want of that which the people alone could produce. This led to a compromise. The populace created the Tribunes of the people. The patricians could neither vote for, nor be elected to this office. A safer plan would have been to abolish the distinction of patrician and plebeian, and change the senate into a purely elective assembly. The conservative element is always a strong one in society. Even the exclusive rights of the patricians were not without supporters among the lower orders. The people, instead of reducing the aristocratic powers to a republican basis, created a government machinery of their own. The two existed together, conflicting, of course, whenever either party felt strong enough. As the populace always were in majority, the senate and patricians worked adroitly in an underhanded way, and as they possessed wealth, the real sinew of power, were still able for a time to maintain their privileges and authority. The next step of the people was what has been styled the agrarian law, and was simply a proposition to redistribute the lands among the citizens. A wealthy citizen, Sp. Cassius, was one of the champions of the people in this demand, and to evidence his sincerity divided a large portion of his surplus lands among the indigent citizens. Against him all the venom of the patrician order turned. He unfortunately held to some opinions, one as to the introduction of aliens, that were not popular. Taking advantage of this and the extreme jealousy of the people against any one who was supposed to be aiming at royal authority, this popular leader was denounced as a dangerous demagogue aiming to subvert the power of the government, and was destroyed by the hatred of patricians and the jealousies of the populace.

The patricians met the demand for a fair distribution of the lands of the republic by specious arguments. They urged that these lands were originally the property of none of them, but were derived from conquest; that if they had been equitably divided at first, and a provision made that they should be, through all time, the property of all the people, it would have been all right. That, however, had not been done. Law and custom had permitted them to drift into the hands of the present owners, who had vested rights in them, and that all these leveling measures could not now be applied without the subversion of all government, and all rights of property. The Tribunes and the people, however, succeeded in sending a commission to Greece to procure a code of law suitable for a free people. These commissioners first returned with a table of ten laws. To gain time, the patricians used their arts on the commissioners, and the latter, who had usurped a great many powers never intended to be delegated to them, endeavored to perpetuate their authority, on the pretext that they had not completed this work. Finally, however, twelve tables of Roman law were adopted. These laws involved assignments of land on a fair prescription for two years, a jury system for trials and other propositions for the popular welfare. The barriers that had shut the people from the highest offices were swept away. Ultimately, the law fixed the amount of land that any citizen should be permitted to own. The theory was that the cultivator, under the state, should, for the time, own and control the land he cultivated. Pliny informs us that Curius Dentatus looked upon the Roman as a pernicious citizen, who was not content with seven acres, and the Roman law restricted each holder, at one time, to that amount. The power of the patrician order, although reduced, was not altogether broken. Restrictions had been placed upon the practice of enslaving for debt. Rome, however, was full of alien slaves, and persons born in slavery. The ranks of slavery were increased from condemned criminals. It is needless to say that labor can never be independent and honorable under such circumstances.

Rome grew in power and wealth. The title, Roman citizen, became, of itself, a sort of aristocracy. It was not confined to the natives of the republic, but was conferred upon individuals inhabiting other cities or provinces. Since the animosities of patrician and plebeian had been partly extinguished by the division of power and honor between them, more than two hundred years elapsed before new conditions menaced the rights of the people. The patricians had been compelled to open the channels to the highest offices to those eminent among the plebeians. The Roman senate, although it was originally aristocratic, contained many of the most eminent Roman citizens of all orders, and, in spite of its faults, maintained a character for magnanimity and greatness longer than any similar body known among men. The changes in the Roman condition gradually undermined the principles of the government. A career of conquest furnished an ample field for the active and ambitious Roman citizens of every grade. The offices of state and the command of the armies now became lucrative as well as honorable. Citizens contended for offices in the state as the road to wealth-producing appointments abroad, and brought back from the positions they thus obtained a profusion of ill-acquired wealth, to corrupt the people, and make themselves leaders of factions. The comparative seclusion of the equestrian order, from political positions, turned them into traders, usurers, government contractors, farmers of revenue; and they thus in turn absorbed the lands and capital, and controlled the labor. The citizens abandoned agricultural pursuits, and flocked to the capital, where the gratuitous distribution of corn, and the splendid shows amused and gratified them. The exercise of their powers, as members of the popular assemblies, gave them a voice in controlling the affairs of the world, and an opportunity of selling their suffrage in the markets, which gradually debauched them. Once more the small farms were swallowed up by the large ones cultivated by slaves. Wealth was permitted to have undue power. In point of fact, the republic was hastening to a sure decay.

At this period a fresh attempt was made to return to the first principles of the republic. The republic had lasted for three hundred and seventy-five years. A popular leader arose, Tiberius Gracchus, who was elected Tribune. He saw and deprecated the decline of virtue and real prosperity. In the early days of the republic the earth was tilled by freedmen, and everywhere there reigned a sound prosperity. The aristocracy, as Livy informs us, had invaded the little homesteads which had given place to vast estates cultivated by slaves. That writer, deploring the condition of the Roman country, said, "Vast numbers of freedmen used to live in these regions, which now remain a nursery for scarce a handful of soldiers, and are only saved from actual solitude by the Roman slave gangs." In one of the oft-quoted speeches of Gracchus, he is reported as saying: "The wild beasts of Italy have their lairs to which they can retreat, the brave men who shed their blood in her cause have nothing left but light and the air they breathe; without house, without any fixed abode, they wander from place to place with their wives and children. They fight and die to advance the wealth and luxury of the great. They are called masters of the world, and have not a foot of ground in their possession."

He proposed to restore or enforce the agrarian or Licinian law, which had fallen into neglect. He inveighed against the practice of employing slaves, and demanded that the laws should be enforced to prevent it. He also proposed limiting estates, as under the original Licinian law, but to reconcile the nobles and rich land owners, proposed that the state should pay them an appraised value for their relinquishment. He also insisted on a law to prevent, hereafter, all commerce in land, or its accumulation in large estates. He considered it reasonable that what was public should be applied to public uses. The project of Tiberius Gracchus was strenuously opposed by the senate and the nobles. Finding that the people were determined on having such laws, they secured one of the Tribunes, who interposed his negative, which stopped further proceedings. Indignant at the course pursued by the patricians, Gracchus now modified his proposition by striking out the provisions for indemnifying those who had accumulated great estates, for the surplus thus to be taken from them to distribute to the people. He further announced several other propositions, among them, one to reduce the powers of the senate. His proposed laws were discussed in all the provinces of Italy, the people generally being on his side, and the nobles and their partisans on the other. After a desperate struggle, the laws he proposed were adopted by the vote of the citizens, the patricians, however, claiming that it could not be constitutionally done after one of the Tribunes had interposed his negative. The senate refused to take the necessary steps to carry it out, and once more proclaimed a dictator. In the midst of great disorder, a mob, or band of the clients and attachés of the senators and nobles, headed by them, broke into the assembly of the people; Tiberius Gracchus and three hundred of his followers were slain. Some of the more active of his partisans were afterwards condemned and outlawed. Thus, in blood, did the nobles destroy the popular assemblies. The senate, with affected moderation, professed to execute the laws just adopted, and even appointed the necessary commissioners, but this was merely to avert another storm. The Gracchi fell one hundred years before the date of the Christian era, and, although ninety-four years of the nominal republic elapsed before Octavius, as Augustus Cæsar, became emperor, the republic had, on the murder of Tiberius Gracchus, received its death blow. The great events and foreign conquests that filled that period, diverted public attention from more vital questions. Never again did there come to the Roman people a leader who was able to preserve the principles of the republic. It was not when the Cæsars ascended the throne that the republic perished. All that was vital in it had previously passed away. It was merely a question between one great tyrant and a thousand small tyrants. It is not the first time a people have taken refuge in a despotism to escape an oligarchy. Nor was the downfall of the magnificent, but guilty empire, surprising. The Roman citizens had ceased to have much interest in Rome, and why should they stain the soil with their blood to bolster a tyrant? The bands of Huns, and Goths and Sclavs, many of whose people had been dragged to Rome, and "butchered, to make a Roman holiday," came, in their own good time, to give the tyrants a new lesson in the gladiatorial combat.

CHAPTER III.

CONDITION OF LABOR AND LAND IN THE MIDDLE AGES.

Aryan emigration to Europe—Allodial title the distinction for freemen—The village council the ancient foundation of government—Division of conquered lands—Women's property rights invaded—The feudal system erected on breach of public trust—Primogeniture—Freemen reduced to villeinage—Game laws for the pleasure of aristocrats—Social rights invaded—Marriages between commoners and nobles declared unlawful—Laws of escheat—The civil list—The "Younger Son"—Banditti—Parliaments represent landowners—Guilds and trades societies—Free cities and towns—Gunpowder as a democratic element—Titles the insignia of luxurious rogabondage.

For some time before the Christian era, and for three or four hundred years thereafter, many hordes or tribes of Asiatics invaded Europe. These have been variously named Goths, Huns, Vandals, Suevi, Alani. Some of these emigrants had been originally from the valleys around the Himalayah mountains and were driven by superabundant population to emigrate. After wandering through the steppes of Central Asia and acquiring the vigor, self denial and warlike spirit incident to nomadic tribes, they finally consolidated under chosen leaders and precipitated themselves on Europe. It has been one of the proudest boasts of ethnological science, to trace the present great nations of Europe to their Indian ancestry. The Aryans could be traced not only by their language but by their forms of society and ideas of inheritance and personal rights. "There was a time," says Professor Max Müller, in his "Languages of the Seat of War," page 30, "when the ancestors of the Celts, the Germans, the Slavs, the Greeks, Italians, Persians and Hindoos were living together beneath the same roof, separate from the Semetic or Turanian races."

It is important to trace the social ideas and principles regarding the rights of property these people brought with them to Europe and the changes that were wrought during the conquering and Middle Ages. The highest authorities generally agree, that originally, the common possession of land characterised all the Aryan races.* The indications are, that allodial land was everywhere the distinctive privilege of freemen. By allodial land is meant, land equally held under family rights, this tenure giving no power to the occupants to reduce or abridge the rights in it of all the family that might come after them. It was, therefore, founded on equal laws of inheritance.

Among the earlier arrivals of the great swarm we refer to, and prior to the Christian era, we read of the Germans. From Cæsar, Strabo and other Roman authorities, we learn that these Germans were scattered in a number of independent tribes. They elected their kings and other rulers from particular families. The lands were allotted to all the citizens every two years.

The ancient foundation of government for all the branches of these people was the village community. The "Village Council" was the voice of law for all the branches of the Aryan race.† It has been suggested that this council has furnished the model for all the parliamentary bodies of the world.

The conquering hordes from Asia first lodged in Northern Europe, driving before them or subduing the thinly settled tribes east of the Rhine and north of the 37th degree of latitude, that being the practical boundary of the Roman empire. Having acquired sufficient strength, these invaders precipitated themselves upon the older governments on the Mediterranean.

* Maine's History of Institutions, page 340. † Ibid., page 388.

When these warlike races overran the Roman Empire and captured her colonies, they were in the habit of making a division of land between themselves and the people they conquered. The Germans and Goths took one-half, leaving the remainder to former inhabitants, while the Burgundians and Visigoths took two-thirds.* The Vandals in Africa appropriated all the best lands.†

The beginnings of these new nations show us a camp rather than a civil government, and military leaders rather than civil rulers. It was a combination of sturdy freemen, however. The old ideas struggled resolutely and for ages, against the changes and innovations of the ambitious and selfish. When the country was divided between the conquered and the conquerors, military forces could not disband. Especially had those on the Roman frontiers to maintain their martial character. The military leaders were elective and had little power save in time of war, and at first no more land than their neighbors. They cultivated their own land. Each soldier had to serve so many days in a year, usually not to exceed forty. The town assemblage was the government, and all debated questions of right or claim were referred to it. In this way the allodial title long struggled against the encroachments of the feudal system. The original laws and customs of these people were to divide their inheritance equally among all children.‡ The Franks did not permit the land obtained by conquest to be divided among females, as they desired to secure military service from all holders. Even among this tribe, lands secured by purchase passed by law to all the family alike, males and females.§ The Visigoths, and other of these nations or tribes, permitted conquered lands to be fairly divided by inheritance among all without regard to sex.

Whether this idea of setting aside woman's rights was the

* Hallam's Middle Ages, vol. i., page 149. † Ibid.

‡ Ibid., page 151. § Ibid., page 150.

product of mere violence or was copied from some of the systems these Indo-Europeans encountered, is not so material as the fact that it soon led to other innovations.

The first five hundred years of war and conquest were not more disastrous to the Roman Empire than to the liberties of the new nations thus peopling the north of Europe. The seeds of much political mischief were sown, and an aristocracy, the worst the world ever beheld, founded. The duty of defending the country, they held, gave the military leaders the right to summon each holder of land to the field. The wars became burdensome and prolonged and could not have been continued but for plunder, which had a demoralizing effect not only on the people themselves but on their social and political system. Public brigandage was common. Chiefs hired or bribed their vassals with presents obtained by war. Hopes of plunder often congregated armed bands of adventurers about the warlike leaders. These, of course, soon became formidable and dangerous to the peaceful fathers of the Village Council. Military service exacted for public defense soon grew into a duty claimed by the chief, and thus by insidious degrees the foundations of the feudal system were laid. The term "Feudalism," Mr. Bell says, is but another name for aristocracy. It was utterly at variance with every social doctrine of the Aryan race.

The war chiefs did not at once rise to full aristocratic power or privilege. Nobility was not known among the Franks until long after the overthrow of the Roman Empire.*

A lord and his vassals were originally a captain and his men. It is noteworthy that these Teutonic folk seem to have acquired some of the worst faults of the Roman Empire they overthrew. The relations of a feudal chief and his vassals closely resemble, and are said to have been copied after those of a Roman patron and clients. It is also significant that

* Hallam's Middle Ages, vol. i., page 159.

many of the titles that originated and grew up in this period, are from Latin words. Thus, duke, from the Latin *duces*, "leader." Counts, from comer (companions of the prince). Marquis, from marcha, "boundary." Earl, on the other hand, is from the Scandinavian, but originally signified elder, like the Arabic Sheik. The Teutonic races, in their early history, detested aristocracy, and yet they, through war, created the germs of military aristocracy. To them a landed aristocracy was also abhorrent, and it required ages of intrigue and violence before these military leaders succeeded in establishing it. Even when the Saxons conquered England, in the fourth century, and drove the Celtic population into Wales and the North of Scotland, gavelkind, or land inheritance by all the members of the family, was their law and custom. Slavery was originally repugnant to the ideas of these people, and, although they took captives in war, they had not created a fixed servile class. Imitating the Romans, they now began to make one. At first the duties of the vassals were not burdensome. They were bound to serve their country in war, and had a personal interest in rendering such service. The land upon which the yeoman gave this military service was his home, and he had an interest in its defence, just as every man had an interest.

At that period the lord had to cultivate his own land. Military power, however, is never slow in taking care of personal interests, and in a very short time the lord enriched himself by taking his retainers on predatory expeditions, chiefly for his own benefit. For military service due, commutation began to be accepted, and whether there was war or not, this gradually grew into rent, and in the same way came to be a perquisite of the lord of the manor. Exactions thus begun, of course, increased, as avarice inspired the chieftain who collected it. In the course of a few centuries, the tenants of an estate began to be considered as a species of slaves. Slaves, to a certain extent, those who pay rent to a great proprietor, always will be. On the continent they were styled retainers, or serfs; in England, villeins. They were, in the course of time, transferred as chattels with the estate.

It is a crime in a father to desire that his son shall inherit a public trust. In empires and kingdoms it has been so common as to be almost universal that a king's son succeeded him. This custom followed no natural law, and existed only because a leader, at first of popular acceptance, had been able to fortify his position so as to render him independent of popular will. The frequent struggles incident to the crowning of new kings, attest the strength of the popular protest against it. This continuance of a family in power, comes, in most cases, from causes equally dangerous to the public interests. No large kingdom or royalty can be formed without a great and potent machinery. Generals, ministers, deputies, ambassadors, judges, captains and so on, down to the most petty officials and scavengers of the royal household, are all concerned in the succession. Whoever is king, each of these must be "Vicar of Bray." We thus see that a powerful combination has been created, which, on the death of the real or nominal head, wants things to go on just as they are, and who naturally take the king's son and continue him in order that they may keep in office. Revolutions, or elections that might rotate them out are not to be thought of. In this way privileged classes are created, hoary corruptions perpetuated, tyrannies cemented, human equality blotted out, and the public interests made the football of every intriguing and ambitious adventurer.

If kingly succession is fatal to popular liberty, an aristocracy by inheritance is a still more fearful scourge. Grafted on feudalism, the law of primogeniture became the insidious curse of European society, stepping across the threshold of home, and over the cradle of childhood, to lay the foundation for a lordly, privileged class. The law by which property descended through the oldest son did not exist among the

Aryan races on their first establishment in the Roman empire.* Not only among the ancient Germans, but among the Hindoos, from whom they sprang, the endowment of the family could not be parted with, except by the consent of all its members. The idea of primogeniture was certainly not obtained from the Romans.† Neither could it be derived from Christian teachings. It was first introduced by the great lords, when they made grants of land to knights, for the performance of knight service, one person, or head, being thus created to represent and pay the service, all his brethren becoming retainers. Such was the original custom, but it led to the concentration of power in the first born as the head of the estate. It took some time, and a good deal of fraud, chicanery and violence to fasten on these independent warriors the yoke of masters.

This unjust discrimination was, as has been shown, in violation of the fundamental customs and laws of the people over whom it was thrust, and was brought about by breach of public trust. John Adams said that, "Since the promulgation of Christianity the two greatest systems of tyranny are the canon and feudal law." ‡ He added a few pages later: "The feudal system was inconsistent with liberty and the rights of mankind." Rousseau styles the feudal system, "The most iniquitous and abased form of government which shamefully degraded human nature," and Lord Kames in "Antiquities," says: "A constitution so contradictory could never be brought about but by foreign conquest or domestic usurpation." While referring to this phase in the history of English titles, and to primogeniture, Adam Smith says: "While land is considered as the means only of subsistence and enjoyment, the natural law of succession divides it among all the children of the family. When land was considered as the means not

* Systems of Land Tenures in Various Countries, page 94.

† Maine's History of Institutions, page 198.

‡ Works of John Adams, vol. iii., page 449.

only of subsistence, but of power and protection, it was thought better that it should descend undivided to one." That is a very ingenious attempt to explain the circumstance by which a few great families absorbed nearly all the land in the country. One would think in reading it that it had been a matter of general acquiescence. Sir Henry Sumner Maine says that "the great development of primogeniture was in the early part of the Middle Ages." *

The term "Middle Ages," I suppose, when it is used with any definite meaning, refers to that portion of European history beginning at the time of the final overthrow of the Roman or Western Empire, and drawing to a close with the introduction of constitutional governments in Western and Northern Europe. In Hallam's History on the subject, he places it between the fifth and fifteenth centuries of the Christian era. In styling it the "Dark Ages" is meant the barbarous or semi-barbarous ages.

When the Aryan races in their great waves of emigration entered Europe, they brought with them the knowledge and use of iron, horses, chariots, cattle, and had made considerable progress in agriculture. It has even been alleged that some of these nations had letters. When the Franks invaded Gaul they found considerable wealth and semi-barbaric splendor.† The wretched squalor and poverty witnessed in the Middle Ages were the fruits of the avarice, tyranny and misgovernment of feudalism. The crimes and degradation of Rome not only paved the way for its own ruin but imparted the virus of its iniquity into the nerves and fresher blood of the Teutonic race. From the fifth to the tenth century of the Christian era there was throughout the greater portion of Europe a decline in all that constitutes national greatness. After the fall of the Roman Empire and the abandonment of Great Britain by its armies, the warlike Picts and Scots, hemmed up

* Maine's History of Institutions, page 205. † Ibid., page 350.

by the Romans in the North of Scotland, invaded the land now occupied by the Britons. The latter employed Danish and Saxon navigators, chiefly from the Danish peninsula, to aid them, and finally the Britons were overrun and conquered by these Anglo-Saxons. They carried with them ideas of allodial title, folcland and tanistry, but this primitive condition had already become imbued with the worst vices of the systems they found in Europe, and a conflict between individual rights and aristocracy began.

For several hundred years England was torn by wars and dissensions. The eight kings were supplemented by many military leaders, each of whom was a king or a robber as far as he had the power. They were largely governed by customs. Some little of the Roman law remained, but without any ruler potent enough to administer it. The local chiefs, Tanists or Thanes, were elective, but the chieftains usually managed to keep the succession in their own family. The rights of the ancient Britons were trampled upon by the Anglo-Saxon conquerors. The Anglo-Saxon people found it difficult to defend their rights against their own military chiefs. Allodial titles and folcland still existed, but largely burdened by feudal duty. The folcmote, or councils of the people, were still a cherished Anglo-Saxon institution, but were steadily being undermined by the exactions of the Thanes, Earls and other titled leaders. The great body of the people comprised two classes: freemen who held land subject to duty of various kinds, and slaves who had nothing. The latter could not be sold out of the county where they lived, and had some few privileges, in fact, they were about as well off as the poor freemen. The slaves were the descendants of slaves from the Roman period, captives in war, and people condemned to slavery for crime. When England was finally united in one kingdom under Egbert, in the ninth century, it was not a closely consolidated government. The nobles were still all powerful, and between them and the king there was continual dissension. Despotic and selfish though the kings were, their power was a check to some extent on the aristocracy, but was unable to strip them of their ill-gotten wealth and authority. Many laws and codes of law are referred to, but complete codes did not exist. The old customs of the people, which yet struggled for existence, were rarely written laws, the latter were the new and supplemental acts of various reigns. The old council of the people, folcmote, had been considerably abridged by the witenagemote, or supreme council, out of which parliament finally grew. The latter was essentially an aristocratic body. Whenever the kings grew sufficiently powerful they struggled to abridge the powers of this assembly. Until the time of Alfred, the nobility had not completely succeeded in becoming hereditary. After his reign they were so, and a son might inherit his "father's county." The Anglo-Saxon law at various times decreed "that no man should continue without a lord." Laws were also enacted to prevent the marriage of the aristocratic orders with the common people, and the children of a marriage between a noble and ignoble person were held to be illegitimate. The freemen who still held their lands under tribute of military service were compelled to accept vassalage under some noble or lose their lands. In addition to the forty days' service, or its equivalent, to a knight, all manner of impositions were continually added. They had to contribute to purchase a knight's right for the earl's son, to contribute to a dower for his daughter, and, indeed, there was no limit to the rapacity of these aristocrats. The nobles continually warred on what was left of the allodial title. It has been customary to charge the worst evils of the feudal system on the Norman conquest. Before that period arrived the agrarian constitutions and village rights of ancient times had been largely swept away. Gradually, the chiefs undermined independent holders, the community became the "Manor," the greater free holders tenants, and the small holders were reduced to the positions of villeins, laborers or slaves. Maine says that villeinage is a tenure rendering uncertain and unlimited services, "where it cannot be known at eventide what hath to be done on the morrow." * Under these circumstances, it took but a few hundred years to reduce more than half of the people to abject slavery. Not only was their substance taken by the aristocrats who thus fattened on them, but every insult and contumely was heaped upon them, and even the sacredness of the rights of husband and wife were invaded.

It has often been wondered at that, in a single battle and almost without a struggle, England was placed at the feet of the Norman conquerors. It was indeed a calamity to the Saxon aristocracy, but why should the people of England fight for such a government as they possessed? Æsop furnishes the fable of the two asses, the most asinine of which urged the other to flee on the approach of an invading enemy. To these adjurations the other ass asked, "Will this invader work us harder, feed us more poorly or beat us more cruelly than our present masters do?" "I suppose not," was the reply. "Very well," said the other, "you may run if you please, but I am going to stay, it cannot be much worse." With the conquest came a supposed change in the title to lands in England. King William claimed the land as his by right of conquest,— a conquest, moreover, made as against all the parties living on it. In point of fact, a systematic spoliation of the great Saxon nobility began with the reign of William the Norman, and continued to its close.† Although the Saxon leaders had absorbed the greater portion of the land, theoretically or practically, some of it was still technically styled "commons," or lands over which the power of the lord was not absolute, or on which a figment of the people's title rested. This nominal public or people's land, the conqueror annexed as crown lands.

* Early Law and Custom, page 334.

† Hallam's Middle Ages, vol. i., page 98.

We look through that chequered and darkened history in vain to find any attempt to restore to the people what had been taken by the Saxon aristocracy. A new nobility was created, consisting of shoots of royalty, favorites and conquerors. Most of the oldest and proudest English aristocratic families date from that period. In addition it is said, that for one hundred years from the conquest no native Englishmen held office in the Church or State.* Some of the Saxon nobles fled and took refuge in Constantinople. A good deal of sympathy has been expended on them in history, but between the Saxon aristocratic robbers of the people and the Norman conquerors the difference was not great. The kings, however, had a stronger hand.

As the Saxon aristocracy had grown into wealth, power and luxury, they refused to the common people the right to kill the wild game, though it fed on the crops raised in the fields of the serf or villein. Even the monopoly of keeping and raising pigeons was assumed by them. These laws grew more stringent under the Normans. The knights, earls and dukes rode about the country with hawk and hound, and no peasant could take or kill the wild beasts of nature. At one time the killing of a stag or boar by a peasant was punished with death.† Nothing could exhibit better the desperate extremity to which they had reduced the laboring people. This gross usurpation continues to the present day. Poor men have been transported beyond the seas for killing a hare. Lands that might have furnished a living for yeomen have been turned into deer parks and preserves, merely for the luxurious amusement of the rich and aristocratic.

The way these kings sometimes procured artisans is worthy of note. Edward III. announced to his sheriffs that he "had created William, of Walsingham, his commissioner to collect as many painters as might be required to finish St.

* Hallam's Middle Ages, vol. i., page 97. † Ibid., vol. ii., page 503.

Stephen's Chapel, to be at the king's wages, but he is authorized to seize and imprison all who refuse to work." *

Such were the foundations of the system, Saxon and Norman, under which an aristocracy reduced the laboring people of England to poverty, hardship and servitude. The Norman kings created fresh nobles as soon as escheats, confiscations or other causes threw property in their hands. Under the Saxons an escheat for failure to perform military duty, or for treason or other offense, could only extend for a certain period, or during the lives of the offenders, as the idea still survived, to some extent, that each generation had certain rights in the land. The Normans, however, made escheats and confiscations perpetual. It is true, that this to a great extent was among the nobles, and the change from one aristocrat to another might be of little consequence to the real cultivator of the soil. This was considered a great grievance among the nobility; hence we find as constitutional governments began to be formed, there was a struggle to prevent the perpetual escheatment for offenses. One amusing circumstance connected with it is the fact that this idea has crept into the Constitution of the United States, and it is held, that perpetual escheat or attainder shall not be inflicted. Lands, with us, are a mere chattel. There is no assertion anywhere of the rights of the next generation in them, independent of the will of the holder. We have no law of entail. If we had laws which provided that the lands held should in each succeeding generation be fairly divided between all the surviving members of each family, this provision against escheat and attainder would have some point.

Growing out of the laws of primogeniture and the feudal system, there came the law of entail. Its purpose is very evident. It grew up in the fourteenth and fifteenth centuries. The law of entail, it will be observed, does not make

* Hallam's Middle Ages, vol. ii., page 351.

the land a chattel. A holding under it is not a fee simple title. It is a life interest, which cannot be alienated from his family by the holder, or subject even to his debts after his death. Had the entail been for the family, and for every family, divisible among all its descendants in each generation, it would have resembled, to some extent, the system these despotic aristocrats had overthrown. The law of entail was really a precautionary measure of the nobles against the growing power of the cities. A new class of rich bourgeois was rising, and it was not desirable that they should own land. This law of entail was also a reactionary struggle against the doctrine of land sovereignty, or "eminent domain." By the latter doctrine, which, in a different shape, has crept into our land system, the monarch claimed sovereign rights in the land. Guizot holds that it is the amalgamation of sovereignty with property that constitutes feudalism. This feudal power might be in the nobles or in the king. When primogeniture and the law of entail were fastened on the feudal system, they irrevocably fixed an aristocracy in a certain line. The folly, extravagance or wickedness of one generation, could not forfeit the perpetual lien that the head of a certain house had upon the industry and toil of the people of a community. To make the matter worse, the policy of intermarrying the noble class only with each other, tended further to consolidate this power, and to create an interest so potent and well intrenched as to defy opposition.

The Norman kings having disposed of all the public domain to relatives, or favorites, and there being thus no rent for public expenditures, proceeded to tax the producing classes, of course, for an additional income to support the government. Not content with moderate and economical government expenditure, hosts of sinecures were from time to time created. Indeed, this soon became a necessity of the aristocracy. After the adoption of the law of primogeniture, the younger sons of nobles became a constantly increasing and dangerous body.

They were the squires and pet men-at-arms, and much of the aristocratic brigandage of the Middle Ages was due to the necessities of this class. Bell, in his history of feudalism, says, that at one time, in France, upwards of one hundred thousand of these armed men were roaming about. They were termed in that country "skinners alive." The younger sons could either sink into villeinage, or be soldiers or bandits. As brigandage fell under the ban of progressing civilization, official positions had to be created for those nearly connected with the nobles. Offices were not only created for them, but for the nobles themselves. Some lord or offshoot of nobility or royalty would have an annual salary from the public purse, as "keeper" of some "seal," or other nominal office. To meet the extravagance of the aristocratic class, immense civil lists of persons, really pensioners on the public bounty, were created, and this burden steadily enlarged from time to time. It is probable that a very few of these gifts and gratuities of government may have been given for meritorious public services, and, in such cases there might have been some small excuse for them, if the money had not been drawn from the revenues of a burdened and overworked people. During the first five hundred years of feudalism in England, the great nobles resolutely resisted the imposition of taxes upon themselves by the king. Not content with drawing great revenues from the natural resources of the country, they refused to bear their share of the public burdens.

In the last few hundred years armies were raised, and immense public debts incurred to obtain and hold colonies. As was once eloquently said, these were paddocks into which were turned the lean and decayed members of the aristocracy. The colonial expense was maintained from the public purse, and the profits so arranged that they went into the pockets of the privileged few. It was boasted that the country was very rich. The laboring classes could not be said to be a great deal better off. Their food, in spite of artificial adjuncts, was really neither so good nor so wholesome. Their holidays and hours of leisure were reduced. The mode of life grew so artificial that it was difficult to manage expenses, and paupers became more common. There was a constant increase of the weak and helpless class. It is a common thing to boast of the wealth and increasing property of a nation, but a nation should never be considered as prosperous or increasing in real wealth unless the improvement is with the laboring and producing classes. The wealth that increases the number of idlers to live on the producers is not beneficent, but is merely the machinery for greater oppression.

It must not be supposed that the growth of this system was not resisted. The laboring classes, although more numerous, are always at a disadvantage when coping with an aristocracy, which, besides other accumulated wealth and power, holds the lands from which men have to get bread for their families. Secret societies flourished. Trades took shelter under organizations or guilds. Each trade had its representatives, and they grew into political power. These, at least, were elective. The lower clergy generally encouraged and aided them. As the landed proprietors usurped judicial functions, secret tribunals were created to punish notorious offenders. In a few vigorous communities, such as Kent, the system of peonage or villeinage was resisted.

Among the powers of the Crown assumed by the conqueror and many of his successors was the power to make laws. The Saxons had relegated all important questions to a general council of notables.

The nobles and country gentlemen, owners of land, had a voice in these old assemblages, and thus, to some extent, this question of taxation was a quarrel between the nobles and the kings. In this state of affairs, the opinions of the people began to be of consequence. Intelligence and general information were increasing. The people in the towns had begun to acquire rights to lands, occupied and common to the town, upon certain payments. Originally, the Saxons were not builders of towns or cities, but were, in spirit, an agricultural, communal people.* Some of the old towns and cities were not abandoned, but the building of English towns and cities as independent communities commenced later. Many of these first clustered around the religious establishments of Christianity. The towns which depended on the crown were liable to certain annual payments. In the twelfth and thirteenth centuries the town officers were entrusted with the collection of its annual payments.† The jurisdiction of the town authorities was enlarged. Privileges were granted them, and immunities, under Richard I., and King John. They obtained the right of electing their own officers, and many powers of self-government, and the power of forming guilds and enacting laws for their control. These guilds were, to some extent, trades unions. Each trade or craft had its organization and officers. They were armed for defense. The municipal privileges of London were recognized in a charter by William the Conqueror. The organization of the trades to a considerable extent, served to protect them against the abuse or brigandage of the nobles. Brigandage was still common. Hallam says that all the nobles of England, France and Germany were robbers.‡ Highway robbery, from the earliest times, was a common crime. Towns were for this reason organized and armed, as were the societies or guilds of the trades, and slowly grew to be an independent power in the realm. Under these circumstances commerce began to be of considerable consequence. When a serf or villein escaped from the country and sought the towns, he could not join a guild until he had resided a year and a day in the town.§ If a serf or villein had not been claimed for more than a year, he could not be forced back into servitude by his master. The population of

* Roger's Work and Wages, page 102. † Ibid.

‡ Hallam's Middle Ages, vol. ii., page 506.

§ Roger's Work and Wages, page 110.

the towns and cities worked usually at trades, or were engaged in business, but it was the custom for many of them to go to the country in the harvest season. Even students in colleges, and persons connected with the government and courts, used to be sent to aid in the harvest.* When the king dismissed his parliament, in the Middle Ages, he sent the nobles to their sports and the commons to their harvest, and the long vacations of the courts and universities, from July to October, was for the purpose of enabling even those engaged in law and letters to take part in the harvest. The growth of commerce and the organization of trades and guilds had much to do with the increase of civil liberties in England. As the towns usually existed in connection with, or close to, religious establishments, the bourgeois were, to some extent, under their protection, and, also, more under the enlightening influences of that period than the laborer in the country.

The value of the bill of rights, secured at Runnymede, has been greatly exaggerated, but very important concessions were obtained, and it would be unfair to deny that the interests of the people were to some extent considered. Trial by jury was not altogether unknown, or something like it, for King Alfred hanged several judges for causing criminals to be executed who had not been convicted by the unanimous vote of twelve freemen, as we learn from the "Mirror of Justice." The Magna Charta guaranteed that no man should be imprisoned without a trial, or convicted until found guilty by a jury of his equals. This was a decided improvement on the judicial modes then in vogue.

Sir E. Coke informs us that the Magna Charta was reaffirmed thirty-two times. He does not enumerate how often it was violated. One of the remarkable concessions of the Magna Charta was, that in the courts and tribunals of the realm, justice should not be sold. In point of fact, the whole ma-

* Roger's Work and Wages, page 122.

chinery of jurisprudence was thoroughly and notoriously corrupt.

While the Middle Ages may have closed with the fifteenth century, it is a mistake to suppose that the evils entailed on the people of Europe terminated at that period. The very worst of them exist to-day, and the aristocracy cling to their ill-gotten privileges and property with the utmost tenacity. In the contest for English liberty, the concessions were wrung inch by inch from a tyrannical king and a powerful and corrupt aristocracy. In the English revolutions the two extremes of society, the monarch and the poorest people, were at once interested in the overthrow of feudalism. In the reign of William the Conqueror, it is supposed that the population of England and Wales was about two millions of people. At that time all the land was held by about one hundred and seventy thousand persons.* The same authority quoted, states that at present, when that population has increased to twenty millions, only one hundred and fifty thousand persons own more than an acre and a half, and that two thousand two hundred and fifty persons own nearly half of the enclosed portions of England and Wales. Such are the fruits of the feudal system to-day. Feudal tenure, in a legal sense, was abolished in the reign of Charles II., but, unhappily, the rules and customs of the feudal system escaped revision. There was no restitution of the lands to the people, and therefore we find the indelible stamp of feudalism on the English land system.

After the conquest of Ireland by the English, besides grants to the English and Scotch settlers, there were additional steps taken to make the Irish land system like the English. Under an Act of the twelfth year of Queen Elizabeth, the Irish lords were empowered to surrender their titles to the queen,—these titles were at that time nominally held under the laws of gavel-

* Broderick's Reform of the English Land System, page 9.

kind,—and having done this, they accepted titles from the queen under the English feudal system and laws of primogeniture.* This malevolent law and the procedure under it shows the vindictive purpose of the English landed aristocracy. A chief, tanist or noble, whose rights were not those of a landholder, thus became one. The common people from being freeholders were reduced to the state of tenants and villeins, and this perversion of rights had only the authority of an English Act of Parliament.

The difference between the German and English systems are due rather to political accidents than other causes. All the Teutonic nations that came in contact with Rome adopted the feudal system. As has been said, all of them were originally communal. In ancient times the German was both a lord and a commoner. He was a freeman and a freeholder. The political geography of the continent of Europe has changed so often, that systems based purely on political power have been broken up. The transition from general ownership to individual and unequal possessions was resisted by the sturdy German. While her kingly authorities were, according to the theory of her law, elective, they soon became, in fact, hereditary. Whether king or lord of the manor, the manor and the office were identified with the land, and under this modification of the original freeman's title by the feudal system, and with the law of primogeniture, the changes gradually came. The process differed as to the manner in which it was received; the steps were the same: first, lands belonging to the community, then military service for defense, then the change from a tenure on military service to private right of the noble to the land, lastly, its transmittal by inheritance to one of a certain family. The difficulties encountered in some parts of Germany were that instead of building up this system on lands that had been conquered and divided, it had to be extended to lands held

*Maine's History of Institutions, page 201.

from remote periods by allodial freeholders. The system began, however, along the old frontiers of the Roman empire. When it was introduced, moreover, part of the lands since occupied were then waste. In each community there was so much arable land, occupied and held in tracts by each family, and lands common to all. The latter, of course, were first subject to political usurpation. The purely military service due from land was longer preserved in some parts of Germany. When the feudal system was first established, short military excursions, especially when the crops were harvested, were not onerous. Under the many terrible European wars military duties became more frequent and burdensome. Military duty, no matter what the length of service, was demanded by the lord of the manor; and, at last, pressed by these burdens, the tenant was forced to relinquish rights the tax on which had become too hard to be borne. Thus the holders under the ancient tenure disappeared and were replaced by mere tenants at will. The Germans, however, long maintained their ancient traditions.

At the time of the Reformation the Germans attempted to regain the rights of which the territorial lords had robbed them. Many of the people very naturally supposed there was some relation between liberty of conscience and liberty of the man. The kings and the nobles might wish to escape the exactions of the pope, but had no intention, if they could help it, of diminishing their own demands. It so happened, however, that after the Reformation feudalism lost much of its power.*

As in England, the first improvements proceeded from the towns. Manufactures and commerce had offered new fields for industry. Many of the free cities possessed great power, and were eminent factors in the change in behalf of the rights of the laboring man. The famous league of the Hanseatic

* Broderick's Reform of the English Land System, page 4.

towns, at one time comprising sixty-four cities and twenty-four towns, showed the increase of this new element of progress and reform. These were often able to put an army in the field.

In Germany, the power of land as a political element did not centre in the empire as was the case in England under William the Conqueror. An innumerable host of princes, margraves, barons, counts and other nobles had concentrated the political power by becoming lords of the manor. The German systems were federations with electorates chosen by these petty princes. The essence of power was with the local ruler; the emperors were weak and their dominions variable and transitory. The separation of the Franks and Germans in the ninth century gave a more distinct character to Germany, but made little change in the condition of the people. Switzerland maintained a spirit of freedom longer, and it was chiefly due to the fact that her people remained freeholders.

The condition of the Scandinavian nations differed from the other European countries. But little is known of their history prior to the eleventh century. The Goths largely displaced the ancient inhabitants, but the native element gave the dominant influence to religion and predatory habits. A bloody paganism prevailed until the twelfth century. Christian missionaries gained some foothold in the ninth century, but they encountered more opposition, and found it a harder task to overthrow the cruel religious rites here than elsewhere. The old Norseman pictured his Valhalla, or paradise, as a place where he drank wine and mead from the skulls of his enemies. They were a hardy, vigorous race, those old sea kings, and pushed the prows of their piratical craft into every sea of the Western world. Besides their incursions into Britain and Iceland they discovered and settled Greenland and the American coast and held it, at least, from the ninth to the thirteenth centuries.*

* Preface to Sinding's History of Scandinavia.

Nobles grew up in Sweden, Denmark and Norway under the same system as in the other countries, but not to the same extent or with the same powers. The landholder and even many of the nobles cultivate the soil and engage in business. The sturdy, independent character of the old Vikings did not brook many restraints. The inhospitable character of much of the country did not furnish the means for very wealthy noble families. The rulers were indebted for their power largely to selection, and the governments of Sweden, Denmark and Norway have possessed less of absolute power, and have been more easily overthrown than other nations in Europe. The governments were of a mixed hereditary and elective character. In early times the peasantry was a species of corporation consisting of freeborn persons who were not only husbandmen and agriculturists but possessed real estate. Above the peasants ranked the chiefs or leaders representing families of influence and of greater property. From these the kings took or created earls (*jarles*) to rule conquered provinces. The peasants and the nobles met at an assize, like the British Druids, round a circle of stones. Here they selected their kings, consulted on war or peace and settled cases judicially. Without the consent of this diet the king could not decide on any matter of importance.*

In all its earlier history Scandinavia was cursed with slavery. Their slavery was of the worst character. The slaves were divided into two classes, native Scandinavians and foreigners. In their many wars and piratical expeditions they made prisoners, who, unless ransomed by their friends became slaves. They also obtained many slaves by trade. The condition of the slaves was very miserable. The ancient Norseman scarcely held them to be men. A slave might be beaten, starved, tormented or even killed by his master, and the abuser go unpunished. A slave could not buy, sell or inherit. They

* Sinding's History of Scandinavia, page 38.

could not take oath or marry. Slaves were mere chattels sold like other wares. They were usually not permitted to carry arms.* The one redeeming trait in Scandinavian slavery was that a kind master would sometimes liberate his slave for faithful service, and slaves when hired out were permitted to retain a portion of their earnings and with this purchase their freedom. Once free, they might acquire land, upon which they took the rank of peasants. This wretched system of slavery continued, as Sinding and other authorities inform us, until Scandinavia became thoroughly Christianized, when slavery was abolished. Sinding also tells us, that as Christianity imbued the minds of the people they gave the women a share in the inheritance of property.

The Spanish peninsula has been the theatre of many strange events. In the days of Carthaginian splendor, this was one of her richest provinces. Rome wrested it from her, and the Ostrogoths wrested it from Rome. Then the warlike Saracens conquered and held it for centuries. Again, the mingled elements of Goth and Latin, after a long and fierce struggle, regained the peninsula. Here the blood of Carthaginian, Egyptian, Latin, Goth and Saracen mingled. Here art flourished, but human freedom was not sufficiently prized. The fall of the Moorish kings did not mean the liberation of the people.

On the restoration of Spanish government the country was parceled among the nobles. A spirit of independence, however, lingered among the people, and towards the close of the fourteenth century, the Spanish parliament, or cortez, was the best in Europe. Her tradesmen were organized into guilds, and her mercantile interests acquired power. The agricultural interests, however, were always under the feet of the nobles. The discovery of America turned the attention of the Spaniards to foreign conquest and adventure. The immense

* Sinding's History of Scandinavia, page 39.

wealth poured into Spain from the robbery of the American nations, appeared to be sufficient to enrich all Spain, and place them above the necessity of labor. The result was the most instructive lesson ever administered to human nature. In the face of these great accumulations industry languished. In spite of the rapid growth of all the nations around her, Spain, if she has not retrograded, has, at least, not kept pace with the other nations of Europe.

Unfortunately for the people, parliamentary bodies in Europe have largely represented land, and as the land chiefly belonged to the aristocracy, the aristocracy ruled the parliaments. In Germany, parliamentary developments are comparatively modern. The electorate of Germany was a convocation of princes. The great free cities had governments of their own. In England, towns, cities and trades had representation. A very important factor in the leveling process, was the introduction of gunpowder in the art of war. Formerly an earl or knight rode about the country with his squire and a few faithful men at arms. They were mounted on good horses, covered with mail, and armed so that a common yeoman, with his halberd and spear had no more chance in an encounter, than a lamb in the hands of a lion. When the plain foot soldier with his musket had become more than a match for the mounted knight, the situation had changed. The effect of gunpowder on the ancient freebooting baron or knight-errant was much greater than the sarcasm of Cervantes. Cannon was first used to bombard the strongholds of the robber barons. As gunpowder was employed in war, civilization advanced.* "When it was found that no coat of mail could keep out a small bullet, the knell of feudalry was rung."

As an apology for all the inequality and injustice that took root and grew up during this period, it is asserted that these

* Bell on Feudalism, page 165.

were the necessary accompaniments of a rude and violent age. This is a mistake. The ancient founders of the nations of Northern Europe, when they first entered Europe, equally divided the land for the use of all the people. With all their rudeness they were a brave and independent race. The honor of having been chosen leaders for defense, was, by an avaricious and unscrupulous aristocracy, prostituted, and the office used first to rob and then enslave the people they were commissioned to defend. The insidious and slow steps to accomplish this, are now matters of history, and stand in broad relief as a lesson to the human race. But for these conspiracies and crimes the European nations might have reached their present position several hundred years ago. The causes were the same which exist in any community where a privileged aristocracy have in their hands the machinery to turn the products of human labor into their own pockets. There was nothing done then which is not in a somewhat different manner being done to-day. The creation of an idle class is always a calamity. Titles are merely the insignia of luxurious vagabondage.

CHAPTER IV.

THE CHRISTIAN SYSTEM AS ITS PRINCIPLES AFFECT SOCIETY AND ORGANIZED GOVERNMENT.

Religious belief a pillar of law—The status and power of Christian nations—Religious political economy—Does Christianity teach socialism—Unholy alliance of church and state—A church founded on capital necessarily corrupt and idolatrous—Dates of the introduction of Christianity to Europe—Monastic orders—Slavery and woman's rights—Polygamy—Reformations—Sects—Denominations—Agnostics and the supernatural—Prof. Sumner's doctrine of a "free state" and the law of "contracts"—Startling effect of "ecclesiastical prejudice"—Dives and Lazarus.

To what extent does religious sentiment govern mankind? Another question: How far do organized religious bodies operate to promote the welfare of the great masses of laboring men? No one will deny the power of religious beliefs in all ages of the world. Men, in all times, have inseparably connected every kind of law with divine authority. Governments, at once the most despotic, dishonest and sanguinary, have never hesitated to ally themselves, when they could, to church or priesthood, in order thereby to prevent their overthrow.

It is estimated that in modern civilized society, judicial proceedings take place in a large proportion of the serious offences committed, such as theft, robbery and murder. In the more numerous petty offences against a high order of morals which show a cruel and dishonest heart, we have evidence that a greater number of persons cherish the spirit that would commit crime, but are restrained within legal limits. Besides these classes of offenders there is a better class much larger than both, estimated in the proportion of five to one, who live on a higher plane. To whatever extent this latter class may be subject to human weaknesses and temptations, they give evidence that they are restrained from the commission of crime and wrong by better motives; by a conviction that sin is morally wrong and degrading, and by the fear they entertain of Divine disapprobation. It will thus be seen that order is maintained in society, and human life and property made safe by the operation of two separate laws, the human and divine, and that one of these in its workings is much more potent and satisfactory than the other. Human law is not made for the virtuous but the vicious. The machinery of human government, although extremely expensive, has been found necessary in the almost unanimous opinion of mankind. It is a happy circumstance, however, that there exists a higher law in the human conscience. Some men call this public opinion, but public opinion is merely another kind of society tribunal which punishes by loss of caste or popular opprobrium. This also prevents the commission of crime by operating on the fears of men and women, and it may be truly said that no tribunal is more unsafe in its proceedings or more frequently unjust in its decisions. But for the class governed by a sense of right, courts and laws against criminals would be impossible; for offenders could not be depended upon to frame or execute rigid laws against themselves. The great anchor of a state, then, is this enlightened conscience of good men and women. From what source does society derive this best element? Some say it comes from the religious sentiment, almost universal in the human race. Some say it comes from education, and that it can be secured by a course of instruction fully informing man of all the principles that should govern society, which will make him act with mathematical exactness in a right direction. Another class, inclined to reject the religious idea as mere superstition, and who are, nevertheless, perfectly well aware that knowledge is not virtue, claim that there is a law of development in the human race, that brought man up from the original mollusk to a monkey, and from a monkey to the wonderful civilized man of the nineteenth century. It may be retorted on the latter that crime is as common in civilized as in barbarous communities and the most desperately wicked criminals known to jurisprudence have been highly educated and enlightened.

It is not too much to assume that the nations of modern Christendom are the most highly advanced nations in art, manufactures, intelligence, and what has been styled free government. The United States, Britain, Switzerland, Germany, France, Italy, Spain, Austria and even Russia, are Christian countries, and so are Canada, Central and South America. By Christian, I mean countries where the Christian religion is either recognized by the state or where a majority of the people profess belief in it. The elder Adams endeavored to commend us to Tripoli by asserting that the United States was in no sense a Christian government. The state, properly, has no connection with the church; it rests its conception of law on the will of the majority. At the same time the great mass of her people are believers in Christianity. Every officer, from the highest to the lowest, qualifies himself for the duties of public place by putting his hand on the Bible and calling God to witness that he means faithfully to discharge his duties. There are a great many intelligent freethinkers, atheists, and agnostics who repudiate God, revelation and religion, and there are many others who reject all the systems of religion known and entertain a theoretical, vague, undefined Theism of their own. Both of these classes are in the minority. While the republic of the United States is therefore not a Christian state, technically, it is a government of the people, and the people are a Christian people. It is, moreover, an offshoot of the Christian governments of Europe, and has in its inception and history been subject to Christian influences. It has not been subject to or influenced by Mahometanism, Buddhism or the doctrines of Confucius or Zoroaster. It ought to be understood, that religion in any country affects not only its professional believers but all within its influence, including the government itself.

Springing from a small despised sect, Christianity has spread until it is the controlling religion of all the nations of Europe, the continents and islands of the two Americas, Australia, a small part of British India, and other colonies of the leading modern nations. The most skeptical will readily admit that its influence over these is very great. Christianity is weak in Africa. Except in the French, British and Dutch colonies, and a somewhat degraded form in Abyssinia, it has little influence over the people of that continent. It will not be denied that Africa presents the most debased population found on the globe. It has been styled the "Dark Continent." There we see governments that are little better than organized murder. The worst forms of slavery and the slave trade exist and flourish. Human life and human labor are worth less there than anywhere else. The personal freedom of the citizen is unknown.

Asia is the next large portion of the world where Christianity has comparatively little power. Up to a very recent period, the Nestorian Chaldeans, and one or two other small communities, were the only native Christians. In Asiatic Russia, of course, the Greek-Christian church is supposed to be the religion of the state. There it exists pretty much as Christianity exists in British India, or in the colonies of any other European power. It is an intrusive idea that may be said to have the sympathy or patronage of the government, and may become a factor of great strength when it thoroughly uproots the native faith, and has existed long enough to instill its precepts into the minds of the people. That period is not yet. In British India, Mahometanism, Buddhism and various other religious beliefs exist, and form, to a large extent, the minds of the people, just as Mahometanism, Buddhism, Parseeism and modern Lamaism are potent in Russian Asia. The

European conquerors learned, in attempting to subjugate Asiatic empires, that it is one thing to get political power, and another to control the minds of the people. For this reason European civilization and European ideas of government make slow progress. There is not a native representative government, outside of colonial influence, in Asia, although it is true, that while elective rulers are hardly to be found, many of the governments only exist from popular toleration. To the encroachments of European civilization, Asia has been, until late years, impregnable. The Asiatic people are in no sense wild or barbarous. Their forms of society are very ancient. Several empires have for ages exhibited a very high degree of art. They have proven themselves capable of maintaining more dense populations than the nations of Christendom have so far coped with. Some of the religions that hold power over them, promulgate a dreamy, but not altogether degraded order of philosophy. The systems of morals taught by them cannot, as a general thing, be styled vicious. Bad systems and societies have become incorporated with them, however, and they have, to some extent, degenerated into idolatry and demonology. In nearly all Oriental religions, church and state are blended; in other words, the rulers have succeeded in uniting the religious beliefs with their systems of government, and the religion thus controlled by tyrants and usurpers, has been prostituted and degraded.

If religion comprised only the spiritual and supernatural, political economists would have little concern with it. Religious ideas, however, enter the domain of morals and law, affecting all the relations of citizens to each other. They operate on love, fear, social duty and human prejudice. The most skeptical will admit that the contemplation of a just and pure Deity has a tendency to elevate the character. Men and women who cultivate this affectionate love and worship are by far the best members of society. On the other hand, it operates also through fear. More men and women fear being damned, than being punished by the civil law. Religion has, therefore, always been a wonderful element of power. Even Thomas Paine admits the great power of religion, and, in his "Rights of Man," says: "All religions are, in their nature, mild and benign, and united with principles of morality. They could not have made proselytes by professing anything that was vicious, cruel, persecuting or immoral. Like everything else, they had their beginning, and they proceeded by persuasion, exhortation and example." He goes on to say, that all mischiefs flowing from them have been caused by the alliance between church and state.

In the Asiatic religions the supernatural predominates. Their codes of morals have not been of a very high order, at least, as compared with those of Christianity. It is true that Buddhism, which has the greatest number of followers, believing in the transmigration of souls, will not, under their moral law, kill animals, as the souls of men and women may be in them, but sets of fanatical murderers have grown up among them. Nowhere in their teachings do we find a high regard for human life inculcated. So far from asserting the universal brotherhood of man, systems of religious caste prevail. These Asiatic ecclesiastics do not encourage progress. The people remain stationary, their religious morals are not openly or secretly at war with the despotism of tyrants. We can, therefore, find the history of Asia written in her creeds; blind submission to fate, ancestor worship and caste prejudice. In the first few hundred years of its existence, Christianity made considerable progress in Asia, in what had been the old Greek and Persian empire. It spread rapidly up to the time of Heraclitus, and had very considerably ameliorated the condition of the people. It had reached far into Central Asia, and even to China. It is difficult to conjecture what the result would have been, if it had thoroughly indoctrinated the great masses of Central Asia. From its very nature, it is usually slow in its growth, and gradual in its progress to power over communities. It inculcates the doctrines of peace, moreover, and thus checks, instead of encouraging a martial spirit. This left it weak to resist the encroachments of warlike and barbarous violence, and, on the Asiatic continent, it fell before the aggressive and military genius of Mahometanism.

It had been held by many that early Christianity taught socialism. It appeared to be the practice of the early disciples and apostles. In the 41st verse of the 2d chapter of Acts, we are informed, that in one day "about three thousand souls were added to the church;" and in the 44th verse, we are told that "all who believed were together, and had all things common." In the 32d verse of the 4th chapter of the same book, we also find "Neither said any that aught of the things he possessed was his own, but they had all things common." In examining the question as to whether Christianity taught socialism, we find, in the first place, that there is nothing in the teachings of the founder of the church enjoining it. It was undoubtedly a convenience for the first organization of the church, in Jerusalem, to have this unity of interest. Then a believer became, to a certain extent, ostracised, without home or friends, and, possibly, for the time, driven from the employment that supported him. The convert connected himself with an organization, the founder of which had just been put to an ignominious death. The chief priests and rulers were not slow to exhibit the kind of treatment they intended to bestow on the new sect. Each convert was also expected in turn, to make proselyting, to a large extent, his business. It was not demanded that the believer, who had any property, should sell all he had and turn it into the common stock, but he was enjoined, if occasion offered, to sell all that he had, and to give to the poor. Ananias was not condemned for withholding, but for pretending to give where he did not. Peter, in reprimanding him, told him that the property was his own, and before he gave it, he could do what he pleased with it. We find, shortly afterward, the apostles enjoining converts to give, as God had prospered them, to the necessities of the saints. A disposition to be largely supported from the contribution of believers was very freely condemned, and it was said, that "he who doth not provide for they of his own household, has denied the faith, and is worse than an infidel." While it was asserted that those giving their time to the ministry were entitled to support, one of the most active apostles boasted that he had, in addition, labored with his hands, and had not been a charge on the church. Originally, says Hartwig, when the Christian communions were formed, all the members contributed according to their ability, to one common fund, for the purpose of good works; with the extension of Christianity, this general display of love abated, contributions became less general and liberal, and as it acquired power, or became allied with the state, changed into regular, and, in some cases, involuntary taxes.* With the single exception of Mahometanism, all other religions, except Christianity, were "limited in their design and local in their range." They were the images of separate nationalities.† The essential doctrine of Christianity is the brotherhood of mankind in all nations. It taught the worthlessness of forms in religion. Its founder denounced hypocrisy, and enjoined a pure life. It held all the moral law of Judaism to be intact. Jesus of Nazareth declared that "not one jot or tittle of the law should pass until all was fulfilled." Adding to these the generous and benignant doctrines of Christianity He broke down the wall that made the Jews an isolated and peculiar people, and sent forth his disciples with this enlightened and renovated system, as a law to all races and nations.

Such were the doctrines carried in a peaceful, missionary

* Brentano's History of Guilds, etc., page 7.

† Hardwick's Christ and other Masters, page 42.

way, into countries both civilized and barbarous, after the death of Christ; and, in a comparatively short period of time, they had spread through a portion of Eastern Asia, Northern Africa and large portions of Europe. What was left of the Grecian empire became largely Christian. Christianity struggled for the ascendant in the Roman empire, under a fierce persecution. There it had to encounter not only the fury of a luxurious, despotic and corrupt court, but the criticism and hostility of a brilliant galaxy of philosophers. Tacitus merely refers to Christianity as a sect of Judaism. The stoics and the epicures alike treated it with contempt. Not only did it have to contend with the interest and the prejudice of the existing religion, but with the low moral condition of a people steeped in vice and corruption. From its earliest history, Roman law had opposed polygamy, and it is stated that for five hundred and twenty years there was no such thing as a divorce in Rome.* Under the empire the marriage tie was less sacred. Juvenal speaks of a woman who had eight husbands in five years. St. Jerome relates an incident of a woman who married her twenty-third husband, and she was his twenty-first wife. Seneca denounced the free divorce system as a great evil. Besides this extreme laxity of the marriage tie, domestic morals in other respects were very loose. Mr. Lecky, in tracing the causes of decay, attributes much to the foregoing, and also dates the decline to the introduction of general slavery at the close of the Punic wars.†

The religion that should have given balance to the state was compounded of a profligate pantheon and the hypercritical speculations of the stoics and epicurians. The people were venal and debased, and society was in a decline so hopeless that nothing seemed to be left for it but the fire and brimstone that had closed the career of Sodom and Gomorrah.

* Lecky's History of European Morals, vol. ii., page 300.

† Ibid., page 302.

Such was the condition of the Roman empire when the apostles of Christianity struggled for its conversion. There was scarcely a doctrine taught by Christians that was not a living caveto against the whole Roman system. It made its way slowly but steadily. Women have always been quicker than men to embrace the doctrines of Christianity. Some of the most distinguished Roman matrons became its converts, and this only served to stimulate the persecution. Households were divided and embittered against each other, for if the Christian doctrine of universal brotherhood should prevail, it would abolish the privileges of Roman citizenship, and open the door to the equality of the people of all her provinces. In spite of these difficulties, the struggling church finally prevailed. Before the conversion of the Emperor Constantine, A.D. 312, it has been supposed, by some authorities, that a majority of the Roman people had become converted. Lecky, in his History of European Morals, says there was not a majority, and the probabilities are that its active, energetic followers, who had to risk their lives for their opinions, constituted much less than a majority.

The Emperor Constantine rebuilt Constantinople, originally Byzantium, A.D. 338, twenty-six years after he had embraced Christianity. It was not until July 9th, A.D. 381, that Bishop Nestorius was nominated as the first Patriarch of Constantinople. The term Pope comes from the Greek pappas and papa, father, or grandfather, and was originally applied to bishops. In A.D. 606, nearly three hundred years after the conversion of Constantine, Pope Benedict III. induced the Emperor of the East to confine the title to the chief prelates of Rome. While the greatness and power of Christianity usually dates from the conversion of the Emperor Constantine, it is extremely doubtful whether its alliance with the state did any good to Christianity. It has been said, on the other hand, that the conversion of the state was the ruin of Rome.

Lecky informs us * that all the evidence shows that the Christian Church went stoutly to work to reform Roman morals. In order to preserve the purity of marriage, it elevated it to a sacrament.† We have only one of two things to believe. Christianity must have failed in all its teachings, such as the universal brotherhood of man, the doctrine of peace, to provide things honestly in the sight of all men, purity, justice, meekness and temperance, or else, having faithfully taught these truths with any degree of success, the elements of Roman power were inevitably bound to crumble.

The Emperor Constantine called the council of Nice, which assembled June 19th, A. D. 325, and sat until August, three hundred and eighteen bishops attending. They manufactured a creed, and attempted otherwise to give a form to the religion that came to abolish all forms. This first great so-called Christian convocation condemned the doctrines of the Arians. General Ecclesiastical Councils were held in Constantinople, chiefly against heresy, A. D. 381, 553, 680 and 869. The church was torn by dissensions on points of doctrine as well as on the exercise of temporal authority by spiritual rulers. The idea of a supervision of nations by the church was probably well meant. This was one great purpose of the exercise of the papal power. Unjust wars were not to be permitted. The papal authority was to be supreme among nations. Good men entertained great hopes that the warlike power of cruel nations could thus be ended. Unhappily, the exercise of political power by the church plunges it into an arena for which it never was designed. In attending to duties of that sort, it usually forgets its legitimate business, which is to convert men and leave to them the task of reforming governments.

Other questions divided the church. All forms of religion have been fertile in schisms. Schisms as to doctrine, and

* History of European Morals, vol. ii., page 316. † Ibid., page 347.

much more frequently, schisms as to form. The question of figures and images in churches was a fruitful source of trouble. Several monarchs lost their thrones, and a few of them their lives, during the struggle to turn images and pictures out of, and into, the Christian churches. How such adjuncts to worship should ever have crept in under the teachings of Christ and the ten commandments it is difficult to imagine. Another innovation was monastic orders. The paganism overthrown in Rome and Greece had an element of asceticism that took this shape under the new religion. The supposed virtue of remaining unwashed and uncombed, in a half-starved condition, in a cave, or on the top of a pillar, derived neither encouragement nor command from the teachings of Christ. Monastic orders were injected into the kind of Christianity that had an early existence in Asia, and were borrowed from other religions. It was the third century of the Christian era before monastic orders were introduced in Europe.* In two or three hundred years they multiplied until they could be found in every city, and until laws were enacted against them. The organized church soon began to own property. Instead of limiting its means of support, according to the plan of the founder, to the voluntary contribution of believers, it aspired to be independent of such accidents. The gifts of the pious were encouraged and held up to be a virtue that would atone for sin. Bequests from dying saints and sinners commenced to be an important mode of adding to the fixed property of the church. The real estate of the church grew to be as formidable as the aristocratic resources of the priesthood in Egypt. The power thus created threatened to become a means of levying a tax on production, for all time, to be drawn, of course, out of the labor of each year, and without the slightest regard for what the coming generation might want in the way of a church organization. No church should ever be permitted to exist

* Lecky's History of European Morals, vol. ii., page 101.

on organized capital. Outside of the place it occupies for worship, all church property should be taxed, and such accumulations discouraged. A priesthood established on the revenues of land or capital is only less objectionable than an aristocracy so created: both are bad. When a church cannot obtain all it needs from the generosity and conscience of its hearers and believers it may be taken for granted that it is time for it, as an organization, to close business. In addition to the general jealousy engendered by the steady accumulation of property in the hands of ecclesiastics, and the inevitable tendency of selfish, designing men to get into and to control such an establishment, the confidence of the people in the priesthood began to be shaken. With or without reason, frightful stories were told about the morals of high dignitaries, and also about the religious orders. Such was the condition of the Christian Church at the close of the first six hundred years of its history. Its instincts and genius should have taught it to avoid all these abuses. The simplicity of Christ's teachings had been buried beneath a selfish and corrupt hierarchy.

So long as Christians were liable to be torn by wild beasts, there was little danger of the church receiving any but genuine converts. An emperor, clothed with patronage, at the head of the church, was likely to have insincere followers. This established religion had to submit to another infliction. The philosophers interjected their theories into it, just as the Philistines put the mice and the emerods into the Ark of the Covenant. They had done this with the old pantheon, why not with the new? They were theorists and philosophical speculators, not repentant sinners. It is surprising that Christianity survived all these calamities. That it did so is no small argument in favor of its divine origin. Organized Christianity had become thus debauched, when the entrance of Mahometanism to the field of thought and morals, A.D. 612, marked a new epoch.

Christianity was introduced, as Bede informs us, into

Britain, in the 64th year of the Christian era. It is well known, however, that England was essentially pagan long after. A careful comparison of the dates of its general acceptance in the countries of Europe, and the initial steps in the civilized progress of these states is instructive. Although introduced into Ireland in the second century, it was not until A. D. 432, that it obtained controlling influence under the teachings of St. Patrick. It was introduced among the Goths in 376, but did not attain much influence until the Gothic people had been formed into their European governments. It was established in France by Clovis, A. D. 496. The Saxons were converted by Augustine in 597; but Christianity was not introduced into what is known as Saxony, until 785 under Charlemagne. Harold introduced it to Denmark in 827, and it was not established in Sweden until the eleventh century. It was introduced into Norway and Iceland A. D. 998. It will be remembered that these Scandinavian nations had a bloody idolatry, characterized by fierce and unclean rites. Christianity was introduced into Bohemia, under Borsiva, A. D. 894. It was introduced into Russia, by Swiatoslaf, A. D. 940 or 942. The Teutonic knights, on returning from the holy wars, A. D. 1227, introduced the Christian doctrine to Prussia, which they had obtained permission to "convert and conquer." Care must be taken not to confound the introduction of Christianity with the real christianization of the masses. A careful study of the nations or countries named will show that a gradual change in their condition, for the better, began with these periods. Slavery, in its worst forms, existed in every one of them prior to that time, and for a considerable period after. Guilds were associations of towns, trades or religious societies, for mutual protection and benefit. They were introduced early in the eighth century, and were fostered by the priesthood. Guilds, and the organization of the people, were the means of introducing juries, about A. D. 886. The system by which a man or a cause could only be tried by the equals of the parties in interest was improved and systematized from that period.

Christianity was the means of abolishing polygamy in the German and Scandinavian nations; indeed, the evil existed up to, or after, the time of Charlemagne. Until Rome had become Christian it never attempted to elevate the character of the people of its provinces. It did not, to any extent, give its colonies political power, or teach them the arts of peace. Christianity, on the other hand, immediately set to work to convert and elevate the people.

During these struggles it must be remembered that the church had a constant war within itself. Prior to the invention or introduction of the printing press in Europe, the doctrines of Christianity could only be taught through the organized priesthood. As nations became converted from barbarous forms of religion, they tried to incorporate into Christianity many of their old ideas. The lack of a general literature rendered it difficult to detect such impostures. Had the Christian Church been able to retain all its purity and simplicity, and had it always used its authority for a good purpose, Europe to-day would have been in a much better condition. As the church grew in temporal power, and began to absorb the wealth of the nations, it excited the jealousy and hatred, not only of the people, but of the civil authorities. Its very wealth betrayed those who were in charge of it into a course of life altogether inconsistent with their professions. A great hierarchy degenerated, of necessity, into forms. An apostle traveling in poverty, persecution and hardship, to preach the doctrines of peace and the brotherhood of man, was one thing, and a great priesthood charged with disbursing the revenues of the church, quite another. Where there is a great temptation to simulate, there will always be an inevitable tendency to substitute idols for a pure worship, ceremonies in the place of a pure life, and forms where the substance is lacking.

The introduction of the art of printing was destined to have a very considerable effect on society and the church. Books, hitherto confined to cloisters, began to be read by the people. At such a time the assumptions of personal sanctity and the power to dogmatise over the minds of men was not safe, and the Protestant religion followed. It was at first a protest against the spiritual authority of the Pope. Reforms in the church were not new before the time of Luther in 1517. The reform of the Albigenses in 1177 was of a similar character, as was that of Wickliff in England in 1360. Huss in Bohemia, in 1405, introduced reforms for the many abuses that had crept into the church. For this action he and Jerome of Prague were burned at the stake. Savonarola in 1498 attempted the reformation of the Papal church in Italy. These were some of the leaders of the great revolutions that swept over Europe, but reformers within the church had steadily striven against its abuses through all ages, and the final separation of the Eastern and Western empires of the Christian Church was due to their efforts. The Greek Church, one of the great branches of Christianity, has been separated from the Roman Church for twelve hundred years; its present seat and centre being in Russia.

After the Reformation the property of the church, accumulated during ages, was stripped from it. Monastic orders were to some extent broken up. The doctrine of indulgences was scoffed at, not only by sinners, but by men who had been educated as priests. In the revulsion all the branches of the church became better. It is true there was bloody persecution, but of course only in cases where the church was closely allied with the state. Stripping the great central church organization of power had a tendency to increase the power and weaken the responsibility of kings. It might have resulted in the creation of strong despotisms in the leading nations but for the rise of the people, the enfranchisement of whom was in considerable degree due to Christianity. Constitutional governments were beginning to be understood. Representative bodies assumed force and character, and from the time of Henry VIII., when the Reformation occurred in England, little more than a hundred years elapsed until Charles I. was beheaded for asserting royal prerogatives against the wishes of the people.

Following the Protestant reformation of Zuinglius, Luther, Calvin and Knox, came a host of other reformers. The hope that universal Christian peace might prevail on the recognition of the spiritual power of the Pope had faded away when new bodies emerged from the Protestant Church to secure if possible the Christian doctrine of peace and good will toward men. The Quakers, eminent for many virtues, have made this one of the prominent reasons for their departure, together with their general protest against all forms, vanity and extravagance. That such a people should have been the subjects of cruel persecution seems hardly credible. Their influence is not confined to those of their own immediate persuasion. The Menonites were originally a species of German Quakers, but on being driven from Germany took refuge in Southern Russia. There for generations they founded a worthy and industrious community, protesting against all wars, and as they have resolutely refused to violate their conscience in this particular, most of them have recently been forced to emigrate to the United States. Then there followed Methodists, Baptists, and many other sects and denominations. As the Protestant churches were unhappily established by the state, the alliance carrying with it poison and corruption into the body of the church, there came still another swarm of "dissenters," who protested against all alliances between the Church and State. The foundation of the great deep of thought had been broken up. The Catholic Church said all this was the inevitable wanderings of heresy, and they pointed to the rapid growth of freethinking and atheistic opinions in support of their theory. Books were written against every kind of religious belief. Priestcraft and statecraft were confounded, and the church having kept bad company, the charge that it was the tool of despotism was not altogether unfounded. Historians wrote books, ostensibly against the Catholic Church, but really aimed at all religion. A profession of skepticism began to be considered as rather creditable to the intellect. Even the Reformed churches seemed to have a tendency to form new hierarchies. Cant and hypocrisy formulate the externals of religion. A "wealthy religious body" is really as much of a deception as a "fashionable church." Neither of them have anything in common with the Man who "had not where to lay his head."

The American and French revolutions treated religion differently. In America the colonists contented themselves by forever divorcing church and state. Everything connected with the former must be voluntary. The French people found a corrupt hierarchy closely allied with a corrupt aristocracy; and, confounding religion with priestcraft, the Jacobin clubs reveled in denying all authority, human and divine. Atheism was rampant. Agnosticism can raise questions, can revile, can speculate; it cannot create rules for life, or build society, or restrain men from the commission of evil; it has nothing to offer but skeptical doubts about all things. Napoleon I. was not a Christian, but he said he could not govern France without religion, and he restored the Catholic Church. One would have thought that the seeds of Atheism had been so sown that such a restoration would have been extremely difficult, if not impossible. Governments had shaken off not only the king and the aristocracy, but had set divine authority at defiance, and were rejoicing in their freedom from all restraint. France indeed had, and still has within her, strong skeptical elements. Her capital is a hotbed for theorists, and her manners tend rather to vitiate than to elevate the tone of Christendom; but in spite of the licentiousness of her press, the lax morals of her capital, and in the face of the teachings of all her philosophers, the masses of the laboring classes of France draw their inspirations of devotion and duty from the Christian Church.

In Britain, Christianity is a strong element of power. Scoffers, skeptics, freethinkers, backed by an army of philosophers and scientists, constantly are at work to explain away much of the accepted data in the formula of believers. While the philosophers and the scientists fill the prints and are heard in the lecture room, the great mass of the British people are really or professedly religious. Here in the United States, in the midst of a universal school system, her books, her pamphlets solid and flippant, the majority of her people are true or nominal Christians. If her freethinkers are not very numerous they are able and adroit. They are propped up by devices called scientific, and schools of philosophy that pride themselves on being rigidly practical. Superstitious belief is pronounced unphilosophic and incredible, the church a convocation of dupes and ignoramuses; religious zeal is branded as hypocrisy, but let no man figure upon the results of political reforms or social changes who refuses to take into account the power of the Christian religion. The teachings of the Man of Nazareth are echoed from ten thousand pulpits each week, the most staid and responsible members of society attend and listen. Innumerable Sunday-schools are instilling into the minds of tender children the ideas and doctrines of Christianity.

Christianity, although still encumbered, was never so free from political demoralization or from being used by tyrants, selfish interests, or all the riff-raff that have "stolen the livery of Heaven to serve the devil in," since the time when Constantine was converted, as it is to-day. If the Christian religion has been reduced in the public esteem or weakened for the accomplishment of good, this misfortune is attributable to the insincerity and unfaithfulness of many of those who have assumed to be its priesthood. Its potency does not consist in its wealth, respectability, or in alliances with the state. All these are a travesty on the religion of Christ. In defending the cause of the downtrodden and the weak; in rebuking wrong in high places; in simplicity and purity its "great strength lies." John Adams wrote: "One of the most calamitous events for human liberty was a wicked confederacy between the temporal grandees and the priesthood, mutually to uphold each other." * For these reasons many defenders of popular liberty permitted themselves to drift into a position antagonistic to the church. In the rigid separation of religion from all civil power the safety of true religion rests, but irreligious rulers are not, as a general thing, safe custodians of the interests of men. Even John Adams, not an admirer of religion, was forced to write somewhat bitterly, but significantly: "I believe it will be found universally true that no great enterprise for the honor or happiness of mankind was ever achieved without a large mixture of that noble infirmity." †

What has been known as the Christian religion has had two sides presented to the world. Its principles and the sincere believers in them, and religious organizations, churches allied to the state, hierarchies and the abuses that have clustered round them. The skeptic sees one face and does not believe in the other. It is true we had professors of religion in the United States who connived at or shut their eyes to the sin of slavery; but it is also true that not only the Quakers, who made the first early persistent protest against this wickedness, but also the devout, earnest Christian people of other denominations, who wished to see no stain on the name of Christianity, by their prayers and efforts abolished American slavery.

In the same way a pure Christianity will always protest

* Works of John Adams, vol. iii., page 450. † Ibid., page 452.

against wrong. When the voice of the Master is heard from the lips of his followers, it comes with a rebuke to selfishness, usury, unfair dealing, oppression of the poor, pride, aristocracy, fashionable religion, hypocrisy, and the folly and wrong of amassing great and unnecessary fortunes. Unless the voice of the church is bribed to silence it will espouse the cause of the struggling poor.

Christendom is the centre of the world's progress and high civilization to-day. It is, therefore, proper to consider how much of that power and success can be traced to its teachings. It is fair to estimate Christianity by its works. Among these are the elevation of women, the abolition of slavery in Europe and America, and of polygamy in Northern and Central Europe. If it has been stained by selfish and hypocritical professors, it has been adorned by sincere and vigorous reformers.

Modern agnosticism discredits what is styled the supernatural in the region of morals. There is a hungering and thirsting for some rule of life outside of the law of God and an æsthetical religion divorced from the supernatural. Separate the church and its worship from the idea of an intelligent, powerful Deity, and you strip religion of its vitality. If it was possible to destroy in the minds of men the belief in a hereafter, and in future responsibility, and make them believe that they were like the beasts that perish, mankind would be hopelessly degraded.

Professor Sumner, in his work "What Social Classes Owe Each Other," says: "The only social improvements which are now conceivable lie in the direction of a more complete realization of free men united by contract." * * * "It follows, however, that one man in a free state cannot claim help from, and cannot be charged to give help to another." * He also says: "The greatest part of the preaching in America

* What Social Classes Owe Each Other, page 26.

consists in injunctions to those who have taken care of themselves, to perform their assumed duty to take care of others." He adds, very naively: "Whatever may be one's private sentiments, the fear of appearing cold and hard-hearted causes those conventional theories of social duty and these assumptions of social fact to pass unchallenged." The professor exclaims, "Is it wicked to be rich? Is it mean to be a capitalist?" and proceeds thus: "There is an old ecclesiastical prejudice in favor of the poor, and against the rich. In days when men acted by ecclesiastical rules, these prejudices produced waste of capital, and helped mightily to replunge Europe into barbarism. The prejudices are not yet dead, but they survive in our society as ludicrous contradictions and inconsistencies." *

This is certainly a very remarkable statement, and we apprehend the professor would find it difficult to fix the date when appeals from Christian teachers, in behalf of the poor, "re-plunged Europe into barbarism." He made a mistake in the term when he used the word "ecclesiastic." Ecclesiasticism has neither prejudices nor principles. It is a mere form, a shell. Religion may be within it, or it may not. It was ecclesiasticism that preached, when he says, "Preaching in England *used* to be all done to the poor—that they ought to be contented with their lot, and respectful to their betters." We are grateful that he said "used to be," as regards England, and thankful that he bears a different kind of testimony as to American Christian teachings. It was not ecclesiasticism, but the religion of Christ, that had "a prejudice in favor of the poor, and against the rich." Jesus Christ, who was certainly not an ecclesiastic, gives for our instruction the story of Dives and Lazarus. He tells us also that a certain man went down from Jerusalem to Jericho, and fell among thieves. The priest and Levite who were "ecclesiastics,"

* What Social Classes Owe Each Other, page 44.

were the professor's "free men of a free democracy," who were under no obligations to neglect their business and waste their capital on a man who ought to have had sense enough to keep out of the thieves' way. The Samaritan seems to have been one of those "crochety sentimentalists" who are afflicted with a false "conventional theory of social duty," but his example will be held up for emulation when political economists of the Sumner school have been forgotten. In an age where selfishness threatens the very existence of society, help alone can come from a better understanding and more general acceptance of the leading idea of Christianity: "Whatsoever ye would that men should do to you, do ye even so to them."

CHAPTER V.

THE MAHOMETAN SYSTEM, AND THE GOVERNMENTS AND FORMS OF SOCIETY FOUNDED ON IT.

Arabia the blest and curst—The robber of the desert a founder of empires—Democratic tendencies of Mahometanism—Its foundation—Plunder and polygamy—Furnished an occupation for the large class who seek to subsist by war or their wits—Slavery legalized—Women degraded—War on property rights of women—Mahometan laws of taxation—Land tenure—Divorce—Wills forbidden—Temperance and abstinence by law—Licentiousness established on earth and deified in heaven—Pure Mahometanism, or Theism—Worship of the Prophet an innovation—Christianity and Mahometanism the only cosmopolite religions—Reformations in the Mahometan church—The Wahabees—Mahdis—Causes of Mahometan decay.

THE peninsula, or region of country lying between the Persian Gulf and the Red Sea, with a thousand miles of frontage on the Indian Ocean, and extending indefinitely northward across the deserts toward the country watered by the Euphrates, has, at different periods, passed under many names, but in literature is best known as Arabia. Ptolemy classified Arabia into three parts or portions, the stony, or mountainous; the desert, or sandy; and Happy Arabia, "Arabia Felix." It is about seven hundred and fifty miles from Bassora to Suez, and nearly the same distance from the Persian Gulf to the Red Sea, the southern part of the peninsula being wider. There is no navigable river in the peninsula. Streams of any kind are scarce, and in the greater portion rain rarely falls; sometimes years pass without it. Along the Persian Gulf there is a strip of land, partially cultivated, into which the drifting sands have constantly struggled to make inroads, but which maintains a varying population. None of the mountains of the peninsula rise to any great height. Most of them are sharp, rugged peaks, "stony land" without trees or verdure. "Arabia Felix" is in the southwestern part. Immediately on the sea the coast is a sandy plain, Et Tehama, but a short distance inland, there are mountains interspersed with fruitful valleys. This is the land of frankincense and myrrh, of gold and precious stones. Niebuhr has enumerated fourteen provinces in the fertile portion of Yemen. In ancient times, Strabo says, it was divided into five kingdoms, and that its chief cities abounded in palaces and temples. Coffee is one of its valuable exports, and from one of its ports, Mocha, many other spices have long been shipped. In all ages a very valuable commerce has been carried across the deserts on the backs of camels, the larger of these animals being able to carry a load of one thousand pounds.

Egypt, Greece, Persia, India, the cities on the Mediterranean and the rich portions of Arabia, all furnish articles thus sent through these dreary regions. Commerce, the carrying trade and the productions of Arabia Felix, yielded subsistence for the people of Arabia. Outside of Yemen, several other provinces had considerable cities and trade. The two most remarkable of these cities, during a long period, have been Mecca and Medina, two hundred and seventy miles apart, in the same geographical district. The latter has some agricultural land around it, but Mecca is a veritable city of the desert, good water, even, being scarce. Oakley informs us that in its greatest prosperity it was about the size of Marseilles. Mecca was known to the Greeks under the name of Macoraba. Outside of the agricultural or spice districts, and a few valleys, the great bulk of Arabia is a rocky or sandy desert waste. Burckhardt, the traveler, informs us that it is the most desolate portion of the globe, and that the natives call it the "empty abode."

Under a tropical sky, and without lake or river to furnish moisture, the atmosphere is dry and burning. The bare, treeless, rocky peaks are little more inviting than the sea of drifting sand. None of her mountains reach the region of eternal snow. A few of them in the southwest portion, several days' journey from the sea, reach an altitude of five or six thousand feet, and such is the peculiar atmosphere of that section, that at times, for one or two months of the winter, snow lies on them, while across the straits of Babel-Mandeb, in Africa, the mountains, reaching nine or ten thousand feet altitude, never have snow. Hot and deadly winds blow over the desert of Arabia, and the whole region is subject to malarial influences that render it difficult for the natives to live there, and fatal to foreigners.

The Arabs have always boasted of their independence, and say their country was never conquered, and that they never paid tribute. Its poverty and desolation is its defense. The Bedouin, who courses over it, is an active, restless, independent man, to whom war is at once a trade and a luxury. He has everything to gain and nothing to lose by adventure. Ockley says that the Arabs have been professional robbers since the days of Job,* and all other authorities corroborate the statement, running back to Strabo and Herodotus. In their military movements they can make a journey of four or five hundred miles in eight or ten days.† The horse is supposed to be a native of Arabia. Their horses are not large, but of a fine and hardy variety. When threatened by an invading army some noted emir would hoist a rallying standard, then all that could be collected would make common cause against the enemy. Whole armies have perished in the desert attempting to pursue them.‡ In this way the wandering Arabs have maintained their independence and

* History of the Saracens, page 9.

† Ockley's History of the Saracens, page 7.

‡ Chrichton's History of Arabia, vol. i., page 64.

a vigorous, self-denying existence. Often pressed sore by famine, they have wandered, with belts tied about their waists, subsisting on a little gum. Besides resisting attacks and preying on caravans, they have often carried their predatory incursions into the richest of the enemy's provinces. The Arabs planted date-palms wherever they could induce them to grow, and this is one of their sources of subsistence. When locusts stripped the country of its herbage they ate the locusts.

While it may be difficult to conceive of a very high order of manly qualities among a nation of professional robbers, all authorities agree that many things esteemed as virtues have been sedulously cultivated among them. Grapes grow, and wine to some extent is produced in their country, and fermented mare's milk was not unknown, but the virtue of temperance has always been rigidly inculcated. Diodorus tells us that the Nabatheans (Arabs) were prohibited by their laws from sowing, planting, drinking wine or building houses, and that the penalty for a violation of either law was death. The 35th chapter of Jeremiah contains similar information. The Rechabites (Arabs) were held up to the Israelites as an example because they had obeyed the laws of their fathers, refused wine and dwelt in tents.

The cities of southwest Arabia and the richer portions have been conquered on many occasions. Even these were so surrounded by deserts that they were hard to take and harder to hold, but they were at different times under the yoke of Abyssinia, Egypt, Greece, Rome and Persia. The victor's grasp on these regions was but frail, however. The roving Arabs always recognized and usually stood by their brethren in the cities, or those living in the cultivated regions. They were, to a great extent, the merchants and freighters for them. The people in the cities strove to keep on good terms with them, and had usually little difficulty in securing their aid for warlike operations when there was a reasonable prospect of booty. It was customary to send for them in all emergencies.

Such were the inhabitants of Arabia who had lived for ages without being enslaved or without being able to found an empire of any note. So they continued until the close of the sixth century of the Christian era. Then a remarkable revolution occurred. It did not arise from the wars or quarrels of kings, nor was it, so far as the original actors were concerned, a revolution springing from accumulated tyranny. What, then, made this poor wandering robber of the desert a builder of cities and a founder of empires?

Mahomet was born at Mecca, A. D. 569. He announced himself as the Prophet of God in 622. At the time of his advent every species of religion, superstition and irreligion flourished in Arabia. Its ancient history is wrapped in some little obscurity, for it was the policy of Mahomet and his successors to prevent any recurrence to its past religion or history. All before Mahomet's time is spoken of as "the time of ignorance." In the time of ignorance they had some pretty elaborate forms of religion. The oldest, as far as known, was the Sabean or worship of the Magi. They worshiped or used as symbols the sun, the moon and the great planetary bodies. They drew horoscopes, ascertained the stars under which people were born, and were devout believers in planetary influences; astrology and theology were there allied.

Before the Christian era, as Diodorus informs us, the Sabeans had a famous temple at Mecca, which was revered by all the Arabians. In fact, pilgrimages were made to Mecca long before the time of Mahomet. The Caaba, or temple, had then, as the temple at Medina has now, a black stone that was reverently kissed. The old temple, as several of the ancient authorities inform us, was a sort of pantheon. It was said to contain three hundred and sixty idols of men, eagles, lions and antelopes, and among these the statue of Hebal, of agate, holding in his hand seven arrows without heads or feathers, the old symbol for divination. It appears to have been a church on such a liberal basis that each tribe or individual could get in gods of their own. The tribe of Koreish somehow managed to get the custody of the Caaba and the care of it came down through several generations to the grandfather of Mahomet. Besides this heathen worship, the Jews had long held foothold in the cultivated and wealthy portions of Arabia. Their settlements date, at least from the time of the first captivity, and in all probability many of them were there earlier. The Arabians and Jews claim original kinship, being of the Semitic stock. In spite of this supposed relationship by blood, there has long been a jealousy and hatred of the Jewish population in Arabia. This chiefly arose from the Jews remaining a distinct people, and the fact that they were traders and usurers intensified the dislike. After the advent of Mahomet the differences became very bitter, for the Jews and Christians were the chief elements of resistance to Mahomet, and but for his calling in the wandering Arab tribes to aid him, their resistance could not have been overcome.

Although Christianity had taken root among the fixed populations of the Arabian peninsula, upon the roving Arabs it did not seem to have much influence, and, in fact, its teachings of peace and good-will toward men and restitution for theft, were scarcely likely to be popular among a race of habitual robbers. The many gods and doctrine of chance in the Caaba, at Mecca, suited them better. Even that religion, to all appearance, left them as it found them.

The causes that lay at the bottom of the wonderful uprising and marvelous growth of Mahometanism will always be a subject of profound study. A people, who for ages did not seem inclined to tolerate a stable or powerful government among themselves, at once became the organizers of powerful governments over others. Poor, without a revenue to maintain or equip armies, in little more than a century they overran and conquered two-thirds of the known world. Rome, in all her glory, trained to conquest by centuries of trial, did not accomplish as much. It is a coarse and vulgar thing merely to conquer; these Saracens, as they were styled, did more. They organized governments and founded empires. To these, moreover, they gave distinctive ideas. A race whose early traditional law forbade them to build houses, founded an architecture the ruins of which still excite the admiration of the civilized world. Its ideas inspired communities of men with new forms of law, religion and government, and though there may be much we must condemn, it would be unfair to deny that it improved the condition of many of the peoples whom it affected. It has long been on the wane, and Christendom complacently contemplates its coming overthrow; but still in parts of Europe, Asia and Africa it is not without influence, and it is estimated that in different nations, even to-day, not less than a hundred millions of people, twice the population of the United States, accept the Alcoran and look devoutly to the tomb of Mahomet.

For what did this system commend itself to the children of men? What are its inherent merits and vices? How did it affect the happiness and prosperity of the toiling masses? How did it affect the interests of labor? What land system did these conquerors, who had no land in their own country, foster or plant in the governments they builded? What effect has it had on the interests of common people in the past, and what is its influence on the interests of humanity to-day? It has been said that the strength of Mahometanism lay in its democratic principles; that men had been enslaved by the patriarchal system; that the elder put his feet on the necks of his younger brethren, and was an absolute monarch,—in fact, absorbing what little property there was, and holding even the power of life and death. The destruction of this aristocracy was said to be involved in the principles Mahomet inculcated, although an open war on the patriarchal state was not made. Of course, this new system opened the door to the enterprise of every man, as there was no provision for an aristocracy. The Mahometan laws of inheritance divided equally between all the sons, but the females were degraded to dependent position.

The first five successors of the Prophet were elected; founding an hereditary monarchy was certainly foreign to Mahometan ideas. The sixth caliph, by intrigue and force of arms, overthrew Ali, the son-in-law of Mahomet. This schism played an important part in the subsequent history of the Moslem. The Koreish chief Moawijah, first an enemy and then a convert of Mahomet, became an active leader of the new faith, and before Mahometanism was half a century old, converted an elective theocracy into an absolute monarchy, and founded the dynasty of the Ommiades.

In judging the governments founded by the believers in the Koran, it is well not only to read the book but to examine the circumstances by which these leaders were surrounded. The Koran itself has been loaded with so much of the supernatural and miraculous, that it is difficult to extricate the real principles it contained from the incredible fictions with which it is encumbered. It is generally admitted that a great deal of the more mystical and miraculous portions were added long after it was first written. Mahomet, in composing the part of it he wrote, was not ignorant of the Bible or the Testament; in fact, he recognized both these books. He embodied no inconsiderable portion of their precepts. The points on which the Koran differed from Judaism and Christianity constituted Mahometanism,—what were these?

Christianity had existed six hundred years. At that time, many even in the Christian Church who accepted its morals and its doctrine in the main, rejected the divinity of Christ. Mahomet promulgated the doctrine, "There is but one God, and Mahomet is his prophet." He did not claim divinity himself, and he admitted that Christ and the great lawgivers of the Jewish Church were teachers sent from God. He seemed to comprehend the necessity of a law that should have the sanction of Divine authority: hence his account of the miraculous transmission of the Alcoran to him. He rejected the doctrine of sacrifice. The Prophet, and afterward the Caliph or vicar of God, officiated in the Mosque and taught therein. There was no priestly order as such. The Muezzin, who called to prayer, was merely a convenience, and all other services were supposed to be best performed by the worshiper himself. If performed by others, no significance was attached to the exercise of such duty. Florian informs us that at first the Mahometans had neither altars, pictures nor place of worship. They have a sabbath of one day for rest and religious instruction. This they borrowed from the Jews and Christians. They selected Friday, and in time it became customary for the caliph to go to the Mosque and pray like other believers, and then address the congregation on their religious duties or duties to the state. Among the more pious Mussulmen, prayer for temporal blessings was not approved. They could pray, however, for the prosperity of their country or success of their cause, and for confusion to all unbelievers.

Rigid temperance was a cardinal feature of the Mahometan system. It was not original with the founder of the religion, for, as we have said, it had long been a law with the Arabians. Mahomet inculcated abstinence from intoxicating liquor as a religious duty; the extreme penalty of death was modified; a man is publicly whipped for drinking, even if he does not get drunk, and drunkenness is punished with the bastinado.* A man who uses intoxicating liquors at all is not considered a good Mussulman; if he persists in it, he is treated as a reprobate. In the early and purer days of the system, all narcotics and intoxicants were included in this prohibition. By the Alcoran and the teachings of the purest believers strict temperance in food is also enjoined, and plainness in clothing. The conqueror of Syria, out of all the plunder taken by his followers, only reserved for himself a pittance of forty cents per day. Another potent general

* Hamilton's Hedaya, vol. iv., page 157.

who had overthrown kingdoms, rode from city to city on a brown camel, with a skin bottle of water, a bag of barley, and a wooden vessel from which to eat. Self-denial, hardship, freedom from pride and avarice were insisted upon. Pilgrimages to Mecca were enjoined in the subsequent teachings of the church, but were not demanded. Mecca, the sacred city, and Medina, the burial place of the Prophet, remained but for a short period the seats of empire. The Koran allows pilgrims, and the faithful generally, during the journey, to make an increase of their substance by trading. This system of pilgrimage was doubtless copied after the visits of the Jews to Jerusalem; one important principle was hostility to usury, and law and custom denounced the usurious profit of capital.

The Alcoran and all the subsequent teachings of the faithful enjoined a constant and liberal charity. Giving of alms was one of the first duties of the true believers. The theory of the zakat, or tax, is that it is a voluntary gift. Contributing for the needs of the state followed in the course of time, and became obligatory. These taxes, or zakat, amounted by law to two and a half per cent. of the principal of certain assessed property. If he desired strictly to accomplish the law, the true believer was required to give in all a tithe of his increase.* As the Mahometan law became systematized the tax varied. The term zakat, in its primitive sense, means "purification," and was an enjoined contribution for the use of the poor. When it grew into taxes, zakat was not due from property until the owner possessed it for one year. The property of maniacs and children was not taxed. It was not enforced where a man's debts equalled his property.† The tax was levied on fixed property. Zakat was not due unless a man owned five camels; for that number the annual tax was a goat. The tax was not due unless a man owned thirty kine, then the tax was a year old steer or heifer. Zakat was not

* Crichton's History of Arabia, vol. i., page 295.

† Hamilton's Hedaya, vol. i., page 4.

due unless the person taxed owned forty goats, then the annual tax was one goat. On horses the tax was "five deeners per cent. on the total value." On all other property or money values the tax was two and a half per cent.* Upon everything produced from the earth, a tithe or tenth was due, with one exception; if land required watering, land near a river paid a tithe, land watered by hand, only half a tithe.

The Arabs of the desert did not practice agriculture. As a pastoral people they rove over a country common to all. Contests often occurred about springs or wells, and the only rule that seems to govern the possession is force. The Arabs knew little about land. Observing the agriculturists in the valley of the Euphrates, the Tigris and the Nile, they despised them as the slaves of the kings and satraps, who drained their substance from them. With the roving Arabs it was a vice to cultivate the soil. Among the stationary tribes of Arabia, subdivisions of the soil were adopted.† These were the people in Arabia Felix. The latter were composed, not only of the tribes of Ishmael, but Jews, Christians, Ethiopians and Phœnicians. In one case it is mentioned that a bush marked the boundaries of two districts, and that a hereditary estate was measured by the distance you could hear the barking of a dog. It is evident that among the best of these people land laws were in a crude state. Mahomet had the Bible, and knew what the Jewish land laws were perfectly. He did not copy them into the Alcoran. In his time the dominions of the faithful did not extend beyond Arabia. He induced the roving Arabs to help him to conquer Arabia Felix. That was the great effort, in accomplishing which, his life closed, he being poisoned by a Jewess.

To some extent the Mahometans accommodated themselves to the customs and laws of the countries they overran. Their

* Hamilton's Hedaya, vol. i., page 25.

† Crichton's History of Arabia, vol. i., page 157.

land policy, what there was of it, scarcely applied to Arabia. In their conquests they only disturbed rights in land for public uses, and from the rest exacted tithes. At first they did not tolerate unbelievers under any circumstances, or, at least, adopted that as their public policy. All land occupied was subject to the zakat of tithes, and, as one-tenth was considerably less than the rulers overthrown by the Mahometan conquerors usually exacted, the cultivators of the soil were to that extent better off. In the main, the Saracenic leaders permitted the people they found in possession of land to retain it, especially if they embraced the doctrines of Mahomet. All unoccupied land in the countries they overran they held to be conquered territory, and gave inducements to any one to settle and improve it, giving them for doing so a continuous tenure in the land, or an occupancy title.* Tithes from the produce had to be paid.

Among the elements that are supposed to have aided in building up the Moslem power were the laws allowing polygamy and the rewards derivable from conquest. Those European historians who are disposed to make the most charitable exhibit for Mahometanism claim that polygamy was almost universal in Asia. That it existed long before the time of Mahomet; that he merely accommodated himself to the circumstance, and that the tendency of the Koran was rather to check the evil. It is difficult to see how such an opinion can be maintained. It is true that polygamy has been an Asiatic vice as long as we have any record, but even in Asiatic countries it never attained prominence or grew into great proportions until the rise of the Mahometan power. Sir Henry Sumner Maine, says: "The people of the Aryan race are monogamous and exogamous, that is, they have one wife, and have a large list of persons they cannot marry. The Mussulman whose ideas originated with the Semitic race, are, on the

* Ockley's History of the Saracens, page 167.

other hand, polygamous and endogamous, that is, he has a plurality of wives, and his law permits near relations to marry.* Maine says it has been noticed by good observers that this comparative liberty of intermarriage was one secret of Mussulman success. In India it offered a bribe to the convert by offering him relief from the rigid Brahminical law.† Mahomet did more than tolerate polygamy: he openly encouraged it. The Koran says: "Ye may marry whatsoever women are agreeable to you, two, three or four." In the compendium of Mahometan law we find: "A man may marry four women, free or slave, any beyond that number is unlawful." ‡ A slave was permitted to have two wives. Among the faithful there was no particular limit to concubines. The worst vice of Mahometanism was that it deified licentiousness. Even Heaven was represented as a place of sensual delight. Home, in its highest and purifying sense, did not exist. Woman was impoverished and degraded. Their ceremonies of marriage had neither dignity nor sacredness. Two witnesses were required in order to make it strictly according to the Mahometan law, but the rule was not universally followed. The most lax systems of divorce were tolerated. Nothing could show their domestic tyranny more conclusively than that the husband should be able in a few words to pronounce his wife divorced.

There are three kinds of divorce known to Mussulmen; first, the "most laudable," second, "laudable" and third, "irregular"; all are conclusive.§ The first of these is when a husband utters the sentence of divorce once. This separates them, but if not repeated after the end of a period, he may re-marry the woman without incurring reproach. By the second form, he utters the three sentences at regular periods of time, or "Tohrs." The third form is when the husband utters

* Maine's Early Law and Custom, page 235. † Ibid.

‡ Hamilton's Hedaya, vol. i., page 88. § Ibid.

the three sentences at once. He says, "You are divorced," or "Your business is in your own hands," or he condenses the three sentences, and says, adding to either, "Count," "count." If a separation takes place, the wife has the custody and care of a young child until it is able to eat and care for itself, then it is under the authority of the father. The Prophet said, "Every divorce is lawful except that of a boy or a lunatic." A man may marry a female slave, but the offspring do not share in the inheritance with the other sons. A woman who is an adult may marry without the consent of her guardian, but, as a usual thing, a woman has but little authority. She is contracted in marriage without her volition, is dependent all her life, and is not among the recognized heirs of her father's estate. In some of the conquered countries, where the rights of women had been respected, she was allowed half a son's share, but in strictly Moslem countries her property rights and her existence were merged, first in her father, and then in her husband. While the doctrines of polygamy may be said to have been firmly established in Arabia, Turkey, Persia, Egypt and Central Asia, the conquerors failed to establish it to any considerable extent in India and some other countries supposed to be at one time Mahometan. This violation of nature has recoiled on the Mahometan system, and is one of the chief causes of its overthrow. Such homes as the Moslem law and custom made can never permanently build up a great progressive race. The degradation of woman will, in the end, produce the degradation of man.

The other element of strength to Mahomet and his followers was the war of conquest. The world was then full of adventurers ready to follow any standard to power and plunder. Teeming multitudes, born under the most adverse circumstances, were constantly swarming from the deserts of Arabia. Like the locusts which came from the "wilderness," where there seemed to be no green thing, they darkened the air by their untold hosts. The shepherd kings who conquered

Egypt were the spawn of this seemingly barren region. Twice, at least, all Northern Africa had been overrun by them before the time of Mahomet. Many circumstances had conspired to produce a great population in Arabia a few generations before the time of the prophet. Warlike Greek and Roman armies no longer marched past her, bent on the conquest of the world. The Chaldean and Babylonian had passed away, and the Syrian and Persian empires were broken. Jerusalem was a ruin on a hill. Times had changed. Over what was left of the Greek and Roman empires, Christianity had settled, and was endeavoring to lead a long enslaved and besotted people by its teachings into the doctrines of peace. Few enemies harassed the Arabs. Commerce was rich and flourishing; the Arabic hosts were ready to swarm.

It was no small inducement to offer a race of professional robbers the conquest and plunder of the world, and to lead them to the task inspired by a fanatical sense of religious duty. They had the elements of power; Mahomet gave the inspiration. They had no organization, and he organized them. Every active man amongst them hoped to become a prince. The civilized world was then weak. At the sieges of Antioch and Damascus the Arabs were reviled for being a despised and beggarly race, who tied a starvation belt around their waists and lived on barley. On the death of Mahomet, his successor, Abubeker, had first the task of reducing the rebels. They had refused to pay the zakat, and those of them who could be reached were crushed and punished. Several new pretenders arose and wrote modified versions of the Alcoran, but were overthrown. Having established the authority of the caliphate at Medina, he sent for the chiefs of the Arabs. An army flocked to Medina and were not slow to remind this apostle vicar that they wanted rations.* He would have preferred to wait for a

* Ockley's History of the Saracens, page 167.

larger force, but it was "go" or "mutiny," and he sent them out for the conquest of Syria. The commander sent the greater part of the first spoils from a fallen city to the caliph at Medina, who distributed them, and this procured plenty of recruits immediately. The Moslem doctrine, that "to the victor belong the spoils," allured to their standard unscrupulous adventurers from all parts of the earth.

It is not desired, in this chapter, to give a detailed history of the conquests of the Saracens. In an incredibly short period they overran Syria, the greater part of Asiatic Greece, Egypt and Northern Africa. The caliph kindly enjoined his generals to be just and even indulgent to all who professed the faith. They demanded that the conquered should embrace Islamism, but they often compounded for a nominal acquiescence and the payment of tribute. This soon swelled the revenues of the caliph and his deputies, and the amounts received seem almost beyond credence. A large portion of the world at the feet of these semi-barbarous conquerors furnished the money to carry on military operations. Spain was invaded and finally conquered from the Goths. Mahometanism was carried into India and even China. The dynasty of Ommiades, seated at Damascus, gave law from the Ganges to the Pillars of Hercules. With the increase of wealth and power came refinement. The scholars of all nations were encouraged to come to the court of the caliph. In Spain, as elsewhere, the Saracen rulers encouraged intermarriages with the conquered people. In Northern Africa, before the Moslem conquest, two races, both of Asiatic origin, occupied the country, the Berbers and the Moors. The former were the oldest occupants; they were or had been allied or mixed with the Carthaginians. The Moors and the Berbers were enemies. Christianity mixed with Paganism existed among them. The Moors, who were of Arabian blood, naturally fused with the Mahometan conquerors. Not so, the Berbers, who were never altogether subdued. When the Saracenic armies were present they would submit, pay tribute and accept the Koran; but when the armies left, went back to their old ways and their old religion. To punish them, severe examples were made and a fortified city built some thirty-five leagues from the site of Carthage, called Kairwan.*

Slavery was one of the curses of the Moslem governments. Like polygamy, it had existed before Mahomet's time; but in founding his religion, instead of uttering teachings and laws against it, he systematized and made it worse. Nor was it confined to the slavery of an alien or despised race. Slaves of every hue and from every clime filled the Saracenic and Turkish bazaars. Even in these modern times, when slave trading has been outlawed in Christian countries, one of the few slave markets left is under the shadow of the crescent. In the earlier days of Mahometanism, the faithful were enjoined not to enslave a believer, but this distinction was not maintained. The prophet recommended the manumission of slaves as a charitable act. The closest relations existed between the slaves and their masters. The child of a free woman was free even if her husband was a slave, and the child of a slave mother was a slave even if its father was free.† The marriage of a male or female slave is not lawful without the owner's consent. A slave was sometimes permitted to carry on business, on giving his master a share of his profits.

Mussulmen are not agreed on the question of the power to make a will. Acting under more modern inspiration, one set of Mahometan lawyers hold that limited wills are lawful; the more rigid hold that they are not lawful, and that the attempt to dispose of property by will is an attempt to dispose of a thing after the title has become void in the proprietor.‡ Even under the constructions that permit of will making, a bequest

* Ockley's History of the Saracens, page 349.

† Hamilton's Hedaya, vol. i., page 436. ‡ Ibid., vol. iv., page 467.

of more than one-third of the property is not valid, while a will made in favor of part of the legal heirs is not valid without the consent of other heirs.* In many Mahometan countries, especially in Hindostan, it has been customary to dedicate houses, lands and other fixed as well as movable property, for the use of the poor and the support of religion. While the Moslem law cut off women, in India and other countries overrun by Mahometans, the separate rights of property of women had to be recognized; but the Mahometan lawyers have steadily opposed and tried to reduce the "Stridhan," or female separate property, even there.† By the Koran, Mahometan traders are exempted from paying impost duties in excess of 2½ per cent. The want of a good land system, affording proper tenure and thus building up an independent agricultural population, was one of the sources of Mahometan weakness. Their governments were only held by taxation, and where plunder ceased to offer sufficient inducements to military adventurers, their power soon crumbled. From the time of the overthrow of Ali, Mahomet's son-in-law, factions divided the state. Finally, the descendants of the family of the prophet planted the dynasty of the Abbassides on the Tigris, and the caliph of Bagdad became the rival of the caliph of Damascus. The Ommiades had been popular in Syria, but never very acceptable to the Arabians. It is needless to follow the feud or recount the frightful massacre of the Ommiades. The dynasty of the Abbassides encouraged learning more than the court at Damascus. One caliph of Bagdad was reproached for putting a Christian at the head of his educational system. Men of learning of all nations were encouraged at Bagdad. If slavery had been forbidden a happier day might have dawned on the toiling people of the Tigris and Euphrates. The rulers were perhaps as good as any that region ever had,

* Hamilton's Hedaya, vol. iv., page 470.

† Maine's History of Early Institutions, page 333.

but they were aliens. Between luxury, effeminacy and slavery the fabric finally crumbled to decay.

It is a mistake to suppose that learning or intellect will supply the place of virtue, temperance, and the vigor that comes of an active and useful life. With ample resources of wealth the caliphs required slaves, not freemen, to do their bidding. They drafted their slaves into a standing army. These were largely Turcomans, a Tartar race that had conquered and occupied Armenia A. D. 760. They were active, restless, brave, and gave the Saracens a great deal of trouble. The caliph had now an army of paid troops his slaves; alas, they soon became his masters! They made and unmade caliphs. More than one commander of the faithful, when he became obstinate, or attempted to control these hireling soldiers, was bowstrung, and a more complaisant sovereign placed upon the throne, and the Saracen empire, that still gave law to a large portion of the world, became the creature of slaves. It is not at all surprising that the Turcomans finally invaded an empire at once so rich and so effeminate. Of an accommodating spirit, the new conquerors adopted the religion of Mahomet or what passed for it.

From A. D. 630 to 1453, Constantinople remained in the hands of those who were at least nominally Christians. It resisted the Saracens in A. D. 675, and again in A. D. 718, when the first fresh wave of Saracen conquest was vainly expended upon it. The Arabians, with all their activity and vigor, were not to conquer it; but the new dominant race of Turks had reinforced the now languid and effeminate Saracens, and after a desperate attempt in 1453, Constantinople fell after a fifty-three days' siege by the sultan Mahomet II. The Turks had now both spiritual and temporal power, the sultan being commander of the Faithful. Genghis Khan finished the last vestige of Saracen power at Bagdad. At the very time the Turks were pressing their armies around Constantinople, the brilliant fabric of Saracen power and genius was being overthrown in Spain, and thirty-nine years after the downfall of the empire founded by Constantine, in the same year that Christopher Columbus discovered the Americas, 1492, Grenada fell, and the last of the Moorish kings was driven from the Spanish peninsula.

It is difficult to estimate the precise effect of Mahometanism on the world's history. Its warlike operations and its exactions of tribute we can estimate; it is harder to weigh justly the mark it has left on our own civilization. The wars of the Crusades and fierce centuries of war under other names, between the Crescent and the Cross, convulsed European nations. There were wars of ideas and social systems, rather than a war of nations. When Charles Martel defeated their approach to France and Germany, he merely expressed the purpose of the European people of that time, as did John Sobieski when he drove them back from the walls of Vienna. Mahometanism had become purely autocratic. It rested on no large body of aristocrats, and for this reason her monarchs were splendid, for they absorbed everything. They established slavery of all kinds, and were enslaved by it. They robbed mankind more systematically than mankind had ever been robbed before, and perished from a surfeit of the spoils.

The Moslem religion changed its character. Reformers arose and tried to turn the people back to a frugal, temperate life. Predestinarianism was one of the old sheet anchors of the original fatalist Saracen faith, but sects arose contending for free will. The more startling reformation was that of the Wahabees, who sprung up about the beginning of the eighteenth century. This, like the ancient religion, emanated from Arabia, and endeavored to reform the empire founded by the Turks. They declared against all the ornaments in churches, figures, or anything pertaining to idolatry which the Wahabees claimed were innovations foreign to the faith. They insisted on the ancient rigid temperance; even tobacco and opium were proscribed. Many of the old simple practices had, as they believed, gone into disrepute, and forms had taken the place of the zealous fanaticism that founded the empire. They said the religion taught by Mahomet had become utterly corrupt, and unauthorized portions inserted in the Koran. They even deprecated the worship at the shrine of the Prophet, or the attempt to represent him as possessing miraculous powers. Mahomet, they held, was but a mortal, and though charged with a divine mission, he was only a prophet, and that all men were equal before God. Take it all in all, there was nothing particularly vicious in the doctrines of the Wahabees, but two causes brought them to trouble. The sultan of Turkey, after the authority of the Turcomans had been properly settled, assumed beside his temporal powers the function of commander of the Faithful. He was the head of the church, as well as the state. In a despotism like the Turkish government, it is hardly to be supposed that its head would acquiesce in the claims of a new pretender to subvert its institutions. The innovations which had been made on Mahometanism were generally profitable ones. They concerned great interests in the church and state.

All the men of good position and means objected to the professed reforms, as such people usually do to any reformation or change. Whatever Abdul Wahab, or anybody else might think, changes were dangerous. The men proposing them were fanatics. Mihidis, or "Mahdis," "Directors of the Faithful," were always arising. They were liable to rise as often as any one supposed he had a divine mission, or could get any number of persons to believe it. There had been one in the ninth century who had given a good deal of trouble, and a good many more, small and great, came after him. The wealthy, powerful and comfortably-established persons in the empire, whatever they might be inclined to believe in a theoretical way, set their faces like flint, against all these innovations, as there was no telling where they might lead. If the personal worship of Mahomet, as a god, had crept in and been established for a few hundred years, these classes, whatever their private opinions, would have resisted to the uttermost all attempts to interfere with it. The other cause for opposition from the Sultan was, that this movement of the Wahabees, in Arabia, looked like a race jealousy, to seize the control of the Mahometan religion from the Turks. After a century of trouble, and no small amount of bloodshed, the Porte was able, some years ago, to announce the final and total overthrow of the Wahabees. It is useless to deny that a deep-seated sentiment, impregnated with the ideas set forth by the Wahabees, has been scattered broadcast over the Turkish empire. The Turkish government would have perished long ago if several so-called "Christian governments" had not been interested in propping it up.

The Bedouin Arabs have for some time been a merely nominal portion of the Turkish Church. So long as they were well paid for their pains, they were zealous enough, but now the Turks, who have the responsibility of government on their shoulders, are compelled to make some effort to check these marauding bands, and the latter are not particularly interested in either the church or the state. "The religion of Mahomet was not intended for us," they say. Referring to its requirements for frequent washings or cleansing by water, they add: "We have no water in the desert, how can we make ablutions? We have no money, how can we give alms? The fast of Ramadan is a useless command to persons who fast all the year round. If God is everywhere, as the books say, why should we go to Mecca to adore him?" The fatal weaknesses of the church of Mahomet were fundamental. While Christianity proclaimed doctrines of peace, Mahometanism proclaimed war. Military plunder and highway robbery, as avocations, are in a decline, and, with them, Mahometanism. Mahomet, although his success in life was due to his wife, degraded women, and this undermined all the governments founded on his ideas. They had no land polity, and did not build up healthy communities. They cling to slavery, when all the rest of the world are setting their faces against it.

In estimating the effects of Mahometanism on the happiness of mankind, the proper way is to see in what condition it found the nations it touched, and the situation in which it left them. Arabia, independent of the spoils it obtained, was not improved by it at any time. Egypt, for a while, rallied under its influence, for it had long suffered under even worse governments. In the first century of Moslem power a canal was cut from the Red Sea to the Mediterranean, and agriculture and commerce seemed to revive. Egypt, to-day, is in a frightful condition. To say that the common people and laborers are poor does not half state the case; they are deplorably wretched. The revenues extorted from them for rent cripples industry, and has more than half destroyed the powers of production of the richest country in the world. Decaying Mahometanism sits on Northern Africa like a nightmare. The navies of Christendom prevent the Barbary ports from being dens of pirates, but the desert is still the abode of wandering robbers. No system of independent, honest citizenship has been founded. There is no encouragement to settle down to steady husbandry, for a fixed habitation only subjects those attempting to have it to the exactions of rulers and the brigandage of the lawless. In all the Mahometan countries in Asia, government and society is in the closing stages of a long decline. The condition of the laboring people to-day is one of poverty, dependence and hardship. It is even true that the people on the Tigris and Euphrates are worse off than the denizens of that region were in the days of the Chaldeans and Babylonians. Security to the laborer does not exist. The Mahometans found them an oppressed people, and they are now more oppressed. In the ancient Greece of Asia and Europe, which is largely the modern Turkey of to-day, the condition is but little less deplorable. An independent, manly body of citizens is not to be found. In spite of the splendors of the first three centuries of the Saracenic rule, the countries conquered have never since been prosperous. Part of Greece has escaped the political dominion of the Turk, but has not yet been able to rise above the Moslem influence of centuries. The European countries, formerly under Mahometan rule, which are now nominally Christian states, are the lowest in the scale of civilization in Christendom. Spain is the last of these states to listen to the demand for the abolition of slavery.

The spirit that made Mahometanism the enemy of aristocracy has long since been lost in a government of petty satraps, deputies and janizaries. In no part of the world is official life more corrupt. Public offices have long been shamelessly sold for presents or cash. The amounts paid for some of the most lucrative of these places is almost incredible. A vacancy is a godsend to a sultan or a pacha. The new incumbent not only pays to get in, but he well knows that he must pay to keep in. A Turkish ruler soon forgets the officer who does not remind him of his existence by valuable presents. Power thus shamelessly bought is exercised with heartless rapacity. The people are pitilessly robbed, and there is no means among them to build up popular organization and power. The aristocrats of Northern and Western Europe, as they listen with alarm to every advancing footstep in the march of human progress, can compare with pride their condition to that of Mahometan countries, where in one-third of the world human rights hardly exist, and, boastful of their position, call all reforms the effervescent froth of an agrarian rabble.

We may be amazed at the rapid decline of a religion once so powerful, but our surprise must be greater that human reverence for the Mahometan idea of the divine should so enslave the judgment, that a hundred millions of people yet accept its teachings, and that at the call of the Muezzin vast hosts still fall prostrate in prayer, with their faces to Mecca.

CHAPTER VI.

LAND AND LABOR IN RUSSIA AND ASIATIC COUNTRIES.

Chattel title to land unknown— Struggles of Turanian and Tartar—Central Asia rendered a desert by misgovernment—Rents and grazing taxes—Tartar greenbacks—India the seat of allodial title and village government—Emperors, kings, warriors and corporations, merely organized robbers—Tax collecting the chief feature of imperialism—The British attempt to plant landed aristocracy in India—Lord Cornwallis—From Yorktown to Bengal—Sale of land for debt formerly unknown in India—Land speculation introduced—"Mutiny"—China and "cheap labor"—Dense population—Chinese land tenure—Hung Ki—Rate of rent—No landed aristocracy—Banks in China—Paper money—Pawnbrokers—Secret societies—Rates of interest—Civil service reform—Opium *vs.* whiskey—Russia a network of colonies—Great and Little Russia—The Mir—The vetche—The village commune—Land systems of Eastern and Western Europe compared—Usurpations of the Tzars—Overthrow of popular rights and government—Recent attempts to liberate Russia from aristocrats and tyrants—Russian politics—Despotism and nihilism.

THE regions referred to in this chapter may be said to embrace half of the tillable lands on the globe. These are worthy of especial attention, for two reasons. First, because within this immense area there exist modes of land tenure different from the systems that have grown up in Western Europe, and, second, because in these regions we have almost every variety of usufruct land tenure. Fee simple or chattel title is almost unknown. Communal title; holdings by house or village communities; land held directly from government upon the payment of a land tax; land from which tribute is exacted for the head of a military empire; all these modes of holding land have existed, and still exist in an infinite variety, over the immense region which stretches from the Dnieper to the Yellow Sea.

We have already sketched the ancient forms of society in that part of Asia lying south and west of the Amu-Daria, or Oxus, and our present purpose is to examine the modern conditions of land tenure as they have been shaped during the past few centuries, and as they exist to-day. It has been scoffingly said by the Duke of Argyle, in his criticism of Henry George,* that in India, where the land is owned by the government, "the poverty of the masses is so abject that millions live only from hand to mouth, and when there is any, even a partial, failure of the crops, thousands and hundreds of thousands are in danger of actual starvation."

To this region we invite the reader. This immense continent of plains, mountains, valleys, rivers and deserts, has been, to a large extent, a sealed book to the people of Europe. One great mountain range, the *Ala-tagh*, has only been known to science for fifty years.† The great steppes and plains of Central Asia, even where not suitable for agriculture, have nourished numerous flocks of horses, cattle, sheep and, toward the centre and south, camels.

Two great races of mankind, differing vastly in their natural propensities, energy and ability, divide between them now, as they did four thousand years ago, the countries in Central Asia.‡ These were the Iranian and Turkish Tartars. The intellectual Iranians, or Persians and Hindoos of the Aryan race, occupied the countries from the frontiers of China to the Tigris. The Afghans are a people of Aryan descent. The features of the people of this race are handsome, the nose small and the beard full. The fundamental quality they exhibit is a disposition to peaceful occupations, especially agriculture. In this they differed from the Semitic nomads west of the Tigris, and in Arabia, and toward the Mediterranean. They also differed from the Tartar, Klapchack, Cos-

* The Prophet of San Francisco, in Nineteenth Century, for April, 1884.

† Hutton's Central Asia, page 319.

‡ Hellwald's Russians in Central Asia, page 94.

sack and other tribes north of them. Usually, the Amu-Daria, or Oxus, was the line between the Turanian and Iranian races.* The latter, indeed, planted their civilization in the valley of Sir-Daria, or Juxartes, as well as on the Oxus. Ancient Bactria was on the Oxus.† The Tartar and Turks, however, often established their authority on the Oxus, and on several occasions they crossed that river, and did not stop their career of conquest until they reached the Persian Gulf. The war between Buddhism and Parseeism was a struggle, not only of faith, but of races, the Iranian against the Turanian.‡ Persia, or Bactria, was the original and persistent seat of the religion of Zoroaster. The region of Central Asia may be said to have been ruined by misgovernment. It has, in former times, maintained great populations.§ The ruins of ancient cities are scattered everywhere. One authority puts the number of cities of Transoxiana at three hundred thousand, but Vambery pronounces this a "gross exaggeration." The productiveness of the country was due to the rivers and irrigating canals, which were so numerous and extensive as to interfere materially with travel and commerce.||

The great northern regions of Asia and Northeastern Europe were the home of nomads, shepherds, hunters and soldiers. They consisted of many tribes, from the Mongolian nomads on the extreme east to the Cossacks and Kirghiz Kazaks. They had no fixed habitations but traveled from place to place with their flocks, herds and families. This hardy, active life inured them to war and conquest. The most noted conqueror of this race was Genghis Khan, who overran Asia, conquering China. His chiefs held Bokhara for a century and a half,

* Vambery's History of Bokhara, page 10.

† Hellwald's Russians in Central Asia, page 75.

‡ Vambery's History of Bokhara, page 14.

§ Introduction to Vambery's History of Bokhara, page 34.

|| Hellwald's Russians in Central Asia, page 78.

expelling the Arab rulers from Central Asia. Genghis Khan tolerated all the prominent religions, Buddhism, Christianity, Mahometanism and Parseeism. A few generations later came Timour the Tartar, of the same stock although not of the royal family. He began his career by being a robber. At one time he had but a handful of followers, and, finally, by intrigue and violence, stretched his authority over Central Asia. He professed to be a Mahometan, but from the description of the Spanish traveler, Ruy Gonzalez de Clavijo, who visited Samarcand in 1403, it is evident that the variety of Mahometanism practiced at his court was not of a very rigid kind. Public drinking of wine, in which the monarch, his guests, and even the ladies of his court participated, was carried to such an extent that public exhibitions of gross drunkenness were frequent.* The same authority informs us that most of the Mahometan sovereigns of Central Asia died of delirium tremens. In his day, Samarcand was the great entrepot of trade for Central Asia. Silks were brought from China, furs from Siberia, spices from India, and various articles from Europe. In China, what was left of the dynasty of Genghis Khan was overthrown by a Chinese adventurer in 1368, who founded the dynasty of Ming. *Choo-yuen-chang*, its founder, had in youth been a common laborer, then a scullion in the temple, then a soldier, and Markham informs us, was "promoted" to be a robber captain. From this elevation it appears that he was able to reach the throne.

We gather, from the narrative of the dignified Spanish ambassador, some few glimpses of the condition of the people. He tells us, that in the deserts of Khorassan the people had no dwelling place but tents; they wander winter and summer. In the latter season they frequent the banks of the rivers and sow their corn, cotton and melons. They also raise millet, which they mix with milk, and this constitutes

* Hakluyt. Markham's Trans. Narrative of Clavijo, page 139.

much of their food. In the winter they seek warmer regions.* These people were Zagatays or Toorkmans. The "Zagatays" were a cruel and rapacious race, and made raids through Khorrassan and other regions. To be in training for these predatory incursions they recruited their horses for a month, and having sent spies out to find suitable victims would, on their report, proceed to the place indicated with the utmost rapidity. It has been alleged that they sometimes rode six hundred miles in six days. They usually attacked the unsuspecting town or village at daybreak, and the struggle was soon over. The people and everything of value were carried off, and the prisoners who were not ransomed, after being treated with shocking cruelty, were sold in the Turkish slave market at Khiva.† These nomads, the Spanish ambassador says, spoke a different language from the Persian, and seemed to be everywhere. Of another of these bands, the Albares, the Spaniard says: "These people possess nothing but their black cloth tents and flocks of sheep and cattle and twenty thousand camels. They pay the lord (Timour) a yearly tribute of three thousand camels and fifteen thousand sheep for the right of grazing in his territories."‡

Markham, in his Life of Timour,§ informs us that the rent was one-third of the produce of all irrigated land. There was, beside this, however, an assessment in addition for the water from the canals for irrigation. Any cultivator who built a tank or otherwise placed fresh land in cultivation, or planted an orchard or trees, had such tracts exempted from taxes or rent for the first and second year. The Sassanian kings of Persia exacted a tax or rent of one-third of the produce. When calamity overtook the crops the cultivator was sometimes able to borrow relief from the government.

* Hakluyt. Markham's Trans. Narrative of Clavijo, page 112.

† Ibid., page 116. ‡ Ibid., page 107.

§ Hakluyt. Markham's Life of Timour, page 30.

In Asia the land tax is the chief source of revenue of all governments, good and bad.

The Hindu kings exacted one-sixth of the produce, and in addition a poll tax. Central Asia, we are told by one of the most enlightened writers on the subject, "has been the foul ditch into which has been emptied all the worst vices of Mahometanism added to the vices of the Tartars."

The land tax in Central Asia was supplemented at all times by numberless other exactions, levied to meet the expenses of wars or the marriage of a son or daughter of the ruler or tax collector. Messengers, troops, escorts and ambassadors, as they traveled over the country, were supported by the people. Don Gonzalez found that these parties were always provided with three times the amount required. The approach of such a party to a town was a great calamity. The traders shut their shops and fled. The first man met was beaten until he conducted them to the chief of the town, who was also beaten if he did not promptly furnish all that was demanded. The people had to watch the stock of the visitors night and day, and make good a horse or camel if one should be lost, and, finally, the orders were to put to death any one who should obstruct these proceedings. Our Spanish ambassador passed through one region freshly abandoned. A "lord" had passed with his army, and because provender was not furnished, they took all the growing grain. On this calamity the inhabitants left the country.

In addition to the rent and grazing tax these Tartar rulers had other sources of revenue. Timour carried away all the artisans and good laborers he could find during his raid through Eastern Asia, and took not less than one hundred thousand of these as slaves to Samarcand. The king had a ferry at the Oxus which was closely guarded to prevent the escape of these slaves. Any one could enter Transoxiana, but no one without a passport could cross it to the south and east. Those who were ferried over paid a heavy toll. The khan also set up gates, or held the passes to India, Afghanistan and China, and all merchants, travelers or others on passing paid a heavy tribute.

Marco Polo and Rubruquis, in their narratives, confirm what Ruy Gonzalez de Clavijo narrates. The two former told so much that was marvelous, that at least one of them, Marco Polo, has passed down to our time as a romancer and liar. Later investigations have tended to restore his reputation as a correct observer. The Venetian traveler visited China during the reign of the Great Khan. His description of the paper money introduced into China by the Tartar conquerors is worthy of note. He describes how the paper on which the national notes were printed was made from the inner bark of certain trees, and cut into pieces "nearly square, but somewhat longer than they are wide." These notes are of many denominations, some of them very small. He adds: "The coinage of this paper money is authenticated with as much form and ceremony as if it actually were of pure gold and silver, for to each note a number of officers, especially appointed, affix their names and signets. When this has been regularly done by all of them, the principal officer, deputed by his majesty, having dipped into vermilion the royal seal, stamps with it the piece of paper, so that the form of the seal, tinged with vermilion, remains upon it, by which it receives full authenticity as current money." *

Vambery tells us that Asia, left to herself, produces hardly anything.† Her irrigating canals have largely disappeared. Some of them in the early times reached one hundred miles from the river. Ten years of warlike disturbance is sufficient to turn the most fertile region into a desert. The ruins of the ancient cities are known by the mounds and heaps of dust and sand.

Hellwald states that the aspiring chief who would found

* Wright's Marco Polo, page 216. † History of Bokhara, page 32.

an empire in Afghanistan, must, as little as possible, limit or interfere with the independence of the tribes. They are largely an agricultural people, holding their lands and governing themselves by the village community system. Shere Ali nearly had his throne overturned a few years ago, upon his attempting to organize his army on the European plan.

An increase of population made a redistribution of land, or emigration, necessary, which latter was often instituted by the town authorities. The system of allowing individual owners or landlords to create a mode of exacting tribute or rent from the land, independent of the state, is very obnoxious to Asiatic ideas.

When it is said that land has been nationalized in Asiatic countries, a mistake is made. No great government has ever risen to develop or elaborate such a policy. The systems of land tenure were older than the governments, and were local. The town or community regulated its own affairs, and, so far as it was concerned, recognized the rights of every one in the community to a share in the lands controlled or occupied by them. This was a law or custom among these people. The questions that might arise as to the amount of land each should occupy, or changes in the occupancy of a family were discussed in the town meeting, and had to be satisfactory to all concerned.

It will thus be seen that the governments of Asia were one thing, and the land system quite another. If the governments had legitimately earned the tax or rent, by affording protection, and providing, as they sometimes professed to do, a fund to relieve the destitute from calamitous seasons, little complaint would have been made of them.

India has always been considered one of the richest and most productive empires of the world. Surprise has been expressed at the extreme poverty of the people at the time it became an appanage of the British government. The Mogul empire, founded by Baber, in 1519, was tottering to its fall before the middle of the seventeenth century. Petty chiefs had arisen in every direction, too strong to be controlled by his successors. They plundered the people mercilessly. All security was at an end. It was in 1658 that Arungzebe deposed his father and murdered his brethren. Four years later Bengal was ceded to England by the Portuguese, as part of the dower of Caroline, queen of Charles II. The Portuguese had at that time, and long after, a commercial standing in the Indian Ocean, and claimed a good deal by right of discovery, but could not, in any sense, be said to possess Bengal. A company of English merchants had been chartered, in 1600, to trade in India. The French created an East India Company in 1664, and both of these corporations, not content with mere merchandising, undertook the business of colonizing, ruling and conquering. A "war" between the English and French companies broke out in 1746. In this war native rulers took part on each side. Native soldiers were enlisted by both companies. The French were substantially beaten in 1760, and after the battle of Buxar the Nabob surrendered the revenues of Bengal, Bahar and Orissa to the British East India Company. So far, the people of India had been compelled to pay rent to military chiefs, called emperors, kings, moguls and nabobs, and now an English company, under a British charter, set up a claim to be universal landlord in three states, and compelled the natives to pay rent. Corporations have done many things in their time, but this was, undoubtedly, the crowning act of corporate impudence. The company extended its power and increased its exactions until parliament became ashamed of its rapacity, or covetous of its authority. The British peers and commons first inquired into its conduct, and then, by Act after Act, stripped it of its privileges, "vested rights," to the contrary, notwithstanding. The impeachment of Hastings was political in its character as much as judicial. The trial of the governor-general, and investigations by parliament, were merely the steps by which that body wrested the empire of India from a corporation and made it a colony of the British crown.

Under a tropical sun the inhabitants of the lower peninsula seem to be enervated and helpless before every species of governmental vagabondism. Violence and war injected Buddhism into the ancient Hindu faith. Alexander attempted to introduce Greek ideas and Greek rulers. By the time Mahometanism had reached India, its dogmas and morals had gone through so many metamorphoses that its founder would hardly have recognized it. Amidst all these vicissitudes and changes, the old Aryan system of landholding remained.

Sir George Campbell, for some time commissioner of the central provinces of India, complains of the extreme difficulty of getting title to land there on account of the complexity of both Hindu and Mahometan laws of inheritance. So many people have a divided interest in the land, that after a man has bought land he is liable to find other owners than those from whom he purchased. This merely arose from the fact that neither Hindu or Mahometan laws were framed for the purpose of selling land. The Mahometan laws of inheritance were very different from the Hindu, as the latter give women equal rights, and recognize, so far as land is concerned, an equal division among all. The variety of Mahometanism introduced by Baber secured a better collection of the taxes, and reduced woman's property one-half, in portions of India. It is therefore not singular that Sir George inveighs against the difficulty of making a chattel title. The only wonder is that he found it possible to make one at all.

In India the government claims and collects rent or tribute from the land. The proportion of grain taken varies from one-half to one-fourth, the former being deemed an excessive, and the latter a light rent. The most common is about two-fifths.* Where irrigation is supplied the share of the cultivator is proportionally less. In each separate community there is, by long practice, a fixed rate of charges, and also of the fees of collectors, which could not be changed except by a very strong government or by revolution. In various insidious ways the deputy, or local ruler, contrives to squeeze the people a little more by encouraging or exacting gratuities, or extra fees, on the marriage of his daughter, or any other similar event that might seem to furnish an apology for it.† Previous to British rule the rent had been commuted to money rates.‡ Hindu, Mahometan and British rulers, alike, claimed rent from the soil of India. Sir George estimates that before British rule in India the most iniquitous exactions were made from the cultivators, especially upon the old residents who had made some improvements, such as digging wells and planting trees, which they could not move away, and would have to abandon in case they ceased to pay rent. These old holders of farms had usually the first choice, but this availed them little when additional exactions were fastened upon them, which they were unable to pay. Outside of rent to the government, the affairs of the people were largely managed by themselves. The bond which holds a community together is municipal. The arable land is divided, each farm being held by the family from its ancestors, provided they pay the rent to the government. The waste and grazing lands are held in common. When sums of money are received from the latter, they go into the common fund.§ A jat village consists of a community of freemen of one caste, held traditionally together. A village may be subdivided into two or three parts, each held by different castes. Every man has his share, which is generally ploughed land.|| The community is managed by a council of elders, who rule only so long

* Systems of Land Tenure, page 220. † Ibid., page 221.
‡ Ibid., page 222. § Ibid., page 223. || Ibid.

as they retain the confidence of the people. These town or village elders conduct all negotiations with the government, in point of fact, their relations with the state are chiefly of a diplomatic character. The elders may or may not get a small perquisite for their trouble. It must be voluntary as they have no means of collecting it. Many republics have been served at one time or other by slaves, usually of a race considered inferior. These East Indian communities have nothing exactly like chattel slavery, but they have usually a small body of servile laborers who do not exercise the same rights as a village proprietor.* These laborers in many cases cultivate a small piece of land, which they hold on the same terms as others, or more usually rent from one of the villagers. They live by odd jobs, and by assisting at the more laborious tasks. They usually consist of those who prefer thus to attach themselves to a village where they have no hereditary rights. In Cashmere and lower Bengal, the villages have less cohesion, and are subject to more changes in their population. Although Mahometanism has dominated in India for several hundred years, the Hindu or Brahminical religion is still numerically the strongest. The former was more democratic and active, the latter more conservative and exclusive. Distinctions in India come from caste and blood rather than wealth.

In the long period of anarchy that occurred between the decline of Mahometanism in India and the rise of the British power, a very considerable amount of land had been abandoned by the cultivators, and these ryots, as cultivators are termed, were in great demand. An Indian ruler, who is only a landlord with limited privileges, depends for his income entirely on the number of active producing ryots in his dominions. The breaking up of the Mogul empire turned loose a petty set of usurpers, whose wasteful rapacity almost ruined

* Systems of Land Tenure, page 224.

agricultural interests in India. War, famine and pestilence had weakened or abolished many of the old villages, and many farms had been taken by new cultivators, who claimed no hereditary right to the soil. The commons, or unoccupied lands, were recognized as part of the heritage of the village for pasture and timber. There was no clearly defined law giving any right of occupancy to non-proprietary holders, or those who do not belong to the village, but there was a distinction perfectly understood that where a stranger coming among them was permitted to improve a farm, as long as he paid his full share of all the burdens borne by the others, he should not be disturbed. The distinction was between such parties and those who moved about from place to place, cultivating patches of land merely on paying the rent. Questions sometimes arose between the old hereditary town proprietors and those who had been permitted to settle among them, and in cases where it was understood by the town that the occupation was not to be permanent, great jealousy was created where such modern squatters or settlers by digging wells, planting trees or making other valuable permanent improvements, attempted to render it difficult for the town to get rid of them if the interests of the community should require it. As a usual thing, improvements on the soil, while they are held to be the personal property of the man who puts them there, gives him no lien on the land, or even continuous right to hold it. When, from any cause, the person holding land, closed his connection with it, he usually removed all the material he had placed upon it which was of sufficient value to warrant his doing so, such as the wood-work, matting, roofing or other movable parts of the building. This custom may have had the effect of preventing the erection of valuable permanent houses; but as evictions are rarely heard of, it is more likely to be the result of the predatory and warlike habits of the various military governments, which have preyed upon, rather than ruled, the Indian peninsula.

The term ryot, while it is used generally in reference to the cultivators of the soil, is not an Indian word, but an intrusive one, from the Arabic, literally, "protected one," and is used and applied indiscriminately to cultivators, weavers, carpenters and laborers. It is said to resemble the English word "subject"; it also means that they do not belong to the government, or official class. The zemeendar, or zemindar, was strictly an officer. He was the representative of the government which levied the taxes or tribute. It is a Persian word, and the zemindars had their chief importance under the Mahometan rule.

The few cases of individual proprietorship of land that are to be found in India are looked upon with a very unfavorable eye. Public opinion reprobates it as the most fatal social or political heresy, and even in their language, the term *landlord* and *robber* are the same word.* The tendency of everything Hindu is to become hereditary; not a discriminating or invidious hereditary claim, to be raised or urged against the different members of the family, for their rights are all equal; but the son of a Hindu, by mere birth, becomes the partner of his father. The zemindar, as a tax collector, came in with the Mahometan rulers, the Hindu mode of collecting the tax being through the elders of the village. The zemindar was not originally a hereditary officer, for there is nothing hereditary in the Mahometan system. When the Hindu became a zemindar, which was sometimes the case, he usually wanted one of his sons to succeed him. In some cases such succession was had, but not as a right, for he was liable to removal at any moment, and had the extremely difficult task of being compelled to satisfy the monarch who received the taxes and the ryot who paid them. Farming out imposts to speculators was not only unpopular, but rarely resorted to; never, save in the case of a weak ruler.

* Systems of Land Tenure, page 230.

The grade of rent, or tax, had long been fixed, and the speculator, in such cases, had to make his profit out of the government. All the collectors, or middlemen, whether contractors, zemindars or governors, were merely agents of the government. There was nothing in the positions of the parties resembling landlord or tenant. Under native rule, the rights of the people in the land, whatever they may be, are not bought and sold in the market.* When a cultivator could not meet his engagements, he might, with the approval of the community, make a contract with another party to cultivate the land and pay his debts. On repaying all that was due under this contract he might be permitted to resume his holding, which was, however, at all times, subject to the rights of any of his family connection. Seizure and sale of land for private debt was wholly unknown.† This idea had not entered into the native imagination.

Such was the system the British found in India. The people had always contributed largely of their substance to sustain the government, and had usually been poorly governed. Indeed, a thoroughly organized, intermeddling, *penetrating* government, with new local forms, it would have been difficult to establish and impossible to maintain. Paying rent they were familiar with. They had paid it to native rulers who had stretched authority over their country; had paid it to Greek, Persian, Turk or Tartar; why should they not continue to pay it to the East India Company, or the British government? They, of course, expected that the government collecting rents or taxes would be willing to let their local affairs alone. The East Indian political expert disliked everything that was not British. His whole instincts drove him to intermeddle. A few of them, to their credit be it said, endeavored to comprehend the Oriental idea of landholding, and even admitted some of its excellencies, but with

* Systems of Land Tenure, page 231.

† Ibid., page 232.

the most of them the system had several great drawbacks, the chief of which was that the British had no stable and interested power in the country that they could lean on. Europeans, who wished to become great planters, had no adequate way of getting land, and the power to increase the revenues whenever the ruler desired was lacking. The idea that had been growing up in Western Europe, of land as a source of wealth, independent of its tillage, and of power and social standing outside of wealth, could not be contented with the East Indian system. All the adventurers and speculators thirsted for the introduction of modern European chattel landholding. One of the most early and noted of British East India politicians was Lord Cornwallis. To console him for his defeats in the war against the rights of the American people, and the humiliation of Yorktown, he was made governor-general of India, in 1786. A short time prior to this, after his return from America, he had been, or tried to be, viceroy of Ireland. His experience on that island was little to his own credit, and still less to the advantage of Ireland, so he was translated to the realm from which Warren Hastings had been deposed. The field before him, while a much easier and safer one than the subjugation of the turbulent American colonies, turned out to be beset with difficulties almost as insurmountable. The British in India at that time had hardly encountered the more warlike hill tribes, and the Bengalee seemed incapable of protracted resistance, but still he clung with the utmost tenacity to his old forms of society. That Lord Cornwallis should neither comprehend nor appreciate the Indian system of land tenure, inheritance and social regulations was natural enough. His conception of progress and refinement were received from the beautiful homes and parks of the British landed aristocracy, and it certainly had little in common with the East Indian system. Men of more ability than he had turned their attention to Indian politics, Hastings was not destitute of ability, and the reputed author of Junius, Sir Philip Francis, was one of the early British rulers in India. Lieutenant-Colonel Dow, of the Company's service, not only translated from the Persian a history of Hindostan, but embraced in it a statement of the errors of the "Company and the proposed remedies" for them. The Company, not content with its revenues from land, had created monopolies in some articles of necessary or universal use. The price of salt was raised two hundred per cent. in this way.* Tobacco and the betel-nut, generally used, also fell into the hands of a monoply. The author of the "Inquiry" states that in 1767 the expense of the Bundabust, or yearly settlement, amounted to twenty-seven and a half per cent. of the revenue, which was shared between Mahomet Riza and the bankers of Murshedabad.† He further states that the place of the Company's resident at the nabob's court was honestly worth one hundred and fifty thousand pounds a year. What this functionary really made it yield him it would be impossible to conjecture. A mode of practically levying a tax on the silver coinage was invented by some bankers, at Murshedabad, and the nabob and the British residents did not scruple to adopt and continue it.‡

Our scholarly lieutenant-colonel, in his "Inquiry," which was intended for the use of the British government, recommends as to religion "a perfect toleration," and says: "We may use the Indians as we can in this world, but let them serve themselves as they can in the next." He recommends the abolition of monopolies and the establishment of a paper currency and submits a proposal to establish landed property in India.§ He asks: "Let, therefore, the *Company* be empowered by an Act of Parliament to dispose of all the lands in Bengal and Behar, *in perpetuity*, for the payment of an annual sum not much less than the present rents." He adds: "Very

* Dow's Hindostan, vol. i., dissertation, page 131.

† Ibid., page 136. ‡ Ibid., page 147. § Ibid., page 103.

extensive possessions in the hands of an individual are productive of pernicious consequences in all countries." He therefore suggests a limit as to the amount that could be purchased, as not to exceed on any account a rental of "fifty thousand rupees a year." Such were the views that led to what is called the "permanent settlement" in Bengal in 1793. The tax-collecting zemindars were manufactured into landlords. The "preamble" to the form of settlement proves that the British administrators were not ignorant of the fact, that the zemindars did not own the land. This creation of landlords in India was adopted as a fixed policy, and its purpose was to establish a landed aristocracy, similar to that of England. By these regulations and the code of laws that accompanied them, land in Bengal, in 1793, was made transferable by sale, and in almost every respect put on the footing of chattel property.* A creditor in Bengal was given the most summary rights to sell for debt all the interest any one had in land, and immediately thereafter great numbers of ryots were sold out. It has been sarcastically said of Cornwallis, that he designed to make English landlords and only succeeded in making Irish landlords. Indeed, the zemindars did not quite comprehend the position into which they were thus thrust. At first it was not attempted to very materially increase the tribute or rent demanded, and the ryots for some time scarcely understood that a fatal blow had been struck at their rights and interests. Instead of the nominal ten per cent. for collecting tribute, the zemindars were by this arrangement to get twenty, and were created lords of the soil. It was difficult to introduce the system. It is true, that a large portion of these tax collectors did not belong to the races over whom it was intended that they should "lord." Dow informs us that when he wrote, towards the close of the eighteenth century, that the zemindars were mostly Persians,

* Systems of Land Tenure, page 237.

Turks, or men from the upper countries. They had been long enough among the people, however, to understand their former relations to them, and, in spite of the settlement, permitted matters to drift on pretty much as they had done before, and there seemed to be almost insuperable difficulties in the way of this "inchoate" aristocracy. The next step was to assume that all of the "unoccupied lands" were the property of the British crown. It will be remembered that, besides waste lands, there were public and common lands used for grazing or timber, but all fell under the same head. It was the ostensible purpose of the regulations for these alleged "crown lands" to secure their improvement, and some semblance of occupation and cultivation, but the grossest abuses and corruptions at once crept into the sale, and foreign holders, mercantile and middle men began to have great estates to be cultivated by a dependent class of hired laborers. At first the zemindars were prohibited by the terms of the Act of Settlement from giving a lease for more than ten years, but these restrictions were very soon modified. Bengâl is still largely Mahometan, and owing to the jealousies between these people and the Hindustanee, the British schemes have had some success, although the system even there cannot be said to be altogether established. In Oude, the British attempted to establish the titles in officers or local nobles called talookdars, but the scheme has not been successful. In the Punjaub the aristocratic scheme has failed in a measure, but very numerous peasant proprietors have been created. In the great central provinces the attempt to make land property has so far almost totally failed. In the northwest provinces the conspiracy to plant aristocracy has been but partially successful. The old ryots have been forced to accept fixed tenures at fair rents. In Assam it has been impossible to introduce the zemindars.

It must not be forgotten, that the British governors of India had been all this time receiving great revenues from the country. In the northwest provinces, even fifty years ago, when the conquered country was not near so great as now, they received twenty millions of dollars annually.* In Northern India, which is largely Hindustanee, the British have been compelled to abandon the perpetuity of land tenure, but they have steadily pressed a system of lease with the privilege of removals. Proceeding from these changes came attempts to induce or force the ryots to raise indigo and opium instead of the old products. Indigo and opium, of course, were more profitable for exportation, and it was the British interest to force their cultivation. This was resisted by the natives, because it was found to have a bad effect on the production of bread for their own people. Leases were made to compel it by inserting provisions to furnish certain amounts of indigo-material and opium with the rent. On the refusal to do this, the rents were raised. Courts, however, had been introduced, and the cultivator, falling back on the rights of his people for ages, carried the case into court, claiming that as long as the fixed rent or tribute was paid the rent could not be changed. Much has been said of the fairness of British rulers in India, but in this scheme to oppress the Indian people, Chief Justice Sir Barnes Peacock decided, "That the ryots were bound to pay a fair rent *in the sense of the highest rent attainable*, that on the increase in the value of produce being shown, there was no limit to the increase demandable, but the real profit of the cultivator," or rack rent. He decreed the full amount claimed. The case was carried to the full high court of fifteen, who maintained the opinion fourteen to one.

Springing from these insidious encroachments, great land leagues have been formed among the people. In some cases whole communities refused to pay rent. A constant struggle has also been carried on against the attempt to form a landed

* Systems of Land Tenure, page 247.

aristocracy. It has been strenuously denied by Sir George Campbell and other British rulers, that the insurrection called "The Mutiny," in that country, was caused by these English land expedients. It is sufficient answer to this, to recall the fact, that wherever the British were expelled, and they were expelled from great provinces, the landed proprietors they had created were expelled with them. In the long career of civilized robbery by which alien rulers have exacted enormous sums from the native people, the British have probably given them many wrongs to remember. There was more than one "mutiny." In 1806, there was a Sepoy mutiny at Vellore, when eight hundred "insurgents" were executed. Again, in 1809, at Seringapatam, and so continuing until the terrible "Mutiny" of 1857, beginning in Bengal and spreading to the remotest provinces. It was not a "revolution," for it was not successful. It was not even permitted to be called an insurrection, but stigmatized as a "mutiny" for which the ringleaders were shot from the mouths of cannon.

Practically, the attempt to found a landed aristocracy in India is still but an experiment in Bengal and can scarcely be said to exist elsewhere. Although twice under Mahometan rule, slavery has never flourished in India to the same extent as in other Oriental countries. There has never been a great servile class, embracing a majority of the laboring people, which would have been the case if the instincts of the people had not been against it. The slavery that did exist was abolished by the British government in 1834, and the East Indian Company, long merely an attendant leech, ceased its connection with Indian politics in 1858.

In spite of the sarcasm of the Duke of Argyle, it would not be fair to attribute either the faults or the calamities of the East Indian people to their system of land tenure. It was, indeed, the one redeeming feature in their unhappy lot. To call the tribute or rent exacted by alien tyrants a "Nationalization of Land" is the most bitter irony. In all the chequered vicissitudes of East Indian history, they had at least escaped the additional exactions of a landed aristocracy, until the British government has attempted to expose them to its burdens and rapacity.

Until recently the vast empire of China has been almost unknown to Europeans, and of its people, institutions and history we are still comparatively ignorant. Not including the vast territories which have been, and some of which still are, connected with the empire, the eighteen provinces of China proper contain a population of from three hundred and fifty to four hundred millions of people.* For this empire a great antiquity is claimed, and without giving credence to a fabulous chronology enough is known to make it certain that it has survived any other government of which we have knowledge. The evidence also lends some color to the statement that China has remained in a comparatively stationary condition for a long time. Her forms of society, or what we call civilization, while they differ in many respects from ours, are, nevertheless, of a high order, and are as far removed as they well can be from those of nomadic wanderers or barbarians. The worst features presented by China are a dense population, much of it existing on limited resources. They are a rice- or grain-eating people; beef is little used. Animal food is only eaten at intervals by the poorer Chinese. Of the animal food consumed, pork constitutes more than half.† Chickens, ducks and other fowls are eaten; puppies, kittens, rats, mice and various animated things are killed and occasionally eaten. Fish of all kinds constitute a staple element of food, and fish are produced in artificial ponds. The Chinese rarely drink cold water, as they consider it unwholesome. Tea and several other preparations are used, but coffee, chocolate and cocoa are almost unknown, and the same may be said of beer, cider, wine,

* Williams' Middle Kingdom, vol. i., page 270. † Ibid., page 777.

porter, brandy, etc.* It is proper to say that in towns visited by Europeans, intoxicating liquors are found. Beef, though to some extent eaten by the richer classes, is never exposed for sale in public market, chiefly from Buddhistic prejudice.† For the same reason, milk, butter and cheese are rarely eaten, and a European usually disgusts a Chinese by drinking milk. In all their cooking, oils and fats are a universal article, and this renders most of their food unpalatable to an American. The proportion of animal food of any kind eaten by the Chinese is smaller than with any other nation living in the same latitude. Cooke and other authorities agree that drinking is not one of the sins of the Chinese, but opium debauches constitute their worst vice.‡ They also smoke tobacco, preparations of hemp and other things. Physically, the Chinese are not so strong as Europeans, but stronger than most of the Oriental races.§ Nevius says that nearly all the men, and many of the women use tobacco, and that where they have been thrown in contact with Europeans they are learning to use ardent spirits.‖ They are not, and so far as any authentic records carry us, never have been, warlike. As Williams intimates, the Chinese are the beau ideal of a nation devoted to the "peace policy." This has led to their being overrun and conquered on several occasions by the rude and warlike Tartars and Mongols, active, beef-eating nomads, from the great plains and mountain regions of Central and Northern Asia. These conquering intruders rarely attempted any important change in the laws, customs or polity of the Chinese. They may be said to have conquered the government rather than the people. After a few generations the invaders grew so effeminate that they were easily overthrown in their turn.

* Williams' Middle Kingdom, vol. i., page 776.

† Nevius' China, page 246.

‡ Cooke's China and Lower Bengal, page 172.

§ Williams' Middle Kingdom, vol. ii., page 91.

‖ Nevius' China, page 250.

Landed property is held in clans and families as much as possible.* Land is held directly from the crown, and not entailed. If *mesne* lords or landed aristocracy ever existed they are now unknown.† The condition of land tenure is the payment of an annual tax. When this is paid, the land and its improvements remain in the family. While the paternal estate may be nominally ruled by the eldest, his authority is subject to the rights and wishes of all the others, as all share alike. The only difference consists in a small amount allowed to the elder for the performance of purely administrative functions.‡ All of the family have a right to live on the estate, and usually do so, the younger sons devise their interest in perpetuity to their offspring.§ No change can be made in this disposition save by some agreement and the payment of an amount acceptable to all parties. In case of any alienation or transfer, there is a government tax, or charge, in addition to the expense of registering. Daughters in China never inherit.|| The proprietors of land record their names in the district where they live, and have from the government a *hung-ki*, "red deed," which secures them possession as long as the tax is paid. For convenience in mortgages and alienations, there is a "white deed," which is from the individual. There are sometimes twenty of these, but they are only valuable when accompanied by the "red deed." As the expense of any transfer through the government is equal to one-third of the rent, these white transfers or mortgages are resorted to. To some extent these *white* and *red* deeds resemble warrantee deed and patent, the difference being this, that when our government executes a patent, it thus, in fee simple, disposes of the proprietary interest. The Chinese official "red deed," on the contrary, is a family lease rather than a deed. The law and custom permits the transfer of these, and the Chinese

* Williams' Middle Kingdom, vol. ii., page 1. † Ibid.

‡ Nevius' China, page 237.

§ Williams' Middle Kingdom, vol. ii., page 2. || Ibid.

government would issue a fresh *hung-ki* in every regular case of transfer if applied for, provided all the necessary steps to secure every interest have been taken. A mortgagee *must* enter upon, pay the taxes and use the property, in order to give any validity to his title.* The laws and customs effectually prevent several tracts from drifting into the hands of an owner *not an occupant.* A mortgage or alienation can only cover the individual rights of those making it, and are always subject to the rights of others. In addition, these mortgages, or alienations, can be at any time cancelled within thirty years, on the payment of the original sum, without interest, the party having had the use of the land in the meantime. This thirty years is supposed to cover the extent and value of the improvements and pre-emptive right which constitute all the individual interest in the soil. A full record is kept of alienations and the amount of tax due. The amount of rent or tax on the land varies on account of location, fertility and other circumstances from $1.20 to $1.30 and $1.50 per acre, per annum.† If the tax is to be considered as rent, it is certainly not high. In Perry's expedition to Japan, he gives the rent or land tax in the island of Loo-Choo as six-tenths to the lord, or ruler, two-tenths to the cultivator, and two-tenths for the expense of supervision and collection.‡ The commodore places the rate of field wages in Loo Choo at from three to eight cents per day. Under the Chinese laws there are provisions for reclaiming lands not under cultivation, and for securing location on new alluvial lands created along the rivers. This can *only be done* on an arrangement made with the government, or under the cognizance of its authorities, and a certain period of time is fixed during which no tribute is paid, as a just compensation for labor in reclaiming land.§

* Williams' Middle Kingdom, vol. ii., page 2. † Ibid.

‡ Perry's Expedition to Japan, page 252.

§ Williams' Middle Kingdom, vol. ii., page 3.

The Chinese may be styled gardeners rather than farmers. The tracts held are small and usually thoroughly cultivated, often with the spade and hoe. The buffalo, or Chinese ox, is used for dry ploughing, and they also employ for that purpose horses, mules, cows, and even goats. Nieuhoff represents a Chinaman ploughing with his ass and his wife yoked together, but Williams, while admitting that this is sometimes done, considers it unusual. No inconsiderable portion of the agricultural labor is by hand, not only because better crops are produced, but on account of the expense of feeding large animals. While the pig and the goat can be fed on refuse and from waste spots of land, a horse or an ox would require as much land to maintain it as several human beings. Everything in the shape of manure is saved and the plant rather than the ground is manured. Terracing, although carried on in some portions of China, is not so common as is generally supposed. Agriculture holds the first rank in China among all the branches of labor. At the opening of the agricultural season there are great festivals, when the emperor and all the princes and grandees hold the plough. Irrigation, not only from the streams, but by hand and pump, is universal. Two or three immense rivers wind through China, their main course being from west to east. These are rivals of the great rivers of America. Their sources are fed from the perpetual snows in the highest mountains of the world, the Himalaya. The "Celestial mountains" stand on the western frontiers, and the *Tengri Tagh* and Ala-tagh are regions of snows, rivers, forests, wild animals, and almost as wild men. The Chinese have penal settlements across the mountain ranges in the valleys of the Ili.* Floods from the great rivers of China are the chief sources of disaster to the agriculturists. The greatest river in China changed the location of its mouth nearly one hundred miles. The result of all this in a densely

* Hellwald's Russians in Central Asia, page 59.

populated country can be appreciated. It is considered as one of the duties of the government to build public granaries, in which shall be deposited a part of the revenue from the land, to support or furnish seed and food for those who have suffered from flood, drouth or other natural calamity. This government duty, like a good many other government duties, there and elsewhere, is, in many cases, more frequently omitted than performed. The necessities of the government, or the covetousness of the officials, tend to keep these grain depots much below the standard, so that when a great calamity comes there is not an adequate supply. In some instances great distress and even mortality have resulted, and officials been decapitated and disgraced, and government shaken to its centre in consequence. Except this provision for natural calamity, China does not possess a pauper system.* The government also makes provision for canals and irrigation. Cooke informs us that there are large numbers of tramps in China. There is a very large class of coast and river pirates, and also orders or organized bands of thieves and robbers.† Besides punishment by whipping, which is common, not less than ten thousand criminals are annually executed in China.

Several authorities agree that infanticide is practiced, especially on female infants, but there is reason to believe that this has been exaggerated. In some towns and cities there is a "baby tower," into which dead infants, wrapped in matting, or other substance, are thrown, and these are from time to time burned out.‡ As the Chinese are usually very reverent and respectful to their dead, it appears this disrespect and indifference to dead infants arises from a superstition that infants dying young have been seized by a devil. The presence of the baby tower may lead to infanticide, but as our Chinese friends make profit, in case of necessity, out of

* Cooke's China and Lower Bengal, page 190.

† Ibid., page 191.

‡ Ibid., page 91.

their children, they are hardly likely to be destroyed in ordinary circumstances. Indeed, we learn that in many Chinese cities, among other charitable institutions there are foundling hospitals with a basket outside in which to deposit infants, and on striking a bamboo the basket is drawn in and no questions asked.* Gray says these foundling hospitals are poorly kept.

Slavery, to a very limited extent, exists in China. Williams says: "It is worthy of note how few slaves there are in China, and how easy their condition compared with those of Greece or Rome." † Chinese slavery is, in point of fact, a mild domestic slavery. There is no great distinct enslaved class. It is by law and custom limited in its character. The power of a man over his child and wife is almost absolute. At an early age a child is worth so many dollars, and a father may transfer whatever rights he has in it.‡ While polygamy, slavery and prostitution exist to some extent, they have been circumscribed in their effects.§ The absolute right of parents to their children and husbands to their wives is so recognized that they can sell them.||

We have already quoted Marco Polo's description of the paper money issued by Kublai Khan. Pauthier reckoned that during that reign of thirty-four years, $624,135,500 of this currency was issued. It does not appear to have been discredited then, and was taken for dues, public and private. His weak successors, however, among their many other acts of misgovernment, issued it to an extent altogether beyond the point at which it could be kept afloat, and Mr. Williams intimates that the overthrow of that dynasty was due to this circumstance. Paper money is not now regularly issued by

* Cooke's China and Lower Bengal, page 99.

† Williams' Middle Kingdom, vol. i, page 413.

‡ Cooke's China and Lower Bengal, page 99.

§ Williams' Middle Kingdom, vol. i., page 285.

|| Nevius' China, page 253.

the Chinese government, although it was during the *Tae Ping* rebellion. At present it is largely limited to the Peking district and government transactions, although the revenues are claimed in sycee silver. There are, however, any number of private banks, and these among other things are permitted to issue paper money.* This practice, we believe, is comparatively modern. There are no banks with special charters, but a bank can be opened by any person or company. These are subject to certain laws and regulations, and are compelled to report their organization.† The circulation of the notes is limited. Some of them are confined in their operations to the city or to particular streets, or even one street. The notes, in a somewhat similar way to those of the bank of England, are endorsed by each holder. Very few counterfeit notes are met with, which is probably due to the limited range of the bills and the mode of endorsement. The worth of the bills depends on the exchange between silver and Chinese coin, and as these fluctuate daily the notes are thus forced home. The system must make a paradise in a small way for stock jobbers. No gold or silver are at present coined in China.‡ The Chinese coin are of equal parts of copper and zinc, or with a small admixture of lead and tin. These coins are styled relatively, tael, mace, candoreen and cash. The silver or gold coin in circulation, which is chiefly the former, are of foreign coins or bars of silver, "*sycee.*" In the southern provinces bank notes are little known or used. Banks also issue letters of credit, and remittance by draft, the system of exchange, is as complete as in Europe. The number of these "offices," or banks, is large in proportion to the business of a town, but the capital only averages two or three thousand taels, which is petty enough. The number of banks in Tientsin is three hundred, and in Pekin four hundred, many of these being branch banks.

* Williams' Middle Kingdom, vol. ii., page 85.

† Ibid.

‡ Ibid., page 83.

Interest in some cases runs as high as three per cent. a month, varying from that to ten and twelve per cent. per annum.* This permission of usury has, no doubt, disastrous effects on poor business men. The horde of petty bankers, however, is constantly under the supervision of the government: they are burdened with taxes, and do not, under such circumstances, succeed in creating a large class of non-producing capitalists.

Next to the banks are the pawnbrokers. There are three kinds of pawnshops. They are strictly regulated by law. The habit of pawning is very general, and the results very disastrous to the poor and laboring classes.† Some of these establishments are extensive; the English forces at Tinghai used one for a hospital, which accommodated three hundred patients. One of the evils connected with pawnshops is the facility they give to thieves.‡ Pawn tickets are offered for sale in the street, and are a constant article of merchandise. As in the case of the bankers, the pawnbrokers have a rigid responsibility. The government compels them to meet their engagements. Pawned articles cannot be sold for three years, and no pawnbroker can go out of business without giving three years' notice. In case of fire originating in the pawnbroker's premises, the pawner claims the full amount. If the fire originates in a neighbor's house, or is conveyed from other premises, the pawnbroker makes up one half.

One tendency of Chinese society is to crystallize into associations.§ Everybody has to co-operate with somebody else, women as well as men. It is a leading aspiration to belong to one of the *hwai*, or societies, to be identified with its fortunes and enlisted in its interests. Societies are formed for all purposes, even for robbery, and to secure protection from

* Williams' Middle Kingdom, vol. ii., page 87.

† Gray's China, vol. ii., page 79.

‡ Williams' Middle Kingdom, vol. ii., page 86.

§ Ibid., page 87.

robbery.* Williams thinks this results from the strong democratic element in Chinese polity. In trade or manufacture men associate. Petty capitalists associate to found banks. Trades associate to protect the interests of their respective crafts. Little farmers associate to buy an ox. Porters to monopolize the loads in certain wards, or chair bearers, to furnish all the sedans for a town. There are also money-lending clubs, or co-operative loan associations.† Even beggars are allotted to one or two streets by these societies, and are driven off another beat if they encroach. Villages form themselves into societies to regulate their matters and defend themselves against powerful clans.‡ Universal organization of towns and trades is the defense of this pacific people. In a country where there is no representative lawmaking body, these societies are all-powerful. Government, indeed, exists by their suffrance. This is probably one of the chief causes of the conservative character and extreme age of Chinese institutions, for while rulers and even dynasties may change, there is rarely any modification in the essentials of Chinese polity.

The Chinese government is absolute. The emperor and his council have power of life and death. They have no landed aristocracy, and no aristocracy founded on money or capital. The emperor's relatives and descendants to the eighth degree are princes and titular dignitaries, but when they get to the eighth degree, they again merge with the common people. None of the royal family are permitted to hold office in the government. They receive stipends. The nearest relatives of the sovereign have an income of between thirteen and fourteen thousand dollars, but have, in addition, a number of attendants to maintain their dignity, which, with

* Cooke's China and Lower Bengal, page 191.

† Gray's China, vol. ii., page 86.

‡ Williams' Middle Kingdom, vol. ii., page 88.

allowances, make the charge to the state, for a few of the highest, from seventy to eighty thousand dollars a year. As the relationship gets more remote the salary dwindles rapidly, the lowest have four dollars per month and rations. Besides these there are some other titular dignities conferred by the emperor as gracious marks of his appreciation, and they are authorized to wear a certain shaped hat, with a certain kind of button on it. None of these titles are derived from landed estates. The recipients are without power, land, wealth, office or influence. The whole scheme of Chinese titular nobility has been adroitly devised to tickle human vanity without giving a figment of real influence or power.

The officers who administer the government under the emperor, and all the officers of the provinces are, at least, theoretically, appointed for literary merit.* China is the chosen home of "civil service reform," which, like her tea and silks, we have imported. The regulations by law for competitive examinations are more elaborate than any other legal canons in China. These examinations are open to all *reputable* persons; that is, they must be of a family which, for three generations, have not been criminals, slaves, executioners, actors, or been engaged in vicious or disreputable callings. Education is mainly sought for official position. Women in China do not receive as good educations as men.† The aspirants, for office are of all ages, from the callow youth to the man of sixty, are shut up during examinations. It is true, the government, when its treasury is deficient, occasionally puts up its offices for sale, but only to be sold to those who have at least respectable literary qualifications. Corruption has sometimes been charged in the modes of determining the result of competitive examinations. Its advantages in a country like China are, that the door of preferment is opened

* Williams' Middle Kingdom, vol. i., page 442.

† Nevius' China, page 238.

to every man; and an inducement is thus given to lead an honorable life. The cohesive power of this element in maintaining the government cannot be overestimated.

It is very true that many Chinese officials are notoriously corrupt. Rapacity, bribery and peculations of every kind are common. The people bear these patiently, because every man believes that he will, some day, be a mandarin himself. With all its faults, as Morrison, Gray, and, indeed, all respectable authorities agree, there is great regularity and system in the Chinese government. Every district has its appropriate officers, every street its constable, and every ten houses their tithing man. While the higher functionaries affect great moderation and dignity, the petty officials, such as clerks, constables, lictors and underlings, are called by the Chinese "claws," because they are supposed to extort. All the leading officers are required to report, by card, to the emperor, twice a month. Commissioners or inspectors are sent by the emperor to see what is going on in all departments of the government. These are his eyes and ears, and action on their reports are not usually arbitrary, but the result of deliberation in council.

While there is no representative body there are two great councils. One of these has to do with the general administration of the civil government, and the other with the army and supervision of the administration of justice. Appeals may be had from the lower courts, but, to a poor man, that is not much advantage. Every man is supposed, of right, to have free access to magistrates and dignitaries, and their complaint to be considered. The councilors supervise the promulgation of canons or laws, which are believed to emanate from the emperor. The members of both councils are selected by the emperor, from the official class, during good behavior. Cooke says that while the government makes appropriation for bridges, canals, irrigation, etc., the mandarins and contractors use a large part of it between them, or for bribes to those who might be able to call their operations in question.* There is great danger, however, of getting a notification to perform *hari kari*, or, at least, be dismissed or banished. When a Chinese official refuses to commit suicide, if notified to do so, all his relatives and their property suffer. The savings of officials have not enabled them to build up a permanent wealthy class.

The Chinese government is weak against foreign invasion or rebellion. In some cases where the government cannot suppress a rebellion, it buys up or rewards the leaders, and thus breaks and destroys their organization. All their neighbors, Manchus, Tartars and Mongols, scoff at the cowardice or inefficiency of their troops. They are great philosophers, however, and the science of military affairs, crude as it is, is far in advance of the practice.

The religion of the Chinese is a singular compound. Confucius was merely a philosopher with fine maxims. Buddhism is the chief nominal religion, and was introduced to China in the first century of the Christian era.† Confucius recognized ancestor worship. Williams intimates that skepticism is much more common than religion of any kind. The Chinese worshipers have been placed in three classes: First, the priests or adepts who abstain from animal food and perform the ritual so as to fit themselves for absorption into something; second, those who cannot comprehend any abstruse speculations, but through religious fervor endeavor to do what they believe to be their duty; and third, the lower orders, who cannot rise above the forms and ceremonies; and this class is largely composed of old women.‡ It has been said that the latter, in their prayers to be transformed at death, ask to be transformed into men. Judging from the way women are treated in China this is not surprising. In the Buddhistic

* Cooke's China and Lower Bengal, page 98.

† Gray's China, vol. i., page 105.

‡ Cooke's China and Lower Bengal, page 121.

temples they have chanting in the morning and the evening, and it is a noteworthy coincidence, that this is partly in the native or Chinese language and partly in the Sanscrit tongue, clearly showing the origin of this faith. The incomes of the monasteries are chiefly derived from the voluntary offerings of the worshipers, partly from allowances or fees for priestly services at funerals and other domestic ceremonies; some of them have been endowed with a small quantity of land, but the latter is of limited amount.* The real worship is ancestor worship. A man's father and grandfathers are in his pantheon. The Chinese believe these absent ones in their migrations are cognizant of all they do, and expecting their sympathy they pray to them and present food at their shrines. This belief has much to do with their whole social and political system. The degradation of their women is the chief cause of the worst elements of the Chinese character. A husband in China can divorce his wife for seven reasons, but is obliged to maintain her if she has no home.†

Practically, China presents to us an organized government ruling the most dense population on earth. Take China as a whole, from the Tien Shan mountains to the sea: By the census of 1812, there was a population of 268 to the square mile, and it is, of course, greater now. By the census of 1881, Bengal had a population of 440 to the square mile, and England, in the same year, 289, to the square mile. In China, the southern and western provinces stood only 154 to the square mile, but in the great plain or lower country, an immense empire in itself, the population was, in 1812, 458 to the square mile, and is now probably nearer 500. If nominal wages are low the price of staple eatables is also low. There is, in fact, less disparity of condition among the masses of China than with Europeans. There is no system of inheritance which tends

* Nevius' China, page 99.

† Doolittle's Social Life among the Chinese, page 75.

to throw property in a few hands, and the fixed polity of the government is to prevent this. The tea, silk and porcelain manufactures are mainly in the hands of the masses, and the tendency of all their customs and political systems is to distribute and scatter, rather than concentrate. The distinction between a farmer and a laborer is not great. Servants are hired by the month at from three to five dollars; cooks by the year. Domestics and slaves are on intimate and social relations with their masters.* The only nonproducing classes in the country are the civil officers, most of whom are kept busy, the army, and a few pensioned nobles. The farms are small, and the buildings and improvements not of much value, and the dwellings in cities are not greatly in advance of those in the country. The material of the houses, which is largely bamboo, can be removed. Except public buildings and bridges, the architecture of China is not imposing. Even the public buildings, if we consider the age of the empire and its population of several hundred millions, are not equal to the architecture of other nations. This at least shows that the efforts of the people are not expended on public works. Labor is cheap, when a girl can be purchased for from fifteen to one hundred dollars, but then she must be clothed and fed. The statements regarding the entire revenue of this empire of four hundred millions of people, are very conflicting, varying all the way between eighty millions and three hundred millions of dollars per annum. Probably the truth lies between these figures. From these taxes all the expenses of the government are maintained, including the pensions or salaries of the members of the royal family, which is the only salaried aristocratic class. If the total Chinese tax amounted to the highest figures given, three hundred million dollars, it would be less than the revenue raised by the United States government, which was some three hundred and twenty-six millions

* Gray's China, vol. i., page 240.

in 1884. Three-fourths of the Chinese revenues are derived from the land tax or rent, a portion from salt and other monopolies,* and the remainder from customs. It must be remembered that the population of China is seven or eight times as large as that of the United States, and, in addition, the Chinese have no state or county tax. Except the tax referred to, the people cultivate the lands without paying other rent. It is plain that they do not suffer from heavy public burdens.

In the past few centuries a new nation has been growing up, stretching far across Europe to the Vistula, and maintaining its dominion across the Asiatic continent to Behring's Strait. It would not be correct to style it a people, for it embraces many peoples. Much of the country included within its recognized boundaries is a wilderness, and vast stretches of icy waste reach northward to the frozen sea. Russia proper has been classified as Great and Little Russia, the former with Moscow, the latter with Kiev for its centre. The Russian country or empire has been created by a system of constantly spreading or continuous emigrations of local communities. Little Russia was the mother country, and was purely Sclavonic. Great Russia was made by conquering and driving out the Finnic tribes and partly by absorbing them. The village is the unit of the Russian system. The village contains nearly everything within itself—agriculture, stock raising, manufactures, and is a well-knit community in all its interests. There is a closely packed village of block houses on each side of a broad street, shut up at the two ends by stockades. It is organized for defense and business. The enclosed space in the street is the common workshop. Cattle stands, threshing floors, barns, granaries, are attached to each block house and mark where general interests end and individual interests begin. The clearing is made in the forests by the joint labor

* Doolittle's Social Life of the Chinese, page 281.

of all, and in the common field each male person has his portion. This is called the *mir*, and defines the early rights known to their landed system. It is a right of each child born in the village. The mir of Central Russia and the gromade of Southern Russia is the peasant's conception of supreme authority.* The village is the nucleus or centre of Russia. In other countries a man with a large family is burdened, but in the Russian village the household gets an addition of the productive domain for every child that is born.† The large land cultivators are men of large families, and few children or none, give a small farm. The village, not the family, was the social unit. Every question is settled before the village mir. These village communes meet under the vault of heaven, chairman there is none. The right of speaking belongs to him who can command attention. If a speaker is acceptable they listen to him and if not he is soon stopped. Sometimes all speak at once. Voting is unknown. The majority does not force the minority. The discussion goes on until all can agree on the action to be taken or some plan finds acceptance. There must be concessions. It is compromise, not coercion.‡ The term mir means more than the council; it means the right of the individual as a part of the village. Parties in Russia differ widely from parties in Western Europe or with us. With the Russian peasant communism in land is designated as the Sclavonian substratum of civilization. They are not ignorant of the land systems of Western Europe, and hold that these have crept in among a people who knew of, or once had institutions like the Russian mir, and made a fatal blunder early in their career, exposing themselves to sure decay, by allowing individual and alienable rights to land. Land, the Russian villager argues, has never been produced but *found*. Rent paid to individuals has therefore no foundation in justice. Only such rent or tax

* Stepniak's Russia under the Tzars, page 2.

† Systems of Land Tenure, page 331.

‡ Stepniak's Russia under the Tzars, page 3.

may be taken from it as is necessary for the expenditure of the lesser or larger community, the village or the state.

There is, therefore, a fundamental difference in the ideas and polity of Eastern and Western Europe. While Little Russia was the mother of colonies and of Great Russia, there grew up around Novgorod great clusters of democratic villages. Russia in the eleventh and twelfth centuries was ultra democratic.* In three or four hundred years it has been converted into a despotism. Russia spread out like a tree. As a village became crowded it sent out a colony far into unoccupied regions. A system of spreading settlements, such as has existed in America for the past three hundred years, has been going on in Russia for a much longer period, but widely differing from it in many respects. In America, the tendency was to the individual; in Russia, to the community. In this manner, like swarms of bees, the great Russian Empire was formed. The mother villages exercised a care and parental authority over the colonies. Even after the lapse of fifty years they assisted them. When young men went to other villages or cities they were commissioned to secure orders for the whole community, and were not expected to confine their efforts to their individual interests. Everything connected with trade was a village matter.

In the south Sclavonic countries there are house communities which have largely been made under Turkish rule.† Sir Henry Sumner Maine says that in the Russian village communities the bond of kinship, though still recognized in language, is feeble and indistinct. Toward the south the related families no longer hold their lands as a common fund, but distribute them periodically.‡ Professor Bogisic says the house communities rarely consist of more than sixty persons. They are as far as possible from being patriarchal despotisms.§

* Stepniak's Russia Under the Tzars, page 24.

† Maine's Early Law and Custom, page 242.

‡ Ibid., page 240.

§ Ibid., page 244.

They are democratically governed. Every member of the body has a right to be fed, housed and clothed out of the common fund. Every daughter has a right to a marriage portion, every son to a portion for his wife, every male a voice in its government.* When placed under the Mahometan law, a daughter took half a son's share. Among the south Sclavonic races women have certain property, like the East Indian stridhan, that descends to women heiresses. The Sclavonian communities have long and steadily resisted individual property that could be alienated.† With house communities as a general rule, land, oxen or cattle necessary for carrying on the business of the community is incapable of alienation.‡ Although to some extent they might be, and often were, these house communities were not natural families as they not only adopted others but were often largely made up from outside persons. They were more democratic than the natural family. Under the Sclavonian usages the house communities developed into the village communities, although in the south, the former have struggled for their identity. "All recent observers of house communities," says Maine, "regret their decline." In the mingling of peoples, and the assertion of individual interests, the house community suffers. A member goes abroad, makes a fortune, and when he returns, the others attempt to induce him to divide. On the other hand, some dissatisfied or ambitious persons desiring to leave are induced by the laws and customs of society around them to demand a distributive share of the assets, so that they can go off and begin elsewhere. Both these causes when supplemented by general law and authority inimical to house communities tend to disintegrate them. The Austrian code has been fatal to the house communities. On the Austrian military frontiers where house communities have been

* Maine's Early Law and Custom, page 252.

† Ibid., page 249. ‡ Ibid.

placed on land subject to military service, under the Austrian system, the chief of the house community grew into a nobleman and lord of the manor.*

In the dawn of Russian recorded history we meet with the existence of slaves, but they were merely prisoners of war. The same Scandinavian or Norman warriors who invaded France, and, ultimately, England, invaded Russia in the ninth century,† and founded a species of monarchy over European Russia, and gave the name of Russ, or Russian. Stepniak says these dukes and the different princes were at first the servants of the people, and not their masters. The vetche, great or small, selected them, and dispensed with their services. They were leaders in war, and their whole function related to defense. There was not, in fact, before the time of Peter the Great, any organized government or system of laws or edicts in Russia. The call of a prince or duke by the vetche was only the first step in his election: the next was the conclusion of a convention, the riada.‡ The riada was a constitutional pact or bargain. It defined the mutual obligations of the contracting parties. Besides the defense of the country, he was to act as judge in great cases, not interfering, however, with the power of the mir or vetche.

The inroad of the Tartars and Kaptschaks under a lieutenant of Genghis Khan, put a stop to the authority of the dynasty of Ruric. They did not expel the Scandinavians, but made them a species of deputies. Their business was not with the Russian people but with the rulers. They compelled the latter to surrender a large portion of the tribute they had taken from the peasantry. These fresh invaders interfered but little with the mir of the villages or the vetche, and left their land system as they found it. This Tartar and

* Maine's Early Law and Custom, page 266.

† Kelley's Russia, vol. i., page 8.

‡ Stepniak's Russia under the Tzars, page 9.

Kaptschak rule lasted for more than two hundred years, when Duke Ivan contrived to overthrow the yoke of the Tartars. In fact, about that time all the governments founded under Genghis Khan were disappearing.

The resumption of authority by the old dukes or princes did no good to Russia. Ivan, in 1482, took the title of Tzar of Muscovy. In 1598, Boris Goodonof, a usurper, issued a ukase forbidding the peasant from leaving his native village without a passport from the government authorities.* Indeed, with the withdrawal of the Tartars the disfranchisement of the peasantry began, but it progressed very slowly. A nobility, the friends, relatives and retainers of the Tzar was soon created. When this was first done the tribute from the land was not increased, but part of the tax was given to the nobles and the remainder to the Tzar. The next step was to set apart certain villages for the nobles over which they had charge, and in this way originated the distinction of Tzar's villages and the villages of nobles. While this new autonomy was created, it did not at first interfere with the mir of the villages or their mode of transacting business, and it was some time before the people became conscious that a great blow had been struck at their liberties. The Tzar finally cultivated part of the villages he claimed by slaves who had been captives taken in war. Ivan IV., by a ukase, defined certain villages as state villages, or villages owing tribute to the government, and certain villages as the personal property of the Tzar, thus claiming what was not his own. A great many villages formerly paying a public revenue to the state now paid it as the property of the Tzar or of the nobility. When Boris Goodonof issued his ukase to prevent the peasants from leaving their villages without the consent of government, it was to check an increased spirit of colonization to new fields, that threatened to leave the nobles and the Tzar without tenants. These encroachments

* Systems of Land Tenure, page 324.

continued until the reign of the wicked Peter the First, who assumed the title of emperor in 1721 and reduced a large portion of the peasants of Russia to serfdom. He degraded the old nobility and created a new, which he supposed would be devoted to himself. These had to reach distinction through grades of military and civil service. Then began the official tchin and tchinovnik so detested by the peasantry of Russia: official classes of the general government, all of whose actions constantly infringed on the rights of the peasants, burdened them with new and heavier exactions, restricted their liberty and degraded them.* In 1715 Peter established the law of primogeniture.

The attempts to improve the condition of the Russian peasantry began with the emperor Nicholas. It is true the emperor Paul, in 1797, by a ukase, restored to the peasantry the right to elect their village heads. The first important act of Nicholas was by a ukase issued in 1848, to permit the proprietors of estates, by treaty, to transform their serfs into farmers. In 1848 he abolished the despotic regulation which forbade private peasants from buying immovable property. He further forbid the sale of peasants without land. When the emperor Alexander II. announced his determination to do justice to the peasants, he found nearly one-half of them, constituting more than a third of the population of the empire, practically slaves, tilling a soil that did not belong to them, without being paid for their labor, during three days in the week, while they had to maintain themselves and families by toiling the other three. The measure of Nicholas to induce the nobility to free their serfs having practically failed, it was now determined that it should be done by imperial decree. The serf had, however, not been a slave in the same sense that an American negro was a slave. He was a kind of slave attached to the land. To give him his freedom and leave the

* Kelley's Russia, vol. i., page 357.

land with the nobles or the Tzar would not answer. It was thus in substance agreed that the land should be divided between the nobles and the peasants. This compromise, like many human devices, proved unsatisfactory. How was the enfranchised serf to hold his land? Was he to hold it as he desired to hold it in a community or village under the mir? It was on this question that parties in Russia divided. The Sclavonian socialists insisted and still insist on the ancient system, and utterly repudiate the western idea of title. In the settlement it had to be conceded that it should be *optional* with the peasantry whether they would hold their land individually or under the mir. Thus was left side by side, noble proprietors who had to employ labor, and a peasantry to cultivate a common estate. The ultimate result of this experiment constitutes one of the difficult problems of the present generation. The disturbances in Russia indicate that enough was not attempted and what has been done has not been done well.

Russia is a comparatively new government. With much new and active blood Russia is still full of irreconcilable elements. So long as a mighty army can be kept in the hands of the Tzar, while a corrupt judicial system and the horrors of Siberia remain to punish liberty-loving men and women, this tyrannical government may continue. Through all their vicissitudes this great Sclavonic people are slowly acquiring knowledge, resources and power, and while to-day Russia is the most despotic government in the world, there is a prophetic promise that it will yet become the most democratic.

CHAPTER VII.

THE LAND SYSTEM OF MODERN EUROPE.

Lavergne—Agrarian legislation of this century—Lawns and deer parks versus cottages—French small holdings—Number of proprietors in France and Britain—Condition of the French peasantry—Exports of England and France—Effect of small farms on wages—Oppressive debts of the aristocracy—Improvements under large and small holdings—Code Napoleon—French law of inheritance—Belgium—Laveleye—Made lands—Gross production of a hectare—Spade husbandry—Short and long leases—Average food of workingmen in Europe—Spain—Aristocracy and decay of husbandry—Average wages—Aforamento—Portuguese tenure—Austria Hungary—Size of estates—Number of cultivating farmers—Tenants and farm laborers—Wages and work of men and women—Italy—Relative population—Number of land owners—Tenants and leases—Rent—Wages—Production—Land tenure in Switzerland, Denmark and Sweden—Number and kind of land owners—Size of estates—Food of working people—Wages—Emigration from Scandinavian nations—Prussia—Per cent. of land owners—Price of land—Abolition of Villeinage—Agrarian legislation—Rent—Food—Wages.

M. DE LAVERGNE, in his work, "Rural Economy in England," credits the great progress in agriculture in Britain in the past two hundred years, to "political institutions, political liberty and political tranquillity." In the sixteenth century a great revolution had occurred in the economical history of England by substituting money rents for personal services. This change in land tenures, while it had a tendency to free the peasant or villein from degrading service and a very offensive kind of personal slavery, also divorced the peasant from the land and to that extent was one of the steps toward closing his interest in it, and creating a distinct title in the land owner, which he has since asserted. In every country of modern

Europe these changes had been going on. In Germany the technical change from feudal tenure is marked by the legislation beginning with this century; but in all these nations radical changes had been effected both in governments and the privileges of the people. Absolute slavery had been first abolished and then villeinage, vassalage, serfdom and the various kinds of limited personal service growing out of rent or duty incident to the cultivation of the soil. The relief the vassal or villein thus obtained from servitude that had become degrading, was unhappily supplemented by the assumptions on the part of the aristocratic class of a fixed title, personal to themselves in the manor, common domains and landed estates, in which the theory had been that all had an interest. The freedom of the individual peasant ought to have been accompanied by freedom to the land. All the conditions on which the lords had any pretense of a claim to it had passed away. The first assumption that the nobles became possessed of the allotted lands was followed up by their attempt to fence up the public commons. These lands had been largely used for grazing, and afforded a privilege for all the citizens for that purpose and cutting necessary timber from the forests. Great complaints were made about these encroachments.* The grass or pasturage, husbandry, and the proceeds of the forests thus became a private monopoly, while communities and villages were also driven out. Nasse, in his work on these inclosures, says that sometimes three shepherds were employed where two hundred men had supported themselves by honest labor. Deer forests were made. Several enactments were issued against these agrarian proceedings of the nobles, but do not seem to have been able to put a stop to them. An Act of Henry VII., cap. 19, is quaintly entitled: "An Act against pulling downe of touns." The lands from the vicinity of which these towns were demolished were, as the Act recites:

* Young's Labor in Europe and America, page 124.

"laying to pasture lands which customably have been manured, and occupied wyth tyllage and husbandry." In Henry VIII.'s time this evil had assumed great proportions. Some men possessed twenty-four thousand sheep, and against the latter Henry had several Acts leveled, by one of which it was provided: "No one, therefore, shall possess more than two thousand sheep, with the exception of laymen, who, upon their own inheritance, may possess as many as they please, but they must not carry on sheep farming on other properties."

In these revolutions, encroachments and changes, which were carried down to a very recent period, the present titles in modern Europe crystallized. In some countries the small holders were still numerous. France, to-day, presents the most wonderful and successful experiment in small holdings, "petite culture." The contrast between France and England is an extraordinary spectacle. It is the opinion generally entertained, which is, undoubtedly, to some extent, true, that the system of small holdings in France has resulted from the French revolution, and been perpetuated, and increased by the code Napoleon. The people of France have always favored small holdings. About the close of the sixteenth century, and while the changes of which we have spoken were going on, the French peasants purchased small tracts, often not more than half an acre.* They were, however, deprived of much benefit therefrom by feudal oppressions, in the shape of numberless fees exacted, and merciless taxation. Not until after the revolution did the present system begin to flourish. The official statistics of France, following the enumeration of 1850, reckon no less than 7,845,724 "proprietors of lands," including houses and lots in towns. Of these, about five millions are rural proprietors, of whom nearly four millions are actual cultivators.† The official tables return no less than 3,799,775 land owners as *cultivators* of the soil, and, of these,

* Systems of Land Tenure, page 294. † Ibid., page 292.

57,639 are represented as cultivating through head laborers, and 3,740,793 who cultivated their lands *in person.* Since 1851, the number of cultivating proprietors has largely increased. M. de Lavergne estimates that there are five million proprietors of whom at least three million cultivate only an average of a *hectare* apiece,—little over two acres. Mulhall, in his work of 1884, gives 154,000 land proprietors in France whose lands average 320 acres, 636,000 whose lands average 50 acres each, and 3,226,000 who are the proprietors on an average of 10 acres each.* He estimates, or gives the number of separate properties, in 1881, at 6,942,974, his statistics showing a considerable increase in separate properties since 1858. M. de Lavergne estimates that there are at present 250,000 who own lands in Great Britain, but some of these are urban and not rural holders. Mulhall, in 1884, gives for Great Britain 180,524 land owners, who own, in the aggregate, 70,279,000, the average number of acres to a holder being 390.† The same authority gives for France three million, two hundred and twenty-six thousand owners who possess five acres and upward, but his figures in both England and France do not include cottars or holders of a few acres. These latter, as has been shown are a very large class in France, but a comparatively small class of independent holders in England. The Statesman's Year Book (Scott Keltie) for 1885 gives the number of persons who own upward of an acre in Great Britain as 321,386, but gives 852,408 persons who own less than an acre (presumably lot owners in cities). By Great Britain is included England, Wales, Scotland, Ireland and the channel Islands. This latter authority estimates that in England and Wales one person in twenty owns land in some amount.‡ In Scotland, one in twenty-five, and in Ireland, one in seventy-nine. The discrepancy

* Mulhall's Dictionary of Statistics 1884, page 269.

† Ibid., page 266.

‡ Statesman's Year Book, for 1885, page 252.

in these different figures quoted, arises partly from confounding lot owners with owners of small farms who live on and cultivate them. Another source of confusion has been in giving the *separate* tracts owned, when in many cases, especially in England, one person owns several of them. In 1884 the population of Great Britain was 35,961,540.* The same authority gives the population of France, December, 1881, at 37,672,048. These two, the most wealthy and enlightened nations in modern Europe, thus offer us a study of much value as to great and small holdings. It will be seen that the great body of British agriculturists are renters, the land-owning agriculturist being the exception, while in France the great body of the agricultural population are land owners, living on their own farms and cultivating and improving their own soil. Again, the number of land owners in England has been steadily decreasing. In France, under the system established by the revolution, and systematized by the code Napoleon, the number of small farms steadily increases. Laborers without lands are continually becoming land owners, and the farms more subdivided. It is, therefore important to examine the results of this small culture in France. This system has continued until, in some of the greatest departments in France, farms of one hundred hectares, upward of two hundred acres, are so scarce that they can be counted on the fingers. The great estates are day by day being purchased by small proprietors. A certain class of political economists have denounced this tendency to small farms as likely to *reduce* the productive powers of the country. Mr. Leslie says "Four millions of land owners cultivating the soil of a territory only one-third larger than Great Britain, may probably appear to the minds, familiar only with great estates and large farms, almost a *reductio ad absurdum* of the land system of the French;" but he adds: "Those who have studied the condi-

* Statesman's Year Book, 1885, page 253.

tion of the French, not merely from books, but in their own country, and who have witnessed the improvements which have taken place in French cultivation, year after year, will probably regard the number with a feeling of satisfaction." * The same writer adds: "The system of small property is daily gaining ground in France," and "The fact that the small cultivating landholder is a continual buyer of land proves that it is profitable." This culture is a species of garden tillage; no inconsiderable portion of the work is done by hand, and this tillage in France has demonstrated, as it has done everywhere else, that the soil produces more, that there is less waste, and that the country is thus better able to sustain a great population. France is a manufacturing country, and yet we find that in 1880 her exports of woolen, silk and cotton goods amounted to (reducing it to dollars) $135,000,000, while her exports of wine, spirits, sugar, grain, fruit, cheese and eggs, amounted to $120,000,000,† the latter being productions of her soil. These exports, moreover, have been steadily and to a large extent increasing in the past thirty or forty years. While France exports grain, Great Britain, in 1880, imported upward of four hundred millions of dollars worth of grain and meat.‡ Bread and meat are cheaper in France than in England, bread standing as four to six, the meats nine and a half to ten. § So far as emigration may show greater distress among the people, while the population of Britain is less by upward of two millions than France, we find that from 1820 to 1882 there emigrated from Great Britain eight million, five hundred and seventy thousand of her people. From France, during the same period the emigration was only three hundred and eighty-four thousand.|| These statistics show very conclusively the advantages of the *petite culture* of France. It is also true, that in the past two-thirds of a century the improvements on

* Systems of Land Tenure, page 293.

† Mulhall's Dictionary of Statistics, 1884, page 180.

‡ Ibid., page 104. § Ibid., page 375. || Ibid., page 168.

the small farms are much greater than they would be if the land was held by renters. The cultivators are not only able to buy more land whenever an opportunity offers, but to improve the condition of what they have. Mr. Leslie says: "There is nothing so delightful as the cottages in France, so clean and so orderly." * Arthur Young predicted that such small divisions would make France a "rabbit warren." It was also predicted that as there would be no wealthy employers the common laborers would suffer and wages decline. The contrary is the fact. The small farm culture in France has increased wages,† partly owing to better production from the soil, and partly from the fact that the laborers have continually been changing to small holders. Mr. Leslie on this subject says that seventy-five per cent. of those who were mere laborers when this system began have become owners of land. It was also said by the political economists that these small farmers would be burdened with debt so as to cripple them. M. de Lavergne estimates the debt on the small properties in France to be only five per cent. of their value. Many of the larger estates in Britain and Germany of the kind on which debt can be placed, are burdened with it to the extent of more than half their value, and but for the law of entail the large British estates would long ago have gone out of the families owning them. In point of fact, owing to the extravagance of the aristocracy, many of them are heavily burdened so far as the life interest is concerned, and it is to this condition of embarrassment and debt of the aristocracy that much of the rack renting by the *noble* owners is due. Sir Wren Hoskyn, in his "Land in England, Land in Ireland and Land in other Lands," says: "The modern doctrine of the most produce by the least labor, is, as applied to the soil, the doctrine of starvation to the laborers."

While the great bulk of France has thus been reclaimed for

* Systems of Land Tenure, page 299. † Ibid.

Frenchmen, there is still a portion cultivated by tenants. At a recent date France still contained in all the departments some fifty thousand landed properties of upward of two hundred hectares, more than four hundred acres.* There are at present upward of one million of tenant farmers in France. There are two kinds of lease tenure. First, leases of three, six or nine years; an occasional rare lease may be for eighteen. Second, the *metayage* system, by which the landlord and his tenant are sharers in the crops. The landlord furnishes the land and part of the capital required to work it, the tenant the labor and the remainder of the capital. The produce is divided and the amount of capital furnished by each varies on account of the locality, quality of soil, etc. In France, whether this cultivation of the soil of landlords is carried on by lease or *metayage*, the terms of years of holding are usually short, and as the tenant has comparatively little interest in the estate he invests but little in improvements. Where irrigation is needed, as it often is in some seasons, the land held by lease or on shares is seldom properly irrigated, while the small farms of the independent holders are so almost invariably. For improvements in the nature of drainage or irrigation no right of compensation of any kind exists.† Under the code some compensation may be obtained by the tenant for unexhausted manures or unexhausted improvements of a certain character. It is fortunate for France that the tendency of her land system is to make the cultivating tenant, if possible, a proprietor. It has been said by careful observers that the present land system of France is one of the principal securities for the tranquillity of Europe. If the French peasantry had been once more oppressed, disturbances would have followed. It is customary to judge the French Revolution by its excesses, and in them to forget the wrongs out of which its fierce spirit grew, and the good results which

* Systems of Land Tenure, page 304.

† Ibid., page 309.

have come from that convulsion. On the 4th of August, 1879, the constituent assembly of France abolished feudal rights and privileges.* About the same time they made their declaration of rights, and in November of that year decreed the transfer of the ecclesiastical property to the state. They abolished tithes, game laws, immunities, seignorial dues, *gabelle* and aristocracy.† In 1792, the national convention took the place of the legislative assembly, and declared France a republic. In 1804, the code of France was published,‡ afterward called the "Code de Napoleon." The code, in so far as it affected the present condition of affairs in France, was but part of the will of the French nation, then and now. The old feudal nobles had been stripped of the estates they had improperly assumed to own, and their exactions from the people ended. Whether by convention, assembly or legislative assembly, all struck a fresh blow at the nobles. So far did the hatred of aristocracy go that those who had not fled into exile or been guillotined were declared aliens. Practically, the work of the convention still stands, and none of the many political changes have been able to modify it. The subdivision of land is facilitated by the structure of the French law, first, the law of transfer, and second, the law of succession. The French law of succession does not altogether deny the power of a parent or head of a family to devise property, but his power over the property he has is limited to an amount equal to the share of one child; that is, with four children he can, by will, dispose of one-fifth of his property, all the rest goes share and share alike to the children, after the widow has received her interest. Nor has he the power to prevent divisions of the land. If one takes an equivalent it is simply a matter of agreement or sale by the party interested. Operating against these forced subdivisions, and as a

* Helprin's Historical Reference Book, page 110.

† Carlyle's French Revolution, vol. i., page 212.

‡ Helprin's Historical Reference Book, page 120.

check and counterpoise, is the disposition to accumulate. The peasant owners are the great land buyers in France.* They are continually buying and adding to their farms. While the policy pursued toward great holdings and the encouragement to small holdings has produced and is producing this result, obstacles have also been placed in the way of mutations in title. Every transaction affecting title to real estate has to be recorded, and in addition there is a tax on sales of six per cent. In selling, moreover, a successor pays tax on the entire value of the property,† without deducting for the mortgage. In spite of this tax these land sales of small quantities are continuous and the price, of course, increasing. We do not find in France, however, a class of speculating non-occupying dealers. The buyers are almost exclusively occupants. Capital is more equally distributed in France than in England.‡ A large amount of the national debt of France is held by these peasant landholders. This was one thing that enabled France to meet her great war indemnity to Germany. In the last half century the French have shown great recuperative power.

In addition to the peasant holdings and the larger holdings of land in France there are upward of four million and a half hectares of land that belong in *common* to various kinds of bodies, corporations, communes and villages. § Of this a considerable portion is forest, managed by the state, and which the interest of all in the country require should be kept as forest, and not divided or placed subject to individual control. Considerable discussion has arisen about throwing the village commons, not including the forest, on the market in small parcels. These commons have given the French peasant villager many advantages with which they are loath to part, especially as there is no sufficient guarantee that each peasant

* Systems of Land Tenure, page 295.

† Ibid., page 304. ‡ Ibid., page 297. § Ibid., page 310.

would get an addition to his little farm proportioned to his share. An entire commune, made up of several villages, own these commons, and the authority of the whole is necessary for a division. These public holdings, therefore, remain as reserved tracts that may be called into individual ownership. In studying modern French society it must be remembered that it is less than a century since France escaped from the thraldom of the feudal system and enjoyed anything like liberty, and she has had much less than a half a century of tranquillity and industrial life. France suffered from the jealousy of the intensely aristocratic and despotic governments around her, and, perhaps, to some extent, from the spirit of violence called into birth by the effort to overthrow her oppressors.

Belgium has a population of five million four hundred and eighty thousand,* and an area of eleven thousand three hundred and seventy-three square miles.† There are in Belgium sixty-three thousand small tenants whose farms average ten acres; two hundred and seventy thousand small freeholds, averaging eight acres; sixty-one thousand freeholds of larger size averaging forty acres and four thousand of what are considered large estates, averaging one hundred and sixty acres.‡ Belgium and Holland are naturally very poor countries. Lavergne says "not a blade of grass grows in Flanders without manure." Flemish small farmers pick up grass and manure from the roadside. As far back as the times of the Romans the inhabitants on the borders of the Scheldt used to visit England to obtain marl to improve their infertile soil. Whether reclaimed from the sea or converted into productive lands from barren sandy wastes, the low countries have certainly been largely made by the people. In addition to the freeholders we have enumerated there are many other petty land holders and cottars. We are told that in 1846 the

* Mulhall's Dictionary of Statistics, page 356.

† Statesman's Year Book, 1885, page 40.

‡ Mulhall's Dictionary of Statistics, page 271.

enumerator's report showed seven hundred and fifty-eight thousand five hundred and twelve land proprietors and five million five hundred thousand parcels of land. In 1878, the enumeration showed one million one hundred and forty-three thousand seven hundred and thirty-three owners of land and six million four hundred and seventy-eight thousand three hundred and forty parcels or tracts owned by them.* It will thus be seen that small land owners have rapidly increased in Belgium. This progressive division of lands has been marked by an increase of rental and a steady advance in price of all lands in the country. The working capital of a farm in England is supposed to be from sixty to seventy-five dollars; in Belgium it is estimated at one hundred dollars. The gross produce of a hectare is estimated at about one hundred and eighteen dollars.† In 1846, there were found fifty-five head of horned cattle, twelve horses and eight sheep on every one hundred hectares, superficial area. In England, not including Wales and Scotland, M. de Lavergne says there are thirty-three head of horned cattle, six horses and two hundred sheep per one hundred hectares, for the same year. The average rent of land in Flanders is, in dollars, about twenty dollars per hectare, nearly ten dollars per acre; the selling price varies from (in dollars) six hundred and seventy-eight to seven hundred and sixty dollars per hectare. Rents and selling prices have doubled since 1830, and such results have not been equaled in any other part of Europe.‡ In the small farm provinces of Belgium, such as Flanders, the land is better cultivated, yields more, has more agricultural capital and sustains a heavier population to the hundred hectares than in other portions of Belgium, there being of agricultural population in East Flanders, two hundred and sixty-three to one hundred and thirty-eight in Namur. Throughout Flanders

* Systems of Land Tenure, page 450.

† Ibid., page 458. ‡ Ibid.

the spade is often used to prepare the soil. In Lombardy it has been computed that in two fields manured in the same way, one being worked with the spade and one being worked with the plough, the returns of the former would be to the latter as sixty-eight to twenty-eight.* The large farmers of Hainault and Namur do not buy manure, as they fancy they would ruin themselves by so doing. The Flemish small farmers invest from fifteen to twenty millions of francs in guano every year, and as much more in other manure.† Belgium contains many manufacturing cities, but in an aggregate population of nearly five millions and a half, eight hundred thousand people are directly engaged in agricultural pursuits.‡ In the portions of Belgium where the farming is carried on between landlord and tenant the usual form is a short lease, rarely over nine years. In the Middle Ages, when much of the land was held under the feudal system, the form for a long time was *metayage*, or a division of the crops between the landlord and tenant, the former furnishing a part of the necessary capital. This has been abolished except in some of the *polders* along the coast of the German ocean.§ Owing to the shortness of the leases the cultivator is not tempted to make improvements of which he would scarcely reap the benefits, and the landlords will not grant longer leases because they expect to raise the rent when the lease expires. The landlords reap all the benefits resulting from the progress made by the entire community in various directions. From the sixteenth century the payments to the landlords have chiefly been in money. The incoming tenant farmer takes possession of the land about the middle of March, the houses April 1st. The laws for the regulation of vacating and entering new leases differ in the different provinces and are generally complicated. In some localities experts are called on to appraise the standing crops

* Systems of Land Tenure, page 465. † Ibid., page 455.
‡ Statesman's Year Book, 1885, page 41.
§ Systems of Land Tenure, page 466.

at the date of the change, and manure already on the ground.* The estimated average of food for a man, per day, in the Low Countries is, of bread thirty ounces, meat four ounces. By the same table we quote it stands in Italy, twenty-eight ounces of bread and two ounces of meat; Spain, twenty-six ounces of bread and three ounces of meat; Sweden and Norway, twenty-two ounces of bread and three ounces of meat. Those we have quoted last are the lowest in Europe. In Britain it stands twenty-one ounces bread, seven ounces meat, and in the United States, twenty-six ounces bread and nine ounces meat.† Of course, such an approximation of food does not include the other articles of diet that may be used. The buildings in Belgium are superior in average value, taking the country through, to what they are in Austria and Spain,‡ where more aristocratic systems prevail. It will thus be seen that the Low Countries, much of which is naturally very poor land, have been rendered as productive as any in Europe, maintaining a very considerable population. The government is a constitutional monarchy; it is not a despotism, and has to consider to some extent the wishes of the people. The parliamentary bodies, a house and senate, are elective by voters who pay a certain amount of taxes. Any citizen of twenty-one who pays about eight dollars per annum taxes can vote for members of the lower house. This makes one in thirteen of the adult males a voter. No man is eligible to the senate who does not pay direct taxes amounting to about four hundred dollars. The senators receive no pay. In Belgium the power of the aristocracy is on the wane. Belgium is following the footsteps of France in the direction of small free holdings for the actual agriculturist. Her cities were long the pillars of popular rights against despotism, but the country is small, surrounded by despotic and encroaching monarchies, and has been inter-

* Systems of Land Tenure, page 491.

† Mulhall's Dictionary of Statistics, page 144.

‡ Ibid., page 237.

fered with too much, from the outside, to give a fair indication of what it might have been if the people had been left to their own instinctive love of freedom. It has been the theatre of war for many a military despot.

Spain is one of the countries suffering from landed aristocracy. There are in Spain six hundred and eighty thousand land owners, their estates average one hundred and fifty acres.* Four per cent. of the population own land not including lot owners. In Spain twenty-two millions of acres are cultivated and ninety millions uncultivated. The Spanish law gives facility to entails, which, with the pride and indolence of the aristocracy, led to the decay of husbandry.† The area of France in 1881 was 204,177 square miles; of Spain at the last enumeration, 1877, 197,767 square miles.‡ It will thus be seen that there is not much difference in the area; while the former maintains a population of thirty-seven millions and a half, the latter has a population of only sixteen millions and a half. The number of head of cattle, including horses, cattle and sheep, stands in the ratio of seventeen in France to six in Spain, by Mulhall's tables.§ Although Spain was enriched by the plunder of Mexico and Peru, and may be said to have been for a long period the European dumping ground for the precious metals from the Americas, we find by the latest statistics there is of actual amount of coin in Spain and Portugal, forty millions of gold and seventeen millions of silver coin, and in France at the same date, one hundred and ninety-one millions in gold, and one hundred and ten millions in silver coin.|| These figures are in both cases of the English pounds sterling, as I have not, in quoting, changed, in this case, Mulhall's tables. The exports from Spain, by the latest tables, aggregate twenty-

* Mulhall's Dictionary of Statistics, 1884, page 267.

† Prescott's Ferdinand and Isabella, vol. iii., page 449.

‡ Statesman's Year Book, 1885, page 443.

§ Mulhall's Dictionary of Statistics, page 76.

|| Ibid., page 96.

one million nine hundred thousand pounds sterling, from France, at the same date, one hundred and thirty-eight million seven hundred thousand pounds sterling. I quote from Mulhall's tables of 1884. One more illustration: the estimated value of lands per inhabitant in France is seventy pounds sterling, and in Spain forty pounds. It is proper to state that estimated values of real estate, except when based on their actual productiveness, are not a safe criterion of prosperity. In France, by Mulhall's tables, the average wages stand per week, thirty shillings; food, twelve shillings; surplus, twelve shillings. In Spain, average wages, sixteen shillings; food, ten shillings; and surplus, six shillings. Laveleye says: "The estates of the grandees have destroyed the small land owners, whose place has been taken by bandits, smugglers, beggars and monks.*

In Portugal the aforamento is a species of hereditary lease by which the right of occupation is granted in consideration of an annual rent *fixed, once for all,* and which the landlord cannot increase.† The aforamento, formerly, was not divisible, and, on the death of the holder, one of the heirs must take it and reimburse the others; or if they did not agree, the leasehold or aforamento was sold, and the purchaser held it on the same conditions. If the hereditary tenant allows the land to deteriorate so as to reduce its value to over one-fifth of the capitalized rent, the landlord can eject him. Besides his rent, the landlord was entitled to a fee or duty whenever the lease changed hands, but, by the code of July, 1867, that, and all feudal dues and charges were done away with, except rent. The same code forbade bequeathing the sole right to one child or person designated, and the division of the lease in equal shares is made compulsory. The aforamento is of early date in Portuguese history, and was introduced by the monastic orders designed to be a check on feudalism. Besides the

* Systems of Land Tenure, page 479. † Ibid., page 487.

noble and aristocratic landlords, private persons occasionally let land at fixed rent, and in consideration of fixity of tenure *and rent*, accept a certain cash sum by agreement, for these perpetuity privileges when so granted. It has been assumed that Portugal is more productive and prosperous than Spain, and the aforamento has been considered the cause. The government of Spain, although a constitutional monarchy, is largely aristocratic. The upper house or senate is of two classes: princes of the blood, grandees whose rent roll from land is equal to twelve thousand dollars, and a hundred senators for life named by the king. One-half of the senate is elective; but the electors must pay a land tax of five dollars or an industrial tax of ten dollars. At the election of 1879, there was one elector to every seventeen of the population.* Spain, politically, may be considered in a transitionary state, and if her people are able to assert and maintain republican institutions, great reforms may be expected. Spain is the only nation in Europe, at present, that has not abolished slavery in her colonies. She has some accomplished statesmen, many of whom are, like Castellar, sympathetically republican.

In Austria, including Hungary, there are eleven thousand noble land owners whose estates, estimated together, average five thousand two hundred acres, the aggregate owned by them being sixty-two millions of acres. There are also three million, four hundred and twenty thousand smaller peasant or farmer land owners, the average acreage of whose estates is twenty-three acres.† Although none of the latter class are among the nobility, many of them may be styled landed gentry. There is, therefore, quite a large body of aristocrats, who derive an income from the land claimed by them, and are in this way a burden on the agricultural laborers of the country. The Austrian empire, exclusive of her

* Statesman's Year Book, 1885, page 435.

† Mulhall's Dictionary of Statistics, page 271.

Turkish provinces, has an area of two hundred and forty thousand nine hundred and forty-two English square miles, and a population, at the last census of December, 1880, of thirty-seven million eight hundred and eighty-three thousand two hundred and twenty-six. In Austria proper, the density of the population is about one hundred and ninety-one to the square mile, and in the rest of the empire about one hundred and thirty-five to the square mile.* In Austria, two million two hundred and seventy-five thousand one hundred and seventeen are returned as farming their own lands, much of it by hired labor; ninety thousand and thirty-six as tenant farmers, and three million seven hundred and thirty-nine thousand four hundred and twenty-one as farm laborers. In all, some six millions of people engaged one way and another in agriculture, with their families, making nearly sixty per cent. of the entire population.† Of the total area of Austria-Hungary, the acreage in crops is forty-six million one hundred and eight thousand and seventy; woods and forests, twenty-three million two hundred and eighty thousand four hundred and twelve acres; meadows and perennial pastures, eleven million three hundred and ten thousand five hundred and thirty-three acres.

The amount of gold and silver coin in Great Britain for each inhabitant is about twenty dollars; in France, forty dollars, and in Austria, a little over two dollars and fifty cents. Coin is not a correct indication of wealth, however. In 1867, Edward Young informs us that agricultural laborers in Austria received per year, as wages, from fourteen dollars and forty cents to nineteen dollars and twenty cents, with board. Women, from four dollars and eighty cents to fourteen dollars and forty cents, with board, but adds that wages have risen since then.‡ In 1870, the daily wages of laborers in factories

* Statesman's Year Book, 1885, page 21. † Ibid., page 24.

‡ Young's Labor in Europe, page 600.

was from twenty-two to forty-eight cents per day, without board, the working hours being from twelve to thirteen per day. Wages have since risen twenty per cent.* Two-thirds of the commerce of the country is carried on with Germany. A good journeyman shoemaker earns about ninety-six cents a day, and a good joiner, from one dollar twenty to one dollar and forty-four cents. Inferior bakers earn about seventy-two cents a week, and board, and head workmen, one dollar and sixty-eight cents per week, with board.† Many of the artisans and laborers are boarded by their employers. The condition of agricultural laborers generally is not as good as in many European countries. When it is considered that in an agricultural population of six million nearly four million are mere laborers, the helpless condition of the lower orders may be inferred. The large body of nobles and still larger body of petty landed aristocrats may be said to consume substantially from one-half to one-third of all the agricultural production. There are two elements in the population, the Eastern or Sclavic, having originally different views of land tenure, but all subjected to the dominant idea produced by feudalism. To make matters worse, the condition of women in Austria is deplorable. All the most menial work in Vienna is done by women, such as cleaning and sweeping the streets, gathering garbage, carrying water, pumping from the cisterns to the upper stories of houses, and even carrying mortar and handling bricks.‡ These are of all ages, young, middle-aged and old, their wages being about forty-eight cents per day, without board. A comparative review of the occupations of the sexes shows that in the industries, manufactures, agriculture, trade, commerce, science, art, etc., there are three million twenty-seven thousand and four females engaged, and three million six hundred and twelve thousand

* Young's Labor in Europe, page 601. † Ibid., page 604.

‡ Young's Labor in Europe and America, page 605.

two hundred and twenty-seven males. Although women almost equally share the grades of labor, we find of independent persons, property owners, factors, churchmen, proprietors, only nine hundred and forty-nine thousand two hundred and sixty-five females, to two million nine hundred and nineteen thousand three hundred and fifty-four males.* The hours of female labor in Austria are also greater than those of male laborers, while the wages are from fifty to twenty-five per cent. less. The greater portion of field labor and labor in factories, mills and mines falls on women. The manner of paying her explains her subordinate position. What is left of the empire, Austria proper and Hungary, have each a parliamentary body, the two united in the person of the sovereign. There are seventeen provincial diets. The poor and laboring people have little or no part in these governments. The government in all its parts is essentially aristocratic,† its powers arising from landed aristocracy and property qualifications. Austria offers a fine field for the political reformer and the advocate of woman's rights.

Italy at the present time possesses a constitutional government which is largely aristocratical, with the elective part based on property qualifications. The executive power belongs to the king, who also practically creates the highest parliamentary body, the senate. That body consists of princes of the royal family, and of distinguished persons who have held office, been noted for scientific or literary ability, or who pay an annual tax equal to six hundred dollars. These are nominated by the king for life. The lower house of deputies is elected by male citizens of twenty-one who can read and write, and who pay taxes to the amount of four dollars; sixty-one per cent. of adult males voted at the election of 1882.‡ Neither senators nor deputies receive any pay but are allowed

* United States Consular Reports, 1885, page 156.

† Statesman's Year Book, 1885, page 7.

‡ Ibid., page 316.

to travel free on railroads and steamboat lines. By the census of December, 1881, the total population of Italy was found to be twenty-eight million four hundred and fifty-nine thousand six hundred and twenty-eight, living on an area of one hundred and fourteen thousand four hundred and ten English square miles, being two hundred and thirty-four persons to the square mile. In Italy there are twenty-seven million acres cultivated land and forty-one million acres uncultivated.* Of her population, one million eight hundred and sixty-five thousand persons own land, the average acreage of whose estates is thirty-five acres and the average value being nearly two thousand one hundred dollars. This list of land owners is from Mulhall's tables, and does not include cottars or persons owning less than five acres. The average value of the cultivated land is about one hundred and five dollars per acre. In Lombardy and Piedmont there are one million one hundred and eighty thousand separate estates averaging sixteen acres, embracing an aggregate of nineteen million acres. In Sicily there are four hundred and ten thousand estates averaging forty acres, and aggregating sixteen million acres. Lombardy, especially, is the small farm region, and is the best cultivated in Italy, and the people are more comfortably situated. Tuscany and Romagna, with an aggregate acreage of sixteen million, have only one hundred and forty-five thousand estates, which average one hundred and ten acres, and Naples one hundred and twenty thousand estates, averaging one hundred and eighty acres and aggregating twenty-one million acres.† One million one hundred and forty thousand proprietors farm thirty-three million acres; one million two hundred and forty-eight thousand metayers cultivate eighteen million acres on a division of crops with the owners, and three hundred and ten thousand tenants cultivate twenty million acres. Where the metayer system exists the state of

* Mulhall's Dictionary of Statistics, page 266. † Ibid., page 270.

agriculture and the condition of the actual laborers and cultivators stand lowest. Tenants with leases stand next. The regions tilled by the proprietors are not only the most prosperous and productive, but the people are in more comfortable circumstances. The average rent, where it is not on the metayer system of a division of crops, is from two to three dollars per acre.

The rate of laborers' wages in Italy is the lowest in Europe.* They eat less animal food than the laborers of any country in Europe, Mulhall giving per diem twenty-eight ounces of bread and two ounces of animal food as the average.† Many of the poor Italian laborers do not eat animal food except on rare occasions. The climate has, of course, something to do with this, and they subsist largely on vegetables and fruit. The diet of the laborers of Piedmont is given by the vice consul as—"Morning meal, vegetable soup; the families of the higher classes of workmen have coffee and milk. Dinner, soup, bread and cheese, or potatoes and codfish. Supper, which is the principal meal, bread, wine, macaroni or vegetable stew. Meat is a rarity and a luxury." ‡ The same authority gives the rate of wages in Turin for a week's work of sixty hours: Bricklayers, $4.20; masons, $3.60; plasterers, $5.04; roofers, $4.20; plumbers, $3.60; carpenters, $4.00; bakers, $4.00; blacksmiths, $3.60; brickmakers, $5.00, and brewers, $8.00; cabinet makers, $3.40; cigar makers, $3.00; hod carriers and tenders, $1.70 per week; draymen and teamsters, $1.50; teachers in public schools, $5.00. Married women very seldom work in factories or at any out-door employment. The wages of female employees is generally about one-half those of the male employees. The American system of boarding is never practiced, everybody keeps house.§ The principal

* United States Consular Reports, 1885, page 149.

† Mulhall's Dictionary of Statistics, page 144.

‡ United States Consular Reports, page 151.

§ Young's Labor in Europe, page 631.

exports are silk, wine, olive oil, fruit, hemp and cotton.* The condition of Italy is not so favorable to the laboring man as France or several other countries in Europe. Without having much more than half the area of Spain it has nearly twice the population. The conditions of land tenure are not favorable to the laboring classes. Large portions of what is produced are consumed by privileged idlers. Politically, Italy is in a transition state. Fettered by the burdens of bygone ages, her people have evinced fresh aspirations for freedom.

Switzerland, although a small mountain region, is one of the most prosperous in Europe so far as the laborers are concerned. Laveleye asks why the Swiss peasant is so much more substantially fed than some of his neighbors, and answers because the Swiss is nearly always the owner of the soil he cultivates.† Swiss working people enjoy full political rights and are taxed like others. Wage workers in Switzerland, however, are required to be at once laborious and denying, and are able to save but little.

Denmark has a population of one million nine hundred and sixty-nine thousand and thirty-nine, living on an area of thirteen thousand seven hundred and eighty-four square miles. The average density is one hundred and forty-three to the square mile. Of land owners there are in this small territory five hundred and fifty, whose estates average two thousand five hundred acres, holding among them one million three hundred and eighty thousand acres. Persons of the rank of farmers number one thousand one hundred and eighty, these also being to some extent a privileged class. Their estates average three thousand acres, making an aggregate of three hundred and sixty thousand acres. Then there are sixty-nine thousand one hundred of what are styled "bondsmen," or farmers, with an average of sixty acres, aggregating four million

* Statesman's Year Book, 1885, page 340.

† Systems of Land Tenure, page 450.

two hundred thousand. "Huusmen," a species of laboring tenant holder, a relic of feudalism, whose holdings average four acres.

In Sweden the population in 1883 was four million six hundred and three thousand five hundred and ninety-six, the area, one hundred and seventy thousand nine hundred and seventy-nine,* being more than four-fifths the size of France, with about one-sixth of the population. Sweden has two thousand six hundred and fifty nobles, who have estates averaging fourteen thousand acres, aggregating thirty-eight million acres. There are one hundred and ninety-one thousand freeholders whose estates average two hundred acres and forty thousand tenants, who each occupy lands averaging four hundred acres.† The average price of land is placed by Mulhall at sixty dollars per acre, and the rent at five English shillings, about a dollar and five cents per acre.

Norway contains three millions of acres of cultivated and seventy million acres uncultivated land. In fact there is a great deal of poor and waste land in all the Scandinavian countries.

Mr. Ryder, consul to Denmark, estimates the daily expense of a family of four persons, a laborer, his wife and two children: Breakfast and supper, four pounds bread, one-fifth pound lard, one-sixth pound cheese, one-quarter pound sugar, one-fourteenth pound coffee and milk, the whole costing nineteen cents. Dinner, which consists of milk porridge, fish and potatoes, or pea soup with pork, about fifteen cents, or thirty-four cents per diem, one hundred and twenty-four dollars per year.‡ He says the condition of the best paid laborers is "fairly comfortable," that of the agricultural laborers one of economy and self denial. This may be judged from his table, in which he gives the expense and income of a laborer and his family for

* Statesman's Year Book, 1885, page 461.

† Mulhall's Dictionary of Statistics, page 271.

‡ United States Consular Reports, 1885, page 165.

a year: rent, $30; food, $123.36; clothing, $10; fuel and light, $12.10; tobacco and spirits, $6.70; total expenses, $183.60; total income, $188.00. Balance for incidentals, $4.40. He gives four families, of which the above is the lowest; for the highest he gives an expenditure of $254.60 and an income of $268.40. The married women attend to their domestic affairs usually, but at times work in the field or shops as the single women do.

The common farmers of Norway till the soil themselves with the assistance of their tenants, a class called "huusmen." * These hire from the farmer a patch of land that will keep one or two cows and a few sheep, for which, and their humble cot, they pay a certain number of day's work in each season of the year. They are so much in the power of the owners of the land that they cannot make reasonable bargains for the payment of rent in money. At home they and their families live chiefly on hominy and barley bread. They scarcely have meat, except, perhaps, at Christmas. Besides the "huusmen," there are agricultural laborers, whose condition, however, is perhaps even better than the "huusmen." † Young places the wages of agricultural laborers, in 1872, at from one dollar and twenty-six to one dollar and ninety-two cents per week; carpenters and blacksmiths, three dollars and eighty-seven cents; weavers in the cotton mills, from five dollars and thirty-two, to six dollars and forty cents.‡ Wages have since risen.

It will be observed that the Scandinavian countries are, to a considerable extent, inhospitable and unproductive, and do not maintain a dense population, only seven and three-tenths per cent. of the land being under cultivation. Manufacturing interests are neither extensive nor considerable. About one-half of the country is covered by forests, timber being one of

* Young's Labor in Europe and America, page 696.

† Ibid.

‡ Ibid., page 693.

the principal exports. The farmer land holders, who are a kind of country gentlemen, work on their farms, and even the petty nobles occasionally work on their estates, but the bulk of the labor is performed by men who have little interest in the soil, and are only connected with it by rent. In 1882, two hundred and twenty-four thousand three hundred and ninety-two persons were returned as paupers, or four and nine-tenths per cent. of the population.* With the exception of sixteen thousand four hundred and twelve Finns, six thousand six hundred Laps, and about twelve thousand persons of foreign birth, the Swedish population is entirely of the Scandinavian branch of the Teutonic family. In 1860 the emigrants from Sweden to countries beyond Europe were only three hundred and forty-eight. In 1865 the number rose to six thousand six hundred and ninety-one; in 1868, to twenty-seven thousand and twenty-four; in 1869, to thirty-nine thousand and sixty-four. The emigration fell, in 1870, to twenty thousand and three, and to seven thousand seven hundred and ninety-one in 1877. In 1879 it was forty-two thousand one hundred and nine; in 1880, forty-five thousand nine hundred and ninety-two; in 1882, fifty thousand one hundred and seventy-six, and in 1883, twenty-nine thousand four hundred and ninety. Over four-fifths of these emigrants went to the United States. It is fair to charge the monopolization of the land by privileged classes with being the leading cause of the condition of the people. The great body of workers are not interested in improving the country; but the people that overran Russia, dictated terms to France, twice overran England, and held great stretches of the American coast in early times, are not destitute of their ancient nerve.

The Prussia of to-day is largely a political creation, and the modern German empire is one of the first great powers in the world. Germany comprises four kingdoms, six grand

* Statesman's Year Book, 1885, page 462.

duchies, five duchies, seven principalities, three free cities, Hamburg, Lubeck and Bremen, and Alsace-Lorraine. The Imperial throne has always been filled by election, but it or its rulers have a tendency to the hereditary principle. Originally, the election was by all the princes and peers of the *Reich*, but the mode was changed in the fourteenth century, when a limited number, seven, afterward changed to nine, assumed the privilege. The old empire was overthrown by Napoleon, in 1806. The present emperor was elected by the vote of the Reichstag of the North German Confederation.

The area of the twenty-five states is two hundred and twelve thousand and twenty-eight English square miles, as against two hundred and four thousand one hundred and seventy-seven of France, and two hundred and forty thousand nine hundred and forty-two of Austria-Hungary. Before Germany obtained Alsace-Lorraine, France was the largest. The population of the German Empire, December 1st, 1880, was forty-five million two hundred and thirty-four thousand and sixty-one.* Not including cottars or persons owning less than five acres, there are, in Germany, two million four hundred and thirty-six thousand persons owning land; the land owners being five per cent. of the population. The average tracts of the landlords given is only thirty-seven acres, but included in that there are some very considerable estates. The average value, if they had all the same amount, would be about four thousand dollars.† In the German Empire sixty-eight millions of acres are cultivated, and fifty-seven million acres uncultivated, which is a large average of cultivated land, although not so large as in France. The price of cultivated land per acre is about one hundred and twenty-five dollars in our money.‡

The original Teutonic community was a body of men who

* Statesman's Year Book, 1885, page 114.

† Mulhall's Dictionary of Statistics, page 267. ‡ Ibid., page 266.

had property in common, among whom any private right or interest in land was connected with public duty or military service. The geographical area was marked out or divided into three marks; first, the common or folcland; second, the arable mark cut out of the common *mark* and apportioned in equal lots, and then the town or village mark, cut up into separate lots.* The individual or marksman stood in a threefold relation to the land, a joint proprietor of the common land, an allòttee in the arable mark and a householder in the township. There was, therefore, under restriction, an inheritance he could call his own in the arable or tillable land, although he was compelled to occupy and cultivate it, and the community determined the mode of cultivation; his cattle grazed on the common pasture, and he cut timber from the public forest. In his dwelling-house and its appurtenances he was absolute lord and master. In another chapter we have shown how, in nearly all the Teutonic nations, the ancient system of equal freeholds was changed, and the lands largely passed into the hands of the lords. In Germany, feudal tenure villeinage, with their accompaniments, came down, to the beginning of this century. Prussia made three great efforts to escape from them, and it endeavored to return to free ownership, *but with unequal possession.*† The first step was taken in 1807, by the abolition of villeinage in so far as it affected the *personal* status of the villein. At that time it must be remembered that all the land in Prussia consisted of the few provinces left it by the peace of Tilsit, which was distributed among three classes, nobles, peasants and burghers. The community was composed of different parties. Some had been formerly slaves, gradually ascending to the peasant class; some had been freeholders and had sunk to villeinage; others held what had been claimed as crown lands by paying an annual service or fee; some had been dispossessed by the

* Systems of Land Tenure, page 351. † Ibid., page 361.

nobles. In the worst form of the villein tenure in Germany, the peasant could be held to unlimited service. At his death the whole or the large part of the personal estate fell to the lord; his children could not marry without the lord's consent, and could be kept an unlimited number of years as *personal* servants. The peasant could be whipped, but his life was protected.* As is usually the case, the calamities of kings and nations is the crucible from which emerges slowly the rights of the people. Frederick the Great, in his terrible struggles to maintain and build up Prussia, found it necessary to recognize to some extent the rights or claims of the cultivator. With all his despotic qualities he undoubtedly improved their condition. This only seemed to hasten inevitable changes. At the time of the reformation the people had endeavored to regain their rights to the land. Feudalism in its worst form was dead, and circumstances made its final overthrow indispensable. The battle of Jena was not, for Prussia, an unmixed calamity. An agrarian spirit was in the air, and not only battles but revolution. The edict of Frederick William, on October 9th, 1807, was ushered in by a liberal allowance of philosophical "whereases," but the substance was, first, providing for the free exchange of property; second, freedom in regard to occupation; third, divisibility of property; fourth, power of granting leases; fifth, extinction and consolidation of peasant holdings; sixth, facilities for mortgaging; seventh, limited entails; eighth, abolition of villeinage. Although M. Morier is inclined to give these events more importance than they are entitled to, they initiated rather than accomplished important changes. Prussia had been scourged by war and stripped of resources: whole villages were lying in ashes.† France had some time before got rid of her aristocratic land holders by a much less elaborate and a much more conclusive plan. Those who

* Systems of Land Tenure, page 365.

† Ibid., page 374.

assisted the weak Frederick William in 1807, were certainly neither communists nor democrats. They were admirers of the English system rather than the French. The first great purpose was to make land a chattel, and their idea of a model farm was a large one with its landlord, supervising farmer, and laborers. They relieved the German laborer or villein of the burden of feudal dues, but as these had largely gone into disrepute some time before, this was not so great a boon. The edict assumed that the noble landlords had certain rights in the soil, the tenant or villein had merely a sort of pre-emptive right of use. Instead of yielding service under the system of feudal tenure, to the lord, the peasant was authorized to buy and pay indemnity to the lord for what the latter was thus to relinquish. In this way the personal right of the lord in the property or estate was recognized, although he really had no right to it. It was essentially a recognition of the lord of the manor's right to the property. If the liberated villein had no money, which was probable, he could buy, get deeds and give a mortgage on the premises he used, and thus pay interest instead of rent or service. As one-half the improvements in the country had been destroyed or laid waste by war, the noble landlords, if their claim to title to the land was good, should have been placed under obligation to put the farms on which the villein furnished them rent into serviceable shape. In making everything salable, moreover, there was danger that the peasant small holdings would be swallowed up by capitalists. On the several questions involved the commissioners and the country at large were divided. To prevent the extinction of peasant holdings, instructions were sent to the provincial governments to give permission for such extinctions under restrictions and only in cases where it was "new peasant land," or land so created within fifty years, and even in such instances half the land so purchased or exchanged must be made into large peasant holdings, and either given in fee to peasant holders or let in perpetual leases. The political economists in these proceedings, as has been said, were men of English ideas. It is generally believed, and justly, that where there is a free exchange of land, the capitalists and large holders will gradually swallow up the small holdings, unless there is a law of compulsory division as in France. In point of fact, the edict of 1807 did not succeed in very vitally changing the form of land tenure in Prussia. It disturbed rather than settled questions. The lord was still owner of the peasant's land, but had not the right to enforce possession or eject the peasant, and the peasant was free but not master of his own labor.* To cure these evils the edicts or legislation of 1811 were promulgated. They consisted of two great edicts, one to regulate the relations between the lords and the peasants and the other purported to be an "edict for the better cultivation of the land." The first edict had two general parts. The one considered the rights of the landlord, the lord's right of ownership, his claim to service, dues in money and kind, dead stock on the farms, easements or servitudes on the land held. The rights of the tenant were claims to assistance in case of misfortune, right to gather wood and other forest rights, claims for repairs on buildings, pasturage on demesne lands or forests.† The commission as a basis laid down, that in case of hereditary holdings neither the service nor the dues could be *increased* and that they *must be lowered* if the holder could not subsist at their actual rate. That the holding must be kept in condition so that the proceeds could pay its dues to the state. Here a distinction is drawn between the claims of the state and the manor. As has been shown, the rights of the manor were originally the rights of the state, or the "eminent domain" for defense. Here we have what had in fact been established long before, the claim of the state to tax or impose burdens, "eminent domain," and the claim of the lord or the ownership of the manor. This merely gave

* Systems of Land Tenure, page 378.

† Ibid., page 377.

the claim of the state precedence. By the terms of the edict, two years were given to the lords and the cultivators, the vassals and tenants, whatever their relative rights might be, to adjust their differences. These were to be adjusted on the basis that the lords should have absolute possession of one-third of the old arable mark and one-third of the common land. For the remainder the peasant was to indemnify the lord, which might take the shape of indemnity of capital, corn or money rent. This has been styled "the agrarian legislation of Prussia," and in so far as it interfered with the peasant's right to the land he lived on, it was agrarian enough. It gave the lord the absolute disposal of one-third of what was really public property, and the right to rent the remainder unless somebody could buy it from him. For the use of his cot the peasant was to pay ten days' labor with a team, or if he had no team, ten days' labor of a man and also of a woman. Where corn rents were not paid punctually the lord of the manor could exact services instead. One of the rights insisted on by the political economists was the unlimited right of disposal. Parents were permitted to divide their estate among their children as they saw fit. Facilities were also given for sales and foreclosures on the principle that if a man had not the means or was unable properly to develop the land, it was better that he should sell to some one who was.

The Prussian legislation of 1850 has been considered more radical, but acted essentially on the same plan. The revolutions or insurrections of 1848 had swept over Europe, and although the despotic rulers and aristocrats had crushed them, there was still a wholesome admonition conveyed by them. By the legislation of 1850 all hereditary holders became proprietors, and the overlordship of the lord of the manor was abrogated. These proprietors, however, or the land they occupied, were held liable for an equivalent of dues and service, which in fact became rent. The land was capitalized at eighteen years' rent, and a species of banks called "rent banks," were created. The government merely lent its credit to put this rent or burden in a tax shape, the lord getting indemnity besides his third on ownership. In France, England and Germany, a great conflict had been going on between the lord, or the *manor*, and the peasant. In England the manor won, the peasant lost. In France the peasant won, the manor lost. In Germany it was a drawn game, the stakes were divided;* but it is easy to see that the lord had the advantage, and the fruits of the most of his exactions and encroachments for ages were conceded to him. In the German empire the instincts of the people are for small and allodial holdings, the interest of the capitalists for large holdings. It is claimed that the number of cultivating holders has not diminished under the chattelization of land. It is too soon to judge it yet, and in any event the cultivating holders do not increase. The rent of land in Germany averages four dollars and a half per acre,† more than twice as much as in Austria and three times as much as in Spain and Portugal or Sweden, and although Italy is much more densely populated than Germany, the rent stands eighteen in Germany to eleven in Italy. In some parts of Germany agricultural laborers' wages are for a man, $67.30, and a woman, $30 per year, with board; day laborer, with board, forty cents, harvest labor, without board, eighty cents per day.‡ The general trades, by the same authority, stand per week of sixty hours: Bricklayers, $4.15; masons, the same, that is without board; carpenters are $4.75; cabinet makers, $4.91; hod carriers, $3.21; tenders, $2.54. In Britain the wages are a little higher. Women perform many menial tasks. Consul Mason, at Dresden, mentions teams of a woman and a dog pulling light carts with very considerable loads.§ As a rule the women are not so well paid as the men.

In presenting the condition of land tenure in modern Europe,

* Systems of Land Tenure, page 389.

† Mulhall's Dictionary of Statistics, page 266.

‡ United States Consular Reports, 1885, page 9.

§ Ibid., page 16.

it will be seen that in nearly all the states of Europe there is a large and aristocratic class that exacts, in the shape of rent, a very considerable portion of what is produced by the laboring classes. The more extravagant the landlords, the greater their exactions from the producers, even to the extent in many cases of crippling and impeding production. Public burdens and the defense of the country are not now defrayed from this rent, but all property, production and consumption are taxed. Enormous armies are maintained by the governments of these countries, ostensibly as a menace to each other, but chiefly to their disaffected subjects. The power of government is largely in the hands of landowners, and they exercise it to protect their own interests.

CHAPTER VIII.

THE LAND SYSTEM OF THE BRITISH EMPIRE.

Cultivated and uncultivated areas—Acreocracy—Extent and value of aristocratic holdings—Number of land owners—Urban and country population—Rent during six hundred years—Prices of wheat and beef—Aristocratic debts saddled on the people—Primogeniture and the younger sons—Loss of cottage and pasture privileges by workingmen—Law of parish settlement—Food and wages—No law to secure a tenant for his improvements—A "retired tenant farmer"—Board and wages three centuries ago—Prices—Watt Tyler—Growth of cities—Manufacture and commerce—Mr. Giffen searching for the laborer's wealth—Mallock—Modern wages—Houses and food—Ireland—Arthur Young—Subjection of Ireland—Landlords in triplicate—Noblemen, perpetual land holders, middlemen and cultivators—Rents in Ireland—Redpath—Tenants and evictions—Number of land proprietors—Battersby and compensation—Argyle and Henry George—The duke as a philosopher and as a sheep raiser—Defense of British aristocracy—Agricultural decadence—Growth of manufactures and commerce—Food produced and food imported—Rival aristocracy of money.

In the third chapter we attempted to show how the aristocratic owners of land in Europe had succeeded in fastening themselves, like Sinbad the Sailor's Old Man of the Mountain, on the shoulders of the laborers of these nations. Who are these land owners? Mulhall says that one hundred and eighty thousand persons own land in the United Kingdom of Great Britain.* The same authority gives the average size of estates at three hundred and ninety acres, and the average value of the estates at nine thousand six hundred pounds. The number of landholders to the whole population being half of one per cent. His table does not include cottars or

* Mulhall's Dictionary of Statistics, page 267.

those owning less than five acres. The cultivated area of Great Britain is stated to be forty-seven millions of acres, and twenty-three million acres are uncultivated.* The average value of the cultivated land is thirty-three pounds per acre, about one hundred and sixty dollars. The value of the land in Britain, if equally divided, would be forty-eight pounds, or two hundred and thirty-two dollars to each man, woman and child. Not being divided equally, we find that twenty-three noblemen, dukes, earls, marquises and lords have estates exceeding one hundred and fifty thousand acres.† As, for example, the Duke of Argyle has one hundred and seventy-five thousand acres; Lord Middleton, one million six thousand acres (one seventieth part of the entire kingdom); the Duke of Sutherland, one million three hundred and fifty-eight thousand acres, or nearly one-fiftieth part of the kingdom. Eighteen noblemen have annual rentals exceeding one hundred thousand pounds, or five hundred thousand dollars, derived from the proceeds of lands. The annual rent roll, for instance, of the Duke of Norfolk, is two hundred and seventy thousand pounds, upwards of one million three hundred and thirty thousand dollars. The Marquis of Bute has a rent roll of two hundred and thirty-two thousand pounds, the Duke of Buccleuch, two hundred and thirty-one thousand pounds, and the Duke of Northumberland, of one hundred and seventy-six thousand pounds. Besides these almost royal revenues, derived from political assignments of the soil, we find, by reference to John Bateman's abridgment of the Domesday book, that in England and Wales, *alone*, there are fifteen hundred and thirty-six persons who own not less than three thousand acres,‡ and that only in a few cases does the rent roll of these estates fall short of three thousand pounds (fifteen thousand dollars), and from that amount, running up to the

* Mulhall's Dictionary of Statistics, page 266. † Ibid., page 272.

‡ Acreocracy of England.

rent roll of the Duke of Norfolk. Mr. Bateman only gives the rent roll of the rural estates. By examining his work it will be seen that several estates are often in the hands of one person, and in this way it appears that several enumerators count the separate *estates* and thus make the number of land owners much greater than it really is. Among the noble land owners, although not the largest, we recognize some names connected with the government. Thus, the Marquis of Salisbury has twenty thousand two hundred and seventy-two acres, and a rent roll from them of thirty-three thousand four hundred and thirteen pounds,* nearly four times the salary paid to the president of the United States, and this tax on the land is supposed to be the property of the Marquis, and all who may come after him, without the slightest reference to the performance of any public duty. The Duke of Bedford has eighty-seven thousand five hundred and seven acres, with a rent roll of one hundred and forty-one thousand five hundred and forty-nine pounds,† about seven hundred thousand dollars per annum. Earl Lonsdale has sixty-seven thousand nine hundred and fifty acres, producing a rent roll of seventy-one thousand two hundred and ten pounds. The Duke of Portland's acres and rent roll are about the same amount.

In addition to the fifteen hundred and thirty-six aristocratic land owners of England and Wales, given by Mr. Bateman as possessing not less than three thousand acres, there is a very considerable number more, who, while they fall below that standard, still have very extensive estates, sufficient to place them independent of exertion, with incomes derived from the natural resources of the country, varying from four or five thousand, to fifty thousand dollars per annum. It will not make the matter much clearer to swell the list of aristocratic names, or enumerate the estates and demesnes of

* Acreocracy of England, page 170. † Ibid., page 14.

princes, knights or lords. From the figures given, the reader can form some kind of an estimate of the fearful mortgage laid on the shoulders of the laborers of England. In no country in Europe are there so few land holders as in the British Empire. Mr. Broderick says: "The number of agricultural land owners was never so small and the population so large." * Besides the noble land owners, there is an army of middlemen, factors, leasing farmers and their adjuncts. The agricultural system of Britain is composed, first, of aristocratic landlords, who, under the law, deduct so much an acre from the producers; second, the leasing or contracting farmers, who employ a capital in the work of agriculture, and make their profit between the rent, the interest they pay the money lenders, and the price they pay for labor; third, the laborers, who get what the leasers and middlemen choose to pay them, and of whom it is only necessary to say that they are very poor and dependent.

During the reign of William the Conqueror, when there were about two million people in England and Wales, there were about one hundred and seventy thousand land owners. Now, when there are twenty millions of people in England and Wales, there are, according to Mr. Broderick, less than one hundred and fifty thousand who own more than an acre and a half, and two thousand two hundred and fifty persons own nearly one-half of the enclosed portion of England and Wales.† There is a real or apparent discrepancy between Mr. Mulhall and Hon. George C. Broderick. A series of official reports, published in 1875 and 1876,.gives a larger number of land proprietors than is given elsewhere. The owners of less than an acre (lot owners outside the city of London, mostly) were eight hundred and fifty-two thousand four hundred and sixty-eight. Of these seven hundred and three thousand two hundred and eighty-nine were in England

* Broderick's Reform of the English Land System, page 9. † Ibid.

and Wales; one hundred and thirteen thousand and five in Scotland, and thirty-six thousand one hundred and fourteen in Ireland. These gave of owners above an acre in England and Wales, two hundred and sixty-nine thousand five hundred and forty-seven; in Scotland, nineteen thousand two hundred and twenty-five; and in Ireland, thirty-two thousand six hundred and fourteen.* The discrepancy between this and the other tables arises from two causes. In the first place the line between urban and rural is in these tables drawn at an acre, while in the others it is an acre and a half. It is also admitted that it was partly caused by enumerating the tracts rather than the owners, several of which belonged to one owner. In France the urban or city population is a small fraction over twenty-four per cent.† and the rural upward of seventy-five per cent. In England, on the other hand, nearly two-thirds of the entire population are urban, or town and city dwellers. In England and Wales the proportion of owners of houses to inhabited houses is one in four; in Scotland, one in three; and in Ireland, one in fourteen.‡ England and Wales, taken by themselves, are more densely populated than any country in Europe except Belgium. By the census of 1881 it contained four hundred and forty-six individuals to the square mile. More than one-fourth of the population of England and Wales is concentrated in London,§ and when we remember the number of her great commercial and manufacturing cities, such as Liverpool, Birmingham, Manchester, Leeds, Sheffield, Bristol, it is not difficult to understand that to-day there is a greater power in England than her agricultural interest.

It is with the agricultural interest we have chiefly to do. We have seen the burdens laid upon it. Those burdens have been steadily increasing for six centuries. Mulhall furnishes

* Statesman's Year Book, 1885, page 252.

† Ibid., page 86. ‡ Ibid., page 252. § Ibid., page 256.

a table of the increase of the rent per acre in England.* In 1230 the land was estimated at a value of about five dollars per acre, the rent two shillings per acre. In 1440 the rent had risen to three shillings; in 1570 to four shillings; in 1660 to six shillings; in 1774 to fifteen shillings; and in 1875 to thirty shillings. In the Statesman's Year Book for 1885, page 253, the estimated average rental in England and Wales is three pounds and two pence. In Scotland the rental is nineteen shillings and nine pence per acre, and in Ireland thirteen shillings and four pence. It will thus be seen that in England and Wales in about six hundred and fifty years the rents had risen from two to sixty shillings an acre. Let us see if produce had risen at the same rates. Mulhall gives a table of the price of wheat for five hundred and eighty years, the average from 1301 to 1350 being eighteen shillings per quarter of eight bushels, running up to 1851; between that year and 1881 wheat averaged fifty-one shillings.† These prices were according to weight of silver, which everybody knows was of much greater value before the discovery of the Americas. Accepting it as a standard, however, it will be observed that while wheat had risen three times in price, rent had risen thirty, or twenty times in price, taking it at the lowest figure in 1440 of three shillings. In the thirteenth and fourteenth centuries wheat, or bread made from it, was the chief food of the people, together with beef and mutton. Six pounds of bread could be got for a penny, a sheep carcass for about a shilling, and a beef carcass ten shillings.‡ Mulhall gives the present standard for beeves of five hundred and sixty pounds, at eight and a half cents, in bulk meat, which would be about forty-seven dollars, for what cost two and a half in the thirteenth and fourteenth centuries, an increase not so great as the increase in rent, but more nearly approximating to it than the grain produced from the land.

* Mulhall's Dictionary of Statistics, page 268. † Ibid., page 476.

‡ Young's Labor in Europe and America, page 85.

During the past five hundred years, Britain in common with the other nations of Western Europe, has been steadily growing in population, wealth, and civilized appliances. I have shown that rent has much more than kept pace with this increase, and the laborer's food thus heavily taxed has risen with the rent, while the soil of Great Britain belongs to a small and progressively decreasing number of persons. This wealth made by the people, stimulated by their genius, and pushed forward by their energy and industry, has thus by a cunningly devised system been absorbed by a small number of persons. The world has seen princely establishments and pampered aristocracies, but never before such an aristocracy as that of modern Britain. Grant that it is an aristocracy of refinement, culture and wealth. The princely residences, stately parks, lawns and country-seats of the British aristocracy constitute a beautiful picture, but it has a reverse dark side.

It is well known to political economists that great revenues are more apt to lead to extravagance and debt than revenues limited by more adverse circumstances. We have called attention to the great incomes derivable from the British land law and land system and it would appear to be an easy matter to live not only in elegance, but to spare a liberal portion of the revenues, so derived, for the benefit of the laboring classes, who have, by cruel methods, been deprived of their share of the common heritage. Upon the contrary, the aristocracy of England seem to be quite as much hampered by their own extravagance as the poorer classes are by their poverty. By a table showing the mortgages on real estate in various countries, these liens amount in Britain to one billion six hundred million pounds, while France, although larger, with a greater agricultural population, carries only seven hundred and seventy million pounds debt.* Germany, another despotic aristocracy, stands even higher than Britain,

* Mulhall's Dictionary of Statistics, page 322.

being one billion seven hundred million. The percentage of mortgages to the value of all real estate in these countries is forty-one per cent. in England, seventeen in France, and forty-nine per cent. in Germany; Holland eighteen and Scandinavia thirteen per cent. It has been claimed by British economists that the English system of agriculture—an aristocratic landlord, a capitalist speculating tenant farmer, and laborers—is the best for high tilth and productive farming; but the export and import tables of France and Britain do not seem to favor this theory. Mr. Hoskyn says that the limited ownership of entail in Britain is unfavorable to improvements.* In other words, the law of entail has created separate interests in the families of the British landed interest. But for the laws of entail and primogeniture their extravagance would have broken up the British aristocratic land owners long ago. The aristocratic idea is to cement the whole property in the Kingdom in a small decreasing class; a conflict arises about the younger sons, not to mention daughters. A reasonably considerate British aristocrat, while willing to perpetuate the pride and power of his family, still wishes and strives to make some kind of a settlement for his wife and younger sons. If he can, he quarters one on the church and one on the army. As the landlords monopolize political power, he gets some official position under the government, or in India, or one of the colonies, for a third. Portions must be had for the daughters. To begin with, most of the landlords attempt a style of living nearly or quite up to their rent roll. Poor man! with an income from an estate, called his, he may have a revenue of twenty or fifty thousand pounds a year, and be at his wits end to meet his obligations. How can he invest much capital to improve his farms merely for the benefit of his oldest son who is to inherit them? If he is not destitute of economy, he saves to make his widow and younger children some provision at his death; and if he should

* Systems of Land Tenure, page 193.

not be able, he tries to induce the eldest son, before he has escaped the influence of home, and is still in the callow state, to tie up the estate with settlements, which forces the new holder to resort to economical practices his father would not adopt. How is the son to save any money to invest in permanent improvements or cottages for laborers. If he expends at all, it is probably in beautifying his country-seat, for that flatters his pride. Hoskyn says: "No well-drawn settlement omits to make provision for the widow and younger children.* The law of primogeniture makes a will for a man which he ought to deem it an insult to be accused of making for himself." Mr. Caird, in writing after a careful survey of the agricultural regions of England in 1851, says: "A far greater portion of it than is generally supposed (by the evidence exceeding two-thirds of the Kingdom) is in the possession of tenants for life so heavily burdened with settlements and encumbrances that they have not the *means* of improving the land they are obliged to hold." The "younger son" question has been the curse of the British aristocracy. Hon. James E. Thorold Rogers, M.P., writes: "The development of the younger son as a social pauper and a social leech is at the bottom of most of the provincial extravagances and all the financial meanness of the English administrations to our own day." † The law of primogeniture, he says further, "perpetuated the poverty of the younger son and the system of quartering him on the public purse." What else *could* an affectionate aristocratic father do? The system of British land tenure permitted him to derive revenues during life from the heritage of the English people, and as he must keep the aristocratic system intact as a constant hereditary leech on the public, why should he not use the public offices for his younger sons, as Rogers intimates, "the post offices or the civil list"? If he robbed Peter for the benefit of his family, why not rob Paul?

* Systems of Land Tenure, page 192.

† Six Centuries of Work and Wages, page 295.

In ascertaining the precise position occupied by the working people of England, it is not only necessary to ascertain the prices of labor and food, but the system of farming by land-owners, and finally, by capitalist leasing farmers. In ancient times the farm laborer, whatever he was or might be styled, had his cottage privileges, pasturage for his cows and other animals on the commons, which, although claimed by the lords, had not been recognized as his property by the people. The sixteenth, seventeenth and eighteenth centuries were marked by the fencing in of these commons by the aristocracy, who thus became the stock raisers. The agricultural laborer who originally held his cottage and home patch without let or hindrance, first had to give so much service for the use of them, and finally was deprived of them altogether. In estimating his wages, therefore, an account must be taken for the loss of his garden patch, his cow, pig or poultry. He at last became merely a house tenant paying rent, has to walk several miles each day to his labor, and his wages must meet all his extra expenses. The landlords originally farmed part of their land. They did so to some extent on shares with the laborers. They furnished stock, and, if necessary, seed. If a misfortune brought a poor crop he was of necessity part loser. A new system was introduced as the land became more valuable, and the aristocratic landlord, less inclined to bear any burdens or responsibilities connected with agriculture; he rented his land to capitalist tenants, who paid him a rent. The rent, or this tribute exacted by the noble claimant from the soil, now constitutes his only connection with it. His only interest is to get the largest income derivable from the acres, claimed to be his, that is possible. With the laborer whose work makes the land productive he has nothing to do. The renter, or middleman, stands between him and the tiller of the soil. This intermediate person is not a laborer. He is a species of contractor or speculator. In raising wheat or other commodities his first expense is rent, that must be paid.

Then comes the expense of implements, stock, seed, and interest on capital invested, and last, labor. Prices confront him on one hand and these items of expenditure on the other. No matter what happens the rent he must pay; his profits must be derived from what he can save out of his other expenditures. He is, therefore, a very cunningly devised "squeezing machine." Rogers says: "The rate of wages is lower when the principal employers are small tenant farmers, if the number of laborers is considerable enough to compete against each other for employment." * The landlord was never so able to screw down his laborers as the leasing tenant. When the change came, from cultivating landlords to cultivating leasers, then came another thing, rack-rent. This first began in the sixteenth century and seems to have continued and increased. If any one is inclined to call in question the great power of laws of inheritance and laws to regulate tenure, the distribution or diminution of land ownership, let him carefully study the British land system. Here we have an aristocracy perpetuated by adroit combination of law. The leasing farmers, or at least many of them, are men of some means. They are business men. They and their families become attached to the homes they lease. This sentiment, among many other things, has been an effective spur to rack-rent. Under fair conditions they would naturally become owners of the soil, but they cannot. As has been shown, the number of aristocratic landholders is steadily diminishing. The system of leases in England has not been as favorable for improvements by the *tenant* as it might have been. In Scotland the landlord often makes the improvements, but they charge their tenants a percentage on the outlay.† Owing to the rapid rise in rents the landlords were averse to granting long leases. Hoskyn says: "The want of a law to secure

* Six Centuries of Work and Wages, page 215.

† Short Talks about Land Tenure by a Tenant Farmer, page 9.

tenants, to some extent, the value of the improvements made by them, and which they must leave, costs the agricultural interests of England millions." * He thinks that leases for a lifetime would offer the highest inducement to such improvements, as every man construes the uncertainties of life in his own favor. So strong is the spirit of enterprise among the farming class in England, that even on short leases they are tempted to make improvements by which they will only partially benefit. The tenancies are generally made up of a number of plots, the time for which they run being different. A farmer will sometimes have five or six separate holdings from the same landlord that expire at different times. This probably arose from the fact that farmers were usually trying to add to the size of their farms, and in this way *small holdings* were absorbed by greater.† Mr. Rogers states, in this connection, that before Henry VIII. confiscated the lands of the church, estimated to be about one-third of the kingdom, the priests, fearing such a result, began to make long leases for forty years.‡ It has been said that the leasing tenant and the landlord have the same interest, which is to exact everything for nothing from the laborer. This is not exactly correct. It is true, the tenant has to keep on fair terms with the landlord so as to renew his leases, but their interest can hardly be said to be identical. "We pull in the same boat," said an English landlord to his tenant. "Yes," was the reply, "but in opposite directions." § The leasers, although a respectable class of some influence and standing, are not the old English yeomen. Most of the old yeoman manor houses were absorbed by the landed aristocracy, and the occupants driven into cities and towns.|| Broderick thinks it would be a public advantage if the old extravagant

* Systems of Land Tenure, page 194.

† Six Centuries of Work and Wages, page 296. ‡ Ibid., page 297.

§ Systems of Land Tenure, page 198.

|| Broderick's Reform of the English Land System, page 8.

landholders could be forced to sell, or separated from their possessions. If the new owner was not encumbered with debts and mortgages he would not be so tempted to oppress and grind his tenants. In fact it is the extravagant pride of the aristocratic landholders that has for ages built up a system of expenditure and a style of living, the maintenance of which they consider indispensable to British civilization.

The condition of the working agricultural laborers, long neglected, should be the first thing to consider. Hoskyn says: "We often hear of the English land system as comprising the landlord, the tenant and the laborer; so, in a certain sense, it does, but no one who considers the position of the laborer in English agriculture will assert that he has any fixed personal tie within the structure." * In point of fact, he is nothing more than a mere auxiliary, more or less in demand at different seasons, subject to the precarious vicissitudes of that demand. Until recent times, the laborer was the recognized inmate of the farmer's home. Still further back than that, the bond that tied him to the soil was the bond of servitude, but it nevertheless connected him with it; his employer was usually the owner of the land he tilled. "Time has changed all this, but the law that freed him from serfdom, stripped him of all interest in the soil. The same English reign that awarded him his freedom marks the origin of the poor law system. Ominous association! He is at present disconnected with all that is known of the progress of society." † The introduction of machinery, while it takes away some of his importance, cannot be said to relieve him from toil. The increase in population is only a menace to his occupation. The increase of wealth, which he does not share, widens the breach between him and the more favored classes. The rise in land and rent only renders it still more impossible

* Systems of Land Tenure, page 201. † Ibid., page 204.

for him to acquire it. Farming by machinery and with capital, on scientific methods, drives the small tenant farmers into the class of laborers, or to the towns. "The law of parish settlement swept away cottages, so the laborer rents a shelter elsewhere and is exhausted traveling to and from his work."* "The laborer is no longer belonging to the glebe. He is free to come and go as he pleases, but without part or parcel in the land he helps to cultivate or any certain abode on it, or in connection with it, for himself or for his family."† Speaking of the present position of the British agricultural laborer, Mr. Fawcett says: "Theirs is a life of incessant toil for wages too scanty to give them a sufficient supply even of the first necessaries of life. No hope cheers their monotonous career. A life of constant labor brings them no other prospect than that when their strength is exhausted they must crave, as suppliant mendicants, for a pittance from parish relief."‡

The statisticians and political economists estimate that the manual labor of an arable farm covers one-third of the entire cost of production. One would think that to pay the laborer one-third, which it is extremely doubtful if he receives, as the item of profit is not included, is not an extravagant estimate, but the farmers are continually complaining about the "costliness" of this item of their year's accounts. Mr. Rogers says: "It has been urged that cheap labor is a necessity for profitable agriculture, which means that the tenant farmers are too cowardly to resist rents which they cannot pay except by the degradation of those they employ."§ Mr. Hoskyn writes: "The condition of the agricultural laborer is something to be preached against as a standing subject of charity, philanthropy, state grants and emigration."‖ He adds: "The farm laborer of England is like a slag thrown out of the fur-

* Systems of Land Tenure, page 206. † Ibid., page 204.

‡ Economic Position of the British Laborer, page 6.

§ Six Centuries of Work and Wages, page 513.

‖ Systems of Land Tenure, page 207.

nace." The most astute of political economists can see no way through his labor to better his condition. Mr. Bailey Denton, in a speech, remarks, "The only way to justify the increase of the laborer's wages will be by rendering the value of the labor greater than it now is." * To show that abundance has been produced, Mr. Fawcett says: "The most conclusive evidence exists that the production of wealth in this country is so vast and so rapidly augmenting that it is idle to say that poverty exists because enough wealth is not produced." † To quote Mr. Hoskyn: "It would be a libel on any class of this generation to charge upon it the isolated phenomenon which the agricultural laborer presents in the midst of growing wealth; standing against it, this growing poverty that is separating the growing life of England." The following is from a speech of the president of the Poor Law Board: "Constantly increasing rates, constantly increasing pauperism, millions of money spent, yet without satisfaction, and, infinitely worse, millions of human beings whose very name implies a degradation, even in their own eyes, as recipients of parochial relief." The "retired tenant farmer," in his "Short Talks about Land Tenure," says: "1. One country is *said* to be *wealthier* than another when the aggregate of money or other articles that will produce money, possessed by its inhabitants, is greater in proportion to their number than that possessed by the inhabitants of another country. 2. One country is more *prosperous* than another when it supports, in proportion to its size, a larger number of persons in greater comfort than the other country, or, to put it more distinctly, *that country is the most prosperous which supports the greatest number in the greatest comfort.*" ‡ C. Wren Hoskyn holds: "The soil was not meant for idle enjoyment even by its unoccupying owners."

* The Agricultural Laborer.

† Economic Position of the British Laborer, page 6.

‡ Short Talks about Land Tenure, page 48.

Under these circumstances we may pause to inquire just the extent of the freedom and independence gained for the British laborer by the struggles of the past six centuries. Charles I., with his bigoted, despotic spirit, tried to restore serfdom and the worst features of the feudal system, but did not succeed. The nominal and final abolition of feudalism occurred in the first year of the reign of the second Charles. The mistake was, that during the troubled times of the commonwealth and the restoration, the lands wrongfully seized from the people were not restored to them. "Those who own the land rule the country," and Britain has been ruled by the landlords ever since, and they have ruled it in their own interests. A careful examination of the condition of the English laborer as serf, villein and hired laborer, does not really show such a progress as English civilization ought to be able to boast of. Mr. Hoskyn truly says, "Dependence has its advantages and independence its charms, but the laborer's lot is so cast as to derive the minimum benefit from either.*" Certainly, the hardest part of his fate has been to leave him a homeless waif. His land, originally, stolen by the noble, the commons fenced up so he could keep no cows or get fuel from the forest, his cottage and garden taken, partly because so long as it stood it was like a ghost of his right to the land, and partly because it disfigured the landscape. In this dilemma about laborers' cottages the government is invoked to lend the public money, drained by taxation, to land improvement companies, empowered by Act of parliament to build laborers cottages on gentlemen's estates.† Dr. Hunter, the medical officer of the privy council, in his Seventh Report, inquires "whether all land that requires labor ought not to be *held liable* to the obligation of containing a certain portion of laborers' dwellings." It is strange that he was not denounced as a "communist," and his report

* Systems of Land Tenure, page 206.

† Ibid., page 207.

as an "incendiary document." Hoskyn asks, "Whose duty is it to provide, under our system of universal tenancy, the laborer with a home that may connect him with his work? The leasing farmer cannot build laborers' cottages." In the first place the land is not his, and if he attempted to build cottages, with gardens attached, it is probable that the landlord would make him pay extra rent for them. Besides, if, in order to be able to pay the heavy rent he is responsible for, he has to reduce the laborer's wages almost to starvation rates, how can he build cottages for the laborers. On the other hand, the laborer is not the landlord's workman. It is nothing to the landlord whence the laborer comes or whither he goes. If any man could invent an automaton to do the laborer's work, and the landlord felt interested at all in labor, he would probably recommend the laborer to try emigration as a relief for all his ills. The tenant's business is to make the most he can during his short lease, and if he can afford it, try to get a renewal. It is the landlord's business to get all the rent he can, so as to meet his settlements and mortgages, and enable his family to live in the position they have been accustomed to. Political society, as it were, is committed to his privileges; has, as the Duke of Argyle says, "recognized such ownership for ages and encouraged it." * After all, the laborer is not the employer's tenant. The man who employs cannot house him, and the man who could does not employ him. The case has thus been cleverly put by a gentleman who understood it: "The question of a cottage for the farm laborer becomes, under our system, one of those detached problems that fall into the waste basket of pure philanthropy." †

In the early part of the fifteenth century the average cost of a laborer's board was nine pence a week. In the famine year 1348–9 it rose to an average of one shilling six pence.

* Argyle's Prophet of San Francisco, in Nineteenth Century, for April, 1884.

† Systems of Land Tenure, page 207.

There was not much variation in the price of board until the issue of base money. In 1542 board and lodging are put at one shilling a week, but in ten years it had risen to an average of three shillings a week. In 1562, 1563 and 1570, Queen Elizabeth makes quarterly contracts for victualling her workmen in the dockyards. In the first year the contract is an average of four shillings half pence; in the second year, four shillings six pence; in the third year, at three shillings eleven pence.* The variation being on account of dear and cheap years. The queen also rented lodgings for the workmen, at two pence a week, the contract being that the men should have feather beds, and that two should lie in a bed, and that the queen should find sheets and pay for washing them, at the rate of one pence a pair. In 1562 the average price of labor was four shillings nine and a half pence a week. In 1565, four shillings half pence. In 1570, four shillings seven pence. In 1573, four shillings eleven and a half pence. In 1577, four shillings ten and a half pence, and in 1578, four shillings eight pence.† The queen having found that which was making her laborers poor was making her poor also, as rents, dues and subsidies were fixed, and the purchasing power of money had fallen to about one-third of its ancient capacity, she had a proclamation drafted declaring that the shilling should circulate at eight pence. Her advisers, however, induced her to suppress the document, fearing that it would be obnoxious to the charge that the crown was trying arbitrarily to enhance its demands against its debtors. In point of fact, it would have enhanced the dues of every creditor and saddled an additional burden on every debtor. In addition to the debasement of the coin, a more potent cause of the failure in the purchasing power of money was the introduction of vast amounts of gold and silver from the Americas, discovered by the Europeans, in 1492, the richest of the American

* Six Centuries of Work and Wages, page 354.

† Ibid.

nations having been robbed during the intervening period. A similar great influx of the precious metals occurred about the middle of this century, on the discovery of gold in Australia and California, and the development of silver mines by improved machinery. The great capitalists of the world finding this reduced the value of their accumulations, have labored to strike down one of the standards, silver being selected, thus to increase the value of what they received from those who owed them. Much of the increase of prices and wages in the past four hundred and fifty years is governed by the decreasing purchasing power of money.

In the days of Queen Elizabeth several laws were enacted affecting laborers, a few of them professedly in their interest. One of these was the law authorizing the judges of the quarter sessions to fix the price of labor in each county. This act continued in force until 1812. Another statute of Elizabeth, 5 cap. 4, enacts "that no person shall work at any trade, mystery or occupation who has not served a seven years' apprenticeship." A list prepared by the judges was issued in a proclamation by Elizabeth, in 1564, as a guide to other authorities. These lists were begun by Burleigh and continued by Cecil. The ordinary citizen is to have nine pence a day in summer, and eight pence in winter. The laborers are to have seven pence in summer, *except harvest*, at which time they have eight pence and ten pence; in winter the laborers to get six pence. With the increased price of wheat and other articles it was required of the laborers, under this list, to give forty weeks' work for that which he obtained in 1495, for fifteen weeks' labor.* In 1593 another table of laborers' wages was fixed, under which the laborer was required to work a whole year to buy what he could have purchased in 1495 by fifteen weeks' labor. In 1610 the Rutland magistrates made their assessment of the price of labor. Under

* Six Centuries of Work and Wages, page 390.

this scale, compared with the prices of the staple articles he had to buy, such as bread, an artisan had to work forty-three weeks to buy what he could have purchased for ten weeks' work in 1495.* It will thus be seen that the quarter sessions magistrates did not let their power lie idle, and it could scarcely be said to be used in the interest of the laborers. Indeed, there was a continual complaint on the part of employers that laborers refused to work, or were unwilling to work, for such wages as they could afford to pay. Another of the enactments of "the good Queen Bess," was to arrest all persons without an occupation, and punish or sell them. It has been stated that it was this statute of Elizabeth that suggested to the Russian despot the idea of reducing his agricultural laborers to serfdom. In 1495 an artisan computing the price of wheat and labor earned a bushel of wheat in a day, and an ordinary laborer, three-quarters of a bushel.† Taking this standard and comparing it at different dates, a pretty fair estimate can be made. One very important matter, however, has to be taken into consideration. In 1495, and long after, the laborers of England had certain advantages, of which they have since been deprived, that added to their productive means of support. The ancient laborer of England, down to the sixteenth, seventeenth and eighteenth centuries, had his cottage and garden, and the right to graze his cow or cows, sheep and pigs on the common pasture. By the increase in population and the subsequent rise in the price of land and rent, the nobles fenced up the common lands, thus distinctly asserting a private claim to them. This was the subject of great complaint at the time, and ought to have been resisted. The landowners, however, made the laws, and the only way of meeting such usurpation would have been by insurrection or armed resistance.

The insurrection of Watt Tyler and Jack Cade were peasant

* Six Centuries of Work and Wages, page 392. † Ibid., page 389.

and artisan insurrections, and although formidable, were suppressed by means of murder, bad faith and treachery, and crushed with the most ruthless cruelty. These earlier insurrections had reference not only to the seizure of the land, but serfdom. The demand made by Watt Tyler and his leading companions, of the king, was one that ennobled those who demanded it. The insurrection was widespread, and an army under Tyler had marched to London, and there was no adequate force to resist it. The young king and the royal family took refuge in the tower, which Tyler notified them he would take unless an interview was granted. Richard demanded what they wanted. They answered: "You will make us free forever, our heirs and *our lands,* and that we be called no more bond or villeins, or so reputed."* The immediate and prompt assent might have aroused the suspicion of these simple, well-meaning men. Richard urged them to return to their homes and leave three men from each town to receive the charters which he promised to give. Many of the insurgents, misled by his promises, obeyed, *trusting to the word of a king.* It is supposed that Tyler, who was undoubtedly a man of moderation as well as capacity, reduced the great force he had because it was subsisted with difficulty. He remained, however, with thirty thousand men to see the pledge carried out. The king put thirty clerks at work to make the charters, and one of them dated June 15th, 1381, is preserved in Walsingham, addressed to the authorities of Hertfordshire. King Richard spoke the insurgents fair, but, it is said, he assured his counselors he would yet take vengeance on them. Whether the king ever meant good faith is uncertain; but as he did not keep it, he deserves no credit. He and the nobles were secretly plotting to get sufficient force together to crush the rebels. The young king was even attempting to escape from London. As the whole country was full of the insurrectionary spirit, it

* Six Centuries of Work and Wages, page 258.

is difficult to see where he could have gone. As the king and his party came near Tyler, the latter told his men to fall back and proceeded alone to the interview, no doubt feeling that in the honor of those who sought this interview he was safe. He was instantly set upon and murdered by the Lord Mayor of London. That the insurgents did not utterly destroy the whole royal party is surprising. The king affected indignation and renewed his promises, and on these promises the armed people were induced to go home. As soon as the king and the nobles became sufficiently fortified, the work of vengeance began. Not less than fifteen hundred of the leaders of the insurrection were executed. The spirit of resistance among the people was not altogether subdued. To make a pretence of escaping the question of dishonor, it was argued that it was beyond the province of the king to free the serfs and free the land. It was the same story, "vested rights." The Parliament of landed aristocrats alone could do that. The king referred the question to them, and they having recovered breath from their fright, resolved "That all grants of liberties and manumissions to the said villeins and bond tenants obtained by force are in disherison of them, the lords and Commons, and to the destruction of the realm, and therefore null and void;" and they added "that this consent they never would give to save themselves from perishing all together in one day." * If all such tyrants had "perished all together in one day," it would have been no great calamity to the realm. In spite of their vainglorious resolve, serfdom was abolished, but only through fear. The "free land" the people claimed was not given to them. The agricultural Englishman, by the very terms of his manumission, was divorced from the mother soil that bore him; when degrading servitude ended, landlordism began. The result through these centuries has proved that they who monopolize the land have ample means for rob-

* Six Centuries of Work and Wages, page 263.

bing human labor without nominal slavery, and in the face of a high civilization these exactions from the people have been perpetuated. The English historians usually distort or speak lightly of the insurrections of Watt Tyler and Jack Cade. They are held up to ridicule now as "communists." What they asked speaks for itself, and must commend its merits to every fair-minded, honorable man. Watt Tyler was one of the most eminent of Englishmen; of undoubted ability and great moderation, restraining his followers from excesses, and only asking for the just rights of the people. It is doubtful if it would add to his fame to place his monument in Westminster, but it is not likely to be done so long as a greedy, landed aristocracy rules England. It was an insurrection of artisans and laborers, and was unsuccessful because it was merciful and moderate, and because the king and selfish aristocrats did not hesitate at falsehood, treachery and murder.

A great change came gradually over England. Driven by tyranny too hard to bear, the most independent fled to the towns. Commerce and manufactures were built up. A power stronger than agriculture arose. The very existence of Britain to-day would be impossible without its commerce and manufactures. As a nation, it imports a great portion of the bread and meat it eats, and pays for them by manufactures, and by performing much of the carrying trade of the world. The manufactures and commerce of England have been built up, not by the aristocracy, but by workmen from the people. Watt, Arkwright, Wedgewood and many others like them, created the modern power in England. Half the people of England find their occupation in the industries such men began. The poor agricultural laborer of Britain has been so impoverished and crippled that he has ceased to be a power in the realm he should have helped to rule. The manufacturing and commercial classes have been too strong to be altogether ignored, and a little power has, from time to time, been reluctantly conceded to them, but all efforts in the direction of doing justice to the people have been defeated by a set of parasitic landholders. It was not the wars of the Crusades, or the French and other wars carried on by the landed aristocratic order for the benefit of the younger sons that built up the power of England. The British empire of to-day is the creation of the working-people of England. The aristocracy, however, has managed to get much benefit from the development of the country. The great commercial activity, and the demand it created, enabled them to double and treble their rents. They thus incidentally were able to place the sturdy burgher of Birmingham, Leeds and Manchester under tribute as they previously had the agricultural laborer. No one can tell the depths to which the agricultural laborer of Britain would have sunk had it not been for the great manufacturing and commercial activity which kept up the price of wages. An examination of the wages of workers in the factories and shops of Britain shows that they are better paid than in most countries on the continent, although the English artisans are not so well paid as the same class in the United States. Robert Giffen, Esq., has endeavored to trace "the progress of the working classes in the last half century" in Britain, and demonstrates that their condition has improved in that time. It would have been wonderful if it had not. Fifty per cent., at least, of the inventions that have added wealth and power to modern civilization have been created in that period. Our railroad system is little more than fifty years old, and steam navigation, practically, not older than the century. The wealth created in that time is perfectly enormous, and it would have been strange if the people, to whom the country owed its production, had not reaped some small advantage. What he *does not* prove, or, indeed, attempt to prove, is, that an equal share, in proportion to their numbers, of this increased wealth, has gone into the pockets of the laboring classes. As everybody knows, including Mr. Giffen, nothing of that kind has happened. Mr. Mulhall, under the head of accumulations in Great Britain, gives the increase of wealth during the decade from 1870 to 1880, as four hundred thousand pounds, or two million dollars per day. This is just as he says, three pence per day to each inhabitant, man, woman and child in the British empire, or forty-five pounds twelve shillings and sixpence each, for the ten years. This amount we will suppose, for the sake of argument to Mr. Giffen and the rest of the political economists, was created by the labor and capital of England. At the rate of five persons to a family, that would be two hundred and twenty-eight pounds two shillings and six pence to each head of a family. Now, does Mr. Giffen, or Mr. Mallock, or anybody else pretend for a moment that the working people found themselves, at the end of the ten years, with that much accumulated capital in their pockets, or anything like it? The most his tables show is that *perhaps* the laborers are a little better fed and a little better clad than they were at a particular period fifty years ago. Will either of these gentlemen tell us in whose pockets this immense accumulation of wealth has lodged? It may be said that the laborer is improvident and intemperate. Are the laborers more intemperate and extravagant than the aristocratic landholders of Britain? It is just to concede that there are many persons in both these classes given to improvidence and excess. He gives a table * comparing the wages at the present time with those of fifty years ago in Great Britain. Carpenters fifty years ago had but twenty-four shillings a week, now, thirty-four shillings; masons, twenty-four shillings then, and now, twenty-nine shillings ten pence; pattern weavers, sixteen shillings then, twenty-five shillings now; Bradford weavers, eight shillings three pence then, twenty shillings six pence now; spinners, twenty-five shillings six pence then, thirty shillings now. That will give a fair idea of his table. Wheat,

* Progress of the Working Classes in the Last Half Century, page 5.

he claims, if not lower, at least, is not higher, and sugar and cotton cloth lower. Animal food has risen more in proportion than wages. House rent, according to his table,* was twenty shillings fifty years ago, forty shillings at the present time. His conclusion is that, comparing prices with wages, there is a "real gain." If he had carefully considered all the items of expenditure he would have found that the condition of the laborer was but little improved,—another fact in reference to his table which refers to the work of mechanics and artisans he has not noted; and it affects its accuracy: fifty years ago there was a great depression of the mercantile interests of Britain, especially among weavers. The introduction of many new kinds of machinery, to the conditions of which the workmen had not time to adjust themselves, had unsettled great manufacturing industries. Thousands and tens of thousands were idle. Public relief and "soup kitchens" were organized in a wholesale way, and this depression continued for a considerable number of years before and after the period Mr. Giffen fixes for the first date in his tables. It is probably true that the British artisan and laborer is slightly better off than he was fifty years ago. Four centuries ago the average English workman was certainly wealthier than he is to-day.† Another thing Mr. Giffen seems to forget, and that is, how far the laboring classes are better off as compared with the wealth of other classes. Another cause and one produced by the depression, a great emigration set in, or rather set *out* from Great Britain about that time. From 1820 to 1882, eight million five hundred and seventy thousand emigrated from Britain; ‡ of these, five million three hundred and seventy-seven thousand came to the United States, and three million one hundred and sixteen thousand went to the British colonies. These emigrants numbered more than one-fifth of the

* Progress of the Working Classes in the Last Half Century, page 14.

† Workingmen Co-operators, page 30.

‡ Mulhall's Dictionary of Statistics, page 168.

present population of Great Britain, and it is safe to say that they were chiefly from the laboring classes. Statistics, by the by, are a very mysterious contrivance. Thus, we find it stated, that the yearly consumption of grain per inhabitant in Britain, is three hundred and thirty pounds; of meat, one hundred and five pounds.* Now, while this amount of animal food is less than one-third of a pound a day, it would be a gross mistake to suppose that the poor artisans and laborers eat even that small amount. The figure is what is termed an aggregate, and is the amount he would have eaten if he had eaten his proportionate share of what was consumed. All Mr. Giffen has been able to demonstrate is that artisans and operatives get wages to-day that can purchase, even according to his showing, just a very little more than they could fifty years ago. With the great majority of the laboring poor, their circumstances, everything considered, are not much better, and that, too, in face of the fact that the wealth and productive power of the nation, as an aggregate, has doubled or trebled. In the same way, Mr. Mallock, in attempting to bring statistics to bear on Mr. Henry George and Mr. Hyndman proceeds to show that in 1843 the gross income of the nation was five hundred and fifteen million pounds; in 1851 it was six hundred and sixteen million pounds; in 1864, eight hundred and fourteen million pounds, and, since 1880, it has reached or exceeded one billion two hundred million pounds.† He then proceeds to ascertain the amount in each of these years that was assessed for income tax, the tax being on incomes of one hundred and fifty pounds or more. He ascertains that in 1843 only two hundred and eighty million pounds of the five hundred and fifteen millions was assessed, and seems to take it for granted that all over the first figures was the income of people having less than one hundred and fifty pounds a year.

* Mulhall's Dictionary of Statistics, page 205.

† Mallock's Property and Progress, page 202.

Absurd as such data must appear, real or approximate, it would not, if true, be a very flattering statement, as the income tax-payers are numbered by hundreds of thousands, and those who do not pay income tax, by tens of millions. In 1851 Mr. Mallock thinks that although the gross income of the nation had increased one hundred and one millions of pounds, "strangely enough," the income tax was no larger. We are familiar with such data in this country. He assumes, however, that the extra income had gone to those in moderate or poor circumstances. When he gets to 1880, with a gross national income of one billion two hundred million, the income tax has only been obtained from five hundred and seventy-seven million, and thus he makes it appear that more than half of the gross income of the nation has gone to those who had less than one hundred and fifty pounds a year. Happy people! This style of statistics is quite facetious. In this country great fortunes of twenty, fifty or even one hundred millions, when viewed through the spectacles of an property tax collector, dwindle from millions to paltry thousands. It may be urged that the British wealthy classes are a high-toned, honest, truthful class, and never resort to subterfuges to reduce their taxable income. One instance was brought to the writer's notice very early in life, and juvenile though he was, he did not forget it. When the window tax prevailed in Britain, a tax of about five dollars a window, for each window over a small number exempted, the then Duke of Argyle kept a few mechanics "adding to" and "finishing" Inverary Castle; as the tax could only be collected when the building was "finished," it was cheaper to continue to build than to pay taxes. I have no doubt that many noble lords and distinguished gentlemen have been in many ways equally ingenious in evading the tax collector, and that income tax returns are rather an unsafe basis for statistical tables showing the relative wealth of parties. Having obtained his statistical basis, however, Mr. Mallock proceeds to erect his superstructure thereon. He places the population of Great Britain in 1843 at twenty-seven millions in round numbers; in 1864, at thirty millions, and, at the present time, thirty-six millions. Taking the basis of wealth to which we have referred, he proceeds, "We know that of this increase of numbers, the larger part, proportionally, is to be attributed to the richer classes. They have increased by more than two hundred per cent., or from one million five hundred thousand, to four million seven hundred thousand; while the poorer classes, on the contrary, have increased but twenty per cent., or from twenty-six million in 1843, to thirty million now. Hence, the same number of them that in 1843 had two hundred and thirty-five million pounds, had, in 1851, three hundred and thirty-six million pounds, and a number that is barely greater by one-fifth, has, annually, by this time, six hundred and twenty million pounds." * By this arithmetic of Mr. Mallock's he has a population of four million seven hundred thousand people enjoying an income of one hundred and fifty pounds. I suppose, allowing nearly five persons to a family, this would give us about one million families. Let us see. Mr. Mulhall's work for 1884 gives the latest classification for 1887, as follows: † It is classified thus: ninety incomes of over fifty thousand pounds (some of these over one million pounds); one thousand and sixty-seven incomes of from ten to fifty thousand pounds; twenty-one thousand six hundred and ninety-one incomes of from one to ten thousand pounds. Mr. Mulhall makes the annual earnings of the British nation one billion two hundred and forty-seven million pounds, and the amount per inhabitant, thirty-six pounds, or about one hundred and seventy-three dollars.‡ He also gives the average income (if equally divided) at thirty-five pounds.§ Going back to

* Mallock's Property and Progress, page 202.

† Mulhall's Dictionary of Statistics, page 247. ‡ Ibid. 246.

§ Mulhall's (table) Dictionary of Statistics, page 473.

Mr. Mallock, he says: "Now if we state this increase in terms of the average income per family, we find that each family among the poorer classes in England had in 1843 about forty pounds a year; in 1851 had fifty-eight pounds, and that at the present it has between ninety-five and one hundred pounds."* He adds: "Of course, this is a general average only and does not correspond exactly to the real facts in the case." We should think not. If we subtract the enormous incomes, running into millions, and the larger number of what might still be called princely incomes, and so on down to the tens of thousands and thousands, all these the incomes of the *non-productive* classes, largely obtained without consideration from the bulk of the national income, the remainder would be the amount received by the middle and lower classes. A large amount of this would be paid to the middle classes, leaving the lowest amount individually to the actual laborers. In the United States consular reports for 1885, just issued, the following prices of agricultural labor are given: In Gloucestershire, England, the average wage, without food or lodging, is in summer, per week, $3.65; in winter, $2.91. Females for ordinary field work, per week, without food or lodging, receive $1.14; females at harvest, $2.13. In Wiltshire and Dorsetshire, males in summer are paid $2.91, males in winter, $2.67, women field workers, $1.46.† These latter are weeks wages without food or lodging. In the Hull district, farm laborers by the year, with board and lodging, get twenty-nine to seventy-two dollars. In county of York, farm laborers, first class, get by the week, four dollars and six cents, with cottage but no board. Second class farm laborers obtain three dollars and seventy cents, without board or lodging. Ploughmen get sixty-eight to seventy-eight dollars per year, with board and lodging; plough boy, forty-eight to sixty-eight dol-

† Mallock's Property and Progress, page 204.

* Consular Reports, 1885, page 81.

lars. Blacksmiths are paid per day, ninety-six cents; joiners, ninety-six cents,—that is without board or lodging, but both receive two glasses of beer a day.* Agricultural laborers in Newcastle hire by the half year for the season's work. For the men by this half year season, forty-eight to seventy-eight dollars are paid; boys, seventeen to twenty-four dollars; females, thirty-one dollars and sixty-four cents to girls, and forty-three dollars and eighty cents for women.† Although not stated this is presumably with board. In Dundee, Scotland, United States Consul Wells writes, that the food of the working classes is "simple and homely, breakfast,—porridge and milk, or tea or coffee with bread and butter and perhaps eggs, small bit of bacon or herring. Dinner,—is frequently Scotch broth cooked with cabbage or other vegetables and beef in small quantities. Supper,—tea with bread and butter. Mill and factory girls who do not reside at home are compelled to live more plainly, their wages being insufficient to procure them the fare here specified."‡ The consul says: "The working classes in Dundee are poorly provided for in the way of house accommodations. There are in the city, eight thousand six hundred and twenty houses, of *only* one room each, occupied by twenty-three thousand six hundred and seventy persons." He speaks of the condition of these single-room "hovels" as places where "five or six human beings are sheltered with nothing to lie on but the floor and covering themselves, when they have an opportunity, with jute burlaps, which they take in to make into hand-sewed bags." The condition of the British laborer and workman two or three hundred years ago was certainly not so utterly wretched. Agricultural laborers, such as the foreman of a farm, get one hundred and fifty-five dollars and fifty cents a year with house, garden, one-half gallon of milk, two and one-half pounds oatmeal and six or seven pounds of potatoes per day. Second

* Consular Reports, 1885, page 82. † Ibid. ‡ Ibid.

and third hands, near Dundee, get one hundred and six dollars and ninety-two cents to one hundred and thirty-six dollars, with milk and meal and sleeping accommodations, with fire in "boothy." Ordinary hands get an average of sixty-seven cents a day. "Outworkers," females, per day on an average, thirty-three cents; during harvest, eighty-seven cents; during potato lifting, forty-nine cents.* In Ireland we find the average wages per year of the agricultural laborers, ploughmen, with board and lodging, ninety-seven dollars and thirty-three cents; without boarding and lodging, one hundred and forty-six dollars. Laborer, with board and lodging, sixty-eight dollars and thirteen cents, without board and lodging, one hundred and sixteen dollars and eighty cents. When, therefore, Mr. Mallock, in order to refute the statements of Mr. George and Mr. Hyndman, says: "We find that each family among the poorer classes of England had, in 1843, about forty pounds a year (two hundred dollars); in 1851, fifty-eight pounds (about two hundred and eighty-seven dollars), and at the present time has between ninety-five and one hundred pounds (nearly four hundred and seventy-five to five hundred dollars), we can understand how fair a statement it is as showing the real conditions of the working classes. But had his figures been even fair and true what would they reveal? The gross income of the nation was, he says, in 1843, in round numbers, five hundred and fifteen million pounds, and had risen in 1880 to one billion two hundred million pounds. Mr. Mulhall puts the income for 1882 at one billion two hundred and forty-seven million pounds; for 1840, five hundred and forty million pounds; for 1822, two hundred and eighty million pounds; for 1860, seven hundred and sixty million pounds.† Thus the gross income of the nation has considerably more than doubled since 1840, and more than

* Consular Reports, 1885.

† Mulhall's Dictionary of Statistics, page 245.

quadrupled since 1822, and it takes Mr. Giffen very close figuring to show an addition to the laborer's income, when, if there had been any fair kind of distribution, it ought, at least, to have been doubled. No more conclusive evidence could be found than even their own statements, to prove that in the great increase of wealth nearly the whole of it had gone into the hands of the wealthy and non-producing classes.

Ireland, so far as land and the land question are concerned, has to be treated as being not a part of Britain, indeed a conquered province that still feels the avaricious hand of the conqueror. We have already stated in another chapter how, in Queen Elizabeth's reign, they made Irish landlords into English landlords. When Oliver Cromwell conquered or overran Ireland, he gave his colonels and captains a very large part of the island. Arthur Young says, when in Ireland, he was informed that descendants of Cromwell's colonels possessed estates drawing rent rolls of ten thousand pounds a year, and descendants of his captains who drew from *rent* incomes of two and three thousand pounds a year.* The last of these forfeitures of the land of Ireland occurred after the battle of the Boyne, when William Prince of Orange banished King James. Young says that at that time, "nineteen-twentieths of Ireland changed hands from Catholic to Protestant." † For this reason, says Mr. Young, who wrote in 1778, "the question of religion has been intimately interwoven with the land question in Ireland." Even though dispossessed, the old owners went through the form of transmitting their deeds to their heirs. It can easily be understood that in this way bitter feelings were likely to be long cherished and although the work of Catholic emancipation in Ireland has taken away many political grievances, other grievances still remain. King William was conqueror at Boyne Water, and did not hesitate to dispossess the old Irish landlords and put in a set of his

* Arthur Young's Tour in Ireland, vol. ii., page 44. † Ibid.

own, but he still was too much in favor of religious toleration to force cruel and proscriptive laws on the people. Six or seven years after his death these were enacted and may thus be summed up: First, the whole body of the Roman Catholics was disarmed. Second, they were incapacitated from *purchasing real estate.* Third, the entails of their estates were broken and the "gavel" of their children. Fourth, if one child abjured that religion he *might* inherit the estate. Fifth, if a son abjure that religion the father hath no power over that estate. Sixth, no Catholic can take a lease for more than thirty-one years. Seventh, if the rent of any Catholic is less than two-thirds of its full value, any *informer* can take the benefit of the lease. Eighth, priests who celebrate mass are to be transported, and if they return, hanged. Ninth, a Catholic having in his possession a horse worth more than five pounds is to forfeit the same to the *discoverer.* Tenth, by a construction of Lord Hardwick they were incapacitated from loaning money on mortgages.* Instead of being surprised at the number of disturbances and rebellions in Ireland, it is only astonishing that there were not more of them. Ireland is a striking lesson of the folly of trying to suppress a religion by persecution. While England and Scotland under a different system have become substantially Protestant, Ireland is not only largely but intensely Catholic. The millions of Irishmen who have during this century emigrated to the United States constitute an important element of the Catholic Church in the United States.

In this way it will be observed that a landed aristocracy, largely alien to the soil, and very largely hostile to the feelings and wishes of the Irish people, was inflicted on the agricultural interests of Ireland. Partly owing to the persecution and ostracism of a majority of the Irish people, it was found difficult to get the lands properly cultivated. Arthur Young

* Arthur Young's Tour in England, vol. ii., page 45.

informs us that in consequence of the small value of land in Ireland previous to the last century, and through a large portion of it "landlords became so careless of the interests of posterity as readily to grant leases to their tenants forever." * The excuse given for executing such leases was that it was very dangerous for Protestants to enter into and execute leases, and as they had to be strong enough for defense, a considerable expense was entailed in addition to the risk, and they would not undertake the adventure on short leases. Under such circumstances perpetual leases were given, but the system continued long after the occasion for it had passed away. Young found that many of these leases had been sublet, so he considers and treats the first lessee as a sort of landlord, which, in fact, he was. As the land and its rent increased in value, or as circumstances enabled those who had all these various liens or claims on it to exact more for its use, the land system of Ireland became, to a great extent, one of occupying tenancy, middlemen landlords, and lords proprietors.† The middlemen claimed that they were useful to the lords, as the occupying tenants were usually so very *very* poor that no "gentleman of fortune would consent to superintend the collection of rents from them." The lords proprietors were usually absentees, living in London, Paris, or at watering places, squandering the money drained from the agricultural laborers of Ireland, often in very questionable ways. Of the middlemen landlords, Arthur Young says: "There is in Ireland a class of small country gentlemen consisting of these profit renters. They generally kept a pack of wretched hounds with which they wasted their time and their money, and were the hardest drinkers in Ireland." He adds: "They are the most oppressive tyrants that ever lent their assistance to the destruction of a country," and "they will not make improvements themselves, and only grant short leases or let

* Arthur Young's Tour in Ireland, vol. ii., part 2d, page 17. † Ibid.

by the year to the real cultivating, occupying tenant, who, under these conditions, cannot afford to make improvements." * He adds that "they screw up the rent and are rapacious in exacting it all. Their excuse for their conduct is that the great lord cannot haggle with such tenants, or take their stuff from them when they cannot pay money." In this way it often happens that these lands are sublet several times, the occupying tenant who works the soil having to pay a profit to each of these middlemen before he and his family can eat what little is left in peace. Arthur Young gave the average rent in Ireland at ten shillings and three pence an acre (in 1778), that is, an English acre. Some of the land rented then as high as one, or even two, pounds an English acre.† Many years before Arthur Young's time, a few of the great landlords gave life leases to German "Palatines," but the scheme did not work well. Young said that the native Irish, if they had an opportunity, would improve the country faster than these Germans had been able to do. It is not difficult to see how foreign emigrants, brought in under such circumstances, would find their position extremely uncomfortable. The same authority stated that at the time he wrote the rent of a cabin, and garden for potatoes, in most of the countries in Ireland, was from one to three pounds a year, the average being one pound eleven shillings and ten pence. A cow's grass rent was from one to two pounds, the average being one pound eleven shillings and ten pence.‡ A garden patch varies from one to half an acre. Sometimes as much as one acre and a half. Small occupying tenants sometimes got leases of several acres of a mountain side, and improved and brought it into cultivation, but had no guarantee for their improvements.§ Some of the middlemen landlords would boast that they spent the part of the rent they got in the

* Arthur Young's Tour in Ireland, vol. ii., part 2d, page 18.

† Ibid., page 43. ‡ Ibid., page 26. § Ibid., page 22.

country, while the lords proprietors spent theirs abroad. As fast as these deputy noblemen fancied they were rich enough, they, too, went abroad and set up for fine gentlemen, and between their debts and extravagance, and the debts and extravagance of the noble lords, the poor cultivator of the soil had a hard time of it. One of the worst features of the business has been that the working-tenant was in most cases in arrears for his rent. He usually undertook to pay all that was possible under favorable circumstances, and the circumstances were not always favorable. In this way he got in arrears with the landlord so far that it was almost impossible for him to get out of debt. If he had good fortune, the landlord got the advantage of it, and if he had fresh misfortune, he went deeper into debt. The under tenants who were in arrears for their rent had to furnish teams to the landlords or middlemen at half price, to haul hay, corn, gravel or turf, and as they *must* go whenever called on, they sometimes lost their own crops when working in this way to pay arrears of rent.* Added to all this there was a class of poor men who could not even rent a small farm, and for whom there was not sufficient remunerative work; Young says: "States are ill-governed which possess people willing to work but who cannot find employment." † He adds: "The oppression of the landlords in Ireland is the chief cause of the misery of the people." The poorest class would build cabins by the roadside or in the ditch, if they were permitted, having no land rented, and lived by doing jobs and hiring. The cabins built by the cottars were usually built by themselves, and were hovels. When a man rented a patch, if there was a cabin on it, he repaired it, and, if not, he built one. That was not a charge on the landlord. I am particular in giving this data from Young, not only because he was a careful and responsible

* Arthur Young's Tour in Ireland, vol. ii., part 2d, page 19.

† Ibid., page 43.

observer, but because it best illustrates the condition of the people, and shows the steps by which the present land system in Ireland was created.

James Redpath, in his "Talks about Ireland," from more recent observations, says "there are 682,237 tenants in Ireland. Now out of these, 626,628, or about seventy-three per cent. are tenants at will and can be evicted." * Mr. Redpath traveled in Ireland a few years ago. He says, in that country there are only eight thousand landowners, including owners of one acre,† and also, I believe, including the holders of long leases, and two thousand of these eight thousand hold more land than all the rest put together, and three thousand of the eight thousand are absentees." These absentees draw every year sixty millions from Ireland. ‡ Mr. Redpath gives as the exact figures of Irish landlordism: six thousand small proprietors; one thousand one hundred and ninety-eight proprietors who own from two to three thousand acres; one hundred and eighty own from ten to twenty thousand acres; ninety own from twenty to fifty thousand acres, and twenty-four own from fifty to one hundred thousand acres. Three proprietors own upward of one hundred thousand acres. § Mulhall gives seventeen thousand five hundred and ten holdings or owners,‖ but it is not stated whether it includes lot owners in towns and villages. Tenants, moreover, have been purchasing under the recent land acts, and I quote from the Mulhall edition of 1884. In it he says that twenty-five thousand eight hundred and forty-nine land cases were adjudicated in the twelve months ending in August, 1882. Mr. Redpath thinks that the landlords ought to be compelled to sell at a fifteen years' purchase on Griffith's valuation, the government advancing the money.¶ The Irish landlords pay taxes on Griffith's valuation

* James Redpath's Talks about Ireland, page 91.

† Ibid., page 90. ‡ Ibid. § Ibid.

‖ Mulhall's Dictionary of Statistics, page 266.

¶ James Redpath's Talks about Ireland, page 98.

Mr. Redpath at one time visited and became familiar with the condition of the West India Islands. He says, that when the British abolished slavery in Jamaica, they refused to abolish absentee proprietorship, which is the present burden and curse of Jamaica. Mr. Redpath observes, that fewer crimes in proportion are committed in Ireland than in England, and also says that many rents are paid in Ireland from money sent by Irish Americans to relieve parents and friends.*

"Mr. Frank Battersby, political economist, etc.," has written a pamphlet to show the *justice* of compensating Irish landlords for the damage done them by the recent land acts. He says: "England has gone far for the sake of peace with Ireland. She has thrown political economy to the winds, restrained freedom of contract in land and denied the landlord's right to do as he pleased with his own." † He adds: "When the new rental in Ireland is fixed, two million five hundred thousand, or, according to Mr. Chamberlain, four million pounds will have been handed over to the tenants out of the pockets of the landlords." For this Mr. Battersby wants the government to go down into the public pocket and reimburse the landlords. In other words, to feed these cormorants out of the left pocket instead of the right. He says that under the Land Act, "the rental of Ireland has been reduced consistently twenty-five per cent. Whatever the results of the recent Land Acts may be, they can only strike an impartial observer as temporary expedients. So potent is the landed interest that any reform that may be demanded by the most urgent political necessities, precipitated by a long line of dishonest abuses, must, according to many, be supplemented by a full recognition of the right of a usurping landlord to hold fast his ill-gotten goods for all time. It occurs to us, that a movement to compel these aristocrats to disgorge their

* James Redpath's Talks about Ireland, page 94.

† Compensation to Landlords by Battersby, page 5.

dishonestly attained gains would be a better thing to do. Unhappily, most of these gains have been wasted and are past recovery. The Duke of Argyle, in his criticism of Mr. George, which is not an argument and little more than a tirade of abuse, among other things says: "Everything in America is on a gigantic scale, even its forms of villainy, and the villainy advocated by Mr. George is an illustration of this even as striking as the Mammoth Cave of Kentucky." * On the same page he says: "The world has never seen such a preacher of unrighteousness as Mr. Henry George." It would not be difficult to point out to the duke a "villainy" and an "unrighteousness" more colossal than either the Mammoth Cave, Niagara, or Mr. George. The British landed aristocrats who, by fraud, violence and murder, seized a large portion of the earth's surface, and exacted for their private emolument rent, or tribute, from their fellow-citizens who cultivated it, may appear to Americans as an "unrighteousness" much more "gigantic." If that was not, then the usurpation of the law-making power as a birthright due them from this stolen property, used for centuries to perpetuate their ill-gotten gains, would certainly be. Not content with this, the descendants of these freebooting sires, have by their pride and extravagance so ground the wretched workmen that they at last are forced to inquire by what right these exactions are made; and in reply the titled landlords pronounce all such inquiries as "villainy" and "unrighteousness," and hold up their hands in horror, as if the bond that bound them to society had not been stained for centuries with crime. We quote from the duke the only thing approximating to an argument: "It is one thing for any given political society to refuse to divide its vacant territory among individual owners. It is quite another thing for a political society, which for ages has recognized

* Duke of Argyle's "Prophet of San Francisco" in Nineteenth Century, for April, 1884.

such ownership and encouraged it, to break faith with those who have acquired such ownership, and have lived and labored and bought and sold and willed upon the faith of it." * That is a very weak attempt at an assertion of right. He claims that his ownership and that of the rest of the British aristocracy has been "recognized" and "encouraged." Who encouraged it? Certainly not the poor people plundered by them. The "political society" that recognized the rights of the British landed aristocracy was a combination of the holders of the lands thus taken. The recognition of a thief by a society of thieves is not usually considered a very good endorsement. Are the worst crimes of government forever to be perpetuated? Is it not the higher duty of a "political society" to see that the people dwelling in a country are allowed to possess their legitimate and natural rights, rather than that a handful of usurping aristocrats should be permitted to extort a luxurious living from them forever. There are two words in the paragraph I have quoted subject matter for inquiry,— the words "labored" and "bought." The duke surely does not mean that he "labored" for the part of Argyleshire he claims, nor can he mean that he "bought" and honestly paid for it. That he has sold or leased and willed "on the faith of it" is probable. He has collected and appropriated to his personal use an immense amount of the production of a vast range of country. He has built a magnificent palace at Inverary, and residences elsewhere, from the proceeds. He and his family have lived like kings from money wrung from an honest and hard-worked people. Perhaps conscious that the aristocratic claim may not be invulnerable he sets up another: "My own experience now extends over a period of the best part of forty years. During that time I have built more than fifty homesteads complete for man and beast. I have

* Duke of Argyle's "Prophet of San Francisco" in Nineteenth Century, for April, 1885.

drained and reclaimed many hundred and *enclosed* some thousand acres." Will the duke tell us how many homestead fires he has forever extinguished? He has, indeed "enclosed" a good many thousand acres. He discovered that it was more profitable (for him) that Argyleshire should produce sheep than men and women, and "enclosed" accordingly; the poor inhabitants escaping to Canada, there to find a region far away from the land of their birth, where they could cultivate the soil without giving the best part of the proceeds to landlords. Many highland villages were thus blotted out by the philosophical and moral duke, who is shocked because people propose to take what he says does not belong to them. But let us examine the duke's claim to his dukedom on the ground of "improvement." He further says: "I find that I have spent on one property alone the sum of forty thousand pounds entirely on the improvement of the soil," * and then he proceeds to say that it has not paid as a speculation. Now let us understand the duke. He must not mix the "color of his title." When he claims the right to exact rent from a good sized portion of Great Britain, taken by force and "recognized," as he pleads, by a "political society," that is one thing, and one that the British people can settle in their own way for the best interests of all. When, on the other hand, he brings in "fifty homesteads complete for man and beast," and forty thousand pounds, the proper way for him would be to make an account current. Set down all that his family have exacted in rent, deducting what would be his individual share as a private citizen of Argyleshire. Then set down all the charges for improvement which added value to the soil, made by him and his predecessors, and deduct this amount from the first figure, or from what he and his had ever taken from Argyleshire. We apprehend, if this kind of a settlement was

* Duke of Argyle's "Prophet of San Francisco" in Nineteenth Century, for April, 1884.

made with the firm of "Campbell & Co.," that their only mode of escape from the result would be to "file a petition in bankruptcy." This literary duke utters another warning, wailing cry. He says: "If all owners of land, great and small, might be robbed, and ought to be robbed of that which society had from time immemorial allowed them and encouraged them to acquire and to call their own; if the thousands of men and women and children who directly and indirectly live on rent * * * are all equally to be ruined by the confiscation of the fund on which they depend, are there *not other* funds that would be swept away?" * The "Prophet of San Francisco" seems to have made as great an impression on the duke as Nathan did on David. This nobleman has written a work, "The Reign of Law." The book considers the "reign of law in the world around us and within us." Should he ever revise it perhaps it would be well to incorporate an utterance of Blackstone's: "No human law is of any validity if contrary to the laws of nature." Hobbes wrote: "The laws of nature are immutable and eternal, for injustice, ingratitude, arrogance, pride, iniquity, acception of persons can never be made lawful." † One more quotation: "The soil was not created for idle enjoyment of unoccupying owners."

The physical and intellectual development of the British Empire, with all its faults, and its ghastly pictures of the calamities of the poor, is still marvelous. Her rural population and her agricultural laborers, although they have unhappily ceased to be a political power, occasionally evince a genius second to that of no people, and an enterprise capable of rising above even their adverse circumstances. Commerce, manufactures and their associate crafts constitute the backbone of the British Empire. The British people of to-day are to some extent cosmopolitan. Her business relations with the

* Duke of Argyle's "Prophet of San Francisco" in Nineteenth Century, for April, 1884.

† Hobbe's Leviathan, vol. iii., page 145.

outside world are necessary for her existence. Of the food her people eat, sixty-one per cent. of the wheat, thirty-seven per cent. of the meat, fifty-eight per cent. of the cheese and butter, not to mention other articles, are imported into the British Kingdom.* London, once a place where population had to be brought to keep up the standard, is now rendered so healthy by improved sanitary regulations as to exhibit a natural increase. There is a German population in London large as that of a first-class town in the German Empire. The Irish population of London is greater than that of any city in Ireland, except Dublin and Belfast. London has absorbed much of the rural population, like the other cities. Agriculture, instead of being on the increase, is on the decline, as more than two million acres of arable land have been converted to pasture in the past few years. Mallock contends that the distress is limited: "Let us make the advance of the poorer classes as partial as possible, and want and misery as widespread as possible, yet, on my calculation, and on my supposition, at least three-fourths of them, during the past forty years, or twenty-two million five hundred thousand out of thirty million have grown, all of them, demonstrably richer." † What this gentleman forgets is that it is with human society as with a steam engine, when an unnatural strain is put upon it the *weakest* parts give way. Mr. Giffen and Mr. Mallock both seem to think that because a few men of great energy are able to rise above all the depressing circumstances that stand in the path of the poor workingmen of Britain, all of them who do not exhibit similar qualities are imbeciles, and should justly bear the lot of poverty inflicted on them. Such a conclusion is not just. Society and law has not to do with the few exceptional cases, but the condition of the great masses, and especially the condition of the poorest and most helpless.

* Mulhall's Dictionary of Statistics, page 207.

* Mallock's Property and Progress, page 207.

The commercial and manufacturing power of England has steadily risen for centuries. It is a great power, but it is not yet the dominant power. There is another unhappy circumstance connected with it. It has developed, and is developing an aristocracy of wealth, differing from the other aristocracy, but still with objectionable features. While that element is conservative, the great working, throbbing business nerve of England is not insensible to the struggle going on with the landed aristocracy. The latter stubbornly temporize and resist. Political economists of the Manchester school do not expect much from the agricultural interest, and seem to think that they can make cotton goods and iron enough to feed the whole British Empire, if the lords and dukes should make every foot of land in Britain a sheep-walk. Let them remember that no country can permanently exist apart from its agricultural resources. If the incubus of the landed aristocracy was removed, and the land divided into small holdings owned by the actual tillers of the soil, it would add infinitely to the comfort, power and wealth of the British people. One of their political economists, Mr. Malthus, wrote: "If a tract of land as large as Britain were added to the island, and sold in small lots, the amelioration of the condition of the common people would be striking, although the rich would always be complaining of the high price of labor, the difficulty of getting work done and the *pride* of the lower classes." *

* Malthus's Principles of Population, page 291.

CHAPTER IX.

THE ABORIGINAL AMERICAN SYSTEM OF LAND TENURE.

Agricultural and roving populations—Tribal government—Aboriginal money and exchange—Tribal boundaries—Homes and hunting grounds—Male and female occupations—Sparse populations—Decay and degradation of the Aborigines under European pressure—Religious beliefs—Rights in land not bought and sold—Communal land, but individual property—Caribbee and Arowaks—Three classes of Aborigines—Land laws of Cherokees and Choctaws—The soil common, but improvements personal property—John Ross—Corn Plant—Bushyhead—Land in severalty prescribed by the whites—Treaties used to secure foothold and land—Repudiated when the Indians grow weak—Washington—Gen. Knox—Chief Justice Marshall—Cass and Jackson versus the Supreme Court—Indian inertia—Zuni and its rich man—A Caribbee political economist.

LITTLE more than two hundred and fifty years have elapsed since European settlements begun in that part of North America now known as the United States. At that time a chattel title to land was unknown upon the continent. The aboriginal inhabitants of all kinds claimed the sovereignty of the regions they occupied, but individual proprietorships in the soil did not exist, and through all their intercourse with the European settlers have been, and still are, obnoxious to their political, social and religious ideas. Considerable confusion and many Indian wars resulted from the early attempts to fix individual and exclusive title to portions of American soil. When the Indians, in the early history of the settlements, relinquished tracts of land to the European colonists, they merely understood by it a joint occupancy by the whites, such as they had themselves. It was difficult to make them comprehend that individuals they had never seen, and who had never even visited the shores of their country, should lay claim to their land.

The native peoples of America differ in many things, radically, from each other, and yet all of them have much in common with the human race elsewhere. Long separated from the people of the Eastern hemisphere, peculiar ideas had developed features of society that seemed remarkable to the first European discoverers. Clashing interests led to hostile feeling, and in subseqüent intercourse our observations have not often been of an impartial or friendly character. We should, therefore, qualify ourselves with a charitable spirit on approaching the subject, and, if possible, cast our prejudices behind us. At the date of the European discovery three distinct or separate classes of society may be said to have existed, and each of these embraced many separate tribes. The first consisted of the organized governments, of which the most distinguished types were those found in Mexico and Peru. The second class would include peoples who lived in communities and villages, chiefly by agriculture, and possessing some manufactures. The third class includes the nomads, or wanderers. In Mexico, these latter were, in the time of Cortez, styled chicamecas. This, Herara informs us, was not the name of any Indian or tribe, but a general term used by the civilized Indians themselves, which meant nomads, or roving men, without fixed habitations. At the time of the discovery, and since, large tribes and nations roved about the central, western and northern portions of North America. It is true that many tribes existed in the regions where these wanderers roved who were not nomads, but lived largely by agriculture, and remained stationary as far as they could. One roving tribe, in early times located as agriculturists, became noted even among wanderers, the Shawnees, or, more correctly, Shawannos, "Men of the bow and arrow." Another people, of comparatively modern aggregation, were stray men from many nations, chiefly, however, from the Creeks.

They located in Florida, and were called Seminoles, or "Wandering men."

The most striking class presented to the European was the nomadic or wild Indians. These rovers of the plains or forest possessed a simple dignity of manner and deportment rarely exhibited by the people of more boasted civilizations. They are, and have been, the most independent people in the world. Forms of society and artificial modes of life do not enslave them. They enjoy the freest government on the earth, for the little authority there is exists merely by the consent of the governed. This is carried so far that, to a white man, it often appears as if there was no government at all. These national or tribal governments never get so large that the popular assembly or council cannot consider and determine all questions that arise. Living largely from the natural resources of the country, consequently driven to scatter for food, and not possessing any centralizing force in their government, it is not wonderful that the country was overrun by wandering bands. Murder, adultery and theft have usually been punished among them. The grades and character of punishment differed. The council considered the matter, and the nearest relative, or aggrieved party, became the avenger and executor of the popular decree. This gave their modes of administering justice an appearance of vengeance rather than law when judged by Europeans. Among these nomadic tribes the same ambition exists for public honor and distinction as found elsewhere. With them, however, the honor conferred by public position was its only emolument. The desire to be a chief, a counselor or even an orator, is great. While they are never boisterous in their mirth, and rarely show even its milder expressions among strangers, they have a fine sense of humor which is often sarcastic. The least civilized and nomadic orators speak with great deliberation and precision. They never hurry and never think of interrupting each other. When the French first settled in Louisiana, one of the chiefs at a council held with them was observed to be trying to conceal his merriment; on being asked what amused him, he at first evaded the question, but on being pressed, said: "These French are like a flock of geese: they all speak at once."

Among the nomads taxes were unknown. Public works were, of course, impossible. Their records were chiefly oral traditions, confided to their best men to prevent interpolations or changes, and their written record, besides inscriptions on the rocks, was the wampum belt, its figures and symbols conveying certain ideas, the years being enumerated by knots tied in the belt. At certain periods and important councils these were brought out, and, by their wise men, read or explained.

While commerce or exchange was largely confined to barter, a circulating medium was not unknown. They never hesitated to use the money of the whites, and very soon understood its value perfectly. Before the European settlements, and, to some extent, since, they used for money, wampum, beads, rare shells, and pieces of copper and salt. The wampum circulated generally among many nations, and had a fixed value, as it required great labor to drill the fine hole through the wampum bead.* The wildest tribes on the continent had the most stringent regulations against the waste of food. When game was killed the parties were compelled to save the whole of it, even portions of the intestines were used for food. In their migrations when rich spots were found containing wild potatoes, rye, nuts or fruits, the discovery was publicly announced by a crier, so that all could participate. When their camp became no longer fresh they removed to another spot, the new location having been agreed upon. They were very jealous of intrusion on lands belonging to the tribe or nation, the wildest nomads had a country they

* Lawson's History of North Carolina, page 195.

claimed. They sometimes claimed hunting grounds as especially their own, and, in case the tribe was strong enough, prevented others from using them. There were also hunting regions not specially claimed, upon which different tribes hunted as on a public or common domain, and also hunting or roaming grounds that were a debatable region. A large portion of Kentucky was in this condition, and thus became the scene of many a struggle, the name meaning "bloody ground." Each of the petty nations, small or great, held the frontiers of their country as sacredly and jealously as the most historic nation. Their traditions carefully referred to their boundaries. Like other nations, many of their wars have grown out of questions of boundary. At the close of these wars the frontiers would be recognized or fixed, and it was considered an affront to pass them without their permission. Such were the modes by which these nations held those portions of the earth's surface that they occupied. The uses they made of it they considered their own concern, and it cannot be said that their tenure lacked anything in form or dignity from the right of country universally held by all nations.

These roving peoples of America thus lived a life of independent freedom, subsisting to a great extent upon the natural productions of a rich country. Barbarous to some extent they were, but not brutish or unmanly. If they had few of the refinements of civilization, they were at least not embarrassed by its cares, or exhausted by its fearfully laborious toil. They lived in the fresh air, and were not condemned to the cellars and dilapidated buildings in which the very poor laboring people of civilized society are crowded. Their shoulders were not bent by working in the coal vein, or stooping over the bench in badly ventilated workshops. The impression that they were lazy is not altogether well-founded, because there is no exercise more exhausting than the chase, and the necessary military occupation of the male inhabitants required much effort, privation and watchfulness. It was for this reason that their women performed many laborious tasks, such as pitching and moving the house or tent, dressing the skins or gathering fruits, roots or berries. This work is performed in the open air, and I question if they work much harder than the wives and daughters of poor laboring men in civilized communities.

While individual ownership of land is abhorrent to all their social and religious ideas, and even the natural productions of the earth are considered common to all, and no pre-emptive right of discovery in them can exist until these have been gathered, it is a mistake to suppose that they are communists. No people guard the rights of mine and thine more jealously, concerning all things they regard as property. Their arms, tents, horses, clothing, indeed, everything they own, is claimed with great tenacity. This distinction of rights extends into the family, where the wife and the children have each their property. While this is true, their hospitality is unbounded, and extends even to their enemies, should they consent to receive them. They never refuse to give to those who are in want, of their own tribe. In distress they never hesitate to go and ask each other, and it is considered mean to refuse, but, at the same time, if one of them permits himself to become a chronic beggar, and refuses to take proper steps to support himself, he is regarded as a common enemy. Some tribes have disposed of such persons summarily. It is needless to deny that their over-lavish giving is a serious check to the disposition to accumulate property. Why should a man struggle to acquire a surplus if the probabilities are that it will be claimed to supply the wants of those in distress. Their acceptance of ransom, or price of blood, in case of a murder or manslaughter, is considered venal, but the question whether it shall be received is determined in council, and it is usually accepted, only in cases where there are mitigating circumstances, or where it is a case between tribes, and is a species of diplomacy, or a humane policy to prevent interminable war. Questions as to the redundancy of population do not afflict them. Astonishment has been expressed at the small population occupying large areas among the wandering tribes. The answer is simple. In the first place, large families of children are rare among them. Owing to the necessary hardships of their mode of life the sickly and delicate do not survive childhood. These causes added to occasional scarcity of food and the frequency of wars, render the vaticinations of a Malthus unnecessary. In general terms, under such a form of society, a dense population and accumulations of great wealth are impossible. It is worthy of note that these wandering tribes, independent of missionary efforts, are all believers in the Great Spirit, or Unknown God. Pure theists; for all their superstitious terms and symbols are mere mythical figures, used to convey an idea *not* to be construed literally. Atheists in any sense they certainly are not. A man going among them and openly denying the existence of a Great Spirit, would doubtless be looked upon with horror, but it is difficult to get them to believe in a systematized religion. The highest forms of society or civilizations in America, such as that in Mexico, were connected with priestcraft, and even human sacrifice, while the lowest and most barbarous were animated by a vague theism.

Next to the nomads or wanderers, comes the class that had more fixed habitations, and depended chiefly on agriculture for subsistence. These, of course, varied a great deal as to their condition, but the larger masses of the population of North America, at the time of the European discovery, were a quiet, industrious set of people, chiefly living in villages and towns, subsisting by agriculture. Narvaez, De Soto and the Huguenots found a people with big fields, "Tallahassee," occupying the Atlantic seaboard. Some of these fields we are told were ten miles long. They domesticated many fowls and a few animals, and even fish, trained to catch other fish * and raised a large variety of vegetables and roots. In the pictures made by Jacob Le Moyne, who was with the Huguenots, the men and women are represented as working in the fields together.† They manufactured and wore clothing. We read in the narrative of De Soto's expedition that these adventurers traveled for hundreds of miles among such people. Often procuring corn from their storehouses, and, finally, that in the mountains they came to a people, the Chalaque (Cherokees), who were almost naked, having a strip of cloth around them, and wearing on their shoulders the dressed skins of the "cattle." Even these people lived in villages, and had small farms in the valleys, subsisting partially by hunting. Some of the purely agricultural aborigines were in a tolerably advanced condition. They built high mounds and kept the sacred fire on them, and had a species of hereditary government in the female line. No individual title to land existed among any of these peoples. They had for each town or village a large field, or more than one, in which every family had a portion that they cultivated. Rights therein were not bought or sold. Each had an interest, and it was the usufruct share interest in a common property. All the products of labor were individual property. They had fixed dwellings, comfortably constructed and furnished. They had knowledge of the precious metals including copper, but not of iron. They had earthenware and wicker-ware of good manufacture. In carefully kept medicine baskets the women had many preparations for medicine and articles for the toilet. They used mediums of exchange as well as barter. Their forms of government, though mainly of popular acceptance, were more elaborate than those of the nomads. Their only taxation was labor for the big fields, public buildings or other necessary public work. Rents were not exacted even by the state. From all indications these partially civilized and in-

* Peter Martyr.

† Hakluyt's Voyages.

dustrial peoples were fragments of more powerful nations undergoing a steady decay. The inroad of the Europeans hastened their destruction. Many of them attempted a resistance, and the superior arms and discipline of the Europeans made the effort very disastrous.

On the West India Islands a condition of affairs existed in some respects different from that on the mainland. The best Spanish authorities inform us that these islands were populated by two different classes. One nation was styled Arowaks, and the other, Caribs, or Caribbees. An examination of their languages will show that these were nicknames they gave each other. The so-called Arowaks, or "meal-eaters," were a peaceful agricultural people, living in villages. They planted corn, and lived upon that and the manioc; the roots from half an acre of the latter will support a family. They also cultivated and smoked tobacco; Peter Martyr informing us that they would pluck it as they walked along, roll it up into a coarse cigar and smoke it. They raised many vegetables and manufactured cloth from plants they cultivated. Their houses were stationary and tolerably comfortable. They had tribal and local governments. Each man cultivated his patch, sometimes in a common field, but often an individual patch. Buying and selling land was not practiced, but they traded in everything else. They were a peaceful, agricultural people, living partly on fish.

At the time of the European discovery no animal larger than a dog was found on any of these islands. They had not only small boats, but vessels of considerable size, in which they sometimes made a fire.

The other class or tribe,—for there appears to have been few distinct tribes among them,—the "Caribbees" (robbers),—for this was the name the suffering, peaceful people gave them in their own soft, musical language,—infested rather than resided on the islands. They were a species of roving pirates, making voyages all over the Caribbean Sea, and visiting both North and South America. They were a cruel, warlike race, addicted to cannibalism. They not only robbed the peaceful Arowaks of all they had, but actually roasted and ate them. One Spanish writer tells us that they took a great many Arowak women and kept them in a separate island to raise grain and fruit for them. This story has often been repeated by the adventurers of the old Spanish main. That the Caribbees plundered as well as roasted and ate the hapless agriculturists there can be no doubt. It was on this account that Columbus proposed to Queen Isabella that these Caribs should be captured and sold into slavery, to aid in defraying the "heavy charges to be borne by her majesty." This, to her honor, she declined, but her successors, colleagues and subordinates were not so conscientious. It was, however, found easier to enslave the peaceful Arowaks, the greater portion of whom miserably perished, many of them dying in the mines. The same kind of slavery was carried on, as far as possible, on the continent, and, it is needless to say, that the industrial, agricultural populations chiefly suffered. In the narrative of Cabezo de Vaca,* who, with two companions, traveled across the continent, from Texas to the Gulf of California, he mentions meeting a company of Spanish soldiers driving three hundred and thirty of the inhabitants, chained together, to work in the mines of Mexico. This was prior to 1520. Whole communities and towns were thus depopulated. Still later, this attempt to enslave the aboriginal inhabitants was continued. At the close of the Tuscarora war, seven hundred prisoners of these people were, in one day, sold into slavery in the city of Charleston. The destruction among the ancient inhabitants was largely from the partially civilized tribes. They suffered in several ways, not only being killed and enslaved, but driven by persecution to become nomads and wanderers. For this reason the nomadic

* Buckingham Smith's Translation Cabeza de Vaca.

portion of the native inhabitants became larger after the European discovery.

The third or higher class inhabiting North and South America at the date of the discovery by Columbus is best represented by the two nations found in Peru and Mexico. These were monarchical governments and theocracies. They had a written or pictoriographic language not inferior to that of many great ancient nations. The power of life and death lay in the hands of the sovereign. Their public buildings were vast and showed in many things high stages of art. They had fine gardens, great aviaries, aqueducts, and a system of messengers or expressmen. Within three days of their arrival, Montezuma showed Cortez a pictoriograph exhibiting the Spanish fleet under Narvaez, then anchored in the Gulf of Mexico. It gave the number and character of the vessels so that Cortez was able to act on the information. They possessed a knowledge of the precious metals, and it was their riches in these that led to their ruin. Many of their articles of clothing were of fine quality. Their feather work has probably never been excelled. They had codes of law, and among other regulations the drinking of intoxicating liquors was forbidden under pain of death. Persons over forty-five years were exempted from the operation of the law, but even in them excesses were punished. Their forms of government were different from those of the Europeans, but, trying them by an impartial standard, they cannot be justly said to have been inferior to the great mass of organized or civilized governments of that age. Agriculture was to a large extent carried on by irrigation. Systems of irrigation were under the management of the government, and the expense of maintaining them was by tax or labor. Land, however, was not sold as a chattel, nor is there evidence that the rulers claimed or gave it away. The services of any or all citizens might be claimed by the monarch. The only privileged class except military leaders were the priests, who were compelled to be simple and abstemious in their lives.

It will thus be seen that in aboriginal America there was no such thing as chattelization of land. It did not even constitute the basis of political power. Each nation or tribe claimed its own territory, but claimed it for the equal benefit of all its inhabitants. At that time individual dealing in land did not exist to any great extent anywhere.

It is to the pitiable claims growing out of right of discovery and right of conquest that the complete chattelization of American land is due. Everything from the gold and silver of the country to the people and the land they lived on was something to steal and sell. In this way the foundation was laid for a system by which certain persons and classes will be able, if it is continued, to levy a tax on agriculture and agriculturists for all time.

Chattel title the aboriginal populations have resisted as far as they were able. The same struggle is going on to-day. Some of the tribes, largely those who were agricultural, were induced to form governments modeled after the state governments of the North American republic. The strongest and most notable are the organized governments of the Choctaws, Chickasaws, Seminoles, Creeks and Cherokees. The latter has a chief and assistant chief, elected every four years, who are simply governor and lieutenant-governor. They have a senate and lower house elected each two years, a supreme court of three judges, and district courts, and an organized school system. Their government is indeed not inferior to that of several of the territories. It is worthy of note, however, that in the written constitution of all these governments the land is declared to be national or common property, equal to all. Its use has never yet been made taxable. Improvements thereon are declared to be the "indefeasible" property of the occupant. Under law these improvements descend to heirs, or may be sold; but if the land is not cultivated for two years, it reverts to the public domain. In addition, the amount that may be cultivated by one person can be reduced by law, so that all may, if they desire, have an equal portion. Monopoly in land is forbidden by the terms of their written constitutions. It is a striking fact that these people, even in forming governments modeled after that of the United States, include their own land system in plain, unmistakable terms. As has been said, monopolization of the earth's surface and taxing the cultivator of land for rent is extremely obnoxious to the ideas of the American Indian.

In taking this course they not only lacked support from the United States government, but have encountered great opposition. They are at present engaged in an active struggle to preserve this system. Every year bills are introduced into Congress, and occasionally one is passed, to compel a tribe to take their land in severalty. Many of their sincere friends even consider this the test of civilization, and seem to think that the true way to civilize an Indian is to enable him to sell land. The aborigine has learned a good deal from the pale face, but has not yet been educated up to the point of thinking that land can be sold as a chattel. The best indication of their feeling on the subject may be gathered from the fact that while there has been a law on the United States statute book since 1862 authorizing and encouraging the Indians to take lands in severalty or to hold them by individual chattel ownership, very few of them have availed themselves of the privilege. It is now proposed to compel them by law to take chattel titles. Some well-meaning people favor this proposition under an impression that if the Indians were forced to adopt this feature of American "civilization" and become private landholders and speculators, they might possibly adopt ideas which, with more reason, have been styled "civilized." The movement, however, receives its chief inspiration from land speculators who wish to get possession of large portions of valuable Indian reservations.

The Indian resists private landholding with great vigor. It is against all their traditions, religion or morals. One of their most accomplished men, John Ross, said: "As far as I am concerned, it would be for my interest to have the land in severalty, for I could make gain of it, but the poor people of my nation would soon be without homes." On August 1st, 1838, at Aquohee Camp, I. T., when the united Cherokee constitution was framed, their proceedings began: "Whereas the title of the Cherokee people to their lands is the most ancient, pure and absolute known to man, its date is beyond the reach of human record; its validity confirmed and illustrated by possession, and enjoyment, antecedent to all pretence of claim by any other portion of the human race."

The first article of the constitution of the Cherokee nation provides: "The lands of the Cherokee nation shall remain the common property, but the improvements made thereon and in the possession of the citizens of the nation are the exclusive and indefeasible property of the citizens respectively who made or may rightfully be in possession of them." * Mr. Bushyhead, the present chief of the Cherokees, in an elaborate article in the New York *Independent* a year or two ago, discussed the question from the Indian standpoint. He called attention to the fact that the lands of the whites were rapidly drifting into the hands of a privileged class, and he predicted the impoverishment of the laboring people, both whites and Indians, by this policy, and stated that his people were steadily improving in condition under their system of holding land in common. The Creek nation, or, more correctly, confederacy, is composed of the fragments of many of the agricultural tribes formerly living in the Mobilian basin. All of these in their old home and in their new one repudiate individual holding of land, and consider it the first step to homeless poverty. They live by agriculture and cattle raising, and although they have been moved about from place to place, sometimes in chains, to meet the demands of white aggression, they are an

* Laws of the Cherokee Nation, page 9.

industrious and rural people. The Choctaws, by their treaty of 1866, were compelled to admit some provisions in it looking to allotment of lands in severalty, but so uncompromising has been their opposition that this has never been accomplished.

The condition of Indian tribes and Indian peoples differ widely, but in one thing they are all alike: entertaining fixed aversion to individual title to land. If they have not been able to hold their own with the European emigrants and their descendants, the reason may be found in the weakness of the tribes and their isolation. While the French and Spanish intermarried with them to a great degree, the British settlers in America did so only to a partial and very limited extent. We thus find in the old French and Spanish colonies large communal or common fields, and a system of local tenure not so widely dissimilar from the native modes. The English and American settlers, on the other hand, as they approached the Indian communities, contemplated their removal and overthrow. The first object in founding a new settlement was the prospective rise in value of the land, and the opportunity of making money in that way. An assimilation, or even partial copying of the aboriginal idea of land tenure, was, therefore, impossible. It is to be regretted that the modes of obtaining these Indian lands were not always characterized by honesty and humanity. Laws were even enacted by the United States to prevent the Indians from selling land, when they were forced to sell, to any party but the United States, it having thus reduced the buyers to one customer, proceeded to use the whole powers of the government to compel them to sell, and then offered them an insignificant trifle for large tracts, bearing no relation to the speculative prices the white purchasers expected to obtain for them. The whole system of acquiring the Indian lands for a century has been one of violence, and the arbitrary exercise of superior power too often supplemented by dishonesty and chicanery.

Indian lands, from the beginning of the government have

usually been obtained by treaty. Such had been the practice under the British, French and Spanish governments. These were merely contracts or bargains, both parties having a voice in them. Since the victims have become weak in numbers and reduced in influence, treaties with them have been denounced and even suspended by law. When the republic was first established it was a question much discussed as to whether Indian treaties should be ratified by the senate. George Washington, in a communication to the senate, September 17, 1789, said:

"It is said to be the general understanding and practice of nations, as a check on the mistakes and indiscretions of ministers and commissioners, not to consider any treaty negotiated and signed by such officers as final and conclusive until ratified by the sovereign or government from whom they derive powers. This practice has been adopted by the United States respecting their treaties with European nations, and I am inclined to think it would be advisable to observe it in the conduct of our treaties with the Indians, for though such treaties, being, on their part, made by their chiefs and rulers, need not be ratified by them, yet, being formed, on our part, by the agency of subordinate officers, it seems to be both prudent and reasonable that their acts should not be binding on the nation until approved and ratified by the government.*

In a letter of General Knox, then Secretary of War, to President Washington, of date July 7th, 1789, he urges fair and conciliatory dealings and says: "It would reflect honor on the new government, and be attended with happy effects, were a declarative law to be passed that the Indian tribes possess the right of soil of all lands within their limits, respectively, and that they are not to be divested thereof, but in consequence of fair and bona fide purchases made under the authority of and with the express approbation of the United States." He says

* American State Papers, vol. i., Indian Affairs, page 58.

further in the same letter: "How different would be the sensation of a philosophic mind to reflect that instead of exterminating a part of the human race by our modes of population, we had preserved through all difficulties and at last imparted our knowledge of cultivation and the arts to the aborigines of the country, by which the source of future life and happiness has been preserved and extended. But it has been conceived to be impracticable to civilize the Indians of North America. This opinion is probably more *convenient* than just." * In a previous letter of June 15th, 1789, he said: "The Indians, being the prior occupants, possess the right of soil. It cannot be taken from them except by their free consent or by the right of conquest in case of a *just* war. To dispossess them on any other principle would be a gross violation of the fundamental laws of nature, and of that distributive justice which is the glory of a nation."

Washington and the founders of the republic uttered, as occasion offered, similar sentiments. When we consider the many reckless modes by which Indian lands were obtained and the subordination of the sentiments quoted from Knox to the interests of those who wished to get possession of these lands, we are forced to regret that all were not animated by equally honorable and humane sentiments. On account of the constant aggressive policy of the white settlers, the Iroquois chief, Corn Plant, in his old age said: "Where is the land upon which our children and their children after them are to lie down? You told us that the line drawn from Pennsylvania to Lake Ontario would mark it forever on the east, and the line from Beaver Creek to Pennsylvania would mark it on the west, and we see it is not so; for first one comes and then another, and takes it away by order of that people which you tell us promised to secure it to us." †

* American State Papers, vol. i., Indian Affairs, page 53.

† Hall and Kenney's Indian Tribes, vol. i., page 98.

The policy steadily pursued by the government was one of acquisition, removal, reduction of reservations, bad faith, threats and aggressive measures, often leading to Indian wars. If the Indians yielded without resistance, hard terms were imposed on them; and if they took up arms, they lost everything. The government never hesitated by presents or honors to induce Indian chiefs and representatives to concede terms such as their people had never authorized them to accept. There has been all through American history two classes of public men. One of these has constantly urged fair dealing with the aborigines; the other has resorted to questionable expedients to secure unfair terms from them. In the funeral oration over one eminent politician of the republic, it was said *eulogistically* that "he had obtained more land for less money than any man who had ever dealt with Indians." The supreme court, when presided over by Chief Justice Marshall, having given a decision recognizing a fair measure of Indian rights, other prominent public men were much exercised. In the cabinet of General Jackson the questions involved in the decision were discussed, and although it was a remarkable proceeding, a *review* of the decision was prepared by General Cass, then Secretary of War, and was read in manuscript to the cabinet and published in the *Globe* of March 31st, 1832.* In this remarkable paper we find the state's rights doctrine very strongly enunciated, and a proposition on another general question which we consider it worth while to copy:

"1. That civilized communities have a right to take possession of a country inhabited by barbarous tribes, to assume jurisdiction over them, and to 'combine within narrow limits,' or, in other words, to appropriate to their own use such portions of the territory as they think proper.

"2. That in the exercise of this right such communities are the judges of the extent of jurisdiction to be assumed and of territory to be acquired." †

* Smith's Life of Lewis Cass, page 249.

† Ibid., page 250.

The only other formula, as a basis of land title, at all equal to it is the celebrated one, "Resolved 1st. That the earth belongs to the saints." "Resolved 2. That we are the saints."

When the Americas were first discovered by Europeans, they were "taken possession of" on the plea of extending Christianity. As the "Christianity" plea had no doubt lost some of its aroma before it reached the administration of President Jackson, "civilization" is made to take its place.

A nation having passed the early and more turbulent stages of its career, is apt to seek for general principles to fortify not only the ideas, but the acts on which it was founded. Higher conceptions of justice usually in the end triumph over lower and cruder. It is and must always be a source of regret to statesmen, that precedents not founded on honor or equity should have been created, and that the title possessed by the American people should be stained by blood and unfair dealing. The ancient inhabitants of the country were in a decline both as to population and power. That decline was greatly accelerated by the European settlements. The agricultural tribes were not only reduced in numbers, but in wealth, industry and standing. Many nations at one time agricultural became wanderers. Tribes were driven from place to place and stripped of their lands so often that it is not wonderful that the spirit to improve their homes died within them. They were deprived of their natural means of support and subject to the degrading influences of pauperization.

There have not been lacking advocates of the theory that their system of tenure was the cause of their misfortunes. There is not the slightest foundation for this. Their mode of land tenure is one that has been common to the great masses of mankind, and was one of the redeeming traits in their social system. It has been urged, with more apparent reason, that they are inert, and lack progressive enterprise. How much of this is natural to them, and how much of it has been created by their unhappy intercourse with the whites, is a grave question. If their people are not characterized by enterprise, and their villages adorned with great monuments of human power and skill, there is a freedom and independence in their arcadian life that has proved seductive to many Europeans. They are simple in their tastes and wants, dignified in their intercourse with each other, and impatient of restraint. While the writer was in the Indian city of Zuni, a few years ago, he was taken to the house of a rich man, the notably "*rich*" man of Zuni. These Zunis are not nomads, but the decaying remnant of what was once a powerful empire. The writer found them a quiet, peaceful, agricultural, pastoral race, almost untouched by European contact. They had one rich man. His condition was a subject of curiosity. In Zuni there were no abjectly poor people. All seemed to live in comfort. On inquiry it was found that the "rich man" had a few thousand sheep, a few hundred head of cattle, and a herd of horses and donkeys. He had no better land privileges than his neighbors, except that his flocks consumed more grass in the neighboring mountains than those of his fellow citizens. It was ascertained that he made no money by usury, interest being unknown in Zuni. In common with his neighbors he had enough ground to cultivate. Others had considerable herds. All seemed to have as much as they needed; he had more. It appeared to have come to him through inheritance and fortunate circumstances. He was not a trader. According to our estimates his riches constituted no very great amount of wealth. He was not a public officer. His adobe house was a little larger, and a little better furnished. His fortune had not lifted him above friendly association with his neighbors. He was hospitable, and, the writer learned, had done many acts of kindness to the less fortunate. His wealth seemed to be neither a reproach nor a menace. I had scarcely expected to find one man better off than another, and

I would scarcely have inquired into or noted his circumstances if my guide had not informed me, in bad Spanish, that this was "the richest man in all that country."

In a history of the Caribbees we have a characteristic speech delivered by a native to a dejected European :

"Friend, how miserable art thou, thus to expose thy person to such tedious and dangerous voyages, and suffer thyself to be oppressed with cares and fears. The inordinate desire of acquiring wealth puts thee to all this trouble and all these inconveniences, and yet thou art in no less disquiet for the goods thou hast already gotten, than for those thou desirest to get. Thou art in continual fear lest somebody should rob thee, either in thine own country or upon the seas; or that thy commodities should be devoured by shipwreck, or lost in the waters. Thus, thy hair turns grey, and thy forehead is wrinkled. A thousand inconveniences attend thy body, a thousand afflictions surround thy heart, and thou makest all haste to the grave. Why dost thou not contemn riches as we do." *

* R. R. Davis's History of the Caribbees, Book 2, chap. xi., page 267.

CHAPTER X.

ERA OF EUROPEAN DISCOVERY AND SETTLEMENT IN AMERICA—RIGHT OF DISCOVERY—RIGHT OF CONQUEST.

European discoverers visit America for gold, silver and trade—A century of robbery, rapine and murder—Comparison between European and American society at date of discovery—Slavery and Las Casas—Dates of actual settlement in the West Indies—Dates of actual settlement in North America—What led to it—Settlements of the Northmen—Discovery a better title than possession—Conquest on pretense of Christianizing—Native rights disregarded—French and Spanish colonies fraternize with the natives—English colonies refuse to mingle—The Indian must "go West"—Attempts to plant white aristocracy—First speculations in sales and gifts of American lands—Popes, kings and parliaments granted land they had never seen—Colonial boundaries—Annexation, wars of conquest—Treaties—Degradation and extermination—The Henderson purchase—Baron Graffenreid—John Locke's constitution—American lords and palatines—Aristocracy—Slavery—Free settlements.

THERE is a common, but mistaken impression, that the industrial settlements in America followed immediately upon the European discovery by Columbus, in 1492. A more careful study of history will show that about one hundred and twenty-five years elapsed before such industrial European settlements actually began. Up to that time both continents and the West India Islands might be said to be infested with European adventurers. Their chief purposes were the search for precious metals, trade in furs or other articles with the natives, and the location of valuable fishing banks, from which food might be obtained for Europe. Indeed, for the latter purpose, the *Basques*, from the French coasts, and other Celtic nations, had visited the banks of Newfoundland, regularly, several hundred years before the time of Columbus.

The Scandinavians had also colonies in Greenland about the tenth century. Had the agricultural occupations of the country been the purpose of the first discoverers, they would naturally have selected spots in both continents but sparsely settled, and not occupied by strong or organized governments. On the contrary, we find Spanish attention chiefly directed to Mexico and Peru, where governments existed that could not be considered much inferior to the Spanish government of that time, except in the art of war. Just before this Spanish inroad on the Americas, her people had been engaged in a long war for the expulsion of the Saracens from the Spanish peninsula. It might be styled the closing part of the wars of the Crusades, for many soldiers, from all countries in Europe, had joined the Spanish army for the expulsion of the Moslems. A martial spirit and martial men had been created, and were ripe for American conquest when the field was opened. The condition of Europe at that time, moreover, was not what it is to-day. Spain, it is true, had then the finest representative government in Europe, crude though it was. The English Parliament was a very different body from the present one. The kings were in the habit of making exactions without parliamentary authority, and, in that age, serfdom was not altogether abolished, and men and women were still included with the transfer of estates, and estimated at so many shillings a piece. There was scarcely such a thing as a pane of glass in the houses of the working classes of England, and only a few churches had them. Chimneys were rare. Many years thereafter, Queen Elizabeth was charged with extravagance, for strewing the royal floors with fresh rushes each week. Only about a dozen vegetables were then cultivated in Europe, while the Europeans found upwards of thirty varieties cultivated in America. In some of our best histories, maize is still set down as one of the American contributions to the European table, a singular mistake, as in Peter Martyr and the works of several of the

Spanish writers of that time, it is distinctly stated that the people in America cultivated and ate "Turkey corn," that cereal having been cultivated in Turkey, and thus known to Europeans long before the discovery. In fact, Humboldt ascertained that maize is nowhere found indigenous in America, or anywhere else, save in the valleys around the Himalaya mountains.

The houses and clothing of the most highly developed nations in America, could not be considered much inferior to those used at that period in Europe. The objective point of the Spanish adventurers was the wealthy empires; the purpose, conquest and robbery. The wild, nomadic tribes of the Americas could not be very successfully enslaved, but of the agricultural people, whole communities and towns were made bondsmen, and miserably perished working in the mines, after the rich empires, such as Mexico and Peru, had been robbed of their accumulations. The inspiring idea of the European adventurers was to get rich and return to Europe. The accomplished and benevolent bishop of Chiapas (Las Casas), whose works were suppressed by the Spanish government for their denunciation of the cruelties practiced on the inhabitants of America, so deeply sympathized with the wretched natives that he suggested the introduction, in the West India Islands, of African slavery, which was then common on the other continents. To its introduction at that time the Americas are indebted for this element of their population, and the history connected therewith.

Although Columbus discovered the West India Islands before he did the coast of the mainland, only one or two of them could be said to be occupied by the Spaniards for one hundred and fifty years. Jamaica had little more than a garrison of Spaniards in 1655, when Admiral Penn conquered it, whereupon it was settled by the English. In 1861 it had thirteen thousand eight hundred and sixty-one whites; eighty-one thousand and seventy-four colored people (mixed) and three hundred and forty-six thousand three hundred and seventy-four blacks. In 1871, five hundred and six thousand one hundred and fifty-four whites; thirteen thousand one hundred and one mixed, and three hundred and ninety-two thousand seven hundred and seven blacks. It is proper to state that in 1850 about fifty thousand of the population perished of cholera.* The dates of actual settlements in the West Indies were as follows: the Dutch settled Tobago in 1632, and the Virgin Islands in 1648. The English settled Barbadoes in 1624; St. Christopher, in 1625; the Bahamas, in 1629; Antigua, Montserrat, Barbuda and Redonda, in 1632, and Auguilla, in 1640.† The French settled Dominica in 1610; Martinique, Guadeloupe, Desirada, Marie Galante, St. Bartholomew, Tortugas and Hermano, in 1635; Grenada in 1650; and St. Vincent, in 1719. The Danes settled St. Thomas in 1671, and St. John in 1717, while it was 1643 before the Spaniards settled St. Martin, St. Eustatius, Sabar and Curacoa. They had, shortly after the discovery, obtained a foothold in Cuba and San Domingo.

Let us examine the European settlements in North America. In 1564, the French Huguenots, on account of their persecution in France, planted a colony in Florida, near the spot on which St. Augustine now stands. The year after, a Spanish governor, Menendez, landed, took the Huguenot fort, and hanged the prisoners as heretics. A few months later, the Spaniards left at the place were hung by a French officer who came to avenge his countrymen. As Spain claimed the North American continent, she established a fort at St. Augustine, in 1565, and there has been a continuous European settlement ever since, which, for a long period, however, did not extend to the adjacent country.‡ In 1584 Queen Elizabeth granted two patents to Adrian Gilbert and Sir Walter

* Haydn's Dictionary of Dates, page 441.

† Lippincott's Gazetteer, page 2386.

‡ Ibid., page 775.

Raleigh, to make settlement in North America. No permanent settlements were effected at that time. In 1607, Jamestown, in Virginia, was settled by the English, but burned by the natives the ensuing year.* It was permanently settled, in 1610, by Governor De La War. At that time all that portion of North America north of Florida was styled Virginia, in honor of Queen Elizabeth, who had granted the original charter. In 1609, Hendrick Hudson, acting under the Dutch, sailed up the Hudson to the place where Albany now stands, and, consequently, the Dutch claimed all the country from Cape Cod to Cape Henlopen.† Conception Bay, Newfoundland was settled in 1610 by forty planters under a patent from King James.‡ In 1608, Champlain, a Frenchman, settled at Quebec, and remained undisturbed until 1613, when the English Virginia colony sent a force to dislodge him. In 1606 James I. divided Virginia by letters patent. The southern part included all lands between the 34th and 41st degrees of north latitude. The northern, called the second colony, also included part of the first, as it ran from the 38th to the 45th. Each of these colonies was to be governed by thirteen men, and, as the territories lapped over each other, to prevent disputes, these separate colonists were forbidden to settle within a hundred miles of each other.§

The Northmen or Scandinavians, as already stated, made settlements in Greenland, in 982.‖ In 1534 the French had sailed up the St. Lawrence river, and went through the formula of taking possession of the country as "New France." Sebastian Cabot, who had sailed along the North American continent from Davis Straits to a not definite point south, in 1497, like the rest of the exploring navigators, went through the form of taking possession of the country for the English

* Holmes' American Annals, page 154. † Ibid., page 167.

‡ Ibid., page 172.

§ Morse's Universal Gazetteer, vol. i., page 115. ‖ Ibid., page 73.

crown.* In 1576, Sir Francis Drake, while cruising for Spanish galleons, discovered and took possession of California for the British, but no settlements were made. The Dutch, claiming, under the discovery of Hendrick Hudson, settled Manhattan, or New Amsterdam, (now New York) in 1614. In 1614 Captain Smith sailed along the coast of "North Virginia," and made a map of it, after which it was called "New England." † In 1620 a portion of the Puritan congregation of Mr. Robinson, with elder Brewster and John Carver, settled at Plymouth.‡ The settlement of New Hampshire dates from 1623. In 1627, a colony of Swedes and Finns landed at Cape Henlopen, and "purchased from the Indians" the land from that point to the Delaware Falls. They, however, called the Delaware river "New Swedeland Stream." Upon it they built several forts and made settlements.§ In 1628 Sir Henry Boswell bought from the New England Council the land around Massachusetts Bay, and founded the colony.|| Maryland was settled by Lord Baltimore, in 1633. In 1630 Connecticut was granted to Lords Say and Brooke, but no English settlement was made there until 1635. In the same year Roger Williams and his brethren were driven from Massachusetts and settled in Rhode Island. The Dutch made settlements in New Jersey, in 1614, and, as has been already stated, the Swedes and Finns made settlements in what is now part of New Jersey, in 1627. The English monarch granted New Jersey to the Duke of York who sold it to Lord Berkeley in 1664. In the same year the English captured Manhattan, or New York, from the Dutch. South Carolina was settled by the English in 1669. William Penn made his celebrated settlement of Pennsylvania in 1682, and made a treaty with the Indians for the relinquishment of a

* Holmes' American Annals, page 17.

† Ibid., page 183. ‡ Ibid., page 199.

§ Morse's Universal Gazetteer, vol. i., page 119.

|| Haydn's Dictionary of Dates, page 32.

small portion of the territory sold to him by the British crown. Louisiana was settled by the French in the same year. Georgia was settled by General Oglethorpe and colony in 1717. The tract of land now known as Vermont was claimed by both the colonies of New York and New Hampshire. When hostilities broke out between Great Britain and the colonies, the inhabitants assembled and formed a "Constitution of Government." It has ever since continued to exercise its powers. The first settlement at Bennington was in 1776. The state was not admitted to the Union under this constitution until 1791.

I am thus particular about the dates because they show that actual European, industrial settlements were not seriously thought of for a long time after the discovery by Columbus. They also show that during the seventeenth century there were active influences at work in Europe driving out a different class of people from those who first came to America for gold or conquest. These causes had much to do with the character of the settlements. A political and religious revolution was going on, and many of the independent thinkers in European countries were glad to seek a new home where they could escape persecution. At that time the English feudal system of land tenure was being modified, and in the reign of Charles was nominally abolished, but the lands of Britain had been left in the hands of their aristocratic owners. The colonists were surrounded by many peculiar circumstances which did not leave them at liberty to devise a perfect system of land tenure, even if they had been prepared for it. Land, moreover, was abundant and cheap; it was not anticipated that there ever would be a scarcity of it.

Following the discovery of Columbus, many of the people of Europe may be said to have become drunk with adventure. Discovery was considered a better title than possession. Spiritual and temporal potentates were alike infected with the idea of giving away or selling the lands of the Americas they had never seen. Whole principalities were generously granted by people who never owned them, and impecunious monarchs paid their debts by laying mortgages on lands to which they never, by purchase or even conquest, had the color of title.

Such was the age of "The right of discovery." The mode of establishing title, under the right of discovery, was for an adventurous navigator to go on shore, in a region hitherto unknown to Europeans, and hoist a flag and take possession in the name of his sovereign, whoever he might happen to be. In the celebrated map of Juan de la Cosa, the companion and chart-maker of Columbus, made in Spain, in 1500, we find the Brazils marked by the Portuguese flag; the larger portion of the islands and continents by the Spanish flag, and the region above and below the mouth of the St. Lawrence is adorned with the British flag. It is a circumstance worthy of note, moreover, that the Cosa map of 1500 gives nearly the whole North American coast line, including a not very correct peninsula of Florida, and the mouths of the Mississippi river. This was twenty years before our historical version of the discovery of Florida by Ponce de Leon, and is a curious instance of the manner in which romance is injected into history. To reconcile it, Mr. Stevens, the Ethnological writer, attempts, in an introduction to a report on the Tehuantepec railway, to show that Juan de la Cosa meant the mouths of the river he represented on his map for the Ganges. How such a writer could have made such a mistake is inexplicable, as it was notorious that Columbus and Cosa, his map-maker, on his second voyage, took an observation at an eclipse at St. Domingo, and fixed the exact number of degrees between that point and Seville. The old Ptolemy maps plainly showed the location of China (Cathay) and, of course, both the men knew perfectly well to a degree the immense stretch of the earth's surface that lay between these points. In fact, Columbus, during that second voyage, wrote a letter to Queen Isabella, in which he said: "This country, your majesty, is not, as many people suppose, an island, but a continent, or rather, two continents connected by a narrow neck of land, and beyond that a great sea much larger than that we have traversed in coming from your majesty's dominions." Of course, Columbus had not sailed over that sea. From personal knowledge he knew little of either continent, but the natives of the West Indies, before he reached them, made continual voyages from continent to continent, across the Caribbean Sea, and the navigators doubtless received much of their knowledge of the subject from them.

Some time afterward Balboa "discovered" the South Sea across the isthmus and frantically rushed into and "took possession" of it in the name of the sovereigns of Spain. In fact, for a long period discoverers were sailing to and fro, hoisting flags and taking possession of countries. Many of them took possession of the same regions, and when a man, founding his right on somebody's discovery, took possession of a locality, there was no specific limit to the extent of his possessions. I am thus particular about the "right of discovery" as this rather absurd fiction has entered as an element into American titles. Courts have gravely discussed it, and persons in authority pondered over the rights thus given to large portions of the surface of the earth. A *right* which seemed to carry the power to expel the native inhabitants, to give kings the authority to make a chattel of an almost unknown region, speculators the claim to traffic in it, and to deny others the privilege of cultivating it without the consent of the discoverer, his heirs and assigns.

The "right of discovery," by its uncertainties, the natural doubt about its record, the mystery as to how much was discovered, or how far the hoisted flag threw its shadow, gave rise to another and kindred right, the "right of conquest." The right of discovery may be styled the pickpocket's right, and the right of conquest the highwayman's right. The pickpocket discovers that a man has a pocketbook in his coat, and by adroit manipulation gets possession of it without alarming or notifying the owner. His possession comes from his right of discovery. On the other hand, the highwayman meets his victim, and by force of arms or greater strength, knocks him down and takes what he has. His title to what he thus gets is the "right of conquest." The right of conquest was not a new invention of European adventurers in America. It had flourished in Western Europe for many hundred years. Lords and barons built castles on almost inaccessible crags, and sallied forth with their retainers, and plundered their neighbors.* The great man of that period was he who could cut a throat if occasion offered, drive in a herd of cattle, or sack a house without compunction. Of course, when persons of this character found a new opening in America, it was to be expected that they would take advantage of their opportunities. The American field, moreover, had several advantages. The natives had not yet discovered gunpowder, and excursions among them were a good deal safer. The chance of reprisals was not so great. In addition to this, Peru and Mexico had better organized governments at that time than some portions of Europe were blessed with, and, as well organized banditti had not flourished on the weakness or connivance of the state, the field was a good deal richer. Human cupidity has written some terrible pages of history, but none which appear more mercilessly cruel, or utterly unwarranted, than the plunder and overthrow of Peru and Mexico. Nor had the conquerors the pretended apology that they carried superior government and civilization. It is stated that there have been upwards of two hundred and sixty revolutions in Mexico since 1821,† not to mention the interminable political confusion before that time. Indeed, it may be safely stated that since the murder of Montezuma, for it was not an execu-

* Hallam's Middle Ages, vol. ii., page 506.

† Haydn's Dictionary of Dates, page 520.

tion, unhappy Mexico has never been so well policed or governed. The amount of gold and silver shipped to Europe was so great that the statistics about it seem incredible. It was enough to upset and unsettle values in the Old World, and laid the foundation for the comparative decay of Spain, by diverting her people from those staid, industrious habits that alone can give prosperity to a nation. Spain was, nevertheless, the envy of Europe. Piratical expeditions were fitted out to cruise on the Spanish main and capture the galleons loaded with bullion. These were the grand old buccaneering days, the term *boucanier* being given because these freebooters chiefly lived on the dry meat of the buffalo, at that time plentifully found on the North American coast. There was no particular discredit attached to the business, one prominent English operator having been knighted for his prowess.

I have endeavored to point out the distinction between the first hundred and twenty-five years of adventure and plunder, and the era of industrial settlements of a better class, beginning with the early portion of the seventeenth century. The era of discovery and robbery had to a considerable extent expended its energies. That period, moreover, had bequeathed some bad elements and precedents as to the rights of property in the New World, especially in land. The theory that the state had the right to determine on what terms the land within its geographical limits should be occupied was upset. Much of the land was disposed of, or pretended to be disposed of, before any American government was established. Much of it was handed and bandied about after a fashion that would not, even then, have been tolerated in Europe, semi-barbarous though it was. It is true, Indian governments of all kinds and grades occupied the country, and their people had lived here from remote periods, but the whole idea of the European settlements was hostile to their rights. The claims of Spain, or France, or England by discovery, were paramount, and the Indian title was something that was to be got rid of as soon as this could be safely or conveniently done. Had it been attempted in any high-handed way, by general conquest, at any time during the first fifty years of settlement, the result, in all probability, would have been the expulsion of the settlers. At the date of the European discovery, the region lying north and east of the Mexican provinces, was thinly populated. The evidences of a more dense population, and a higher stage of civilization, still confront us, but at that period had mainly passed away. A few great nomadic peoples broken into tribes and bands, traversed the west, the north and the east. The country was rich in game, nuts and fruit. Many of the inhabitants cultivated a little maize, and were in one place this year and in another the next. Neither their religion nor their political ideas gave their governments a centralizing force. They were attached to their free, independent modes of life. Their councils were advisory rather than dictatorial. A chief had no power save by the consent of those he ruled. There was no means of enforcing his authority, and it was liable to terminate at any moment. Wandering as they did, conflicts between the different tribes and bands were frequent. Bloody tribal feuds existed. Confederacies in a few cases had been created, but these were chiefly between the people of the same blood, and exercised no general authority capable of organizing resistance. Clustered around the Mobilian basin were the broken fragments of a hundred different races and tribes, many of whom were in stages of decline. A few of these peoples cultivated orchards and fruit, and domesticated many animals and fowls. They had no great cities, but agricultural towns and villages. Long after the date of the European discovery the sacred fire still burned on their great mounds or high places.

The languages of the nomadic tribes of the north and west were crude, and indicated little progress in society or thought;

they rarely generalized, had no such words as "tree" or "cattle," but every beast and every tree had its name. Not so with many tribes or fragments of nations found clustered near the lower part of the great river. Nearly every form of grammatical construction can be found among them. The same law of emigration which obtained in the old continents seemed to have governed here. Nation after nation, and tribe after tribe must have floated down with the current, silt and drift, on the great river, and left their heterogeneous and broken fragments in the delta, or in the low wet lands of Louisiana, Alabama and Mississippi. Tribes and nations not so far advanced, and not so mixed or fragmentary, but still subsisting chiefly from agriculture and fishing, stretched up, far northward on the American coasts. Besides the great nomadic nations heretofore referred to, many tribes and nations once located in certain portions of the country, on being driven from their homes, became, to great extent, nomads and wanderers, nor could they very well help it. On their arrival, the whites were continually pressing and driving them back, and they were thrown in contact with the interior tribes, who, in turn, regarded them as intruders. Having, in many cases, been enemies formerly, fresh feuds were easily engendered by this conflict of interests. While there are a few instances where the contact with the whites benefited or improved their condition, upon the whole, the effect on the native American tribes, has been in every way degrading and disastrous. The date of the European settlements was to them the commencement of ruin. These people, to a large extent, ceased to be agriculturists because they had no security for the crops they might plant, nor could they hope to remain in any location. Permanent improvements, and any advance in their condition was always looked on by the whites with jealousy, as increasing the difficulties of getting rid of them.

After the era of plunder and gold mining had partially subsided, the Spaniards commenced permanent industrial settlements. They were not driven out by religious persecution, for Spain was always Catholic, but, in common with other nations in Europe, her people suffered from the social and political changes that were going on, and to many emigration was a relief. In some respects their colonial settlements differed from the French, but they, too, intermarried with the natives, and there was an absorption and blending of some of the peculiarities of each. In some portions of Spanish America, certain parties still boast of pure Castillian blood. This, however, is rare. A few of the native Indian nations and villages, on the other hand, do not intermix with the Spaniards, but there is no wide gulf fixed as to their modes of life. In driving down the Rio Grande, for instance, the coachman will tell you that this "is an Indian town," and that "a Spanish town," but there seems to be but little difference between them in dwellings, dress or habits. The Spaniards have chiefly occupied countries where agriculture could only be carried on by irrigation, and they adopted the modes and regulations of the aboriginal inhabitants. The ancient building material of the country was largely adobe or adobe and stone, and the Spaniards build almost similar houses. The more wealthy Spaniards merely erected larger houses, and they are a little better finished and furnished, but of the same generic character. What is true of both the French and Spanish settlements, is that in occupying the country, the expulsion of the Indian does not appear to have been necessary, or to have been contemplated. In both cases the French and Spanish governments endeavored to foster an aristocracy. Great grants of land were given to prominent Spaniards for military service or money. The Spanish settlements in America began in a conception of aristocracy and although without titular distinction (beyond mere military titles) have remained essentially aristocratic. In this condition these Spanish colonies are found to-day.

The British colonial system was different. Their settlers

did not intermarry with, or mix in a friendly or homogeneous population with the natives. In the Byrd manuscript, that philosophical and facetious old Virginia colonist deprecated the circumstance, which is specially noted by him. He thinks it unfair that the English in taking their land should not have taken their daughters with it.* There are a few exceptional cases. In Virginia, the case of Pocahontas. The Scotch and Irish settlers of Georgia who went there with Oglethorpe, also, to a considerable extent, became mixed with the Southern tribes. The McGilvarys and McIntoshs of the Creek nation, and the Rosses, McDonalds, McNairs and Adairs of the Cherokees, are notable instances, and have had marked effect on the progress of these tribes. In these cases it is to be observed that such Europeans were absorbed by those two nations, and became part of their people, and active participants in their policy. There was, with the American and Indian tribes in general, no mingling of the two races, or any system encouraged or tolerated for a conjunction of interests or mutual absorption on fair terms. "The Indian must go" was the prevalent policy, and it has written a record stained by bloodshed and bad faith.

One of the most important consequences of the "right of discovery," was the system of treaties with the Indian nations and tribes. The "crown" of each nation having colonies claimed the right of title by discovery, and, from the crown, the colonies claimed powers and privileges under the same head. All parties were perfectly well aware, however, that there was an occupancy right that covered the country. At first many of the colonists endeavored to purchase from the natives the right of occupying certain locations, or propitiated the tribes with presents, so that they would permit the settlements. As has been shown, none of the Indian tribes understood, or for a moment approved of, or adopted the theory that the land

* Byrd's Manuscript, History of the Dividing Line, page 5.

was an individual chattel, or that the purchasers could have perpetual, exclusive use. They were, however, very jealous and careful about the boundaries of the lands belonging to their own people. In defense of their boundaries they did not hesitate to go to war, and they tenaciously clung to their possessions in all the contests about frontage, in council and negotiation. The title, however, was the title of the nation, and could only be disposed of by the nation. William Penn had purchased a tract of land from the British Crown, and, conscientiously believing that this really gave him no title to the Indian property without their consent, he, by treaty, purchased land where Philadelphia now stands, from the Indians. They, of course, merely understood that for these presents they gave the right of settlement at that place to Mr. Penn and his people. They certainly did not contemplate a fresh irruption of settlers, and continued arrivals of innumerable colonists that should over-run not only the country they occupied, but regions now constituting Pennsylvania which were claimed by other tribes. In the same way as stated, the settlement of Swedes and Finns on the Delaware, bought from the Indians all the land from Cape Henlopen to the Falls of the Delaware. Unless it was under the Dutch right of discovery of New York, they had no fiction of a right of discovery to fall back on, and, indeed, they had to make their peace with the British proprietors as best they could.

It very soon became apparent to the rulers in Europe, who were interested in real estate in America, that it would never do to let everybody make bargains or treaties with the Indians, or the right of discovery and even the colonial patents would soon amount to nothing or get mixed up with these purchases by individuals and lead to inextricable confusion. Treaties were then made by the European governments with the governments of the Indian nations for cessions of land from time to time as the colonies progressed. Under the most stringent regulations individuals were prohibited from making purchases or bargains with the Indians, and even the colonists were forbidden from encroaching on the Indian lands, or making purchases or treaties with them except under royal authority. The colonial governors, acting under specific authority, issued patents to tracts purchased or granted in some cases. Besides the companies holding the colonial charters, many other companies obtained and purchased considerable tracts, chiefly for speculation. Many prominent colonists thus obtained tracts, some through the colonial governors, and some directly from the British privy council. A royal proclamation was issued in 1763 forbidding the territorial governors from granting patents to lands beyond the head waters of rivers flowing into the Atlantic. Title predicated on the royal right of discovery and the right of conquest has been treated with the utmost gravity when questions growing out of it have been under consideration by the supreme court of the United States. It is to be regretted, and a few hundred years hence it will probably be regretted more, that fictions about such rights should have figured so prominently, and that in treating these questions the court had not chiefly considered the principles and spirit upon which the government and constitution had been founded. Chief Justice Marshall, the most eminent of our jurists, indeed held that the right of discovery only gave an exclusive right to purchase from the Indians, as against all other nations, and in this he was doubtless sustained by the laws and practice of all the governments. The power to extinguish the right of discovery by the right of conquest, as in the case of the British over the French, and the Dutch does not seem to be called in question by anybody. The colonies by the war of independence succeeded to all the rights the British had, and, by the purchase of Louisiana, to all the rights of the French.

In her treaties with the Indians the United States has, besides paying a trifle for the land she obtained, been in the habit of sacredly guaranteeing the Indians the unmolested possession of the remainder. This the French and English had done before them, and in all these cases the rights thus guaranteed were observed until these governments wanted some more land. Adequate payment to the tribes for the land relinquished was never made. The treaties were often made by the Indians under a species of duress, probably at the close of an Indian war, or a war in which the Indians participated, or under circumstances when some kind of a settlement had to be accepted. Many men claiming to be statesmen have often participated in these purchases of Indian lands for a trifle of what they were worth. A pernicious idea that the lands of the country were something that kings and republics, states and individuals, could speculate in and make gain of, infected the general mind. Long after the adoption of the federal constitution political parties were rent in twain on the subject of selling the public lands and distributing the proceeds among the states. The curse of the first discoverers and conquerors seemed to rest on the soil. The adventurers came, and after they had stolen all the gold and silver they could lay their hands on, attempted to steal the continent and make it a football for speculators. It was a chattel to pay debts with, and barter and give away by those who would not deign even to set foot upon it. Had their influence perished with them it would not have been so much to be regretted, but it made a chattel of land after a fashion the world had not yet seen, and it poisoned and blinded men's minds on this question of great public policy.

Some singular precedents were created by the colonists. North Carolina, by an act of her colonial legislature, *extended* her boundaries to the Mississippi river. Why she did not extend them to the Pacific ocean is incomprehensible. Not the least wonderful thing is that she succeeded in getting her claim to this property considered, and obtained payment for lands in a large portion of Tennessee. A Virginian named Henderson visited what is now Kentucky and purchased a tract from the Cherokee Indians. The transaction appears from the first to have been open to objections. Many years after, when the treaty of Hopewell was made, the Cherokees claimed a considerable portion of the lands of Kentucky, when the commissioners produced the deed or paper conveying all of that region to Mr. Henderson. Tassell, one of the delegates, borrowed some paper from the commissioner and made a map showing the rivers and their boundaries, a fac-simile of which is in the American State Papers, and said that the signature of Oconestoto to the deed was a forgery. Henderson, he said, had only asked for a little land on Kentucky river to feed his horses on. Tassell described it by a small round circle on the map. The commissioner informed him that all the parties to the deed were dead, and as the titles of a great many settlers were involved, it must stand. Tassell then replied, they "would let Kentucky go," but he "was sorry Henderson was dead; he would like to have told him he was a liar." *

When Henderson first made his purchase, the matter was brought to the attention of the Virginia colonial legislature, and as Henderson was a Virginian that body patriotically claimed the country for Virginia. They considerately allowed him about a third of it for himself, taking the ground that such a portion was worth a great deal more than he gave for the whole, and after determining that the sale was not perfectly good so far as Mr. Henderson was concerned, resolved that it was conclusively good so far as any or all Indians were concerned, and then proceeded to dispose of the remainder. This was the foundation for no inconsiderable number of land titles.

Virginia also claimed property interests in the northwest territory in Ohio and Illinois. Connecticut likewise had a claim to land in Ohio, partly growing out of their right to

* American State Papers, vol. i., Indian Affairs, page 42.

extend their boundaries to the "South Sea," and partly owing to settlement under Manasseh Cutler, and both states in 1802 ceded their *jurisdiction* over their reserves to the United States. Connecticut disposed of the lands styled the Western Reserve in Ohio, by sales.

In establishing the British colonies in North America they were marked by the circumstances of the settlers and the spirit that animated the settlement. The founders of the colonies north of Maryland were people driven from Europe by persecution. They were protestants against long established ideas, and their protestant spirit crops out in the colonies they founded. Aristocracy among them soon perished. The people were and are sturdy, laborious and economical. In many of the Southern states aristocracy was carefully planted and encouraged. The colony of Carolina was planned in Great Britain. There were to be counts for the counties and palatines and barons. John Locke lent the scheme the aid of his genius, and wrote the constitution of government that was designed to be adopted. In North Carolina, when the Carolinas were divided, a similar idea was fostered. One of the founders was a Baron Graffenreid, who actually attempted to establish his barony, and came very near being burned at the stake by the exasperated natives.* Virginia was blessed by her shoots of aristocracy and her "first families" still cling to the relics of a decayed greatness. Lord Baltimore remains the patron saint of the tournaments of Maryland. Large landed possessions were acquired, and are still retained in these sections. As the average emigrating European, even then, was averse to peonage, and able to set up for himself, the aristocracy would have pined for a class to lord over, had it not been for African slavery. At first common, to some extent, in all the colonies, it soon languished in the great

* Baron Graffenreid's Letter in Williamson's Tuscarora War, vol. i., page 285.

central and eastern portions and passed away. In the South the system grew to a great aristocratic oligarchy. The poor whites who could not own slaves gradually sank in the scale, for no labor can be respectable where slave labor exists. Georgia, in the beginning, was not blessed or cursed with slavery. The conscientious Oglethorpe resolutely opposed it. His followers coveted the privileges of the adjoining colonies, and kept up the agitation until they carried their point, and the founder of the colony shook the dust from his feet against them.

The colonial era really laid the foundations of what there is of an American land system. It began with royal claims based on discovery, and ended in conquest and speculation. Through all the checkered years from 1610 to 1776, the foundations of European settlements in America were planted, and grew into power. The essential feature of the land polity seemed to be that in this New World each man should get as much land as he could, and if he did not sell it to some successor, his family should have the exclusive right to use it forever. Escaping from the aristocracy and despotism of Europe, each man hoped he could found an aristocratic family of his own. Tenure was not based on a recognition of human rights, but on privilege. The richer and more aristocratic colonists desired great estates and the spread of an aristocratic landed system. Such institutions met the favor and received the patronage of the home governments. Poor settlers and colonists had little power and were anxious to secure all the land they could.

It must, indeed, be conceded that nothing save a strong liberty-loving spirit among the people prevented a worse system than we inherited. The assertion of human rights was broad enough in the Declaration of Independence to constitute the principles of a free government. It is to be regretted that a permanent, equitable land tenure was not established.

CHAPTER XI.

HISTORY OF THE LAND POLITY OF THE UNITED STATES.

Land tenure shaped in colonial days—Conflicting colonial claims—Continental Congress—Plea to pay expenses of Revolutionary War from public lands—First land bounty for soldiers—Proposed northwest colony—Washington's landed estates—The Walpole Land Company—The Ohio Company—The Quebec bill—Ordinance for the northwest territory—Madison's comments—First modes of land sale—French commons—John Adams—Property in soil the foundation of power—Land sold from 1796 to 1885—Proceeds in money—Less than a year's customs and revenue—The surplus funds—The years of great land speculation—Borrowing public money to buy public lands—Distribution of the proceeds—Graduation bill—Grants of lands to states—To schools and colleges—To canals—To corporations—Pre-emption law—Homestead law—Great and small land speculators—Squatters—Residue of public lands—Frauds under a bad system—Texas and her lands—Mexican grants—Letter from the commissioner—Aggregate homesteads filed and taken—Timber culture grants—Area disposed for bounty land warrants—Number of farms in the United States—Number of landholders—Of renters—Of farm laborers—Gradual transfer of land from settler to land speculator.

In founding a republic on the admitted equality of the human race, and on the inalienable right of all its citizens to "life, liberty and the pursuit of happiness," there is nothing in the mode of disposing of the public domain or the adjustment of tenures in these United States that is worthy of being called a land policy. As we have seen, the greatest of ancient nations have been overthrown by the evils following land monopoly. Where equal tenure of the soil passed into privilege, a tax on production was thus levied to sustain an aristocratic non-productive class. In Western Europe feudal landholders had entered into a struggle with chattel holders, both being assertions of individual right to the soil. These different opinions about tenure were transplanted to the soil of a new continent where the right of discovery and the right of conquest had already called in question equal human right. Out of these conflicting materials American tenure was shaped.

During colonial times the land was not treated as something to which all the men who might live on it should have an equal right. Land was sometimes acquired for use, but more frequently for speculation. Ignorant even of the geography of the country they disposed of, the original colonial charters were formed in language, much of which now appears ridiculous, and led to conflicts in regard to title. Many of the grants covered the same ground and nearly all of them terminated at the "South Sea," or Pacific Ocean. When the colonies succeeded in achieving their independence the territorial question was a very disturbing one. Virginia claimed not only Kentucky, but a large tract north and west of the Ohio. New York claimed a great deal of the same country by virtue of cessions from the Iroquois, or six nations. These people rambled over a considerable portion of the United States, and a cession of their territory and jurisdiction was rather indefinite. Massachusetts and Connecticut were pertinacious in asserting their rights to some of the territory that lay between them and the "South Sea." A conflict also existed between New York and Pennsylvania in regard to their Western territories.

The creation of a northwestern colony had long been a disturbing element between influential parties in the colonies and the mother country. A company called the "Ohio Company" had been formed in 1748 by Thomas Lee, Lawrence Washington, Augustine Washington and others, for the colonization of the western country. They obtained from the crown a grant of five hundred thousand acres in the region of the Ohio, and the French and Indian War was precipitated by their attempting to open a road to these western valleys. A royal proclamation was issued in 1763, prohibiting colonial governors from granting patents for land beyond the sources of any of the rivers that flow into the Atlantic Ocean. This proclamation was ostensibly to pacify the Indians by reserving for their use the lands west of the Alleghenies, but behind it lurked another policy,—that of organizing colonies only on the seaboard that could be retained in the interests, commercially and otherwise, of the mother country. The governor of Virginia had no jurisdiction outside of his own province, but he was authorized to grant from "the king's domain" two hundred thousand acres to officers and soldiers who had served in the French and Indian War, provided the claimants applied to him personally for land warrants. These grants were, for every field officer, five thousand acres; for every captain, three thousand; to every subaltern or staff officer, two hundred, and for every private, fifty acres. This was one of the earliest military land grants in this country. These grants could be made in "Florida," Canada or elsewhere in ungranted crown lands. George Washington, who was entitled to five thousand acres in his own right, and who in conjunction with others bought up the claims of various parties, ultimately received at least thirty-two thousand acres of this tract. Governor Dunmore had, in the first place, issued patent to Washington for upward of twenty thousand acres on the Kanawha and Ohio rivers. In the schedule of property appended to Washington's will, the value of the parcels owned by him was noted in 1799, in his own hand. According to this memoranda he had in Virginia, 27,486 acres, thus valued at $124,880; on the Ohio, 9,744 acres, valued by him at $97,440; on the Great Kanawha, 23,341 acres, estimated at $200,000. In addition there are smaller tracts in Maryland, Pennsylvania, New York, in the Northwest Territory and in Kentucky. In all, 70,975 acres, which he deemed at that time to be worth $464,807. He had, also, lots in Washington, Alexandria and Winchester. I refer to this statement as indicating the relations to real estate of a Virginia gentleman of that period. It had been the policy of Britain in several of the colonies, notably Virginia and the Carolinas, to encourage the formation of large landed proprietorships and thus create territorial nobility, or country gentlemen. This mode of disposing of land had a good deal to do with what followed. It is all the more to Washington's credit that, although he owned slaves and was by his surroundings necessarily connected with large landholding interests, he cordially joined in forming a republic predicated on the doctrine of the equal rights of men. The lands of the colonies were being absorbed, and even the "back lands," called "crown lands," were in various ways getting into market. A very instructive advertisement over the signature of George Washington is in part copied from the *Maryland Journal* and *Baltimore Advertiser* of August 20th, 1773:

"MOUNT VERNON, in VIRGINIA, July 15, 1773.

"The subscriber having obtained patents for upwards of twenty thousand acres of land on the Ohio and Great Kanawha (ten thousand of which are situated on the banks of the first-mentioned river, between the mouths of the two Kanawhas, and the remainder on the Great Kanawha, or New River, from the mouth, or near it, upward in one continued survey) proposes to divide the same into any sized tenements that may be desired, and lease them upon moderate terms, allowing a reasonable number of years rent free, provided within the space of two years from next October, three acres for every fifty contained in each lot, and proportionately as above, shall be enclosed and laid down in good grass for meadows, and, moreover, that at least fifty fruit trees for every like quantity of land shall be planted on the premises. * * * * To which may be added, that as patents have now actually passed the seals for the several tracts here offered to be leased, settlers on them may cultivate and enjoy the lands in peace and safety notwithstanding the unsettled counsels respecting a new colony on the Ohio; and, as no right-money is to be paid for the lands, and quit rent of two shillings sterling a hundred, demandable some years hence, only, it is highly presumable that they will always be held on a more desirable footing than when both these are laid on with a heavy hand."

The advertisement enumerates that the "portage" from the "Powtowmack" by Cheat river and the other branches of the Monongahela, will be reduced to the compass of a few miles. The quality of the lands are extolled, and it is signed "George Washington."

In 1766 Benjamin Franklin and others organized a company called the "Vandalia," afterward the "Walpole Company." The company was composed of thirty-two Americans and two gentlemen of London; one of these was Thomas Walpole, a prominent London banker. The petition of the company to the British privy council, in 1769, asked for a grant of two million and a half acres of land between the 38th and 42d parallels of latitude, and east of the Sciota river. Franklin urged the matter in London. It was stated that the company offered more for this grant than the whole region back of the mountains had cost the British government at the treaty of Fort Stanwix. There was another company which was once more styled the "Ohio Company," that was ultimately merged in the "Vandalia." A rival company under the name of the "Mississippi Company" was organized by gentlemen of Virginia, among whom Francis Lightfoot, Richard Henry Lee, Arthur Lee and George Washington were conspicuous. The Walpole petition was first rejected and afterward granted by the crown, August 14th, 1772.

The British government had been strongly urged for some time before the Revolution to create a colonial government on the Ohio, west of the mountains, but appeared to be reluctant to do so. The royal order of 1763, prohibiting the colonial governors from granting patents beyond the head waters of streams running into the Atlantic, as has been said, ostensibly to keep peace with the Indians, had behind it a purpose to limit the territorial claims of the older colonies, and also to prevent any great population from growing up in the interior. A prominent member of the British government wrote a report for the privy council against the policy of creating such colonies. It was held that the colonies on the sea-coast were all connected in their business closely with the mother country, but if a colony or colonies were built up in the interior their interests would soon become inimical. The report indicated that it was the policy of the mother country to secure the production of raw material, which could be easily transported in the colonies, and the retention of these colonies as consumers of British manufactured articles. A rich interior colony could not afford to ship its raw products such a distance from the sea, and would soon be driven to manufacture. Whatever the reason was, the prohibitory order of 1763 was never rescinded. Something very different, however, was done. By an act of parliament, in 1774, the crown lands northwest of the Ohio were transferred and annexed to the royal province of Quebec. This measure was extremely unpopular with the colonies as several of them claimed portions of the country, and various enterprises, as we have partially shown, were on foot for its development, in which individual colonists were interested. This Act was no doubt intended, first, to put an end to the claims of the colonies on the Atlantic seaboard to that country, and also as a check to all schemes of private settlement. This "Quebec Bill," as it was called, was referred to in the Declaration of Independence as "their acts of pretended legislation." The Declaration of Independence made an end of the Quebec bill, as of various other things. At the outbreak of the Revolution, Virginia "annexed" a region of "the back country," which it then called the "County of Kentucky," and when Colonel George Rogers Clarke, in 1778, captured the military posts at Vincennes and Kaskaskia, during his expedition, Virginia once more proceeded to "annex" the lands beyond the Ohio, which it styled the "County of Illinois.

At the close of the Revolutionary War the territorial question was a very distracting one. Besides the claims of Virginia, Massachusetts and Connecticut claimed a portion of these lands under their original charter, which extended to the "South Sea." Many argued, as a question of justice, that all of this undisposed crown land should belong to, or be subject to, the action of Congress, and the proceeds used to defray the expenses of the Revolutionary War. It is a circumstance worthy of note that Thomas Paine and other Revolutionary leaders strenuously urged this view of the case. In point of fact, the old scrip, or war debt, was received in payment for land, until 1806.* The claimant colonies were, at first, not at all inclined to relinquish these territorial interests.

The Continental Congress was simply a representative body of the colonies, assembled for general defense. Feeling the necessity of some organization, the articles of confederation were adopted by Congress, November 15th, 1777, but were not finally agreed to by the colonies until March 1st, 1781. In the condition of the country at that time, engaged in a war with England, the delay of several of the colonies was critical. One of the main causes of dissension was the disposition of the "Crown Lands." Rhode Island, New Jersey, Delaware and Maryland objected to the disposition of the lands, as it stood in the articles of federation. Rhode Island proposed an amendment to the articles of confederation, "declaring that all lands within these states, the property of which was vested in the Crown of Great Britain, should be disposed of for the benefit of all the states in the confederacy;" but, adding, that the "jurisdiction" over these lands should remain with the states where they might be, or which might be adjudged to possess them. New Jersey took similar ground, only that the proceeds of the lands should be used to defray the expenses of the war. Delaware took a like position. Maryland instructed her delegates, forbidding them to ratify the articles of confederation until the land claims of the states were put upon a different basis. In fact, Maryland insisted that the undisposed-of crown lands should be subject to the decision of Congress. New York still claimed a portion of the West-

* Donaldson's History of the Public Domain, page 205.

ern lands through treaty with the Iroquois. The other claimants were Virginia, Connecticut and Massachusetts. But for the critical condition of affairs it is more than probable that the matter would not have been adjusted as it was. The small colonies were naturally jealous of the larger. Among the causes of apprehension it was anticipated, that if the states of Virginia, New York, Massachusetts and Connecticut had their claim to these lands confirmed, the sale of land would greatly enrich and strengthen them, and thus they would not be burdened with taxes, and emigration would tend to these states, and they might even absorb a part of the population of the weaker states. New York and Massachusetts were the first to yield, and, finally, Virginia and Connecticut agreed to the supervision of Congress, and to submit their claims for territory or indemnification to that body. Connecticut succeeded in retaining the Western Reserve in Ohio, which was as large as Connecticut. Part of this she disposed of to indemnify citizens who had been burned out during the war, and the remainder was sold, in 1795, for one million two hundred thousand dollars, and the proceeds chiefly used for educational purposes. Connecticut did not cede the jurisdiction over these lands until 1802. Under the early ordinance a place was agreed on to draw the land by lot for the thirteen states, but this was repealed in 1788.

The Congress under the confederation having thus acquired the territory outside of the colonies and early states, proceeded to take steps in reference to these common territories. The constitution was not framed or the government organized. The articles of confederation, whatever they conferred, contained nothing in them giving eminent domain to Congress. The provisions of the Ordinance of 1787 for the government of the Northwest Territory were new and bold expedients, both adopted before Congress was governed by constitutional limitations, or had a recognized field of authority. It was the first and only period in the history of the country when a policy to preserve the land for all the people might have been inaugurated. It is true that the public mind was infected with the idea that the land was something to sell. Nearly all of the difficulty grew out of the questions who should dispose of it, and who should have the proceeds. Doubtless there might have been a feeling among the framers of the ordinance that the public expected it to be sold to pay the debt caused by the war of the Revolution. Many of the leaders were aware of the importance of the land question in a government of the people, but between the powerful interests of the great estates that had been created, and the general desire to realize money from the land to pay the war debt, the opportunity was not taken to secure the lands of the country for cultivating holders. All financiers of that early period looked upon the public lands as a resource to be cashed to pay the war debt and obligations.*

The ordinance for the Northwest Territory is spoken of as a compact. A new policy was inaugurated by this Congress without a constitution, covering some of the most important interests of the future government. It will be observed that so far as jurisdiction and government for the Northwest Territory were concerned, the governments to be established were essentially temporary. Everything connected with it refers to new states to be created by the people. There has been no small disputation as to the authorship of the ordinance. That ordinance dedicated the Northwest to freedom. It was the first "free soil" legislation. It provided for establishing land titles, townships, schools, religious liberty, and was the essential outline of free states. With so much in the work to commend, it is unfortunate that a broad foundation should not have been laid to secure the soil for the tillers thereof, and to prevent an aristocracy from being founded on land monopoly. Hayne, Benton, Coles and other

* Donaldson's Public Domain, page 196.

Southern gentlemen claimed the authorship of the ordinance for Thomas Jefferson. Webster claimed it for Nathan Davis, of Massachusetts. It has been stated that it was suggested in a letter from George Washington to Mr. Duane, of New York, chairman of the Indian committee, written March, 1784. Madison, while admitting the necessity of some action, said, in an article in the *Federalist:* "They have proceeded to form new states, to erect temporary governments, to appoint officers for them, and to prescribe the condition on which such states shall be admitted into the confederacy. All this has been done, and done *without the least color of constitutional authority.*" Mr. Madison does not censure but urges the necessity for establishing constitutional government. It has even been held that this bond of common authority over these territories, as the property of the whole, and as a means of satisfying army claims, and meeting the debts caused by the war, was one of the strengthening powers that kept the early states together. By a resolution of 1785, squatters were warned against making unauthorized settlements, and settlements were not permitted on unsurveyed lands.* As it stood it initiated what there is of a public land policy. The mode adopted then for the sale and conveyance of land was much more primitive, and, it would appear, less guarded than now. By the Act of March 3d, 1791, it was provided that the governor of the Northwest Territory should be authorized to allot lands to settlers, or provide for disposing of "granted lands" in *amounts* "*according to his discretion.*" The lands were to be paid for. An Act of April 1st, 1806, authorized the governor and judges of Michigan Territory to lay out a town, including the then burned town of Detroit, and ten thousand acres adjacent, and to adjust all claims for lots therein, and to execute deeds for the same. The Act of March 3d, 1791, confirmed to Vincennes and other of the

* Donaldson's Public Domain, page 197.

old French towns their lands held in common. These commons, however, were not permitted to remain "common property," but were under pressure of the chattel system and an Act of April 20th, 1818, sold to individuals, and the proceeds given to schools. In spite of its abolition by law, the writer remembers the old common or "big field," at Kaskaskia, as late as 1840, where each head of a family had his portion of enclosed land to cultivate. The tendency among Americans was to individual chattel holding. Few seemed to think of any changed condition, or of any interest but the present. It is true, some profound thinkers undoubtedly considered it, but the tendency was the other way. On July 20th, 1790, Alexander Hamilton framed a plan for the sale of the public lands. He stated the purpose to be twofold: the first, financial, for the sale of the land; the second, to accommodate the inhabitants of the Western countries. He classifies the probable purchasers as moneyed individuals who may buy to sell again, companies for settlement and individual emigrants. No lands should be sold except where Indian title had been extinguished. Purchasers could buy five hundred acres, but individual settlers only one hundred acres. Larger tracts were to be set apart for sale in townships not less than ten miles square. Any sized tract might be purchased under "special contract" or agreement. Enough of the available land was to be held back from sale to meet applications of holders of scrip, or of holders of the securities of the loan then proposed. The price of lands was to be thirty cents per acre in gold, silver, or public securities. Credit should not be given unless the tract was at least ten miles square, in which cases one-fourth of the purchase money must be paid down. Surveys were to be made at the expense of purchasers or grantees, who were also required to pay fees for patents, which were to be issued by the President.*

The elder Adams, in his defense of the American govern-

* American State Papers, vol. i., Public Lands, page 8.

ments, says: "Property in the soil is the natural foundation of power and authority. Three cases of soil ownership are supposable. First, if the prince own the land he will be absolute. All who cultivate the soil, holding at his pleasure, must be subject to his will. Second, where the landed property is held by a few men the real power of the government will be in the hands of an aristocracy or nobility, *whatever they are named.* Third, if the lands are held and owned by the people, and *prevented from drifting into one or a few hands,* the true power will rest with the people, and that government will, essentially, be a Democracy, whatever it may be called. Under such a constitution the people will constitute the State."

He also wrote: "An attempt was made to introduce the feudal system and the canon law into America." * Mr. Adams publishes a letter from Turgot to Dr. Richard Price, dated Paris, March 22d, 1778, in which Turgot says that in America due attention has not been paid to the great distinction, *and the only one founded in nature* of the two classes of men, those who are landlords and those who are not.† The American method of treating the land question did not escape the observation of reflective minds in Europe. In the same letter, evidently in reference to the idea of territorial possessions as discussed in the confederated Congress, Turgot says, "The pretended interest of possessing more or less territory vanishes when territory is justly considered as belonging to individuals, not nations."

A few years later the French Revolution swept special privileges away. Mirabeau was expostulated with as to the policy of establishing small farms in the hands of the cultivators, but while he admitted that great farms, mechanically managed, might produce food at a cheaper rate, and perhaps more products, he contended that the general interests of the

* John Adams' Works, vol. iii., page 464. † Ibid., page 280.

mass of the people, especially the actual agriculturists, were advanced as well as secured by the system of small farms. The practice of the United States government has been to sell land to individual purchasers, giving fee simple title. The first sale of public lands reported, was in 1796, when the proceeds amounted to $4,836.13. Next year the sales had risen to $83,540.60. They increased, and in 1811 they had reached the amount for that year, of $1,040,237.53. In 1818 they reached $2,606,564.77. The two years when the sales of public lands produced most, were 1835, when the receipts were $14,757,600.75, and 1836, when the proceeds reached $24,877,179.80. In 1881 the proceeds of public land were $9,810,705,01. From 1836 to 1884 the sales had dropped to one, two and three million dollars a year, except that in 1855, the year after Kansas and Nebraska were open to settlement, when they ran up to $11,497,049.07. During the six war years they were very low. In 1861, $870,658.54. In 1862, $152,203.77. In 1863, $167,617.17, and in 1864, $588,333.29. In 1865, $996,553.31, and in 1866, $665,031.-03. The total amount received for sales of public lands from the beginning of the government, including the sales of 1884, amounted to $230,285,892.38.* It will thus be seen that the total proceeds of the sale of half a continent amounted to less than one year's revenue of the government in the years 1882, 1883 or 1884. Under the plan of Hamilton as afterward modified, and until 1810, lands were sold partially on credit. Up to that date 3,386,000 acres were so sold, producing the sum of $7,062,000,†

Small, although the proceeds of these sales have been, they were sufficient to create considerable disturbance. In the early history of the government there was a constant struggle about the proceeds. As the older colonies, that became states,

* Spofford's American Almanac, 1885, page 66.

† Donaldson's Public Domain, page 204.

had the control of the land within their limits, the new states desired to have it also. Of this, the older states were jealous, as they considered it part of the public patrimony. Between the proceeds of public lands and the steady increase of customs tax, a considerable surplus revenue was accumulated in the treasury, and this locking up of money was supposed to reduce the circulating medium of the country, to the detriment of business. Thomas Jefferson, in his second inaugural address, in 1805, proposed a distribution or "repartition" among the states, and also recommended a corresponding amendment to the Constitution, so that this fund could be applied, in time of peace, "to rivers, canals, roads, arts, manufactures, education and other great objects within each state." Jefferson objected to a gradual reduction of the revenue, and said, "Shall we suppress the impost and give that advantage to foreign over domestic manufacture?" The surplus and expected surplus, however, dwindled away, under various causes, during the last term of his administration. In 1809 Gallatin announced a deficit. Mr. Madison, during his administration, vetoed a bill called the "Bonus Bill," on constitutional grounds, which proposed to distribute a surplus for roads, canals, etc. Many statesmen of that day preferred schemes of distributing money among the states, to be applied by the states to improvements, rather than allow Congress to disburse it. Some even proposed that the surplus funds should be distributed to maintain the state governments instead of raising taxes, a proposition of a remarkable character. To prevent locking up needed currency, the surplus funds, or receipts were placed, first, in the United States Bank, and then, by Jackson, in state banks. These banks paid two per cent. to the United States on all amounts above what related to the demands of the government or their retained capital, and loaned funds at ten and twelve per cent. interest to private individuals. The great sales of land in 1835 and 1836 were chiefly due to land speculation. A considerable quantity of the land was purchased with borrowed money. That it was not due to an unusual increase of immigration is evident. The emigration in 1835 was 45,374, and in 1836, 76,242. In 1837 the emigration increased to 79,340, but the sales fell from nearly twenty-five millions to $6,776,236.52. In 1851 the emigration had swelled to 379,466, and the sales of land produced $2,352,305.30. It is estimated that $34,100,610.75 of the sales of these two years were to speculators not agricultural purchasers.* The purchasers borrowed from the banks. The money paid for land would then be deposited by the land officers in the bank, and again loaned out to another man to buy land with, and so on.

The laws for the sale of public lands and the regulations under them were modified after the time of Hamilton. The price was raised. Contests arose out of the old colonial, state, and other grants, which had to be adjusted. The great latitude allowed territorial officers was curtailed. The system of private entry was introduced, and thus in different ways the public lands were disposed of during the first half century of our history. In 1849 and 1850 swamp land acts were passed, by which Congress agreed to give the swamp lands to states for their reclamation. From that date up to 1884, 71,938,140.37 acres were selected by the states under the Act, and there have been approved and confirmed to them 57,794,258.14 acres. It is generally admitted that the fraudulent practices connected with swamp land locations have been quite as great as by any mode of disposing of the public lands. The number of swamps drained and reclaimed by this process have not been noteworthy exhibits in the improved productive industries of the country.

On the 1st of January, 1837, there was an actual surplus in the treasury of $41,468,859.97. On the 23d of June of that year an act was passed to distribute or loan this money,

* History of the Surplus Revenue, page 139.

all except five millions, to the states, according to their proportion of Congressional representation. By the terms of the Act the money was to be paid to the parties the states designated to receive it, on delivery of certificates of deposit bearing five per cent. interest. When it was urged against the measure that it was unconstitutional to raise revenue for distribution, it was answered that this was not derived from revenue but from the sale of property (land) which belonged to the people. On the 1st of January, 1837, fourteen banks of New York city held $12,294,067.80 of government deposits. In less than four months $6,168,854.60 were withdrawn from them for distribution. The amendment of the Senate to make the distribution by Congressional representation rather than upon the census was to give the Southern states more than they otherwise would get. In addition, the states that had an excess of representation got more than their share. If it had been paid, per capita, to freemen, it would have been three dollars and eigty-two cents to each freeman in Delaware, and one dollar and forty-nine cents in Illinois. South Carolina would have had three dollars and ninety-four cents, and New York one dollar and seventy-six cents. The money was not distributed per capita. Some states added it largely to their educational funds. Some expended it in improvements. In Illinois it was mostly sunk in unproductive railroads together with no inconsiderable portion of the proceeds of the state credit. One amusing circumstance connected with it in Illinois, was, that the legislature considerately voted a portion of it in money to those counties where the improvements were not to be made. The bewildered officers of these counties did not know what to do with it. Some of them attempted to place it in local improvements, but the popular plan was to loan it out to such citizens as wanted to borrow it. On these occasions the county seats were besieged by a crowd of borrowers who came there to get the money and endorse for one another. Altogether the history of the distribution of the surplus revenue is worth more as a lesson in political economy than it was as a financial venture.

Various experiments were tried to divert the proceeds of the sales of public lands. At first, one section in a township was granted to the states where there were public lands, for school purposes, being one thirty-sixth part of the whole. Later it was increased to two sections of each township, or the eighteenth part. These were sold by the states or local school boards. They were very generally sold on credit, usually at ten per cent., and, finally, eight per cent. interest, the proceeds as paid going into the school fund. While much school land was bought by speculators there were usually parties living in the neighborhood who purchased it to add to their farms or secure it for their children. It was sold for three or four times the price of government lands, the local policy being not to dispose of it until all or the bulk of the public lands were sold. Another expedient was the Graduation Act, or Acts. Lands which had for a certain period been in the market at the "upset" price of one dollar and twenty-five cents per acre, were gradually reduced until, finally, they were sold at twelve and a half cents per acre. Large tracts in several of the Western states were so sold some thirty years ago, and, although the purchaser was required to swear that the land was for his own use and benefit, this was really no obstruction to subsequent private sale. States succeeded in securing grants for colleges, universities, normal schools and internal improvements. These were disposed of under state law. Of the grants to states for educational purposes, in addition to the school sections, 1,814,769,-656 acres were given to twenty-one states and nine territories, and to the same for other schools 68,083,914 acres; for universities, 1,265,520 acres; for agricultural colleges 300,-000 acres were set apart, for each member of Congress and senator in the states, and scrip was issued therefor, which has been in the market and gone into the hands of speculators.

To deaf and dumb asylums, 44,970 acres.* The states to whom these grants were given contained the public lands. There were also granted to the states of Indiana, Ohio, Illinois, Wisconsin and Michigan, 4,405,980 acres for canal purposes. Congress also granted for internal improvements to the states of Illinois, Mississippi, Alabama, Florida, Louisiana, Arkansas, Missouri, Iowa, Michigan, Wisconsin, Minnesota and Kansas, from September, 1850, up to March 3d, 1873, very large tracts of land. It is impossible to state correctly just how much as there is a considerable difference existing, and unadjusted between the amounts claimed and the amounts certified, but, in round numbers, they have received, or will receive, some fifty million acres. These lands, it will be observed, were, and are, to be disposed of by the railroad companies, on such time, terms, amounts of acres and conditions as they shall see fit, thus throwing immense bodies of land for purely speculative purposes on the market.

Besides these grants to states, Congress began to give grants *directly* to corporations. Corporations had so far been state institutions, acting under and with state authority. The corporations receiving grants from Congress of the alternate sections, to the distance of twenty or twenty-five miles from their line of road, were the Union Pacific, Central Branch Pacific, Kansas Pacific, successor to Denver Pacific, Central Pacific, Western Pacific, Burlington and Missouri River Co., Sioux City and Pacific, Northern Pacific, Oregon Branch of Central Pacific, Oregon and California, Atlantic and Pacific, Southern Pacific, and Southern Pacific Branch line.† It is impossible to tell exactly what these great corporations are entitled to, first, because some of their claims are unadjusted, and secondly, because many of them have delayed the certification of these lands, as they did not wish to have them taxable until they had disposed of them. Some idea may be

* Spofford's American Almanac for 1885, page 324. † Ibid., page 353.

formed when it is stated that the grant of the Union Pacific is estimated at twelve million acres, the Kansas Pacific and Denver Pacific, at seven million one hundred acres, the Central Pacific, eight million acres, the Northern Pacific, forty-seven million acres, the Atlantic and Pacific, forty-two million acres. These enormous tracts, equal to the area of several states, are, in their disposition, subject to the will of the railroad companies. They can dispose of them in enormous tracts if they please, and there is not a single safeguard to secure this portion of the national domain to cultivating yeomanry. The modes of selling by the United States have not been much better. The preemption law was passed in 1841, the avowed purpose being to restrict the land to actual settlers. If such was really the purpose of the law, it was ill-adapted to secure the desired end. The settlers are required, indeed, to make some improvements on the tract, but the improvements made are trifling, and, after title has been secured, there is nothing to prevent the sale of the tract, or the sale of fifty tracts, so secured, to any one. Besides, the law admits of frauds in the mode of securing land. On the 20th of May, 1862, the Homestead law was enacted. About the only difference between the preemption law and the homestead law is, that the man preempting has to pay one dollar and twenty-five cents per acre, while the homesteader only pays some few dollars in fees, and is required to live, or keep up an appearance of living, on the tract for five years. Neither of these laws possessed or pretended to possess any safeguard to prevent the land drifting in large quantities into the hands of speculators and capitalists. In addition, large tracts of land were from time to time thrown on the market. There was usually a pressure on the part of settlers to prevent this, and also a pressure on the part of purchasers and land speculators to secure it. Immense quantities of bounty land warrants have been issued and sold. These can be used by preemptors in paying for their land, as they were transferable, but in addition, when the land, by proclamation, was offered for sale, any one could buy it at the auction, or if not bid off at the auction it was open to purchase, for cash, at one dollar and twenty-five cents per acre, unless within railroad limits, when the price was doubled. Bounty land warrants could also be located on it. Speculators and capitalists bought up millions of acres of public land in that way. Areas equal to whole states are thus held, the only check on the practice being state taxation. To avoid this the railroad land grant companies had an amendment enacted into a law to the effect that they should not obtain their patents until they had paid a small fee to defray the expense of surveying. This they took care not to pay, or only to pay as fast as they could sell tracts to some purchasers, on which occasions they paid the surveying fee and obtained deeds for the portions they sold. In this way they have held millions of acres for speculative purposes, waiting for a rise in prices, without taxation, while the farmers on adjacent lands paid taxes.

It will be seen that in all the stages of the American land history there has never been any adequate effort to secure the public land for the continuous use of the cultivators of the soil, in proportions just to the interests of all. No steps have been taken to prevent the land from going into or remaining in the hands of unoccupying holders or preventing the creation of a landlord and a tenant class. No steps have been taken to secure a subdivision as population increased. In the United States land has simply been a chattel. A legal certificate of title may pass through the hands of a dozen persons, none of whom have ever seen the land. A man in New York, who has never seen an acre ploughed, may own half of one of our greatest states and draw revenues from it without once setting foot on it. Land was cheap and easy of access to all. The farmer and land speculator entered into competition for it, and behind them both, profiting by their accidents and necessities, the capitalist is, and has been, gathering it up. It has been a game of great speculators and little speculators, and the land has steadily drifted out of the hands of cultivating occupants.

Besides the capitalist who invests in land, on the theory that a country rapidly increasing in population, will insure greatly enhanced value to land, we have another class of speculators. They are not capitalists, for their chief stock in trade is precedents. They are not "actual settlers," but they are middlemen, who go between the government and the actual settler who really, in good earnest, improves and cultivates the soil. They have been called "squatters." They are really dealers in that vague commodity—"inchoate titles." They do not squat for the purpose of making a home, but for selling claims. With them an affidavit is a mere form. They calculate to sell without preempting, partly because they rarely have money, and partly because it might interfere with their business in future transactions. If they do preempt at all, it is to close a sale, the terms of which are already made, and they move off to a new field to renew their operations. In the early settlement of Kansas, one armed company of thirty-two men took every timbered claim on a valuable stream that ran through three counties. They laid foundations of four logs, marked the trees on the claims, and had squatter organizations in each township. They hovered over them to and fro, occasionally building a rough cabin or plowing a few furrows, but their chief business was to find customers. The revolver and bowie-knife were the certificates of title. There was an unwritten legal fiction behind them, however, that has entered largely into the pioneer land system of the United States: it is the doctrine that when a man discovers a tract of land that no other man has appropriated, he acquires a certain kind of right to it, acquired to the exclusion of all other persons in the United States. He acquires a right in it altogether independent of the question whether he intends to make a home of it; acquires it without the slightest reference to its ultimate and permanent improvement. This right of discovery is a doctrine famous in American colonization. The squatter does not climb a hill, hoist a flag and take possession in the name of any king or potentate, but he notches and lays four logs together, makes a "blaze" on one of them and puts his name,—or if that be inconvenient, some other man's name,—with a date showing when "this claim was taken;" then he straps his revolver a little tighter, and sends his defiance to the civilized world. There are many other squatters not so violent, who do things in a more respectable way, but who are still essentially "dealers in inchoate titles." I cannot call the earnest pioneer, seeking a home, a squatter. He may be styled one, but he goes into a wilderness, finds a home, improves it, cultivates it and raises a family. He deserves well of his country, even if he obtained the right to use the land for nothing. Still he ought not to be permitted to make himself the medium for transferring the land to capitalists, and should have no right to exclude all other men for all generations.

A great deal is now said by the people; among congressmen, committees of Congress, commissioners and land office officials about the "abuses" of the "preemption law," of the "homestead law," and of the "timber culture laws." There have been abuses enough, but the system under each of these laws, in its best estate, was sadly defective and bad. The preemption and homestead laws professed to do what they did not. The theory was that the land should be reserved for the cultivators of the soil. Neither law secured that end. I have been very much at a loss, in different stages of my land experience, to determine exactly the sentiment in the public mind that has prevented a wise and far-reaching adjustment of the public land question. It could hardly be an accident. The first idea would be that the speculative and real estate interest was too strong to permit of wholesome, permanent legislation. Such a view of the case is not without foundation, but there may have been something else. Perhaps it was thought by men, not destitute of capacity, that it was desirable, as early as possible, to have all the public domain in private hands, and by making it a chattel, providing for its easy transfer without let or hindrance, they believed all could be thus accommodated. If the hat-maker became disgusted with silk, felt and beaver skins, he could sell his blocks and smoothing irons, and buy eighty acres. If the pioneer, who imagined an Arcadia, with the genial farmer sitting under his vine and fig tree, got tired of mauling rails, breaking prairie with oxen, and the ague with quinine, he could sell his "place," together with what a young squatter once proposed to sell, "his embedimeuts," and try to get a position as a clerk in a store. American character is not only enterprising but versatile. Young America might cry "scatter and divide all this national real estate; tangle it with no bars; make it easy to get and easy to sell, and thus it can best serve all interests." I have endeavored to define and exhibit what I have reason to suppose is a strong underlying sentiment. In regard to it I would only say that such a system might do in the squatting era, but we must survive the squatting era. There is a future coming to the American land system with changed conditions.

Let us look at the commissioner's last report. He says: "In the early settlement of the country, when the broad expanse of the public domain was unsettled, a *liberal* system of laws was adopted providing for an easy acquisition of individual titles, and even down to later periods the object apparently sought was to hasten the disposal of the public lands." * Referring to the evasions and frauds under the preemption and homestead laws, the commissioner writes: "The prevailing tendency of legislation has been to remove restrictions rather than to impose them, and Acts have been passed pri-

* Report of the General Land Office for 1884, page 18.

marily for the relief or benefit of settlers which have been availed of to the defeat of *settlements*, by the facility afforded for the aggregation of land titles in speculative and monopolistic possession;" and adds, "It is my opinion that the time has fully arrived when wastefulness in the disposal of the public lands should cease, and that the portion remaining should be economized for the use of actual settlers only." To show how *opportune* the time is, he continues: "The time is near at hand when there will be no public land to invite settlement or afford citizens of the country an opportunity to secure cheap homes." * In the same strain: "Deducting areas wholly unproductive and unavailable for ordinary purposes, and the remaining land shrinks to comparatively small proportions."

I have before me the report made October 22d, 1885, by the present commissioner, Mr. Sparks, in which the following language is used: "I found that the magnificent estate of the nation, in its public lands, has been, to a wide extent, wasted under defective and improvident laws, and through a laxity of public administration." † "The policy of disposing of public lands as a means of raising revenue has long since been rejected by enlightened views of public economy." ‡ Had such "enlightened views" been long potent, we might have had a better land system. In the same spirit, he remarks: "The preemption system was established when land was abundant, and no motive existed for the assertion of false claims. It was *then* a measure of protection to actual settlers against the absorption of lands by private cash entry." § Further, I find: "The near approach of the period when the United States will have no land to dispose of has stimulated the exertions of capitalists and corporations to acquire outlying regions of public land in mass, by whatever means, legal or illegal." ||

* Report of the General Land Office for 1884, page 17.

† Report of the Commissioner of the General Land Office, for October, 1885, page 1.

‡ Ibid., page 75. § Ibid., page 67. || Ibid., page 79.

To quote him once more: "At the outset of my administration I was confronted with overwhelming evidence that the public domain was made the prey of unscrupulous speculation and the worst forms of land monopoly." * There is nothing too strongly stated in the report. In fact, the American public scarcely realize the near approach of the time when the public domain will afford us no facility for the expansion that has, so far, saved us from the evils the system we have created must entail. We look at the figures showing acres and acres as still remaining, and forget that the productive land is gone. Long miles of mountains, and sandy plains and cactus desert remain, without soil, rain or water; even the squatter would shrink from such regions. That a part of it may be utilized hereafter, when greater density makes it a necessity, is probable, but these must be comparatively small portions here and there. The deserts of Arizona, Southern California, Utah and Nevada are arid wastes of the most desolate description. Rivers lose themselves in them and are drunk up by the quenchless thirst of these burning plains. The sand is carried in whirlwinds hither and thither, and even the cactus is often parched and sere. Sharp, rugged, treeless and apparently waterless peaks shoot themselves up like islands on the wilderness. The mirage, peculiar to the dry atmosphere, makes the rocky peaks look as if they were smoking and burning. Then there are miles on miles of bare, rocky, treeless mountains, not high enough to be snow-capped, and upon which rain rarely falls. Such is no inconsiderable portion of the heritage that on the maps and on the books of the general land office figure as the public lands of the United States.

In his report for 1884, the commissioner says: "The forest areas of the country are rapidly diminishing, and the timber

* Report of the Commissioner of the General Land Office, for October, 1885, page 48.

lands of the United States will, under existing laws, soon be exhausted." * He adds: "To a great extent these (timber) lands are now appropriated by illegal preemption, and commuted homestead entries made without settlement, except that of lumber camps, and without improvement except the cutting and removing of the timber for commercial purposes." The present commissioner suggests that "Wise and speedy measures should be adopted for the preservation of forests. * * * To this end I recommend the immediate withdrawal from appropriation, sale or disposal of all public forests, and of lands valuable chiefly for timber, subject to future legislation." † Commissioner McFarland, in reference to mineral land, said: "Coal lands, the government price of which is ten and twenty dollars per acre, are illegally obtained at the minimum price of non-mineral land. The government loses the difference in price, while the public lose in the increased price of coal, the land being thus acquired and held." Speaking of the modes by which capitalists obtain large tracts by using the names and affidavits of fraudulent preempters, he says: "Meanwhile, vast stretches of uncultivated land are everywhere observable, claims to which are held, or titles to which have been acquired, in evasions of restrictions of quantity that may lawfully be appropriated by single individuals, and without complying with the conditions of settlement, improvement and cultivation required by law." ‡ And, on the same page: "The numerous methods of disposal now existing, and the laxity of precautionary measures against misappropriation, are resulting in a waste of the public domain, without the compensations attendant upon small ownerships for actual settlement and occupation."

The commissioner refers to the Act of May 14th, 1880, which doubtless was enacted in the interest of our squatter

* Report of the General Land Office, 1884, page 18.

† Report of the General Land Commissioner, October, 1885, page 84.

‡ Report of the General Land Office, 1884, page 18.

friends: "The effect of this statute," he says, "is to invite speculative entries for the purpose of selling relinquishments. The practical result is, that when a new township is surveyed, large portions of the land are at once covered by filings and entries, relinquishments of which are offered for sale like stocks on the market." These are the vices of a bad system. They exhibit the steps taken to throw the domain of the country into a few hands. The frauds under the homestead and preemption law are only a little worse than the laws themselves. In this way, and for a mere song, mischief is being made for coming generations, and conditions of society, fostered contrary to the genius of the American republic. These frauds merely show that the speculative purchaser cannot wait for ordinary methods.

While the public lands, after survey, were in such a condition that they could only be taken under preemption or homestead law, large tracts have time and again, as demands for investment in land pressed, been thrown on the market by presidential proclamation, and whole townships taken, every unclaimed acre being appropriated by non-resident holders or speculators. The railroad grants furnish a partial supply to meet the land hunger of investing capitalists: even these do not satisfy the land speculators. Frauds, always perpetrated to some extent, have assumed the wholesale proportions stated by the commissioner. Large tracts have been going into the possession of alien holders. They cannot, it is true, purchase or get title under the preemption and homestead laws, without declaring their intention to become citizens, but there is nothing to hinder an alien from buying at second hand all a straw preemptor or commuting homesteader works through the crevices of a loose law. No alien should be permitted to own a foot of land in these United States. In addition to this, there are sales from private parties, railroad companies and Mexican land grants, not to mention the domain of the state of Texas.

Texas was the only new state admitted to the Union that was permitted to hold possession of or control the disposition of her public lands. After asserting her independence of Mexico she remained a separate republic for a very brief period, and when admitted to the Union succeeded in retaining control of all her domain. The use Texas has made of this power is scarcely such as to tempt Congress to repeat the experiment. Bad although the Congressional modes were, the Texas modes were infinitely worse. Instead of securing the land for actual settlers, reckless grants of it were made to every corporation or proposed enterprise. Land scrip for all kinds of service was issued, until it sold at a few cents per acre, and this scrip fell into the hands of speculating purchasers. So much scrip was issued that, enormous though her area is, there was not land enough to take it up, and for several years parties have been engaged in trying to secure a piece of the adjacent territory to locate the scrip on. In point of fact, there has, in all the West, been a strong element, both in politics and business, deeply interested in land speculation. This has largely shaped land legislation, or had it shaped in its interests. From the suggestions of land speculators have come the loose modes permitted by Congress in legislating on land.

Other fruitful sources of mischief in a few of the Southwestern states and territories, including California, have been the Mexican land grants. At the close of the Mexican war a large amount of territory was annexed by the United States. In the treaty of Guadaloupe Hidalgo it was provided that all rights and interests existing under Mexican law should be respected and maintained by the United States. This referred chiefly to the interests and property rights of those Mexicans who were thus absorbed into the United States. One difficulty not then foreseen, lay in the fact that the American and Mexican land systems were in many respects widely different. There had been grants of land by the Spanish Crown. Grants by the viceroys in the different territories. Grants by the Mexican republic and its officers. These grants, moreover, were of a widely different character. The tillable land was usually in a town grant, where each citizen had his share of cultivated land, usually on some river, and paid his water-tax (for irrigation) to the local officer, or "Acequia Keeper." Even when the grants were made in the names of the few first settlers, they were intended for the benefit of all who might follow. Then there were grazing grants, for that purpose alone, sometimes to individuals, but usually for the common use of communities. All mines were royal or government property. The farming grants and the grazing grants conveyed no right to mineral, as the latter could, on discovery, be worked by any one on payment of the royalty to government. It can readily be seen that to apply the American land system to these grants would work confusion. The American land laws contemplated purely individual rights. The land sold or conveyed was a chattel. Ownership was restricted to no special purpose, and it was not complicated with the rights of others. In addition to these differences, the boundaries of the grants were rarely made from surveys at the time, but often were the summits of mountain ranges, not well defined; the best of them admitted of a great deal of latitude in surveying. There was a certain class of general grants, of a few leagues square, and another class much larger. Private grants were sometimes made of a vast tract to some military leader or favorite, but while it included the lands and commons of the people, their rights by the Spanish law were independent of his, and could not be absorbed by him. To confirm the entire grant to him would place whole towns or villages at his mercy, or convey their property absolutely to him, ignoring their rights. The original Spanish and Mexican system as designed, was intended to secure the rights of all, but drifted into a condition of affairs similar to that created by the feudal system. In each community or town there was a prominent man who had great herds and these ate up the general pasturage. This functionary usually kept a store, and traded so that every one was in debt to him. If there was a mill, he or his family owned it. Under the old Mexican law many of the poorer people were his *peons*. In New Mexico the Americans ironically called these personages "Dukes." The annexation of that portion of Mexico caused a good deal of confusion on account of these conflicting Mexican and American ideas. The "dukes" not being able to retain laborers as peons, after annexation, took the former peons' share of the tillable land in collection of debts, and even their orchards and gardens in the villages. Individual grants that had never been heard of before made their appearance. Originally the Spanish records were well kept, but revolutions and political changes destroyed many. At one time in Santa Fé an immense quantity of old records were sold and scattered as waste paper. An Act of Congress was passed July 22d, 1854, providing for the settlement of these claims through their presentation to the surveyor-general, and through him to Congress. Little progress was made toward a settlement. Among the claims presented it was darkly hinted that some were manufactured. Settlers in either of the states or territories affected by this class of claims were at a loss to know where to locate. In his first work, Mr. Henry George said that California had been cursed with Mexican grants. Grant holders would watch settlers and miners and have a location made to include their improvements.* In that work, he states, that not one-fourth of the land sold by the United States went into the hands of cultivators.† In his report, the land commissioner says, that in thirty years seventy Mexican claims have been confirmed by Congress. Ninety-four are pending before that body, while an unknown number remain on the files of the surveyor-general. Some of the maps of

* Our Land Policy, National and State, page 14. † Ibid., page 4.

New Mexico show claims that absorb nearly all of the valuable land together with a good deal of worthless country. Travelers in that region, if they are supposed to be inquiring with a view to purchase grants, are often shown carefully preserved papers with the seals and signatures, to all appearance, of viceroys or governors long since dead, conveying great tracts of unknown and unsurveyed districts.

In hastily sketching the modes by which large portions of country in these United States have been segregated from the body of the public domain, and vested in certain individuals or corporations, "their heirs or assigns," I have endeavored to give the various processes. There is still a popular delusion that American agricultural lands are largely in the hands of cultivating farmers. Proud of a supposed boundless domain our citizens have been unconscious that an absentee landlordism has been growing up, that threatens to become almost as bad as the feudal system.

In a letter to the writer from Hon. W. A. J. Sparks, commissioner of the general land office, of date January 7th, 1886, in reference to the total number of entries of the following character made from the first operations under the law, the commissioner says that there were "computed from the commencement of business to June 30th, 1885, of original homestead entries 714,599, embracing 90,462,499.58 acres, and of final homestead entries 257,395, embracing 31,895,-464.27 acres." It will thus be seen that of the acres included in the original entries, but little over one-third was taken by the perfected entries, and while some of the former of course, were abandoned, it is a legitimate inference that a large number of the cases not perfected were held or used for some kind of speculative purpose. The total number of timber culture entries he gives at "132,275, embracing 21,716,747.89 acres." Up to the date given the amount of land "located by military bounty land warrants was 61,080,-670 acres;" a very considerable portion of this sixty-one million acres was located by purchasers of military bounty scrip for land speculation.

The number of separate farms in the United States does not indicate the number of *owners*, for one may own a good many. Thus the statement that in 1880 there were 4,008,-907 farms in the United States, containing 536,081,835 acres, with 284,771,042 acres of improved land,* must be accepted with some limitations. The value of the four million farms is placed at $10,197,096,776.00, while the estimated annual product for 1879 of "all farm productions, sold, consumed, or on hand," is $2,213,402,564, being considerably over one-fifth or twenty per cent. of the estimated value of these farms.† The same authority gives the number of persons actively engaged in agriculture in 1880 as 7,670,493.‡ The number of farmers or planters, 4,225,945," § which is only a small percentage more than there are farms, must not lead to the impression that these farmers or planters are owners of the soil they cultivate, or that each of them has a *separate* farm. Of farm laborers, not farmers, there are 3,323,876, the remainder of the seven million six hundred and seventy thousand being dairymen, overseers, stock drovers, and miscellaneous employees.

These figures are more significant than at the first glance appears. Of the 4,008,907 farms in the United States, we find, in the same table, that 2,984,306 are returned as being held by cultivating owners; || and this is stated somewhat triumphantly as an evidence that the actual cultivators are largely the owners of the soil. In the first place there is confessedly 1,024,601 farms held by renters, or upwards of one-fourth of the whole.¶ For a nation not yet out of the squatting era, with some public lands still left to take, the

* Tenth Census, Statistics of Agriculture.

† Spofford's American Almanac for 1885, page 373.

‡ Ibid., p. 274.

§ Ibid.

|| Tenth Census, Statistics of Agriculture, page 28.

¶ Ibid., page 29.

fact that more than one-fourth of the farms in the whole country have already drifted into the condition of landlord and tenant, would in itself be sufficiently alarming; nor are these all small tracts, the record showing that 291,703 of these rented farms contain from one hundred to several thousand acres of tillable land, the small rented farms under ten acres only numbering 51,184. These figures, however, do not by any means tell us the whole story. Besides the farmers who by themselves and families cultivate the soil, there is a large number of farms cultivated by capitalist owners, who do a supervising or wholesale business by the labor of wage workers, styled "agricultural laborers." By the figures we have given, while there are 2,984,306 cultivating land owners, there are 3,323,876 farm laborers, men who do not even rent land. The census gives the average acreage of improved land to each farm at seventy-one acres, but of the farms of and under one hundred and sixty acres of land, the average improved land falls under forty acres. That may be accepted as the average size of farms actually cultivated by the occupants and their families with but occasional outside help. There are 92,212 farms not rented, of from five hundred to several thousand acres, owned, we may say, by capitalist owners. Of farms having in cultivation from one hundred to five hundred acres, there are 1,416,618, nearly a million and a half of farms that we can certainly consider are largely owned by capitalists, and are chiefly cultivated by laborers.* We can thus see where the three million three hundred and twenty-three thousand "agricultural laborers" are employed. The single item of capitalist farmers includes one-half of the "cultivating owners." Above the standard of farms that are *actually* cultivated by the owners, say farms of from fifty to a hundred acres of tilled land, there are 804,522. Of the labor performed on these, it is

* Tenth Census, Statistics of Agriculture, page 28.

probable that fifty per cent. of it is done by hired laborers or wage workers. Of farms containing of cultivated land fifty acres and less, there are, all told, 670,954. These latter farms, it may be assumed, are chiefly cultivated by the occupant farmers. If the independence and prosperity of our agricultural population is of any moment, these figures demand immediate consideration.

It will thus be seen that of the 7,670,493 persons in our country engaged in agriculture, there are 1,024,601 who pay rent to persons not cultivating the soil; 1,508,828 capitalist or speculating owners, who own the soil and employ laborers; 804,522 of well-to-do farmers who hire part of their work or employ laborers, and 670,944 who may be said to actually cultivate the soil they own; the rest are hired workers.

Another fact must be borne in mind that a large number of the two million nine hundred and eighty-four thousand three hundred and six farmers who own land are in debt for it to money lenders. From the writer's observation it is probable that forty per cent. of them are so deeply in debt as to pay a rent in interest. This squeezing process is going on at the rate of eight and ten per cent., and in most cases can terminate but in one way. The ninety-two thousand two hundred and ten farms, which contain cultivated land of not less than five hundred acres, and running into the thousands, gives us an incipient landed aristocracy of close on a hundred thousand persons. These large farms are rapidly increasing in number and in size. The bonanza farms of the West have been chiefly created from the railroad land grants, the speculating owners gradually buying out the small farmers on the alternate sections. On these farms everything possible is done by machinery. Hired laborers do the work for fifteen or twenty dollars per month for a few months, and seek odd jobs during the remainder of the year; they are fed in a barrack of a boarding house. Mr. Moody notices the absence of women and children and says: "In no case was the permanent residence of a family to be found upon them.* These large farms held by speculating owners are not confined to the West. Col. Church, of New York, collects the rent from one hundred and eighty farms, most of them large. Col. Murphy left an estate of two million acres. The Standard Oil Company owns a million acres. An Irishman owns in Illinois more than fifty thousand acres, and derives an income from it of about $100,000, and there are a number of others who already possess large landed estates. The one million four hundred and sixteen thousand six hundred and eighteen holders of farms which contain cultivated land of over a hundred, and less than five hundred acres, while they include farms that may be cultivated by active farmers who employ some help, are, to a large extent, held by owners who, so far as the great majority of them are concerned, cannot be considered laboring owners, but they are now, or soon will be, in circumstances to live on income from the land without labor. These form a large basis for a future aristocratic class.

Profiting by the loose modes of permitting the soil of the country to go into the hands of speculators, the aristocrats of Europe have become landholders of great estates in this republic. The Duke of Sutherland, as we have seen, is the largest landholder in Britain. He owns four hundred and twenty-five thousand acres in the United States. The Marquis of Tweedale has one million seven hundred and fifty thousand acres. Sir Edward Reid & Co. own about two million of acres in Florida. A Scotch company, made up largely of titled gentlemen, have half a million acres in that state. A similar English company owns three million of acres in Texas. At the present time some twenty millions of acres of the lands of these United States are held by alien holders, capitalists and noblemen, in farms or holdings of not less than fifty thousand acres each, not to mention a very large amount in holdings of a less acreage. The Mexican law was more provident than

* Moody's Land and Labor, page 54.

ours, for it prohibited alien landholding. Such has been the pressure of late years, that large tracts even there have been and are going into the hands of capitalist holders, or they, at least, are getting some kind of an interest in them.

In estimating the ownership of the productive land in the United States, it must not be forgotten that the large farms constitute no inconsiderable part of the whole, as it would take many small farms to equal one of the large ones. The small holders are changing from freeholders to renters and agricultural laborers. Another fact: there is a rapidly growing class of large labor employing renters or middlemen. By the census no less than twelve thousand three hundred and thirty-eight are reported as renting farms of cultivated land containing from five hundred to several thousand acres, and two hundred and seventy-nine thousand three hundred and sixty-five of these who rent from one hundred to five hundred acres of arable land.* These employ numbers of "agricultural laborers." Such figures are far from encouraging, if we are still to entertain the hope that American freemen are to be independent holders of the soil on which they place their feet. We have, at this time, almost as many tenant renters as there are in the British Islands. The very worst forms of renting and metayer tenancy prevail. We have no legislation to secure the rights of the renting cultivator, and none to induce or protect necessary agricultural improvements. Our whole land system has been nothing more than a piece of carelessly put together machinery, adapted to further the ends of land speculation. Besides, the amount sold for cash, or granted to states and corporations, the operations of the preemption and homestead laws have largely aided the transfer of public lands to other holders. The essential condition of republican independence through freeholding by the cultivators we have not secured, and have no means of securing.

* Tenth Census, Statistics of Agriculture, page 29.

So long as any public land remains, the power of the landlord will not be supreme. In his remarks in the "Statistics of Agriculture," General Walker says, that "the amount of arable land still remaining subject to occupation under the homestead and preemption acts, is barely sufficient to meet the demand of settlers for a year or two to come."* What then? Of those who must live by farming, not much less than half of the agricultural population will have neither land, nor money to buy it, and must make the best terms they can with landlords. Nothing but prompt and vigorous steps can save the republic from the endless mischief and inequality that will follow by the creation of an immense body of agricultural renters and laborers subject and tributary to the landholding class.

In France, with an area about as large as one of our states, and a population on December 18th, 1881, of 37,672,048, Laveleye estimates not less than five million landed proprietors who own less than twenty acres. Of the population of France by the Statesman's Year Book for 1885 nearly one-half live by agriculture. Formerly the population of the United States was more rural or agricultural than it is to-day. By the census of 1880 we find that of males over ten years 14,744,942 are employed in all occupations, and of these 7,075,983 in agriculture.† Mr. Mulhall, in his table showing the relative population of town and country in the United States, only counts those as urban who live in towns exceeding twenty thousand in population. Thus in 1800 the urban population was only six and four-tenths per cent. of the population. In 1820 it had fallen still lower, and was four and eight-tenths per cent. of the population; in 1840 it was nine and one-tenth per cent., in 1860 it was thirteen and five-tenths per cent., and in 1880 eighteen and two-tenths per cent. of the population.‡ With the rapid in-

* Introductory Remarks to Statistics of Agriculture, Tenth Census, page xxviii.

† Tenth Census, Statistics of Population, page 712.

‡ Mulhall's Dictionary of Statistics, 1885, page 362.

crease of city population that has been going on for the past thirty years as a guide, it is safe to say that in 1886 one-fifth of our entire population will live in cities of more than twenty thousand inhabitants, as compared with less than a twentieth some sixty years ago. There is also a very large population in towns of from three thousand to twenty thousand inhabitants, who are entirely detached from agricultural pursuits.

In 1790 there was only six cities in the United States of from eight thousand to twelve thousand inhabitants. Now there are one hundred and ten of such cities, and in all two hundred and eighty-six cities running from eight thousand to upward of one million. The * city population in 1880 by this standard was twenty-two and a half per cent. of the entire population, and it certainly is twenty-five per cent. now. The fact thus appears that practically much more than half of our people live in the country. Country population is supposed to be the independent "bone and sinew" of the nation, and it is among this hitherto independent agricultural people that the changes which seriously affect their standing resources and power have been so rapidly going on.

There are many causes which have led to the sale of farms by the original settlers to capitalist owners. The transition from a primitive and simple rural life to an artificial society has had much to do with it. Many will remember when the families on farms produced and manufactured the greater part of what they needed. The men worked in the field with comparatively few implements of improved or expensive machinery. The women wove, spun, and made the clothing. I do not mean to say that there is not a great superiority in the modern appliances and clothing purchased in the city. The difficulty has been that many were unable fully to cope with the commercial responsibilities thus entailed on them. Above all, the temptation to run in debt has increased with the facility for

* Tenth Census, Statistics of Population, Introduction, page xxix.

getting into it. Eight, ten, and twelve per cent. interest on debts created for articles of luxury and machinery, much of which might be dispensed with, have ruined many a man. The capitalist stood ready to buy up the farm. Our people, too, have been blind to the danger. All thought there was "plenty of public land." If a man lost his farm, he could easily get another. The writer visited a large prairie with his father more than forty years ago. Only a few farms were then located round its edge. The bulk of it was at a later period sold under the graduation bill for some twelve and a half cents per acre. A few years ago, in traversing a lane running through this prairie for a number of miles, it was found to be all in enclosed farms of tillage, meadow or pasturage. On inquiry, the greater part of it had changed hands, some of it more than once. The prices had risen to forty, fifty, and in some cases eighty and one hundred dollars per acre. The improvements constituted only a small part of that valuation. About one-third of the farms were held by cultivating owners, the remainder by renters. Some of the owners of the rented farms were in the county seats, some in St. Louis, and some lived "East." It is unfortunately the case that a great many of our people are not bound by strong local attachments. Many of them sell and move on the first good offer for their farms.

It may be true that the reverses now reducing so many of our farmers to the condition of tenants and laborers are calamities for which the more fortunate are not to blame. It will be said that this impoverishment has been caused by indolence, extravagance and intemperance, and that this reduction of our agricultural workers from freeholders to dependents, while a calamity, is one for which the victims alone are responsible. Although there are undoubtedly cases of misconduct and mismanagement, the writer is convinced that the evils are wide-spread, expanding and continuous, and spring from general causes which ought not to exist. Extravagant and intemperate people are not very common among agriculturists. More of those two vices will be found in five per cent. of the people who live by their wits than in a hundred per cent. of the farming population. No classes are more intensely laborious than our working farmers. From daylight until dark their toil is heavy and unintermittent. When night comes most of them are too tired to read or enjoy themselves. Their food, although wholesome and solid, is very plain, and their clothing far from luxurious. If their circumstances are compared with those of the money-lender who shaves their notes, or even his agent, the contrast becomes painful. The peculiar economy under which our American agriculturist labors, seems to be an experiment of competition between him and the ryots of India and the peasant farmers to the north of the Black Sea, as to which of them can lay down wheat at the lowest price in Liverpool. If fifty per cent. of the money the American wheat brings was not consumed by railroad managers and middlemen it would not be so hard for the farmer. His necessities frequently compel him to divide the little he receives with the usurer. He cannot compete at all when he pays high rent. He is often embarrassed by obligations for "improved machinery," much of which is poorly made and comes to pieces before it is paid for; to these must be added the heavy burden of taxes unjustly and improvidently heaped on him. His present fate leads us to imagine what will be his condition when all the public land is gone, and when there will be added, rent and rack-rent, constantly increased, to meet the luxury and extravagance of aristocratic landlords.

The above causes are all leading to a system of land tenure that, with a great population, will be terrible for the working poor. One thing is certain, such a form of landholding and a free government cannot exist together. The question is whether we have nerve enough to correct such abuses in time, or shall "Land Monopoly" and "Land Speculation" be the epitaphs on the tomb of American liberty?

CHAPTER XII.

CORPORATIONS.

Unsatisfactory statistics of corporations—Corporations known to Roman law—Early town corporations—East India Company—Supposed legal powers of corporations—Plea of vested rights—A legislature cannot grant power that strips its successors of authority—Public and private companies—Corporations a subordinate power of the State—Eminent domain—Railroads public highways—A curious charter—Craftsmen employers and corporate employers—Money as an employer—Crafts, guilds and trades unions—William Pitt—Imaginary political necessity for cheap labor—Organization of capital in corporations—The organization of labor—John Stuart Mill on co-operation—Consolidation among the autocrats of transportation—Stocks, assets, liabilities and income of railroads—Miraculous expansion of capital under the fingering of corporations—Revenues of railroad companies—A greater power than the State—Army of employees under direction of a few—National debts—Corporate debts greater than all public debts combined—Banking on the confidence plan—Dealers in money becoming jobbers in labor—The accumulated property in the country and who owns it—Piratical stock jobbing—Rights of individuals and powers of the State threatened by corporations.

THERE is no subject of similar importance that has been so utterly neglected by statisticians and census-takers, as corporations, beneficiary societies and companies. It is true that the Census Reports of the United States comprise enough on other subjects to appal the most heroic reader. We have the exact amount of humidity, in inches, that might, could, would or should fall on every square yard of the United States. The number of hens that cackle in American barn-yards, and the number of eggs that they *ought* to have laid, we know; but as to the number of corporations, companies, societies, associations, the extent of their capital, of their authority, of their property, we do not know, and there does not at the present writing appear to be any way of finding out. A power has grown up in our country, and become a great estate of the realm, claiming to be deputized to exercise some of the most questionable powers of government; charged with owning and controlling to a large extent the legislative bodies of the country; making laws and by-laws deeply affecting property rights and even the lives and safety of the people; and yet their history, their real statistics, their ways and their works appear to be wrapped in impenetrable mystery. While we have tables giving the number of some kinds of corporations there is not a list, official or otherwise, of all the corporations, companies or organizations of men in the United States, or one that gives an accurate and comprehensive idea of their nominal and real capital, much less of their inner secret history. In Poor's Manual we have the statistics the railroad companies choose to furnish to the public. From these we learn that at the close of 1884 there were 125,379 miles of railroads in the United States, of which 3977 were constructed during that year. The "share capital" was $3,762,616,686 and the funded debt $3,669,115,772. The other forms of debt equalled $244,666,596. The total capital and indebtedness of all kinds aggregating $7,676,399,054.* No person would think for an instant of accepting this as a complete and honest statement of the real capital and debt of these roads. It only serves to deceive the public, in so far as they believe it, as does the statement on the same page that the cost of these roads per mile "*measured by their stock and indebtedness* equalled very nearly $61,400 per mile." Mr. Poor informs us of "securities being issued at the rate of two or three dollars for every dollar of cash paid." † He very properly adds in another place: "The country is now about its lowest depths as far as railroads are concerned."

Besides the railroads we have insurance companies, manu-

* Poor's Manual for 1885, page 1. † Ibid., page 5.

facturing companies, banking companies, telegraph companies, telephone companies, friendly societies with property and responsibilities, lodges, charitable institutions incorporated and otherwise, trades unions, guilds, independent military organizations. These organized bodies we find everywhere. They absorb immense amounts of the national wealth, and they affect the individual prosperity to an extent we can hardly realize.

Of a few of the less dangerous of these combinations, of a social and friendly character, which do not attempt to use their combined capital as a lever on the public, we have some little knowledge. However mysterious the ways of insurance, the statistics of insurance are to some extent before us, but even their modes of transacting business are far too incomprehensible, especially their expenditures and investments, to be tolerated in such a class of institutions. The more powerful and wealthy corporations carry on their business largely on the "confidence" plan, their honest and exact statistics are not recorded. The very exhibits they make are only calculated to deceive. Without wishing to appear unduly suspicious there is something worse than mere mystery about them. Corporations are unduly sensitive, suffer from business modesty, and shrink from the public gaze. They do not permit their right hand to know what their left hand doeth. It is really astonishing that the state governments and Congress should not have insisted on a public record of their operations, in all matters even the most minute, that in any shape involves the public interests; in fact, there is no reason why their pecuniary and official history should not be exactly recorded and its data be public property. Statistical almanacs we have, but you may wade through them in vain to gather the exact facts in regard to corporations in the United States. The ponderous census does not pretend to give the statistics and history of these companies, and even, so far as concerns railroad companies, only gives a little of the outside data.

We have a statistical bureau that is at once voluminous and mathematical, but lean and barren on the statistics of corporations. The Statesman's Year Book does not give the facts, and you can only glean some superficial information such as the companies are willing that the public should possess. It gives the number of miles of railways built in all parts of the British Empire, and the amount of capital supposed to be absorbed by it, but the names or number of the companies, their liabilities, responsibilities and power we have not, and the record neither states nor pretends to state the business proceedings of these public corporations. Neither there nor in Mulhall can you find anything about the corporations of the United States, for the United States has furnished nothing official on that subject. It is true we have the Pacific railroad reports, but they give us very little data, and the little they give seems to be, unhappily, too much for public credence.

Although incorporations are generally supposed to be a modern contrivance, dating their birth and growth during this century, such is not exactly the case. Incorporated companies were known to the Roman law, and, although differing as to their power and the modes of exercising it, from those of the present time, they still assumed sufficient authority to expose them to the hostility of the government. The early history of contracts is almost exclusively to be sought in the history of the Roman law, in the Roman "*societes omnium bonorum.*" * The equestrian or aristocratic class, when driven from official positions, organized business companies to control capital, and were the great contractors when corn and other largesses were bestowed upon the people. Whatever their vices were, and they were not destitute of them, they did not attempt, as modern incorporations do, after being created, to claim independence on the plea of vested rights. In England

* Maine's History of Early Institutions, page 233.

in the Middle Ages, towns and cities received charters from the king, and thus became corporations with certain powers. The government of the city of London began under a charter from the king. Most of the cities and towns obtained governments in a similar way. Although, at first, not very clearly defined, the powers of these city or town incorporations were over matters purely local, and did not interfere with the authority of the general government. The purpose, however, of all such city and town corporations was of a public character and not private emolument. The most wonderful company, organized for private emolument was the British East India Company. When this corporation was originally chartered the design was to authorize it to carry on trade in the Indian seas. The company purchased a small quantity of land for a trading station on the East India coast, and from this beginning gradually conquered a large part of India. It exercised powers of all kinds, created companies and monopolies under it; usurped powers of government; taxed, levied armies, and did other objectionable things, as corporations are liable to do, until the British parliament made an end of it, "vested rights" to the contrary, notwithstanding, and assumed the government of India for itself.

In our own day corporations have become so universal and domineering, have acquired, and are acquiring such authority and wealth that it is well to examine carefully into them, to see how far the powers they are exercising are consistent with the public good. According to the best legal authorities the following powers are assumed to belong to an incorporation. 1st: The power of perpetual succession. 2d: The power to sue and be sued, and to transact all business within the intent of the grant of power; to have and use a common seal, and to make by-laws, not inconsistent with law, and in the strict line of their business. 3d: A corporation or company must strictly confine itself to its legitimate powers; thus, it is *ultra vires* for a bank company to build a railroad; nor has a railroad company any authority to usurp any of the functions of a bank, and neither of them have the slightest authority to assume any municipal function, or to determine any question which is within the province of the courts. 4th: A corporation in this country is a subordinate part of a state government, a creature of a state government. It has been claimed that the general government has nothing to do with them, but in so far as Congress received, by the Constitution, the power to regulate commerce between the states, all corporations are to that extent subject to its jurisdiction, and can be perfectly governed in all matters of interstate commerce by such authority. 5th: Every company or corporation, whether by general law or special charter made amenable or not, is subject to the powers of the state. It is the creature of the state, created only on the supposition that it was for the benefit of the public interests, and liable to be changed, altered, amended or abolished by the state.

One of the dangerous pleas or claims of powerful modern corporations is that they acquire certain vested property rights by the expenditure of their money under their charters, and that the state or general government can pass no law at variance with their interests. If there was the slightest foundation for such an impudent claim, charters should never have been granted, and, in fact, never could have been given; for the constitution of a state confers on no general assembly that may happen to meet under it the power to part with the authority granted to the legislature as a successive body. Such things have been attempted more than once. For instance, the parliament of Ireland had power to meet and enact laws for Ireland. Each successive parliament, as elected, had power to pass laws or to modify or repeal any law of a previous parliament, but one of these assemblages had no power to abolish parliament. Thus the act of the Irish parliament, brought about by English influence or English corruption, abolishing the Irish parliament, was in excess of its powers. They took away from the people the power to elect a succeeding parliament, which was a power superior to their own. No one would pretend that a state legislature could abolish the state government by an act, or strip the legislative assemblies that were to succeed it of a single one of the powers delegated to it by the constitution. In the same way, while corporations are creatures of and subordinate parts of a state government, there never can be constitutionally given to them a power or privilege which the same power cannot take from them. A town government is an incorporation, and it has been customary for legislative bodies, they being competent, to grant to such certain powers and privileges. Thus the authorities incorporated may be authorized to issue licenses to sell liquors, or to burden the people with certain debt, or to make a specific disposition of all or portions of the public property, but no lawyer will pretend that the legislative body which granted such powers may not modify or withdraw them. What most of our great and unscrupulous corporations want to do is to have all the independence of a private person, and, also, all the power of a public corporation; nevertheless, they are mere creatures of the law.

There are private companies with none of the powers of a corporation. A, B and C enter into company to make hats, and transact their business just as John Smith would do. Like an individual, they are subject in every particular to the law, whatever it may be. The law may even change some of the conditions under which they make hats. Congress, by a modification of the tariff, may render it impossible for them to continue in business; or the state legislature, by taxation, or some enactment in the general interest, may seriously embarrass them. Yet, if A, B and C should insist that they put their money in the hat trade with the understanding that the former conditions would continue, that their business is being sacrificed by this change, that these laws should not affect them, that they are in violation of their "vested rights," and that if such legislation must be persisted in, Congress or the legislature should pay damages to them, everybody would laugh at them. A, B and C are not authorized to "make by-laws" any more than John Smith, who might, it is true, write a string of moral maxims and paste them in his hat for reference, but they would have no more authority than he choose to give to them. A, B and C cannot condemn and appraise, and take possession of the shoe shop adjoining, to make an extension necessary for the business of their own hat shop; neither can they run the wagons that deliver their hats over the garden or field of P or Q. A railroad corporation gets that power on the theory that the railroad is a *public highway*. The state grants this power to the corporation, a subordinate public authority under it,—a creature and *weapon* of the legislature. If any one wants to know how the state got that power, the reply is that it gets it on the theory of "eminent domain." That was the theory on which William the Conqueror seized and disposed of the lands of England. After the battle of Hastings he claimed to be "the state." Now, whatever the merits of the doctrine of "eminent domain" may be, and they will be discussed hereafter, there is, of course, no just comparison between a state that properly represents the people, and William the Conqueror. I refer to it merely because the legal system that partially governs us originated then. Eminent domain was eminently obnoxious to the Anglo-saxon ideas. It was quite as obnoxious to the Anglo-saxon nobles, as it was to the Anglo-saxon people, for each of the former wanted the eminent domain himself. Under the system as it has grown up among us, the state is the supreme owner of the land. A state may tax the land to any extent it may require, or it may condemn any portion of it for public use. In this latter case equity requires the state to indemnify the individual, and this should always be determined judicially; but while this has been conceded, it does not affect, under the doctrine of eminent domain, the right or power of the state to tax it two or one hundred cents on the dollar, or, in other words, to take it all.

The doctrine of eminent domain, when you come to examine it as a legal proposition, is an assertion that the state is the primal and highest owner of the land, and that the individual has only limited and defined rights in it, which may be regulated by law. This has always been the theory of our land system, and is substantially Mr. Henry George's platform. So thoroughly has this been systematized and recognized in the history of our government, that when a new state is admitted into the Union, carved out of the public domain of the United States, it is customary to have what is styled an ordinance or contract between the new state and the United States, by which the new state agrees *not to tax* the lands lying within its boundaries belonging to the United States, until the United States has disposed of them. For this relinquishment a consideration is given, being usually two sections of land for school purposes, in each township, and, as the general law stands, five hundred thousand acres for internal improvements, and additional amounts for universities, agricultural colleges and normal schools. In these agreements the power of the state to tax is affirmed, and also the doctrine that the "eminent domain" is in the state, and not in the general government. Over the territories Congress exercises a proprietary right, under that clause of the Constitution authorizing it to "make all needful rules and regulations for the territory and other property of the United States." This clause, by the bye, has been stretched a good deal, and it is a very grave question, considered judicially, whether the assertion of "eminent domain" over the territories can be constitutionally maintained. Every one will understand that such a power as "eminent domain" cannot exist in two authorities at once. It has been the practice of our government to recognize that a state in the Union, once created, by virtue of its existence, possessed the eminent domain, and the United States does not relinquish and convey to it that authority which is alone supposed to be derived from the people, but, on the contrary, the federal government comes to it on the threshold of its existence and seeks to make a bargain with it, that it shall not, for a certain period, tax federal property in land within the state, and pays a part of this property in land to the state for such exemption. The reader must carefully bear in mind the distinction between the proprietary right and the "eminent domain." The "eminent domain" is the highest title. Subordinated to it is the proprietary title, and thus, under the theory of our system, the highest and first title to all the land of the state is in the people of the state, and the proprietorship under it a limited one, subject to legal regulation.

In this way an incorporated railway company secures from the state the authority to build a railroad across the lands of any man, without allowing him to say what shall be the width of the tract, the direction it shall take, or fix the price of his own property. The machinery furnished by law for securing remuneration for damages, or property so taken, is rarely of a kind to insure any exorbitant price; usually, the amount allowed is far less than the individual owner would like to sell such land for, if the matter was regulated by "supply and demand," and in many cases the amount paid is entirely inadequate. The theory largely is that the building of such a road is a matter of public interest, and that heavy damages should not stand in the way of the enterprise. A railroad is a public highway. It is on this theory alone that it has been or could have been built. In the charter there is merely delegated to the corporation a certain public function. Many people think this should never have been done. In several European states the government practically controls the railroads. It will at once be seen that when a corporation puts its money in a public highway called a railroad, it does not thereby secure an independent power or right to continue to exercise a public function. So far as it exercises any authority, it is a delegated power, limited as to time and everything else connected with it, and subordinate to the interests and will of the people. It is not to be supposed that the law or the people will deal inequitably by any interest, but it will never do to permit corporations to call in question the right of the public to regulate, modify or abolish the corporations it has created. Vested interests and rights are always subordinate to public interests and rights. The claim, often impudently made, that by investing money in a public highway, called a railroad, the managers acquire a vested right to regulate and manage it, independent of the law-making power of the people, is not to be tolerated for a moment. The people, and by the people we mean the law-making power, may permit a company, for the time being, to manage the road with as little interference as possible, but that is always merely a toleration, on the presumption that they are performing the duty well for the public interests; but the power always remains with the people to resume the functions they have delegated.

Corporations, when created, have never hesitated to extend and magnify their powers, or to usurp functions not belonging to them. One company, that afterward filled a large place in railroad enterprises, was originally chartered by the legislature of the state of Pennsylvania, to "Irrigate and plant vineyards in California, or in any other state or territory of the United States, except Pennsylvania." Finding California an unsatisfactory field they purchased or negotiated for a railroad charter in Kansas, from a company that did not possess the authority to make such a sale, and proceeded forthwith to build what is now one of the important roads of the country. A town company succeeded in getting a bill through a territorial legislature, authorizing it to purchase, lay out in lots, and sell two thousand acres of public land, when an Act of Congress forbid the sale of more than three hundred and twenty acres for such a purpose. Companies have been organized to manufacture salt, and after starting manufacture in one locality, have acquired salt lands elsewhere with no intention of making salt there, but simply to prevent any one else from making it, they thus create a monopoly.

Officers of railroad companies are continually intriguing to get possession of the coal lands of the country, and to so arrange the freights on coal as to create a monopoly for their friends, to the public detriment. Salt and petroleum interests are sought to be monopolized in the same way, and unless prompt steps are taken to check it, the country will be, before many years, at the mercy of a few monopolists, who will be able to control the price of fuel, salt and petroleum. Organized capital, under a company or corporation, managed by officers, if it exist at all, ought always to be a subordinate *public* authority. This organization and aggregation of capital has brought about one of the greatest revolutions, affecting human labor, in modern times. In England, until recently, a master workman or employer was required to be a thorough craftsman himself. Usually a thriving handicraftsman who had acquired credit or means to carry on business was the employer. He thoroughly understood the details of his own work, was in full sympathy with his workmen, was a member of a guild or trades union, and subject to its regulations, which were made for the good of the trade. In England, in the last century, the woolen manufactures were carried on by small masters, often in their own houses, at times cultivating a garden or patch of land, which, besides air and exercise, furnished many cheap comforts. A careful inquirer states that in 1806 there were about three thousand five hundred of such small manufacturers in the vicinity of Leeds.* As a rule there was one apprentice with the master for every two or three workmen. The way was then opened for any good workman to become a master or employer. A young work-

* Brentano's History of Guilds and Trades Unions, page 105.

man of good repute could always get credit for enough wool to start him as a small master.* The introduction of machinery in 1790 was the first thing that worked a change in the condition of the small employers, and a more radical and worse change was made, .when, instead of the master or employer being a handicraftsman, the employer was simply a capitalist, or worse yet, a company of capitalists. With all their abuses craft guilds maintained a number of regulations which protected workingmen. The overthrow of the guilds was due to the rise of large capital and its investment in manufacture.† Trades unions are the successors of the guilds. Under the old guild regulations no person was to "exercise a trade," or could be a master employer unless he had served a seven years' apprenticeship at the trade. No journeyman was permitted to work with a man who had not so served, or who was not a member of the guild.‡ The usurpation by organized capital of the functions of a master tradesman, manufacturer and head craftsman, was one of the important levers to press the mechanic and laboring man into the dust. Many who had formerly been masters became wage workmen forever. Most of the avenues by which a mechanic and craftsman could elevate himself to an independent position were closed. The mere capitalist employer is a modern invention, separating employer and workman. It will be argued that the introduction of machinery in manufacture and the arts, requires greater capital than the old master workmen had or could get. It has also been argued by one school of political economists that the true theory was to manufacture the largest amount at the smallest cost, so that buyers could get things cheap. In this way the capitalist employer very soon got in the habit of employing children and apprentices. The journeymen were always the first men discharged. Competition grew up among these capitalist employers as to who could sell cheapest. This

* Brentano's History of Guilds and Trades Unions, page 106.

† Ibid., page 97. ‡ Ibid.

competition reduced mechanics and workmen to poverty. The mere capitalist employer knew little of, and cared less, for the workman. His purpose was to sell cheap, whatever became of the mechanics. He was independent of the trade. It was not his business to employ the finest skilled artisans. Shoddy, poorly made-up articles, cheap workmen, low wages, these are often the stock in trade of the capitalist employer. If a competing corporation or firm sell articles at a low rate, he must grind down his laborers and sell his goods at the same price. Beside the disastrous effects of this system on the regular crafts and trades, poor needlewomen make shirts for a few half-pence, and other articles of clothing for a pittance that cannot keep soul and body together, in order that Mr. A may under-sell Mr. B, and one factory has to curtail the wages of its workmen and workwomen in order that it may compete with some other company that has put the price down. It may be said that there is no safe way to prevent this, and that unbridled and unregulated competition must be permitted to go on, reducing the workingmen and workingwomen to poverty. One of the most eminent British statesmen, William Pitt, as will be seen by examining the debates of the British House of Commons, when the Arbitration Act was pending, said: "The time will come when manufacturers will have been so long established, and the operatives not having any other business to flee to, that it will be in the power of any one man in a town to reduce wages, and all the other manufacturers *must* follow. If it ever does arrive at that pitch, parliament, if not sitting, should be called together, and if it cannot redress these grievances, *your power is at an end.*"

While corporations in the present day are created and developed largely in the interest of aggregated capital, it is worthy of note that corporations and guilds a few centuries ago, were aggregations and associations for the defense and protection of labor. These labor-protecting corporations are, indeed, the oldest known associations of men among European nations. Guild is supposed to be of ancient Celtic etymology.* Religious guilds, which were partly political, and partly to organize and strengthen poor people, were almost contemporaneous with Christianity. The beginning of craft or trade guilds was from the commencement of the eleventh to the middle of the thirteenth centuries.† Town corporations or governments were still older, and were largely created to resist the freebooting nobles. The guilds succeeded generally in securing authority to regulate trade instead of the officers of the towns. These two kinds of organization and authority were sometimes in conflict, but as they both derived their power substantially from the people, they operated as a check upon each other. The purpose of the guild organization of any particular craft, was to promote the interest and independence of that craft. The soul of the craft guilds was their meeting every week, month or quarter. The control of the sale of the most necessary provisions, such as bread, meat, drink and fuel, was the special care of the town corporations. The guild of each trade or manufacture regulated the production of articles, the prices, mode of sale, and had laws to prevent imperfectly educated workmen from being employed to the detriment of those who had served regular apprenticeships. The guild sometimes forbid its members from carrying on their trade with borrowed capital,‡ so jealous were they of the interference of capital with their occupation. At Tournay, in 1365, it became necessary to forbid usurers from carrying on the weaving trade. The incomes of the craft guilds were derived from small entrance fees of wax for the churches and taxes which were levied for special purposes as they occurred, such as to provide for the death, misfortunes, or pilgrimage of a member.§

If a master workman withheld wages from a workman the

* Maine's History of Early Institutions, page 232.

† Brentano's History of Guilds and Trades Unions, page 55.

‡ Ibid., page 74. § Ibid., page 64.

guild compelled him to pay. They only permitted a certain number of apprentices for so many journeymen. In England they had more power in regulating wages than the judges of the court of sessions, although the latter were backed by Act of parliament. In all the manufacturing countries of Europe, the most ancient guilds were the weavers. In Germany, the wool weavers guild rose to consideration early in the eleventh century. One of the oldest German charters, referring to craft guilds, was granted 1149. A fraternity was formed with the consent of the judges, sheriffs and aldermen, and henceforth all within the town who wished to carry on the trade were obliged to join the society.*

In Germany and France the working classes were completely organized for defense, and the welfare of their trades. In many parts of Germany guilds existed until this century. In the fourteenth century we have evidence of organized strikes among the workmen, and enactments against them, referring causes of dispute between employers and workmen to the guilds for adjudication. Various causes are assigned as the reason for the decline and overthrow of the guilds. Complaints were made that abuses crept in, and that in many cases they were used to advance selfish interests. In 1484, the Emperor Sigismund complains that membership had to be "grossly bought," † and that in the town council "the crafts followed only their own advantage." He recommended their abolition. The imperial decrees in Germany against the guilds were rarely carried out, as the guilds supported each other.‡ Henry VIII., of England, who had previously stripped the churches of their property, in his expiring days, under pretense of holy zeal, robbed and stripped the guilds of their property.

Such were some of the causes that led to the decline of the

* Brentano's History of Guilds and Trades Unions, page 52.

† Ibid., page 75. ‡ Ibid., page 81.

guilds; but the chief cause of their overthrow was the accumulation of large capital, and its investment in manufactures.* For a time the guilds struggled against that potent enemy, "capital," taking refuge in and using the religious guilds or societies to secure immunity. Upon the final overthrow of guilds, trades unions took their place. The guild had possessed ancient forms. Its meetings were a species of feasts. They possessed, or claimed a religious element, and they were long recognized as corporate authorities of some standing. The trades unions referred merely to the trades and the craftsmen. As the transition in business established capital as the master, that master, whether an individual or company, was not required to be, and, in fact, rarely was, a member of the trades union. Capitalist employers usually denounced them. The committees of the House of Commons were not favorable to the "trades institutions." The followers of such movements were usually spoken of as "poor deluded wretches," and in a parliamentary report of 1806, one great *fault* of such a society was said to be: "That its inevitable result would be progressive rise in wages of all kinds of workmen."† Adam Smith, who did not much favor parliamentary regulation, said: "Whenever the legislature attempts to regulate the differences between master and workmen, its counselors are always the masters." In point of fact, the first legislation of a definite character in England was enacted for the purpose of *reducing* wages. The great plague of 1348, and the consequent depopulation, brought the interests and conflicts of the laborers and employers to a crisis. Even the clergy took advantage of it to raise their fees for masses and prayers. Merchants and traders proceeded to raise the price of their wares, and the workingmen endeavored to secure a general rise of wages. This led to the notorious statute of laborers (23d and 25th King Ed-

* Brentano's History of Guilds and Trades Unions, page 99.

† Parliamentary Report of 1806, page 113.

ward III.), in which it was ordained that no workman should take more, or employer pay more than they did before the plague.

While the purpose of the enactments which fixed or provided for fixing the price of wages, was to prevent the rise of wages, when the change from employers who were handicraftsmen to capitalist employers took place, the workmen sought the protection of the law to prevent the reduction of wages. Added to the natural cupidity of capitalist employers who had little intercourse with or sympathy for the workmen, the sharp competition of manufacturers and their desire to undersell, became a continual menace to wages. The desire to be able to sell a garment for four shillings that had been produced and sold for five was constantly tending to lower prices, and the manufacturer who reduced the rate of wages might say with some plausibility that he could not afford to pay his workmen more. Added to this, in Great Britain, there grew up from all these changes a condition of affairs that might almost be styled a public policy. A large manufacturing and city population, constantly increasing, at this time nearly two-thirds of the empire, has to be supported from bread and meat *not* produced in the country. To meet this foreign expenditure, it was indispensable that they should find a foreign market for their manufactures. To do this the articles *must* be sold cheaper, and in this way the necessities of a public policy were added to private cupidity as a reason for the reduction of wages. It is still an unsolved problem how long a nation can continue to grow, on a very limited area, with a large population, constantly growing, the fundamental basis of its existence being that other nations shall furnish them raw products in exchange for manufactured articles. Political economists will hardly deny that a nation which attempts to exist by shipping raw products and buying with the proceeds the manufactures of other countries, "tends to poverty and the degradation of its people." How long new countries will be found thus to support a purely manufacturing nation, is for Great Britain a grave question. Her advantages are great accumulations of capital, which have been able to some extent to control the purchasing power of money, and this power holds the manufacturing interest of Britain in its grasp. British capital plays the usurer to all the world, deriving great revenues from interest. England has also the advantage of performing a large proportion of the carrying trade of the world, and thus is able to turn exchange in her favor. To these may be added *cheap labor* as a necessity, viewed from the economic standpoint of capital. Valuable improvements in machinery can give little advantage to any one nation in contradistinction to others, for more than one nation has contributed improvements that give power to labor and facilities to trade; in any event these useful inventions soon become general property. Cheap labor and the concentrated influence of capital, directed by a few, cannot in the end maintain a prosperous people. We find that as capital became the employer of workmen, repressive laws began to be enacted against combinations of workmen, mechanics institutes and trades unions. Brentano says, "The workmen having fallen into great distress owing to capitalized masters instead of workingmen masters, they petitioned parliament in 1778 for a legal regulation of wages." * The Act 13th, George III., c. 68, provided that on demand being made the price of wages was to be established. Other acts about the same time contained similar provisions. It will be observed, however, that as the guilds had been driven out of existence, the new law gave the mechanics institutes and trades unions no voice in determining the price of labor. Besides the reduction of wages there were many other abuses from which the mechanics and workingmen suffered. The calico printing trade capitalist employers used apprentices almost exclusively, and the few skilled journeymen they

* Brentano's History of Guilds and Trades Unions, page 118.

employed were discharged on the slightest stagnation or pressure.* The frame-work knitting trade had formed a society in 1663, but from 1740 to 1750, the trade being controlled largely by capitalist employers, was so overstocked by "breadless apprentices" from the parish, who had served their time, that it brought the workmen very near starvation. It is stated that there was often but one coat in a shop which was worn by the workmen in turn as each of them went out. A Northamptonshire master named Moss refused to employ a workman possessed of a good coat, declaring that the best workmen were only to be found in ragged ones.† About the close of the last century and the beginning of the present, as capitalist owners began to have control of trade and manufactures, laws were enacted against "combinations of workmen." In 1800, by Acts 39th and 40th, King George III., c. 106, all such combinations were prohibited, and penalties were provided punishing violations of the law. The workingmen felt their helpless condition, and by meetings and monster petitions endeavored to influence parliament. The employers and business corporations and companies entered into the conflict with them. Brentano says that in 1803 they spent twelve thousand pounds petitioning and presenting their case to parliament.‡ It must be remembered that the laboring men in Britain did not vote, and, in fact, some of them do not vote even at this date. Beside positive hostile legislation, the trades unions and mechanics institutes were treated with ridicule. A set of flippant and reckless writers and would-be political economists denounced every scheme for the elevation of the workingman as "agrarian," or "Utopian." Capital, organized, and under a system of partnerships, companies and corporations, became all powerful. A few men give direction and power to vast sums of money, and are able to wield even

* Brentano's History of Guilds and Trades Unions, page 123.

† Ibid., page 116. ‡ Ibid., page 111.

greater power by an artificial and colossal system of credit. Modern corporations give organization to capital. These multiply its power, and the laborers are denied the privilege of organization for defense. If corporations, organizations and companies are needed for anything, surely they are needed to protect and maintain the value of labor. It is fashionable to denounce labor organizations, however. A cold-blooded school of political economists have grown up who hold that such organizations interfere with the laws of trade, and that everything, the price of labor included, must be subject to the crucible of business competition. According to these the cheapest mode of production is the only excellence, and all organized efforts to raise or maintain the wages of craftsmen, mechanics, and laborers, are dangerous interferences with the natural laws of trade.

When political economists preach the doctrine of "competition" to a skilled mechanic who finds himself unable to support his family from the wages paid him, they forget the circumstances of the skilled mechanic. His craft is his stock in trade. In England, and to a great extent in America, he cannot, in a period of distress, take refuge in the ancient and natural occupation of agriculture. The land has all been monopolized by landlords. Even tenants' leases have become a sort of monopoly. "He cannot dig, to beg he is ashamed." What is free competition between masters and workmen to him? He is, indeed, entirely at the mercy of the capitalist employer. Capital is organized, the laborer is not.

Under these circumstances an impartial reader will easily see the necessity of organization to protect the interests of labor. In union there is strength. If we are to have corporations, companies, associations, institutes, partnerships, at all, let them by all means be organizations for the benefit of workingmen. Such were many of the early corporations. Town and city corporations in the Middle Ages were for the protection of the burgesses, artisans, mechanics and laborers in the towns, against the armed aristocracy. They it was who abolished villeinage, and wrung Magna Charta from King John. The privileged orders were always opposed to such organizations. They ridiculed and satirized Watt Tyler and Jack Cade, who merely strove to make freemen of the enslaved yeomen of England. They scoff at their memory to-day as socialists and levelers.

The highest and perhaps the only legitimate use for corporations is to concentrate and systematize the influence of workingmen. To make them so strong that their dictum shall be felt, and, if necessary, to derive lawful authority for certain legitimate actions and procedures. John Stuart Mill says: "Hitherto there has been no alternative for those who lived by their labor, but that of laboring either each for himself alone or for a master. But the civilizing and improving influences of association, and the efficiency and economy of production on a large scale, may be obtained without dividing the producers into two parties, with hostile interests and feelings, the many who do the work being mere servants under the command of the one who supplies the funds, and having no interest of their own in the enterprise, except to earn their wages with as little labor as possible."

"The speculations and discussions of the past fifty years, and the events of the last ten, are abundantly conclusive on this point." * * * "That the relations of masters and work-people will be gradually superseded by partnerships in one of two forms; temporarily, and, in some cases, association of the laborers with the capitalist; in other cases, and, perhaps, finally in all, association of laborers among themselves." * Speaking of several successful associations, he remarks: "The vitality of these associations must indeed be great to have enabled about twenty of them to survive not only the anti-

* Mill's Principles of Political Economy, vol. ii., page 352.

socialist reaction, which for the time discredited all attempts to enable work-people to be their own employers, but the trying condition of financial and commercial affairs from 1854 to 1858. * * * Of the prosperity attained by some of them, even while passing through this difficult period, I have given examples which must be conclusive to all minds as to the brilliant future reserved for the principle of co-operation." * As an additional argument in favor of the management of manufacturing establishments by the workmen, Mr. Mill says: "Capitals of the requisite magnitude, belonging to single owners, do not, in most countries, exist in the needful abundance, and would be still less numerous if the laws favored the diffusion instead of the concentration of property;" and further: "It is most undesirable that all these improved processes, and those means of efficiency and economy in production which depend on the possession of large funds, should be monopolized in the hands of a few rich individuals." †

It will be observed that Mr. Mill admits law ought to favor the "diffusion" rather than the concentration of capital, and that it is not in the public interest that manufacturing and commercial business should be in the hands of a few rich men. It will be conceded that association is powerful, and while there may be a grave question as to the expediency of permitting capital to organize and acquire corporate powers, and to concentrate its strength, there can be little question about permitting industrial laborers and craftsmen to organize for the better protection of the interests of labor. Nearly everything that has been accomplished in elevating the people of modern Europe was brought about by organization and co-operation. A tyrant, whether he be a landed aristocrat, or a money-controlling capitalist, can always manage and use poor laborers if he can take them individually. It is when they

* Mill's Principles of Political Economy, vol. ii., page 371.

† Ibid., page 510.

are aggregated in guilds, trades unions, associations or institutes that they become powerful. Of course, these are liable to abuses like all societies, companies or corporations, but that is no argument against the legitimate exercise of their powers.

In modern times corporate franchises, as they are granted and carried on, are chiefly for the benefit of capitalists, or those who direct capital. Banking, insurance, railroad and large commercial and manufacturing corporations are all intended to give greater power and greater profit to accumulated capital. At the present time the tendency is to concentration, and the absorption of small enterprises by great concerns. A few rich and powerful railroad men practically control the transportation of the country. Nearly all of these made their enormous wealth by combinations to put up and down prices, watering stocks and other operations that ought to have been under the ban of penal law long ago. If it could be possible to obtain statistics to show us just how much fairly earned cash was actually put in railroad enterprises, and how much of what is styled their "stocks, assets, liabilities, mortgages and indebtedness" is an artificial creation, the lesson would be very instructive. Meagre although the reports of the tenth census are, they inform us that there are one thousand one hundred and sixty-five railroad companies which *report* an aggregate capital stock (paid in) amounting to two billion six hundred and thirteen million six hundred and six thousand two hundred and sixty-four dollars.* Poor's Manual for 1885, states that the share capital for 1884, equalled three billion seven hundred and sixty-two million six hundred and sixteen thousand six hundred and eighty-six dollars.† This sum, much larger than the national debt, we can hardly realize as being invested in railroads, by Americans, in little more

* Compendium of Tenth Census, part 2d, page 1264.

† Poor's Railroad Manual for 1885, page 1.

than half a century. Upon this, by the census report of 1880, there is a funded debt of two billion three hundred and ninety million nine hundred and fifteen thousand four hundred and two dollars, and a debt not funded of four hundred and twenty-one million two hundred thousand eight hundred and ninety-four dollars, in all obligations incurred outside of stock amounting to two billion six hundred and sixty-one million one hundred and fifteen thousand two hundred and ninety-six dollars.* The figures given by Mr. Poor, for 1884, are a funded debt of three billion six hundred and sixty-nine million one hundred and fifteen thousand seven hundred and seventy-two dollars, and of other forms of debt, two hundred and forty-four million six hundred and sixty-six thousand five hundred and ninety-six dollars. The aggregate of liabilities against these enterprises is, according to Mr. Poor, seven billion six hundred and seventy-six million three hundred and ninety-nine thousand and fifty-four dollars,† or, if we are to believe the managers of these concerns, they have expended on them seven billion six hundred and seventy-six million three hundred and ninety-nine thousand and fifty-four dollars. Nobody believes anything of the kind, however. The amount of stock that was actually paid in honestly, dollar for dollar, would constitute a very small item, and, if to it was added the amount of money honestly borrowed on mortgage and honestly expended for the road, we would have a true aggregate of what these roads cost. From the figures the companies furnish us should be deducted all stocks not actually paid; all money borrowed that was not honestly expended on the road, so as to add to its productive value, and all watered stock, bonuses, amounts paid for pretended services or other modes of pensioning their own officials. In point of fact, railroads have borrowed the corporate dignity and authority

* Compendium of Tenth Census, part 2d, page 1260.

† Poor's Manual for Railroads for 1885, page 1.

of the state, only to be better able to plunder the public, and rob the honest stockholders, where there are any. The figures they furnish give no idea of the amount actually raised for and expended on these roads. One branch of the Union Pacific Railway, for instance, let a contract to build a considerable portion of its road for thirty-three thousand three hundred and thirty-three dollars per mile, when it is notorious that the road could have been, if it was not, built for about eleven thousand dollars per mile. The government had endorsed and become responsible for bonds to the extent of sixteen thousand six hundred and sixty-six dollars per mile, and the company was authorized to issue a *preferred* mortgage to the same extent, which should come in as a lien ahead of the government, these two together making the amount for which the road was *nominally* constructed. What was done with the *stock*, if any of it was ever really paid in, does not appear, further than as it exists among the "liabilities" of the company, and among other "obligations," which together amount to upward of sixty thousand dollars a mile, a pretty big stone to be tied around the neck of any enterprise. We have omitted to mention a land grant of some twenty or twenty-five sections per mile, the value of which would not be overstated at one thousand dollars each; the sale of these does not seem to have had the effect of reducing the volume of its obligations. In truth, what is called "stock" is, to a large extent, fictitious. The leading telegraph company in the United States has a stock capital of eighty million dollars, of which a Senate Committee in 1884 reports: "Nearly the whole of it has arisen from stock dividends."

Money lenders, or investors, soon learned to be shy of "stock," and subsequently they learned to be a little shy of mortgages, for mortgages in many cases did not represent capital invested any more than stock. That the roads should have survived these operations and not sunk into universal bankruptcy is the only miraculous thing connected with the business. It exhibits a marvelous recuperative power in the transportation industry of the country. By reference to the reports that come to us through the tenth census, of the one thousand one hundred and sixty-five railroad corporations, six hundred and twenty-three have earned a net income or profit on their stock; one hundred and sixty-nine companies had not yet commenced operations, and three hundred and seventy-three either created a deficit, or made the income balance the expenditures.* The same page, to some extent, gives us the resources of these railroad companies, or rather of the men who manage them. The total income being $661,295,391, the total expenditure $415,508,485, and the net income or profit at $245,786,906.† The net income or profit is stated at 4.91 per cent. of "stock" and funded debt. Mr. Poor, for 1884, gives the gross earnings as $770,684,908, and the net earnings for that year as $268,-106,258.‡ Crude as these figures are they show us conclusively what would be the history of American transportation with roads honestly and economically built, and justly managed and administered. The whole agricultural population are groaning under the burdens of extravagant charges for transportation caused by the nefarious system that has controlled our railroad corporations. We can easily see where the colossal fortunes of modern times, which have no parallel in ancient history, come from. This system of railroad corporations is but in its infancy. Of the eleven hundred and sixty-five companies which pretend to represent upward of seven billions of property, two-thirds of their capital never existed anywhere but on paper, in all probability, far more than the half of these roads are controlled or under the influence of less than twenty men. These railroad corporations have, by the report of the census, an income twice as large as the government of the United States, and by the reports of Mr. Poor for 1885 a still

* Compendium of the Tenth Census, part 2, page 1264.

† Ibid.

‡ Poor's Manual of Railroads for 1885, page 3.

greater amount. They disburse for expenditures and salaries fifty per cent. more than the government, and they dispose of a net income or profit of two hundred and sixty-eight millions. Not including those who construct the roads, but only those operating them, an army of 418,957 persons are employed by them,* and allowing five of the population to be represented by each man, not a great deal less than a twentieth part of the population of the United States is dependent on this interest. The record shows of accidents, 2541 persons killed and 5674 injured by their mode of operating the roads. After paying expenditures, the net earnings for 1883, or profits were $291,-587,588; of this amount $171,414,258 was paid as interest on bonds and $101,579,038 was paid as dividends on "stocks." What became of the other eighteen millions and a half is not set down by Mr. Poor. To show the great power of the managers of these corporations, Mr. Poor states that "an increase of net earnings equal to one mill per ton moved by the New York Central, would add $1,970,087." †

In contemplating this immense system, governed by men possessing large corporate powers and defiantly assuming that the law-making authority should not attempt to control them, we must be at once convinced that mistakes have been made in giving them the authority they exercise. It is indispensable for the public interests and safety that at the earliest possible moment every part of their business be placed under the strictest regulations of law. Had these companies faithfully administered the trusts confided to them, had they never watered stocks or placed mortgages on these properties without adding to their value, or done the thousand and one things that have scandalized railroad management, still a dangerous power of capital is here created, inconsistent with the public interests.

Had it not been for the enormous credit systems built up in

* Compendium of the Tenth Census, part 2, page 1266.

† Poor's Manual of Railroads for 1885, page 8.

this century, the creation as it is would have been impossible. The national debts of all the leading modern nations have increased rapidly during this century, and very rapidly since 1848. The modern debts of the nations of Europe were largely contracted, and were the results of the outbursts of democracy which occurred in Europe and America within a century. The struggle for popular liberty in Europe was at first submerged by military despotism, then the restoration of monarchies; next came the fresh outbreak near the middle of the century, which was quelled by the great standing armies.* The average annual increase of national debts of leading nations has been $489,335,079.† If they continue growing at that rate, the same authority adds, "until the close of the present century, they will have reached the enormous sum of $32,583,781,254." Of this it is only necessary to remark that such a debt can never be paid. It is a mortgage placed, or attempted to be placed on the shoulders of coming generations, largely to maintain by despotic means, governments obnoxious to the people, and inimical to their interests.

The national debts, however, are but an item in the drafts this generation is drawing on posterity. In our own country we have the state debts, to begin with. From 1820 to 1838, $174,306,994 of state debts were contracted and stock issued.‡ From 1833 to 1840 it was found almost impossible to float state debts in Europe at any price. The interest was often not paid. In 1842 an attempt was made to get Congress to assume the state debts. This had been done once before, but under different circumstances. An Act of Congres was passed August 4th, 1790, by which the United States assumed the state debts which had largely been created in meeting the expenses of the Revolutionary War. By the report of a committee of Congress in 1843, the state debts were estimated at $207,894,-

* Tenth Census, vol. vii., page 267.

† Ibid.

‡ Ibid., page 525.

613.35, many of them having failed to pay interest. In 1883 the state debts aggregated $241,010,334 of funded debt, and $22,878,019 of unfunded; total state debt, $263,888,353.*

It is worthy of note, that of the amount of funded debt, thirteen southern, or formerly slave states owe $143,120,370, and the state debts of nineteen northern or former free states are $96,844,820. Delaware has a debt of $864,750, and Kentucky is practically out of debt, as is West Virginia. Colorado, Illinois and Vermont are free from debt. Forty years ago Illinois was so hopelessly in debt as to be considered bankrupt. It will thus be seen that in one portion of the country state debts have not increased in the past fifty years, but as an offset to this there has been created in that period an immense volume of local debt, such as county, township and city debt. The state debt is indeed small compared with the local debt; it has been largely incurred in aid of corporations. This is not all, the most valuable franchises of our towns and cities, such as wharves, highways, privileges for gas and other manufactures are falling into the hands of these corporations, which at once seek to make them monopolies. Beside the great volume of local debt the corporations created within the last fifty years have run into debt enormously. By the report of Mr. Poor for 1885, already quoted, the funded debt of the railroads of the United States is $3,669,115,772,† or, in other words, these corporations in that period have, outside of the stock they subscribed, the ostensible purpose of which was to build the roads, incurred a debt and saddled it on these enterprises, fifty per cent. larger than the national and state debts all put together. Of that three billion and a half of evidences of funded debt, it is probable that one billion, or ten hundred millions, have found their way into the pockets of the railroad manipulators, armed with corporate charters.

* Spofford's American Almanac for 1885, page 105.

† Poor's Manual of Railroads for 1885, page 1.

What the debts of the other corporations in the United States are, it would be impossible to conjecture, as there is little or no means of ascertaining. In issuing the local, city, township and county debts great opportunity was offered for building up the fortunes of manipulators, and creating capital for the corporations. The securities sold for little and the interest was large. The whole system of modern stock jobbing was to a great extent founded on it, and it is difficult to tell which is real and which is fictitious capital.

Our banking system is largely in the hands of companies and corporations. They aspire to control the circulating medium of the country, and to "regulate the value of money" instead of Congress. In September, 1884, there was in operation 2664 national banks. Their resources are placed at two billion two hundred and seventy-nine million, their capital stock being five hundred and twenty-four million dollars,* which shows that they do business to four times the extent of their capital stock. Their books, of course, balance: Up to November 30th, 1882, there was some opportunity to get a little data as to the state and private banks, but the repeal of the Act taxing bank capital and deposits swept away the last chance of throwing light upon the operations of these concerns.

In 1882, by the reports at that time attainable, there were 4473 state banks, and they had a capital of two hundred and twenty-eight million four thousand dollars, and had received deposits of seven hundred and seventy-nine millions of dollars,† and were thus enabled to do business on more than three times the amount of their capital. Beside these there were forty-two savings banks with a capital of four million, which had received forty-three million five thousand dollars in deposits, and six hundred and twenty-five savings banks without capital, which had received nine hundred and fifty million two thou-

* Spofford's American Almanac for 1885, page 91. † Ibid.

sand dollars as deposits.* Hence it will be seen that a great many of the operations of the corporations are conducted on paper. The stock of the railroad, telegraph lines, etc., could not be said to have built the roads. In many cases it was a myth, and in the few cases when it entered into construction it cannot be accepted as a cash investment dollar for dollar. Those who have managed the corporate powers have been enabled to create great debts, and to manipulate, speculate in, and use these paper securities. The result is shown in the fact that all the large railroad and telegraph operators are the principal stock jobbers. They have commenced absorbing the weak and small companies. The chartered recipients of public corporate authority turn that authority against the public. An incidental result of this abuse of trust is that they use the assets of these corporations, or, their inflated paper to get possession of outside properties.

A clever writer once advised a man who was in a hurry to be rich to "invent a pill." In modern times the favorite plan is to invent a mining or insurance company or corporation. There are, of course, many solvent and worthy insurance companies, but the chief assets of no inconsiderable number are an office, agents and a prospectus. So long as money comes in very freely the institution flourishes, but when the time for paying policies arrives, they either go into bankruptcy, or try to compound with the policy holders, and get them to accept twenty-five or fifty per cent. of the amount due. "Mining companies" are the "wild cats" of these days. Their business is not so much mining in the bowels of the earth, as in the pockets of those to whom they sell "stocks." If every person who has been duped by them would cry aloud, there would be a fearful sound heard from Maine to California.

Mr. Mulhall, in 1882, states the aggregate wealth of the United States to be eight billion three hundred and thirty-

* Spofford's American Almanac for 1885, page 91.

nine million pounds.* He divides it thus: Land, is set down at two billion one hundred and fifty million pounds. Houses, two billion seven hundred and eighty million. Railways are put at one billion one hundred and ninety million pounds. Cattle, at three hundred and seventy-eight million, and "sundries," at one billion eight hundred and forty-one million pounds. So far as land and farm improvements are concerned, Mr. Spofford, quoting from the tenth census, puts the value of farms in the United States, including land, fences and buildings, at ten billion one hundred and ninety-seven million ninety-six thousand seven hundred and seventy-six dollars.† The two tables of Mr. Spofford and Mr. Mulhall do not cover the same data, as the former includes only the farms with their houses and improvements, while the latter estimates "land," which may be improved or unimproved, and puts houses in a separate column. Accepting Mr. Spofford's statement of the value of all the land and agricultural improvements in the country as ten billions one hundred and seventy-nine million dollars, we find that the railroad corporations have incurred a funded debt of three billion six hundred and sixty-nine million, which is more than one-third of the entire amount. Mr. Spofford, in the same table just quoted, puts the estimated value of all farm products for 1879, "sold, consumed or on hand," at two billion two hundred and thirteen million four hundred and two thousand five hundred and sixty-four dollars. As the railroads largely draw their resources from the agricultural interests of the country, this railroad debt may, not without reason, be considered as a burden placed upon this annual production. To permit these railroad corporations to create a debt, vying with the debts of the greatest nations, and then claim the right to tax transportation on railways, that were constructed as public high-

* Mulhall's Dictionary of Statistics, page 471.

† Spofford's American Almanac, for 1885.

ways, to pay for them, is a very serious matter. All the fictitious charges they can so place upon them, they will assert to be "vested privileges." While the United States has been rapidly paying off the national debt, created by the war to preserve the Union, these railroad companies continue to increase their debts. As the people have to pay these debts just as surely as they pay the national taxes, it is certainly time that this immense irresponsible system was put completely under the iron hand of law.

The statistics of all public corporations, or companies, or firms, doing general public business, such as banking and insurance, should be public property. No matter what his integrity, no man ought to be permitted to do business with other peoples money on the *confidence* plan. Companies doing insurance and similar business should never be permitted to expend more than a fixed percentage of the sums they receive for insurance policies, in salaries and expenses, as only a certain amount is safe and consistent with honest business. In railroad operations, watering stock, borrowing money to pay dividends, or make bonuses, expending the funds of the company for anything but its economical and real expenses, making false contracts for construction, loading the enterprise with debt to prevent the stockholders from paying their subscriptions; bargains between the men managing the road and express companies, to let the latter get all the profits of transportation, and schemes of the latter to share these profits with the officers of the road, to the detriment of the shareholders and the public, concealing or misrepresenting the true business condition of the company; all these and many other common artifices of railroad companies ought to be declared penal offenses, and punished accordingly.

Railroad corporations when in charge of a public highway, should, in every respect, be closely and rigidly subject to law in all their transactions. There ought to be complete codes, state and national, of railway law. The rates of freight and fare should be regulated by law just as bridge, road or ferry tolls have been. No bond, mortgage or debt should be a lien on the road unless the money derivable therefrom was fully expended in building it, and no stock should be considered a lien or encumbrance on the road unless paid up and fully expended in its construction. Roads, moreover, should be compelled to connect conveniently with each other; to run their trains to make time connections, and to carry for every other railroad on equal terms. These incorporations and companies should pay exactly the same taxes on their property that all other citizens do, assessed at the same time and in the same way. No law should ever be passed exempting property from taxation, except incomes and property below a fixed standard.

If any one is inclined to think that such enactments would prevent the building of railroads or would cripple or retard them, he is mistaken. If railroads can be properly and economically built in our country for eight, ten or fifteen thousand dollars per mile, and were so built, they would be a good investment, and would, at greatly reduced rates for freight and passage, furnish a fair compensation for necessary laborers and employees, and a legitimate profit on the capital expended. If such legislation would put an end to Wall street jobbing in the stocks and securities of railroads it would be a public blessing. It is absolutely indispensable for a healthy and moral state of business that it shall be impossible to make great fortunes dabbling in stocks. All these fictitious and fraudulent modes of getting money must cease if we are to have a just standard founded on honest labor. Besides its evil effects on business, the pernicious example of fortunes made without effort, by stock-jobbing and gambling, is disastrous to our people; disguise these inflations as you will, they inflict burdens the people must ultimately pay. If all the inflated price of such stocks could be stripped from them, if nothing but the dollar actually expended could be represented, the "shrinkage" would be no public calamity.

This may be styled paternal government. One of the oft-debated propositions among practical statesmen is as to the legitimate functions of government. It has been held, and not without reason, that governments should confine themselves to certain duties necessary for peace, order and protection to life, property and reputation, leaving the individual as free as possible to carve his own fortune with the minimum of government interference. This, however, must be considered in connection with the conditions and necessities of highly civilized society and dense population. It is denied, and justly, that a man has a right to bring up his children in ignorance; it is denied, and justly, that a man has no duty to perform to the poor, ignorant, weak and helpless; it is denied, and justly, that a man can be allowed to do anything that is against the interests of the majority; it is denied, and justly, that a man should be permitted to make gain by false pretences, dishonest bargains, unfair combinations, or in any manner save by the measure of honest labor and honest equivalents. If, however, the most extreme views as to government non-interference were taken, it cannot be pretended that a corporation, a creature permitted to exercise certain public functions, should not be rigidly governed by law. There are a great many things the individual must be controlled in by the will of the majority, and when the individual combines with other individuals for purposes of gain, everything connected with such operations should doubly be the subject of public control and scrutiny. No partnership, company or corporation should be allowed to exist with unlimited gains and limited responsibility. No public organization should exist without *publicity*. Corporate privileges are a public trust which ought to be resumed by the people whenever they have become subversive of public interests. The time to all appearance is rapidly approaching, when peace, order and security may demand the abolition of such delegated powers.

CHAPTER XIII.

SHADOWS OF THE COMING AMERICAN ARISTOCRACY.

The fetters of want—American and French republics—Free and slave labor in the young American republic—Aristocracy as first planted almost submerged—Failure of political amendments to secure equal power to landless freedmen—The exodus—Capitalist and wage worker—Duke of Argyle—Necessity of maintaining republican simplicity—Great increasing wealth—Where it goes—Rich, middle and poorer classes—Wages and incomes of tradesmen—Aggregate accumulated wealth—What workingmen have no interest in—What they have a small interest in—Gradually ceasing to own lands and lots—Statistics of labor and of employees, professional men and capitalists—Family and individual property—Laws of inheritance—Life—Property—Reputation—Interest and compound interest—The cumulative power of capital—Atkinson on national debts—Paper credits carry on business—Profits of directing energy—Capital which is used, and capital which is of little use—Non-producing classes always an aristocracy—We must cultivate respect for honest poverty.

IT has been truly said that man, like the horse and the ass, can be subdued and led by the mouth. When the opportunities for procuring a livelihood are equal, men have little to fear, but when governments, instead of protecting the rights of all citizens, invade them and place the bounties of nature in the hands of monopolists, then men step across the threshold of active life in a great degree helpless. The inexorable necessity for food, and the constant pressure of other wants are the bridle and halter which, under our artificial forms of society, are too apt to be the forerunners of aristocracy and despotism. We pride ourselves on the possession of political freedom, and boast that we live in a country that knows no distinctions among men. The American republic was founded on the theory of the equal rights of all its citizens. It was the first result of the great democratic wave that swept over Christendom toward the close of the last century. The spirit of revolt and independence had been brewing for generations. The American colonists were largely refugees fleeing from despotism and aristocracy; the first had taken political power, independence and dignity from the people, and the latter had monopolized the soil of their native land, rendering it impossible for them to live there, save as serfs or renters. It is not surprising, therefore, that the new government they formed was the incarnation of protests and hopes long smothered. To form a nation independent of the British sovereign was one thing, to establish a government on the basis of equal human rights, quite another. Then, as now, they had conservatives and radicals; there was also a little leaven of weak, undeveloped aristocracy, but all gave way before the democratic ideas of government which, among English-speaking people had been struggling against king and aristocracy for three hundred years. The Declaration of American Independence was therefore considered the triumph of liberty and equality among men.

Inspired by its success, the French revolution followed. The European field was very different. France was in the last stage of political dry rot. Kingcraft and aristocracy had almost eaten up an unhappy people, but the rulers themselves were verging on imbecility. Kings and aristocrats were destroyed. Finding the church allied with the state, instead of assailing priests religion was assailed, and humanity held up its hands in horror, as the bloody guillotine cruelly revenged the terrible wrongs of centuries, and proletarians shouted that there "is no God," because they could not find Him among the French hierarchy. In the rest of Europe, tyrants, moneyed interests, conservatives and even moderate, timid liberals were alarmed. A reaction set in, but France was tenacious of her purpose. This hotbed of sedition and anarchy became dangerous; war was declared against it. The young republic became a great camp. Every crowned head and every aristocrat in Europe was against France. Such odds have scarcely ever been seen in war; but behind despotic organizations a smoldering democratic element in Europe looked on France as the forerunner of liberty, and for a time Europe was under her feet. Even Jena wrung from the Prussian government the land reforms of Stein and Hardenberg. France, not satisfied with a war of defense, entered upon a war of conquest: the republic was merged in the empire. The code of law, which really was the code of the revolution, became the "Code Napoleon." Titles may have been created, but feudalism was not restored. Hatred of landed aristocracy was firmly anchored in the public mind, the policy to divide the country in small farms owned by cultivating farmers was fixed, and democratic laws of inheritance secured the result. The "Holy Alliance" crushed the empire, but through all the vicissitudes of France the seeds sown by Mirabeau, Seyes and their colleagues, have fructified. In 1848 another democratic uprising convulsed Europe, but this time kings and aristocrats were prepared, and enormous armies crushed it. Reforms have been slowly doled out to appease the angry spirit. Gigantic armaments are maintained at an expense which threatens Europe with universal bankruptcy. In spite of all these, the doctrines of equal human rights and reforms in land tenure were never so much discussed as they are to-day. The war against despotism and aristocracy was checked, but it is not over.

While this was going on in Europe, what was happening in America. Very considerable estates had been permitted to go into the hands of certain families, especially in the South Atlantic states. The preservation of African slavery after the formation of a free republic aided the creation of a Southern aristocracy. The great estates were cultivated by slaves. It had been an old idea with many men pretending to be republicans, that the menial labor might safely be performed by an alien and servile class in a republic. Had the "accidents of war" and the "mills of the gods" not made an end of slavery it would not have taken many generations to place all the non-slaveholding population under the feet of a terrible oligarchy. Another thing would have happened. The little slave plantations would have been absorbed by the great ones. The sympathies of the poorer class of white men who did not own slaves were secured in the interests of slavery in the Southern states by appealing to their prejudices against the negroes. At the close of the war, everything that constitutional amendments and law could do to place the negroes on a political equality was done. No steps were taken to enable them to become owners of the soil. Neither were measures adopted to secure the disruption and division of the great estates. The result ought to be a most instructive lesson to us, and fully illustrates the idea announced by John Adams, that "those who own the land will rule the country." In spite of constitutional amendments and civil rights bills, the great landowners of the Southern states rule that portion of our republic. If each of the colored men had been encouraged and aided to possess a homestead of even forty or twenty acres, and measures been taken to disentegrate and divide the great estates, the result would have been different. The attempts of the colored people to emigrate from the Southern states, where they were born, to more inhospitable Northwestern states, were merely efforts to get land. It was a struggle to escape from the fate of settling down as tenant-holders under their former masters. Most of them are too poor to buy land. The dependent condition in which they are placed does not afford them much opportunity to improve their fortunes. The present unsettled condition of affairs in the South reduces land values, even to speculators, and offers the nation an opportunity to make landholders of the colored people. It is to be regretted that so few of them are able to avail themselves of the present low prices to become landowners. Unless there is some change in the existing system the time is not far distant when the lands in the South will be held at a high price, and heavy rents will place permanent burdens on the shoulders of the cultivators of the soil, and furnish the means to sustain a privileged, luxurious, non-productive and aristocratic class.

In the Northern and Western states, as we have shown, the steady tendency is to permit the lands to drift into the hands of capitalist holders. When the public land is taken up, which will be very soon, the absorption of the land by the owners of accumulated capital will be greatly accelerated. So far, capitalists have made larger profits from other investments. The rapid multiplication of fortunes in business enterprises has distracted attention from land. Those who wish to found wealthy families will soon seek the enduring monopoly of land as the safest and most permanent basis for an income, and will find few obstacles where the land is a chattel, and small holders are continually liable to be embarrassed. For a comparatively trifling amount the government permits this individual monoply of the soil, and guarantees the power to collect a revenue from occupying cultivators "forever." The power to exact this tax from producers is the thing we call a fee simple title. So long as there is no law prohibiting the owning of land except for cultivation, limiting the amount which shall be held, providing for its redistribution, and forbidding its aggregation, land will inevitably go into the hands of capitalist holders. Whetted by the desire to obtain greater revenues and more dignity, the owners of the large farms will soon own the small ones. The producing yeoman farmer will sink to the condition of a renter or laborer, and the longer this state of affairs lasts the more difficult it will be for the farmer to become once more an owner. Land when so held will be held at high prices. The landlords will have great influence and be the dominant power in the country, no matter what the government may be called. We are now laying the foundations of landed aristocracy, and unless something is done to check and prevent it, our country, in spite of its boasted freedom, will become a country of landlords and aristocrats, ruling over and subsisting on tenants and laborers.

Another thing is happening. Capital is absorbing the manufacturing power of the country. We have no longer trades controlled by tradesmen and mechanics, but capitalist employers and wage workers. We are slowly placing the power of all our means of transportation in the hands of capitalists, and the tendency of the system is to permit them to become monopolists. It is the same thing with canals, telegraphs and many other necessary adjuncts of civilization. Bankers, insurance companies and stock-brokers claim the privilege of controlling money and regulating the supply and demand of the medium of exchange. It will not be denied that the result of these things will be to produce great classes existing by their daily labor, wage workers and a smaller class of capitalist landlords and proprietors of franchises living on capital, and having the power to fix the wages of labor, and determine what shall be the condition of the working classes.

Of this state of affairs our aristocratic European neighbors are not oblivious. Seeing the tendency in that direction in America they take more kindly to our institutions. For several years shoots of aristocracy from the Old World have traversed our country and become afflicted with land hunger. No alien should be permitted to own a foot of American soil. If a man intends to become a citizen our government permits him to take a homestead. A foreigner who never intends to become a citizen, can, unfortunately, buy all he wants at second hand. Bad as it would be to have our farmers paying rent to native landed aristocrats, it would be still worse that they should pay annual rents to a foreign landlord. We have already enumerated some of the alien landholders. About fifteen years ago a tract of land was bought in Kansas from the Pacific Railway Company by an association or combination of English gentlemen, for aristocratic settlement; they never intended to become citizens of the United States, and called their town Victoria. Much larger tracts than that have since been purchased, many of them quite lately. In his reply to Henry George, the Duke of Argyle, with these facts doubtless before him, sarcastically sneers at people in the "many new worlds where kings are left behind and aristocracies have not had time to be established." * The British aristocracy no doubt view the aristocratic tendencies of society in America with more than complacency. In his reply to Mr. George, the Duke refers to an act of courtesy tendered him by that author in terms an American gentleman would consider rude. Superciliousness of that kind may be the privilege of noblemen, but leads us to regret that in devoting their estates to sheep the cultivation of gentlemen may sometimes be neglected.

Proud of our free republic and confident of security so long as men hold the ballot, we have been much too skeptical as to the insidious advances of an aristocracy. We cannot fail to observe that the daughters of some of our most wealthy citizens seek and form marriage alliances with the titled nobility of Europe. Steps are also taken by most of our very rich men to avoid having their property divided at death by concentrating the greater portion on one son, thus seeking to introduce the infamous law of primogeniture. It is true that no inconsiderable portion of our would-be aristocracy is what is styled a "shoddy aristocracy," vain, selfish, undignified and comparatively illiterate. These parties are only worthy of contempt for their ridiculous airs. After all, their conduct is not so reprehensible as that of an educated, wealthy citizen, who, merely because he possesses a great fortune, is recreant to

* The Duke of Argyle's Reply to Henry George, in the Nineteenth Century for April, 1884.

the principles of republican liberty, failing to preserve that dignified and sturdy simplicity which ought to be the pride of every American. Law cannot give tone to society; we need a purified public opinion which will sternly maintain republican dignity. These matters may appear to be trifles, and yet they are not without significance. We must not lose sight of the danger of confounding aristocracy with titles. Landed aristocracies in Europe were mainly established by usurpation, violence and fraud. The title of duke, marquis, or lord, is merely to overawe and mislead. It gilds and conceals the steps by which a man has seized and holds the monopoly of a county or a province. So long as human beings are weak enough to worship and tolerate a nobility, the crimes of an aristocracy will be possible.

Our American aristocracy did not start that way. It has to creep into existence in a republic in which all are ostensibly equals. The wealth of the country increases at present faster than it ever did before. In Mulhall's tables he puts the wealth of the United States in pounds sterling, which is not much less than five times the amount in dollars as follows: In 1850, £1,686,000,000; in 1860, £3,866,000,000; in 1870, £7,074,-000,000; and in 1880, at £9,495,000,000.* Mr. Spofford's figures vary somewhat from these. For 1850 he gives $7,135,-780,228; for 1860, $16,159,616,068; for 1870, $30,068,518,-507, and for 1880, $43,642,000,000.† We will use Mr. Spofford's figures. One curious circumstance will be found by referring to Mr. Spofford's table. In 1850 the wealth estimated at $7,135,780,228 is assessed for taxes at $6,024,-666,909, while in 1880 the wealth put down at $43,642,000,-000 is only assessed at $16,902,000,000. It will thus be seen that the great increase of wealth seems to be accompanied by greater facilities for keeping it off the tax roll. Mr. Spofford,

* Mulhall's Dictionary of Statistics, page 470.

† Spofford's American Almanac for 1885, page 21.

on page 105 of his almanac, gives the taxable property in the United States at $19,180,484,203. These figures he obtained from the state officers of the thirty-eight states, many of the reports coming up to 1884 and two of them to 1885, when it is presumable there was a considerable increase of property over the return for 1880. By the census tables as reported for 1850 and 1860 the value of slaves was given in fifteen states and dropped in 1870 and 1880. In 1850, with this value of slaves included, the wealth of the United States if equally divided per capita was $308 and in 1880 the price of slaves being excluded the wealth was $870.* In other words there was an increase of wealth in the United States, equal to $562 to every man, woman and child in the country, or, counting each family as consisting of five persons, a wealth per family of $2810. In the present state of our statistics we are not in possession of accurate data as to where this great increase of wealth has gone, but if we consider the condition of wage workers in 1850, and the condition of wage workers in 1880, in the United States, it is extremely doubtful if the laborers are any better off, or even as well off to-day as they were then. In 1850 wage workers had occasionally a little property. In our own observation we are firmly persuaded that more of them, in proportion to their number, had homes of their own at that time than have them now. It is to be granted that the number of persons included in what is styled the "middle classes" has probably increased, although nothing could be more vague than the term "middle classes" in the United States. We will borrow a mode sometimes used by British statisticians, and fix a salary or an income of $1000 for the head of a family as indicating the "middle classes." In a table of Mr. Spofford's condensed from the state reports † and which includes the wages paid to bakers, blacksmiths, bookbinders, bricklayers, cabinet makers, carpenters and join-

* Spofford's American Almanac, page 21. † Ibid., page 103.

ers, laborers, porters, painters, plasterers, plumbers, printers, shoemakers, tailors and tinsmiths, we find that only one of them, the plumbers, with their wages computed at the highest rate in the highest market, Chicago, reaches $1040. The table in this case is a weekly wage to working plumbers in Chicago varying from $12 to $20 a week. At the latter rate I have computed it. The laborers run about $350 per year. The "middle classes" in the country would probably include employers, business and professional men, merchants and middlemen generally, whose income was from $1000 to $10,-000 per year, and whose property did not exceed $100,000.

While this "middle class" in Europe may have increased in numbers and wealth, as claimed and boasted by Mr. Mallock and Mr. Giffen, it is not the opinion of the writer that this class in the United States have accumulated much more than their proportion of the increased wealth. Adding these to the still wealthier class, including millionaires, all of them with their families fall considerably below the tenth part of the population. A number of very great fortunes have been created out of the accumulated wealth, and while the middle classes have increased in numbers, and have had some additions in wealth, nine-tenths of the population have not increased in wealth in proportion, and a very large number are absolutely poorer. Such a result shows the growth of an aristocracy of wealth. Mr. Mulhall, in a table, gives what he styles "the component parts of American wealth," that is, the wealth of 1880. Land and forest are valued at £2,150,000,000 (pounds sterling). Cattle, £378,000,000. Railways, £1,190,000,000. Public works, £527,000,000. Houses, £2,780,000,000. Furniture, £1,385,000,000. Merchandise, £155,000,000. Bullion, £157,000,000. Shipping, £60,000,000. Sundries are put down at £713,000,000.* This latter must include banking capital, telegraphs, telephones, insurance companies

* Mulhall's Dictionary of Statistics, page 469.

and the capital of a great many other undescribed interests. Vague as the table is, it gives us some slight clue. Of the aggregate Mr. Mulhall gives of nine billion four hundred and ninety-five million pounds sterling, as the wealth of the United States, there are several heads in which the workers for wages have little or no interest. These are in the capital of railways, cattle, public works, merchandise, bullion, shipping and sundries. Under the latter head a small amount may be credited them. Twenty-five years ago laborers and wage workers had a few cattle, but now these classes own little under this head. Of the two billion seven hundred and eighty million pounds in houses, it is correct to assume that the wage workers in proportion to their number, do not own as much value in houses as they did in 1850. The concentration of the value of houses and lots in the hands of capitalists has been rapidly going on during the past twenty years. Of the sum of £2,150,000,000 in land and forest it is fair to estimate that of this there is no large amount in the hands of wage workers; there is a considerable amount in the hands of poor agricultural laborers still, although the process of transferring land through mortgages and otherwise, to capitalists, is rapidly going on. In the writer's observation, in the West, during the past ten years, of homesteads, to secure titles to which requires five years' occupancy, almost forty per cent. of these farms are alienated or mortgaged within two years of the time of securing title.

Our system of economics in the United States therefore presents several dissimilar and apparently contradictory features. First, the opportunity offered to a poor man to get a farm or piece of land to improve on easy terms, and, second, a commercial and economic system, under which capital is steadily acquiring the land, controlling manufactures, railroads, telegraphs, and accumulating fortunes in the hands of a comparatively limited class.

The population of the United States in 1880 was 50,155,-

783. Of these, 17,392,099 were persons, employed in agriculture, professional and personal services, trade, transportation, manufacturing and mining.* Of those thus employed, 2,647,157 were females, and 14,744,942 males. No inconsiderable number of the latter were lads and boys over ten years. Persons thus employed probably represent an actual population of at least forty-seven millions. The number engaged in agriculture is set down at 7,670,493.† Those who are classed as performing personal and professional services number 4,074,238. To prevent these latter figures from giving an incorrect impression it is necessary to state that they include 1,859,223 laborers, 1,075,653 domestic servants, 44,851 barbers, 77,413 employees of hotels, 121,942 laundresses and launderers, besides a great many other laboring employees or wage workers. The actual professional classes, clergymen, lawyers, doctors, architects, artists, journalists, claim agents, teachers and scientific persons only aggregate 470,475. Those engaged in mining and manufactures are stated to be 3,337,112, of whom all but a small number are wage workers. In trade and transportation 1,810,256 are engaged.‡ The census shows 3375 railroad officials and 415,582 employees. Officials of insurance companies 1774, and bankers and brokers, 15,180. Of those engaged in trade and transportation upwards of a million are merely wage workers. Officials and managers of railroads, banks, insurance companies, and brokerage all together do not number more than 20,000, and only a small number of persons really control them. Of the 800,000 persons engaged as traders or middlemen, considerably more than half are clerks, laborers or other employees, and the tendency in all the branches of trade is to merge the small trading houses into large establishments usually owned by a company. Except in a few Western states the land has

* Spofford's American Almanac for 1885, page 277.

† Ibid., page 274.

‡ Ibid., page 277.

been monopolized, and a mechanic or artisan, if discharged, cannot support his family from the natural products of the earth. Even the fisheries on seas and rivers are becoming private property. Places for shelter as homes are monopolized. If unable to pay rent the laborer cannot rear an humble hut on the common; everything is closed to him, but the chance of finding employment from a master. Trades unions have not the power of law to sustain them. Lawmakers play fast and loose between employers and employed: they profess sympathy for laboring men and legislate in the interests of accumulated property. All these are the steps by which an aristocratic class in the United States is being formed.

Through the transmission of property from one generation to another, aristocracies may be made or aristocracies prevented. In many ancient countries property was family property. In certain conditions of society the relations between man and man were summed up in kinship. The fundamental assumption being that all men not related to you were your enemies or slaves.* The kinship tie was in some countries cemented by religious rites and strengthened among those who worship dead ancestors. In the Brehon law the word Fine (or family) is used for the children and descendants of a living parent. The Sept, the "unit" of ancient Ireland, and the "joint and undivided family" of the East Indian law, constitutes the combined descendants of an ancestor long since dead. All these absorbed strangers by marriage or adoption. With these the property was the property of the whole. No one could be deprived of his interest. No one's share could be disposed of without his consent. No person could by will deprive any other person of his equal rights. In fact, making wills was almost unheard of. As women often married and left the tribe, their interests and rights were long a subject of dispute and conflict. In large portions of India,

* Maine's History of Early Institutions, page 227.

to-day, a woman's interest in the land, which is merely a usufruct with the improvement, cannot be alienated without her consent. There a married woman's separate property is called the "Stridhan," which the modern English Indian courts decide to consist of the property given to her by her family, at marriage, or by her husband. This she holds independent of him. The ancient Hindoo law went much farther, and the modern compiler of the Hindoo law includes what they may have acquired by inheritance, purchase, partition, seizure or finding.* The Mahometan rulers of India, although they did not altogether overthrow the ancient law and custom, endeavored to introduce their own ideas. Mahometan laws of inheritance have often obtruded themselves to the disadvantage of women. The old Mahometan law of inheritance divides the property in minute fractions among the males. As Mahometanism encountered conflicting ideas it adjusted itself to various conditions, however. In many Mahometan countries the daughter takes half a son's share, but if these cases are carefully examined they will be found in countries where the old law and customs were much more liberal to woman. Any inequality in the rights of women and men found in India, may be traced to Mahometan interference. Among these ancient countries of the Aryan stock, the Allod was the share a man took in the appropriated public domain. It came to him as a right. The idea of willing it to him or from him was not thought of. The Roman law was intrusive and aggressive. It left its marks wherever the Roman foot was planted. The Romans distinguished between real and personal property, or rather between property that could pass on a bargain between individuals and that which required record and a conformity to law. The distinction was *Res Mancipi* and *Res nec Mancipi* when it did not require the conveyance of "mancipation" or release. *Res Mancipi*

* Maine's History of Early Institutions, page 323.

included land, slaves, houses, oxen; everything else went under the other head. By the Roman law a woman became the ward of her husband, like a daughter. All the wife's property passed absolutely to him. Under this oppressive system a custom grew of contracting a sort of civil marriage. The wife absented herself from her husband's home three days and three nights to avoid the *Usucapion,* which would have absorbed her property. There was a provision covering this kind of contract in the Roman code of twelve tables. A strong influence was brought to bear to make these marriages less respectable, and as they could be terminated at the will of either party, some color was lent to this idea. It ultimately became the common Roman marriage, however. The Roman law and the theoretical principles of the Roman government originated from philosophical Greek theories. We can easily trace the portions of Roman law that have been thrust into our social and political system. A singular custom grew up in Europe several hundred years ago of giving the widow a life interest of one-third in her husband's real estate, and a certain share of his personal property. It grew out of the conflict of different regulations on this question. With some nations the woman took share with her husband's family; in other cases she held her own property in her own right. In India, under Hindoo law a childless widow had a life estate in her husband's property. This was an ancient custom with many nations, affording the surviving member of the household a life rent in the property that had belonged to both. Out of this provision came the practice of Sutteeism, by which the widow offered herself up as a sacrifice to the manes of her husband. The custom was a comparatively modern innovation. It had its origin in sheer selfishness, and as a general thing only affected childless widows. The male relatives of the deceased husband could not come into the property until her death, consequently they insisted that her sacrifice was due to the love she bore her deceased lord, and her refusal was often treated with such criticism and abuse that it drove the poor woman to the funeral pile. The "widow's third" of modern Europe and the United States is something essentially different from the widow's life estate in the property of her husband. It undoubtedly grew out of a disposition to make property a chattel, and to substitute individual rights as the representatives of property for the rights of compact groups of individuals or families. It was to some extent a compromise between the rigid Roman law and the ancient Aryan custom. Under the Roman law as finally matured, parents were under statutory obligations to make settlements on their marriageable daughters.* In the Sclavonic household and town communities, the daughters were entitled to a settlement and maintenance. In whatever way it originated the "widow's third" has come down to us and prevails in most of the states. Kansas is an exception, the widow taking one-half of all her husband's property, real and personal. In 1787 Congress in passing a law for the government of the Northwest territory provided for the equal division of property among the children and a life rent of "the third" of the real estate to the wife. The distribution among descendants was to be per stirpes, not per capita, but this law merely governed intestate cases, as the father could make by will a different disposal. The one thing it indicated was hostility to the law of primogeniture, but as a principle for the transmission of property it was crude and the ideas not original. In the past three or four generations there has been a constant tendency to the individual control of property. The old custom of equal family holding, or of equal rights in property inherited, has been as completely invaded by this assertion of individual will over accumulated property, as the same system had been by the monopolization of the land by the oldest sons, under the law of primogeniture. The inheritance of

* Maine's History of Early Institutions, page 336.

property lies at the foundation of the state. We have seen that in Europe it created an aristocracy constantly increasing in wealth and diminishing in numbers. Wise laws of inheritance may prevent an aristocracy, and in our republic statutes should be framed for that purpose. Our laws concede too much to individual will in determining the transmission of property from one generation to another. It has been urged that a father's power to disinherit is a wholesome check on the errors of children. This is undoubtedly a mistake. Young men or women who have been taught to form, or neglected so that they formed, bad habits, are only more entitled to help, and so far as the state is concerned a father has no right to create privileged classes. Long leases have been effected, the increased values of which were to inure to the benefit of a man's grandchildren even though his own children remain poor. All such dispositions of property are against public policy and should be prevented by law. Real estate should, in its future disposition, never be subject to individual will, but in everything governed by a policy of its highest uses for the people, and the distinct assertion of the equal rights of every person, in every generation, in it. So far as any disposition of property to descendants is concerned it ought to be governed by rules of perfect equality. One single element of our law of inheritance will show how these inequalities have crept into it. We divide per stirpes and not per capita. A man has accumulated a large fortune and lived to an old age. He has, we will say, two sons. One of these has eight children and one has two. The fathers of these children die before the grandfather, and are never able to control or inherit any of his property. If it was distributed per capita, each of these ten grandchildren would get equal portions, but we distribute it under our law per stirpes, one-half goes to two grandchildren and the other half is divided between eight, and all these persons bear the same relation to the owner of the property. The tendency of our laws and customs is to the assertion of the broadest power by the owner of property not only while living but after he is dead. To carry out this idea more fully, everything, even land, has been reduced to the condition of a chattel. That a man should enjoy a large liberty, during his lifetime, over property made by him, and within the bounds of possible honest acquisition, may be partially admitted. The assertion of individual will in controlling the disposition of property has been carried too far for the public interests. Why should this despotism of one person be clung to tenaciously as an American doctrine? When a man dies he has, strictly speaking, but one right, and that is to be buried. It is natural that he should wish his wife, his *partner*, to be comfortably maintained if there is property left. This, if he does not do, *the law should do for him*. Consistent with that he should wish that all of his descendants at his death should share equally in at least part of what may be left to distribute, and if he does not do this the law *should do it for him*. If he has made a large accumulation of personal property instead of seeking to perpetuate it in his family, an honorable and proper public spirit should lead him in the general public interest to give a portion of such remainder for necessary public institutions, charities, educational establishments or relief for the poor, and if he does not do so the *law should do it for him*. This could easily be done by taxation on bequests or taxation of estates for these purposes, increasing taxation in such ratio at each fresh bequest of the same property until it had melted away, and compelled the third or fourth generation at farthest to be entirely self-supporting. The writer thinks the public interest would be served by not permitting it to go beyond the second generation. The other side of the question is how far such regulations would effect production. A man struggles, toils, submits to privations to acquire the means to render himself comfortable and independent in his old age, and to give something to the children he loves. If he has not this inducement he would not so struggle to acquire. When a man deliberately contemplates making and leaving a fortune for his children so that they will never need to work, but be maintained from accumulated capital as part of a *non-producing* class he *conspires against the public interests.* It is more than probable that he also conspires against the best interests of his children. To aid them in starting in life with a fair prospect ought to be the highest stretch of filial or patriotic duty. Hereditary fortunes are not only inconsistent with our political institutions, but with the public interests and safety. So far as possible our laws of inheritance, our tax laws, and our laws to prevent fraud and overreaching in business should be framed under a fixed and persistent policy, the end of which should be to prevent the accumulation of great fortunes and also to prevent their perpetuation. Land should never in any sense be subjected to disposition by will. The sooner we dispossess our minds of the idea that land in itself is property the better. The right to cultivate it may in some cases be subject to transmission. Certain rights in improvements thereon may exist, but should never be permitted to become alienating liens. Whatever tenure or right of occupancy the state determines shall be held in land ought not to be governed by the usual laws of inheritance, for a family has no more right to monopolize the land than the individual. Families may desire a continuous occupancy, and when their claim covers no more than an equitable share, it may be in the public interest to give it to them. Sufficiently long tenure must be allowed to insure the most productive cultivation and the highest *necessary* line of improvements, but in any case subject to the rights that all the people possess in the land. It is a favorite theory of a modern school of political economists that it makes no difference to the public who owns the land, that the only consideration is under what system will it produce the most. If there is abundance of bread, meat and other articles raised the public will obtain them. The cheaper they can be produced the easier will the public get them. That artisans, manufacturers, laborers and tradesmen derive the best advantages from land in this way, and since all cannot be farmers the subject of land ownership is an unimportant one, the only question being as to whether those who own or control it will have it so conducted as to produce, for the necessities of the public, the greatest amount at the lowest price.

At the first glance this is a seductive theory, but it will not bear a moment's scrutiny. To permit a non-producing class of citizens to fasten themselves on the land and drain from it one-third or one-half of all the produce to maintain an idle class in luxury is not a good economic arrangement for the producer and consumer. The landlords live on and tax both the other classes. Even if all this exacted rent was taken from the wages of the laboring agriculturist, it is not for the interest of the artisan, mechanic, craftsman or manufacturer, that the agriculturist should be so impoverished as to be unable to buy manufactured articles. It is not for the interest of either class that a wealthy aristocracy should be built up to undermine their rights, steal their liberties and sentence them, their women and their children to be an inferior class in the community. It is believed that small farms well cultivated by resident holders produce more than great farms cultivated at wholesale by machinery. In a dense population nothing but small farms cultivated, in every nook and corner, with the close care of even spade husbandry, can support the people. Above all, the happiness, prosperity and independence of the laboring agriculturist is a matter of vital importance to all other tradesmen. If the face of the earth must be sold, the public interests require a policy that will prevent the land from becoming high priced or difficult of access to those who wish to cultivate the soil. Small farms, slight barriers in the way of an interchange of occupations, the destruction of speculative values in land, these are in the line of the highest and best public economy.

The question has been asked, Has government any right to interfere with the accumulations of the individual? It has also been said that the legitimate business of government is to keep the peace, prevent robbery and murder, and otherwise let men alone. The highest function of government is to preserve life, property and reputation. Life cannot be preserved when the conditions necessary to maintain life are unscrupulously and grossly violated. Would we consider the man a more cruel murderer who runs a knife in the heart of his victim in a moment of anger, or the man who by selfish, unfair and dishonest practices starves his fellow man or drives him to despair and destruction? The law-making public is indeed concerned in preserving the lives of all men. That public is also concerned in seeing that the bodies of men are not exposed to slow starvation, physical diseases or moral corruption. Man owes his fellow man more than "mere civility" and society cannot fully protect life without protecting all the conditions of the highest life attainable.

Property rights cannot be protected until we ascertain to whom the property honestly belongs. No one would argue the propriety of defending a thief's right. Shall the highwayman and pirate come into court to demand protection for their acquisitions? Shall the gains of fraud and deception be maintained to the detriment of those who honestly earned the proceeds of labor. In making the protection of property one of the first duties of law, we should regulate by it every question touching the interests and rights of property. Civilization is infested with a class of unscrupulous and avaricious persons who make enormous fortunes that could not be acquired by honest labor or perfectly honorable mercantile transactions; make them, in fact, by tricks, unfair concealments, misrepresentations, conspiracies, selling things for what they are not, or for more than their worth, and having thus acquired great wealth are loud in their declarations that organized society and laws exist but to protect them in their possession of such gains. Society is organized for the equal protection of all its members, and its duty in regard to property is to see that those who really made it are protected in its use.

Reputation calls for protection quite as much as life. This public trust has not always been faithfully executed. The assassin of reputation should be promptly and severely punished. Society also owes it to the honest laboring masses that their position be maintained as honorable among men. Those who are compelled to perform long hours of arduous toil, who have barely a sufficiency of coarse food, and are sheltered with their families in one or two small, ill-ventilated rooms, are scarcely in a position to maintain themselves with that respectability that ought to be enjoyed by the laboring American citizen.

When we reflect that the average duration of a generation is about thirty-three years, and that once in that period or, at most in a few years longer, all the accumulated wealth of the country changes hands, we see one of the portentous influences which, under wise law may preserve property in equal portions, or found an aristocracy. It will readily be admitted that property inherited and property accumulated from toil and saving, stand on a slightly different basis. That which a man fairly produces by his labor he is usually tenaciously inclined to claim the right to dispose of. Where he saves it and adds it to the accumulated wealth of the community he desires and during his life he may be allowed to control it, subject, however, always to the interests and safety of the state. When he seeks to make some disposition of it which shall, after he is dead, affect the interests and well being of the state, other questions and other interests come in. It is not just that one man should toil and live penuriously in order that another may live in luxurious idleness. When a misused life, human cunning and ingenuity are devoted to such a task, laws should be framed to render such self-immolation unprofitable and unsuccessful. The new generation has earned nothing. It is the duty of every man as a faithful and patriotic citizen to perform his share of labor and produce something which shall be a fair equivalent for the food he eats and the clothes he wears. Assuming the right to build up independent fortunes for those who never earn them is assuming the right to create an aristocracy. So long as we permit and encourage the greatly cumulative power of money through usury, we multiply the opportunities that aid in building up such a system. A dollar if permitted to run at compound interest would, in a certain number of years, absorb all the accumulated wealth of the world. To get a closer illustration, Mr. Spofford, as we have quoted, places the value of property in 1880 in the United States at $43,642,000,000 (forty-three billion six hundred and forty-two million). There is that amount of wealth outside of labor, a fixed capital, to use or inherit. Now while money loaned on short time on commercial paper may be obtained for three, four, five or six per cent. per annum in these United States, the laboring man does not borrow much at less than eight or ten per cent. If all accumulated capital produced equally at eight per cent. there would have to be taken out of the product of labor in each year the sum of three billion, four hundred and ninety-one million, three hundred and sixty thousand dollars, before labor could pay the debt due accumulated capital. At four per cent., interest on this property would amount in each year, to one billion seven hundred and forty-five million, six hundred and eighty thousand dollars, or five and one-third times the revenue of the government of the United States for 1884. In 1884 the total domestic exports of the United States was $775,190,-487.00. In other words, it would have taken all the exports of the United States for two and one-third years to pay four per cent. interest for one year on the accumulated capital of the United States. Mr. Spofford gives the total amount paid in wages in 1884 in all the manufacturing establishments of the

United States, at $947,919,647.00.* It would require nearly twice as much to pay four per cent. interest on the accumulated capital in the United States. We find by consulting a table of the same gentleman, compiled from official returns, that the "estimated value of all farm productions, sold, consumed, or on hand for 1879 was $2,213,402,564,† a large part of which would have been required if we were to pay four per cent. per annum on all the accumulated capital in the United States. These figures demonstrate that *all* of the accumulated capital does not add to itself four per cent. on its value each year. If it did it would soon cripple labor and production, and in a very few years at most destroy them. The same thing would happen which Mr. Edward Atkinson thinks will necessarily happen to a large portion of the national debts of Europe before the end of fifteen years. He certainly cannot be accused of conspiring against the rights of property. In his preface to a recent book, he says,‡ "Since the beginning of the present century the public debts of Europe have increased from two billion six hundred million dollars to twenty billion dollars. This debt has been accompanied by the issue in many states of paper substitutes for money, and either by that method, or some other summary way, the repudiation of a large part of it may become a necessity before the end of the century." In other words, a paper debt, no inconsiderable portion of which never represented anything, has been at work in the multiplying process until it threatens itself with destruction. Well might Mr. Atkinson say on the same page, "So long as such a debt exists it works a false distribution of wealth," and he quotes, "One of the greatest living statesmen of England said her national debt was the chief cause of her pauperism." Let us reflect that we, too, have an immense inflated paper capital professing to represent railway, tele-

* Spofford's American Almanac for 1885, page 30. † Ibid., page 373.

‡ Atkinson's Distribution of Products, page 4, Preface.

graph, municipal, insurance and mercantile stock, and an endless variety of paper wealth, all of it calling for interest and dividends. "As long as this exists" it "works a false distribution of wealth." The foregoing criticism applies to our banking system. Nine-tenths of the business of the country is carried on by checks, drafts, certificates of deposit, bills, acceptances and other paper. While a part of this represents a tangible something no inconsiderable part of it does not. It is a paper credit system kept afloat by dealers in money. Every now and then there is a panic which tumbles many palaces of card board and paralyzes business, throwing wage workers out of employment. Even when the banks do not break, many men are drawing interest on their debts. The rates of interest for bank accommodations are lower in the Eastern states than in the West. In the latter eight, ten, twelve, and even twenty per cent. have been paid. It might be a better plan to pay the brokers a small percentage for taking care of money. The alleged advantage of permitting bankers to loan other people's money is that the circulating medium is thus not locked up, but relieves the necessities of many business men. A safer mode would be to organize companies or co-operative societies of workingmen, for manufactures as well as trade, and all the surplus money possessed by them, as well as their credit, could be used to carry on the business without a drain of interest to middlemen. By the present system a percentage is taken out of each manufactured article, and in this way reduces the wages of workingmen, as it is classed with the cost of production. It is no part of the policy of a capitalist employer to combine with other capitalists to keep up the price of labor. The cheaper he can buy labor the better he can undersell. We hear many complaints from employers and speculators of this class that their business does not pay, or that the profits are insufficient. If we compare the condition of the merchant and manufacturing princes, their magnificent houses and equipages, with the condition of their wage workers, we can easily see the untruth of such complaints. Their profits may not quite come up to their avaricious desires or unbridled ambition, but are sufficient to prove that it is only through organizations of workingmen to control business that the laborers can obtain a fair share. Mr. Mallock says that great wealth is produced by two things, machinery and the power of directing labor and capital. He intimates that if these get the lion's share they are entitled to it. Let us see. Machinery has been a contribution of genius for the benefit of the race, and after giving certain profits for a few years to the inventors, these inventions become public property. There is certainly no reason why they should be monopolized by capitalists to the detriment of the laborer, and that is just what has happened. Machinery should give corresponding benefit to all portions of society. Let us consider the "directing power" as an element of wealth. The "directing power," we take notice, is usually "intelligent" enough to direct to itself the lion's share. There is, perhaps, no instance on record where the "directing power" took an income for personal expenses equal to the amount paid an intelligent mechanic. This "directing power" of Mr. Mallock's is the very thing that requires regulating. Its profits should not be permitted to exceed a fair compensation, and "management" is not a sufficient apology for impoverishing the workman to amass a great fortune for the manager. The elements of production to-day are labor, capital and machinery. The existence of machinery ought to inure to the benefit of the laboring class except the mere amount to purchase and keep it in working order. The share of capital in production must be subordinate to the interests of labor. Usury ought to be under the ban of law. Capital is of two kinds. The capital which is produced for use and used by the man who owns it, such as houses, cattle, horses, vehicles, furniture, machinery, &c. Then there is the capital a man has accumulated that he does not personally need or use. Out of this he expects to make an income from those he permits to use it. This is the kind of capital that requires the supervision of the public, or it will impoverish all labor and create an aristocracy among men. This is the kind of capital which in the complicated civilization of modern times has grown to be, not the third but the first estate. It has created in our day what is the essence of all aristocracy—a class thriving on the labor of others. Ancient nations of power and character have legislated against this evil. There never has been a period when surplus capital possessed the power, consideration or profitable resources enjoyed by it to-day. Let it not be said that we overthrew King George to crown the "Almighty dollar."

It may be said if we place discouragements and obstacles in the avenues through which men make great fortunes, that these fortunes will not be accumulated. We reply that it is not for the public interest that they should be accumulated. It has been said that if capital is restricted it will not be able to infuse great activity into manufacture, and we respond that capital should never control manufacture. The rarest artistic skill is the gift of the mechanic; the division of profits has been the task of the capitalist director. The public are not so much concerned in the proposition how one million can be made into twenty millions as in the prosperity, comfort and independence of the working masses. Law should first sift out pretended capital from real, and useful articles of capital from mere blood-sucking capital. In measuring the profits of surplus wealth the only safe standard can be its benefits to the laborer, and as a preliminary we should see that men do not draw interest from their debts. It matters not what they may be called, non-producing classes are an aristocracy. That aristocracy not only taxes but degrades labor. A competency honestly earned to be expended in old age is the just fruit of an honorable life. All else must be subject to restrictions. The lines of distinction between rich and poor have become almost as exclusive as caste in India. The dominion of morals should be as potent in preserving human happiness as the dominion of business or law. Let us, therefore, foster an American spirit of equality and simplicity, so that a useful and honorable man, no matter how poor, will be respected as one of our worthiest and best citizens.

CHAPTER XIV.

REMEDIES.

Is the body politic disordered—Great wealth cannot insure national stability—Inequality in condition steadily developing—Workers not getting their share—What has caused the unequal distribution of wealth—In the early republic no great millionaires and few beggars—Number of monopolies embraced in land monopoly—Allodial title—Two pleas for rent—Can improvements constitute an alienating lien—Bastiat—The natural and indestructible powers of the soil—What rights in land are in accord with public policy—Length of tenure necessary to secure high improvements—Land should only be held by occupying cultivators—Reduction of farms with increase of population—Money should be refused speculating investment in land, or investment to secure rent—Henry George's plan—Tax and rent must not be permitted to increase the price of bread and meat—Tax must come out of accumulated capital—Large farms and landholders—Land speculation and wholesale farming should be taxed out of existence—The destruction of artificial land values no calamity—What is just and what is practicable—Cyrus Field and Henry George—Timber lands—Grazing lands—Mineral lands—Railroad land grants—Various communal experiments—Mormonism—Icaria—Robert Owen—Fourierism—Shakers—Oneida perfectionists—Individualism and socialism—How are wages to be raised—Combination and organization—Law, the servant of labor—Assassination and dynamite the suicide of labor interests—What is the legitimate business of government—How to control railroad and other corporations—Justice but not pauperism—Public improvements—Homes for workingmen—Will-making and inheritance.

WHEN a physician has been called to minister to a sick person, his first purpose is to discover the disease with which the patient is afflicted and then the steps to be taken to insure a return to health. We have at the present moment in these United States a good many physicians who are trying to make a diagnosis of the diseased body politic and various remedies have been proposed. Quite a number declare that the disorder is merely hypochondria and that it exists only in the imagination. To the charge that there are inherent evils, imbedded in our land system they reply that land is free to all in the United States, easy of access and easy of disposition, none are deprived of it and none are bound to it; and when it is urged that laborers are poor and becoming poorer, they reply that wages are higher in the United States than in most countries, and that if laborers are poor it is their own fault. It is, therefore, a debatable question whether or not affairs are in a healthy and prosperous state, and the republic, organized to secure the permanent interests, on a perfectly equitable basis, socially, economically and politically of all its citizens, now and hereafter. Many have grave doubts as to the future condition of the people under the social and business relations of society we are establishing. A hundred years ago, when our government was formed, the United States contained but little more than three millions of people and has now between fifty and sixty millions. Should it continue to increase in the same ratio for another hundred years our population would exceed that of China. We have endeavored to point out the fate of the working classes in many great nations. We have seen that evidences of splendor and power do not secure a permanent state or popular happiness. The history of most of these nations show us that as communities aggregate great wealth the people become divided into rich and poor, this disparity is rendered more striking and acute in highly artificial and luxurious forms of society. The causes of this difference of condition spring from the avaricious and aggressive spirit of a few members of society. The oppression of the poor has usually been brought about by violence, or long years of cunning, chicanery and fraud. We find in many states of society that wicked laws and customs have sanctioned slavery and combinations of men have made servants of a great number of their fellow creatures. We also find that by conspiracy, treachery and murder, men called kings with their confederates organize what they call a government in order that they may be better able to plunder mankind and carry on war, thus placing whole countries under their dishonest and despotic feet. Certain individuals succeed in securing peculiar privileges and monopolies from unwise and tyrannical governments, by which they are able to extort from their brothers a large proportion of their earnings, creating a modified kind of slavery. We observe in other conditions of society, possessors of accumulated wealth preying upon the poor and needy, taking advantage of their wants and necessities to impoverish them as wage workers, paying them only what will purchase poor food and shabby clothing for that labor, the produce of which enables the capitalist to continue and extend this phase of slavery. Thus in all forms of human society and at every period of which we have a record, there have been numbers of selfish, violent and unscrupulous men continually striving to enrich themselves at the expense of others. This they have always done, and this, we may take it for granted, they always will do if they are permitted. For all these abuses the only remedies must come from enlightened law or revolution. The majority can never safely assent to injustice against the weakest member of society, or carelessly permit privilege to a few.

When we contemplate the growing inequality of condition of the people of these United States, we discover that the "inalienable right" to "Life, liberty and the pursuit of happiness," has been and is being subverted. In the earlier history of the republic, so far as the white population was concerned, this inequality was not so great. In primitive times in the United States, and, indeed, for nearly half of its existence, great fortunes were almost unknown, and beggars were so rare that people considered it a privilege to give to them. Now there is a great change, and that change is steadily and rapidly progressing. As the accumulated wealth of the nation increases, the distinction between rich and poor widens. The remuneration paid to wage workers is so small that it affords little opportunity to save, or provide means of support during enforced idleness or for the necessities of old age. Every now and then large numbers of able and worthy citizens and laborers are thrown out of work. Tramps increase until our lawmakers go back to the days of Queen Elizabeth to find models for statutes against them. Numberless useful inventions simplify manufacture and render the production of every needful thing easier, but they do not lighten the burdens of the laboring poor or add to their wages; on the contrary the profits of machinery only increase the number and enhance the riches of the non-producing class. It is useless to deny that all these facts exist. In spite of our wealth and advantages, the circumstances of our wage workers are not improving. Possessors of a competence may complacently deny it, and say that the dissatisfaction among laboring men, strikes and all the murmurs at the burdens of rent and the inequalities of society, are merely the turbulence of demagogues promulgating socialistic and agrarian theories. Political economists of the Ricardo school tell us that capital produces wealth, and consequently takes the greatest share of it, and that this is the natural and just condition of society. Contracts rule and "a bargain's a bargain every part." Competition for shares of the proceeds of labor they argue is the mainspring of society. The weak and the strong, the wise and the simple, the selfish and unselfish, the cunning and the straightforward, the honest and dishonest, all must join in this avaricious scramble, and each take what he is able to get, and what he gets is the just measure of his deserts. According to them, it is in violation of all sound doctrine for law to step in between a laborer and his employer. Government only interferes with and hinders the "eternal law of trade" when it endeavors to fix the hours or price of labor. They contend that law attempts to do an unphilosophic thing when it tries to regulate interest, or presumes to denounce the cumulative additions of capital as "usury." They pronounce the doctrine that man is entitled to "Life, liberty, and the pursuit of happiness," a mere "glittering generality," and declare with Malthus that "man has not a right to subsistence when his labor will not fairly purchase it."* Lastly, we have the doctrine of Professor Sumner, that man owes his fellow man nothing "but civility"; that man is not a social being dependent largely on his fellows, but that individual rights, individual interests, and the measure of individual power, have, in this modern dispensation, swept brotherhood away.

In spite of such assumptions the body politic is diseased to this extent, that the men who do the hard work are not getting their share of the increasing property in the country. It is equally true that privileged classes are being created in this "land of equality" by the unequal distribution of wealth and the unnatural accumulation of large fortunes. The writer differs from some authors on the subject, in that he does not consider these evils solely attributable to the monopolization of land, although that has much to do with them. The land system we have permitted in this country is, indeed, very bad, but its worst evils have not yet had time to develop themselves. As far west as the Mississippi river, the land is, indeed, monopolized, and a great deal of it beyond that river; but as there is still public land to buy or locate, the worst troubles from land monopoly are yet to come. What has already happened may be summed up under two heads: First, the amount of land already monopolized in the heavily populated states has, on account of its being restricted to certain individuals and the increasing demands of a great population, risen enormously in value. This "unearned increment" our law and custom have conceded to be the property

* Malthus' Principles of Population, page 421.

of the men to whom these special privileges were given; and this, as Mr. Atkinson would say, "works a false distribution of wealth." The second evil is: that the high price thus created in favor of the monopolists has made land so dear that poor people cannot buy it. This condition of affairs has converted the poor men who wish to use land or houses into *renters*, and those who own land into non-producers. An incidental evil is that where the working man, who raises grain, has only to support his own family, he can afford to sell produce cheaper, but where he has to support a landlord and his family for the privilege of cultivating the soil, bread and meat become dearer. In this way, when men who do not cultivate the soil are permitted to buy or to own it, there is merely sold to them the privilege of exacting from it and through it a perpetual tax on meat and bread. Before the producer can use his crop there must be taken from it a large portion to support a non-productive class. This tax enhances the price of what is produced, and it is a tax the poorest man cannot escape. In the earlier days of the republic nearly every man owned his own home, whether it was a house and lot or a farm; now a large part of wages go toward rent. If an artisan or mechanic is dissatisfied with his wages and condition he may still, provided he has the money to carry himself West, go to a few Western states and territories and become a farmer. This, however, is frequently accomplished with great difficulty. The "free competition" between a wage worker and an employer in our Eastern cities is anything but fair. With the capitalist employer it is a proposition between a greater and a less amount of profit, with the laborer between taking what his employer will give him and starving to death.

The monopoly of land is the worst, and most far reaching special privilege ever granted to individuals. It includes the monopoly of coal for fuel, timber for building, petroleum and light, salt, and every building material. There is nothing a man eats or uses that is not taxed by this monopoly. Strictly speaking, land is not, and never has been property, it is simply privilege. Brentano asks: "What is land but an opportunity to get an income?" *

"In the sweat of thy face shalt thou eat bread, till thou return unto the ground; for out of it wast thou taken; for dust thou art and unto dust shalt thou return." † The human race is indeed a portion of the earth. The flesh and bones of myriads of human beings who have passed away are incorporated with it. The bodies of myriads yet to come will spring therefrom. All men cultivated land originally or obtained their living from it. Did the fact that a man cultivated any portion of the globe give him any individual right to it. Let us see. It was necessary that man should obtain a temporary use of the soil, to produce corn from it for his family. This, then, being an absolute necessity, carried some kind of right with it. Did it carry an exclusive right, and if so, on what ground, and for how long? In the introductory chapter we have shown that claims to own or control a portion of the earth have only been recognized as rights emanating from governments. Aggregations of men claim a country. We have seen that by the law and custom of the Aryan race, from which sprang the nations of modern Europe and the people of these United States, that they originally regarded the land as common property. Allodial title measured the uses of the earth. The tillable land was fenced, broken and put in shape to produce crops, by the joint labor of all. Each family had an equal interest in it. Every member of each family an equal share. It was the same with the pasture land and unimproved forest. As population increased other acres were added to it, fresh colonies made, or the old land equally subdivided. In each generation no one

* Brentano's History of Guilds and Trades Unions, page 128.

† Gen. iii. 19.

was permitted to have more than his share. There was no room for monopoly, and none for land speculation. The man of the preceding could not say to the man of a new generation, who had been born and grown up: "This is mine; I improved the share I hold; it was accorded to me. You have no part or lot in it. You must find a new place for yourself." Such action would have been a monopoly growing out of a limited, recognized right. It would have been the monopoly of one generation against another. The holder might have claimed the right to give it to one of his sons to the exclusion of all his other children. The law and custom originally said this he should not do. This equal occupancy, in which there was no special privilege, no monopoly, was, undoubtedly, the ancient mode of holding and cultivating land. Then *rent* was unknown, and the "Doctrine of rent" unheard of. It would have been impossible to apply even Mr. Francis Walker's rendition of Ricardo's doctrine: "Rent arises from the fact of the varying degrees of productiveness in the lands actually contributing to the supply of the same market, the least productive land paying no rent, or a rent so small that it may be treated as none. The rent of all the higher grades of land is measured upward from this line, the rent from each piece absorbing all the excess of produce above that of the no rent land."* Among our Aryan ancestors there was no one authorized to collect rent on any pretext. There was no class living on rent. There was no generation attempting to put the use of the land out of the reach of succeeding generations.

There are two claims for the right to exact rent. First, that there was a man in some one generation who found a tract no one else was occupying, and took possession of it and held it by right of first discovery. Such is the theory on which all preemptors', squatters' and "first holders'" rights are

* Land and its Rent, page 21.

founded. Strange, although it may appear, the doctrine is not without its supporters. This title, if asserted by an individual man, not connected with any government or organized society, would be good until two other men came along, or even one, bigger and stronger than he was, who should dispossess him. To be good for anything, therefore, this "right of discovery" must be recognized by a government strong enough to protect the claimant in it. The government or organization is society, the union of all, the whole. It exists to protect the rights of all. There is no other apology for its existence. How shall "the whole" grant a monoply to one or two on the pretext that it is for the interests of the whole? We have seen that when the primitive forms of society acted on the land question they never allowed individual claims to spring up. The ownership of the few asserted against the many is a comparatively modern contrivance. The right of a man to cultivate a piece of unclaimed land amounts just to this: his temporary use of it cannot destroy the rights other men have in it. It can give him no moral claim to it for an indefinite period. Other men have as much right to live upon the earth as he has. If one man can drive another from the part of the earth's surface he claims, the poor landless man can, in the same way, be driven from every foot of the earth. He has in fact no right to live, and the very privilege of living must be obtained from another. No government or form of society has a right to create such a monopoly. The highest interests of society demand that such an attempt be set aside. Neither has any government or form of society the right to create a privileged class, who, on the pretext of owning the land, shall exact an income, to be paid by all succeeding generations to their heirs and assigns before the people of any generation can be allowed to live on it. This, whatever it may be called, is landed aristocracy and is obnoxious to the principles of the American government.

The other claim for the right to exact rent is that improvements have been placed on the land, and that it took so much capital to make the land productive, that the person expending it acquires a right to the land. This claim to have the perpetual ownership of the ground on account of improvements placed thereon is also a modern idea. In China, parts of India and other countries where the equal right of all to the land is recognized, improvements are never permitted to become an alienating lien upon it. In China, for instance, when the changing floods on the rivers have produced a piece of land not previously in cultivation, a man applies to the local authorities for the right to improve it. He is allowed to take it and is awarded the use of it for a few years, usually two, tax free, for breaking it in. At the end of that period it is subject to the same conditions as the other land in the country. The East Indian mode is much the same. With many it is claimed that improvements constitute ownership. One defender of the individual right to hold land went so far as to say that an acre of cultivated ground was as much a manufactured article as a yard of cloth. If a man seized wool, jointly owned by him and ten others, he could scarcely pretend that weaving it gave him an individual title to the cloth. Mr. Walker draws a distinction. He says: "We note, then, that what shall be paid for the use of land may consist of two parts, rent proper, the remuneration for what Ricardo called the original and indestructible powers of the soil; and fictitious rent, which is in truth nothing but interest upon capital invested." * We lay it down as a fundamental maxim that no man has a right to sell or rent the "original and indestructible powers of the soil." The government that undertakes to give to him the power to do this commits an outrage on the people. The interest a man may have in improvements placed on the soil is something different, as Gen-

* Land and its Rent, page 35.

eral Walker correctly states; that this latter should ever be permitted to assume the proportions of a permanent lien is a monstrous proposition. M. Bastiat says, "If rent is paid for the indestructible powers of the soil, then, indeed, landed property is robbery." Bastiat founded his theory of rent, or property in land, on the ground of "service" rendered. The man who used the property, or paid the rent, did so because the property was more valuable to him for the *service* rendered on it. In examining the question as to the ownership of improvements on land, it is necessary to keep certain facts distinctly before the mind. A man's property is in the *improvements,* not the land. Improvements are made with the expectation that they will render it more productive. The proper remuneration, therefore, comes from the increased production. How much of a title can a man derive from improvements? To this we emphatically answer, not any. As the land equally belonged to all in the first place, he must have derived, by common consent, the right to improve and use. Without permitting improvements to escheat land, it is proper between the man who puts improvements on land and the community, that he should be allowed a sufficient length of time to use it to pay him for his improvements out of the proceeds, or a sufficient length of time in which he could be reimbursed if he managed the business well. This, however, would not give him, in equity, the right to improve or use one foot more of the land than would be his share if the whole was divided among the community. If he takes more he is deriving benefits from what belongs to somebody else. A retired "Tenant Farmer" in England, who writes "Short Talks about Land Tenures," says, that on a twenty years' lease, at a fixed rent, the tenant besides paying his *rent* can pay for all the improvements he puts on land so as to make it in the highest degree productive. One of the Kansas wheat farmers, Mr. Henry, of Abilene, informed the writer that he could buy land for ten dollars per acre, pay for the breaking, harrowing and all the expenses of raising the first two crops of wheat, and out of the produce pay for the land and have a margin of profit.

Let us take a piece of government land at $1.25 per acre. Breaking prairie, costing we will say two and a half dollars per acre, and then the expense of seed, harrowing, drilling and harvesting the first crop of wheat. It certainly would require at that rate only a few years to pay for the land, improvements, and even for such buildings as are usually erected. In the old style of forest or woodland clearing, where the land was fenced, the improvements were estimated, when the writer was a lad, at not exceeding ten dollars per acre. The rental of such improved lands in earlier times was about two dollars per acre. It would not thus take many years to remunerate the man who made them for these improvements. Indeed, it may very safely be asserted that at the end of ten years, the owners would have paid for the improvements and if the farm was well managed would have a large margin of profit. It is also probable that unless these farms were much better managed than they have generally been, a person about to occupy and cultivate them would prefer to have the land in its rich, wild, natural state than to take it worn out, with decaying fences and houses that would cost more to repair than they are worth. Again, men in our towns and cities lease lots to build houses on. I have in my mind a long row of brick houses built on twenty years' leases. One of these a double three-story building is erected and a ground rent paid of $600 per year. At the end of twenty years the property and improvements revert to the owner of the lot. Before the lease the land had produced nothing. It was improved in this manner because the city was rapidly increasing in population. The person leasing showed the writer his figures, by which after deducting for insurance and repairs he had the part of the building he occupied rent free, and would receive sufficient on the remainder to pay his $600 ground rent and also for the erection of the building in eight years. Allowing a certain percentage for times when rent might not be paid, he made his calculation of having a free use of one portion and paying the improvements in ten years at least, leaving him the proceeds of the second ten years for profit. These figures give some idea of the value of improvements. On what plea then can the mere improver of land appropriate the "unearned increment." Improvements, therefore, justly give no title to land. The maker places them on it at his own risk and must be paid for them only out of the increased product caused by them. This drives us back for a right to tax land, an annual continuous rent, to the right one man has to sell the "natural and indestructible powers of the soil."

It has been urged as the strongest argument for a chattel title to land, and for perpetual ownership by one family, that under a less certain tenure valuable improvements will not be made. The evidence submitted proves this to be a fallacy. Some of the farms longest occupied in the United States are far from indicating continuous improvement of the highest order, while, on the other hand, a mere chattel holding by unoccupying owners has done more to retard improvement throughout the country than anything else. It is equally true that occupying tenures, leases, or rights covering one or a few years, offer no inducements to make the best improvements, and will not secure pay for them, while yearly tenancy, *metayage*, or short leases, only tend to waste the natural powers of the soil. A law securing family holding, for occupancy and use, if framed carefully so as not to interfere with the rights of others, might be the best. The small farm holdings in France indicate a high order of improvement, as concerns productive tillage and home comforts. Some little is due, and as much as justice would warrant should be given to the affection a family may have for home. It is the inevitable, and not unfortunate condition of the race that a large family on reaching manhood and womanhood branches out from the domestic roof. The pride of maintaining the old family homestead in one of the sons is apt to lead to injustice to his brethren and sisters, or pecuniary embarrassment to him. This family attachment to places is not very strong in our country, and however much we may respect the sentiment should never be permitted to become a monopoly usurping more than the natural share of a family, thus preventing others from having a home. To secure the best improvements there must be adequate security that they will be repaid at what they are fairly worth. Cultivating owners of small farms may possess the best improvements and processes, but under such a system we need not expect, and should not deplore, the absence of aristocratic palaces, patrician lawns and deer parks, or magnificence sustained by lordly revenues.

It will be asserted that in the United States the land was bought and paid for, and that government fairly conveyed it to the individual owners "forever." Admit the lack of wisdom in the transaction. Admit that it was a usurpation of power for the men of one generation to forestall or rob the men of the next generation. Admit the plea that the price was altogether inadequate, and that the public have a right to go into court and claim exemption from the oppressive burdens of this agreement on the ground of "want of consideration." The question remains, how far have these transactions embarrassed a just settlement between man and man? In Europe the case is somewhat different. There the aristocratic owners got possession by violence and fraud. They did not get what they call their land by consent of the legitimate owners, the people, at any time. They endeavor to fortify their position by the plea that some of the land has gone into the hands of innocent purchasers, and that, therefore, the whole system should be still longer tolerated; they forget that the purchaser could buy nothing but what a robber had to sell.

In the United States it will be said that the matter stands on a different footing. Let us examine this. The bulk of the land was sold for about $1.25 per acre. A great deal of it has been granted in homesteads on the payment of trifling fees. For forty years, or since the passage of the preemption law it has been sold chiefly for occupation and actual settlement. This was part of the contract and anything else was an evasion of the nominal terms. When sold for one dollar and a quarter per acre the government did not pretend to part with it for what it was intrinsically worth. That was really a mere fee to pay for the extinguishment of the Indian occupancy right, for surveying it, for protecting it from savages by the United States troops, and for making and keeping records.

Land in its original state, as conveyed by the United States in new states and territories was comparatively valueless. Its only value at first was to use and cultivate. Its speculative value grew out of the increased population of the country. It might be worth only ten cents an acre when there were a few thousand people in a state or territory, and worth one hundred dollars an acre when there were one or two millions. The difference is what John Stuart Mill calls "unearned increment" and he said the national legislature would be justified in appropriating it for the benefit of the whole people who created it. Again, it may be not unfairly argued that the government turned it into the hands of individuals to cultivate on payment of $1.25 per acre at a time, and under circumstances so far as the body politic was concerned, when there was still an abundance of land for every other man to take. It was not a monopoly under these circumstances. In many states such conditions have passed away, and in all of them they will soon pass away, and this privilege granted for a trifle may, and is certain to be an oppressive monopoly. It is an engine daily becoming more destructive to the public interests. We are then justified in assuming that the "eminent domain" in all these lands is in the people of these United States,—that it was bought subject to that power? That it was bought subject to the right of the people to tax it as they pleased? That it was bought subject to the right of the people to make such disposition of all or any portion of it, as the public interests or safety demanded? That it was bought subject to the provision that the people had the right to enact laws of inheritance that would work a "fair distribution" of it, and that, in law and equity, the interests of the great body politic transcend now and always, the private rights of the individual?

There is another, a more intricate, and a graver question. We recognize two kinds of accumulated property, "real" and "personal," the former land, the earth's surface, the latter articles of manufactured or produced property and money. Should accumulated money ever be permitted an investment in land? or an investment in land a man does not buy to cultivate, but from which he and his heirs expect to derive a perpetual revenue? Granting this power in our form of civilization has been a fatal mistake. In the first place, giving such a privileged monopoly adds to the profits of accumulated capital, raises the rate of interest, weakens the resources of the poor laborer, and extends the power and influence of money. When, in addition, capital is permitted to appropriate the "unearned increment," or increased value caused by population and the exclusive privileges of this system, we allow it to double, quadruple or multiply itself tenfold out of the wealth produced by labor, thus "working a false distribution of products." The remedy for this is to prohibit forever any man from buying or exchanging land, except for purposes of actual cultivation, the tenure inseparable from actual cultivation by the owner or holder. By thus preventing accumulated money from placing perpetual liens on industry, and its owners not only from taxing their own generation, but posterity, to support a non-producing class, living on rent, we reduce the inordinate gains of accumulated money, and drive it into more useful fields of actual production.

Mr. Henry George says: "I do not propose to purchase or to confiscate private property in land. The first would be unjust, the second needless. Let the individuals who now hold it still retain, if they want to, possession of what they are pleased to call *their* land. Let them continue to call it *their* land. Let them buy and sell and bequeath and devise it. We may safely leave them the shell if we take the kernel. *It is not necessary to confiscate land, it is only necessary to confiscate rent.*" * He adds: "By leaving to landowners a percentage of rent, which would probably be much less than the cost and loss involved in attempting to rent lands through state agency, and by making use of their existing machinery, we may, without jar or shock, assert the common right to land by taking rent for public uses." † In India, the British government has been trying for three quarters of a century to make the rent or tribute-taking Zemindars into landlords. Mr. George proposes to make the landlords of this country into Zemindars. We will quote him a little farther: "We already take some rent on taxation. We have only to make some changes in our modes of taxation to take it all." "What I, therefore, propose as the simple yet sovereign remedy, which will raise wages, increase the earnings of capital, extirpate pauperism, abolish poverty, give remunerating employment to whoever wishes it, afford free scope to human powers, lessen crime, elevate morals, and taste, and intelligence, purify government, and carry civilization to yet nobler heights, is *to appropriate rent by taxation.*" ‡

We do not think it would be candid or just to Mr. George to charge him with any insincerity or evasion. To write

* Progress and Poverty, Lovell edition, page 292. † Ibid.
‡ Ibid.

about taking the "kernel," and leaving the landowners "the shell," and in the same breath leaving the landowners in possession, trenches on the facetious. In order to "appropriate the rent by taxation," it would be necessary to enact a law which would prevent the landowner from taking *another* rent in addition to the one paid to the state. Or to secure the arrangement he proposes of leaving the landowners a percentage of the rent for leasing and looking after the lands, it would be necessary to prevent him by law from taking more than a fixed per cent. Otherwise the owner would simply add the taxes to the rent, and thus either increase the price of products or diminish the wages of laborers.

Taxation of land is very common; indeed, universal in this country. In some states what we call "real property" pays the great bulk of the taxes. The writer does not think that any one ever heard of heavy taxation reducing rents. On the contrary we have numerous examples of tenants who pay rents in cities complaining of excessive municipal taxation because it raised their rents. Mr. George, however, is perfectly right, in this, that the power of the state to tax lands and the policy of taxing them heavily may be the means of preventing non-resident landowning and putting an end to land monopoly. In the power of taxation we find the necessary lever for bringing about a change in land tenure in this country. That is doubtless what Mr. George means; but to carry out his system he must see that the tax falls on *rent* not land. If the nominal landowner is to be a leasing and collecting agent let him receive what landlords pay their agents now, five per cent. of the rent, and let the rent tax be ninety-five per cent. of it. The law, moreover, would have to be framed with very great care or the world would soon witness an astounding decline of rents and increase of "bonuses" to the agent landowner. A more perfect remedy would be a heavy tax on landowners who do not cultivate the soil and an equal burden placed upon landlords. To prevent great landowners from extending the system of large farms tilled by wage workers or laborers such farms should also be taxed heavily, and the sizes of farms that could be held by one person diminished from time to time, thus securing small holdings. Laws to prevent the creation or extension of great farms ought to be enacted at once. It should be the fixed policy of the people of the United States to have no landlord over the occupying cultivator of the soil unless that landlord is the state. The liberty, independence and happiness of our agricultural yeomanry cannot be preserved unless this is done. Limited tenure to actual cultivators is best, but if title to land be insisted on, at the death of every land owner the law should *compel* the land to be divided. The ambition and covetousness of the human heart will always tend to the accumulation of land in the hands of an active individual, and there must be some counterpoise or check to the aggregating process. This can be most successfully done by compulsory laws of inheritance. A heavy tax on all shares of inherited land in excess of say one hundred and sixty acres, to be gradually reduced, when necessary, to eighty acres, forty acres, twenty acres, or even five. Make land holding unprofitable whenever lands are held in larger amounts than can be cultivated by actual occupying laboring farmers, or when they are held in greater amounts than would furnish a sufficient number of farms for all persons who wish to cultivate the soil. Let it be a settled purpose that in these United States landlordism shall be rendered so unprofitable that it will cease. If it is to be our desire to put the land in the hands of small holders, a heavy tax on such holders would be extremely impolitic. It would be a mere tax on bread and meat.

Such a course might reduce the nominal price of land, but that would be no misfortune. The destruction of speculative land values would not make the country any poorer. The land would produce just as much afterward as before. As has been previously stated, millions of dollars in supposed slave property were on the tax roll, but were taken from it before the close of the late war. In spite of these hundreds of millions of property thus apparently lost by the action of government, nothing was really destroyed. It merely swept away a vicious institution, which, as Mr. Atkinson would say, "worked a false distribution of wealth and of product." If all the speculative value was swept away from land, the country would be just as rich, and its wealth would be more justly distributed. If all the fraudulent and fictitious stocks, bonds and mortgages of companies and corporations could be destroyed by one legislative act, and nothing left save the actual cash paid in and honestly expended, there would be no destruction of property. So far from being poorer, the country would be a great deal better off.

We have, at this time, to consider, not only what would be the wisest and best system of land tenure for these United States, but what is the most feasible way of reaching such a result. If we had a new government to construct and a virgin soil to dispose of, untrammeled by the manufactured privileges of landowners, the wisest foundation would be the doctrine that the surface of the earth belonged to all the people, and that one generation could place no liens upon it to the prejudice of the next. Allodial or family tenure is safer than individual chattel tenure. All the details in regard to length of leases and mode of making or compensating for improvements should be managed by the people of each organized township. Free facility ought to be given for exchange of occupation, as a necessary condition of independence, and any man should be able to cultivate his share of the soil when he desired to do so. Whatever advantages accrued from land tenure ought to be so distributed that each citizen, whatever might be his occupation, would get the benefit of them. There should always be a spot of earth on which every man born in this world could build his home, however humble. If in the crush of increasing population all else was used for raising bread, public parks and even the pleasure grounds of the rich should be taken to furnish a foundation for these homes. No man ought to be able to obtain a living by selling the "natural and indestructible powers of the soil," or foist himself as a non-producing member on society, under the special plea that somebody had sold him the privilege of collecting rent.

While we recognize the justness of these general principles the practical question is how best to reach such an end, when a large portion of the country has been disposed of as a chattel, under law enacted by the representatives of the people. The power to suddenly destroy all the individual privileges in land the people in their sovereign capacity undoubtedly possess, and if it was a necessity for the preservation of the state, or the preservation of the people, they would be justified in exercising it. It was once tenaciously held, even by enemies of the system, that the government, having recognized property in slaves, could not abolish it without fully indemnifying the owners. Slavery was abolished and he would be a bold man who would propose to create another debt to compensate the owners. We do not say that a man forfeits his right to hold another man as a slave because he did not properly buy him, or honestly pay for him, but we object to the transaction because a man is something he should not buy. The United States was freed from the burden of slavery as a war measure. The private ownership of lands will be claimed as a vested right and it is a question how far the government has been complicated by its transactions. In Great Britain, for example, the aristocratic landowners obtained what they call their title merely by conspiracy and violence, and have for many years been enriched by it. To create a great debt as a burden on the people, to buy their title, would merely be to transfer the burden from one shoulder to the other. In our country chattel title to land has the color of law and may claim the sacredness of a bargain, but its owner cannot be said to have an equitable title to the "unearned increment" caused by population, or the privilege to hold land without cultivating it.

It may be taken for granted that the people of these United States are not going to make another great debt in order to get money to buy back all the land, and then proceed to rectify the mistake by which individual claims and individual monopolies were created. A proposition to take possession of the land, and confiscate individual titles, in the present condition of affairs, is not likely to be popular. Practical remedies lie in another direction. It would, however, be entirely proper and consistent to provide by law that lands in this republic should only be sold to occupying cultivators, and this to include, not only the public lands of the United States, but all lands. Cultivation and occupancy by the holder should be one of the conditions of tenure. In order to reduce large farms to small ones, and in this way make every cultivator a landholder, one of two modes could be adopted: The law might limit the acreage to be held by any one person, the other plan would probably be more easily accomplished and lead to less confusion. Fix a small minimum acreage which would be but lightly taxed, or, better still, not taxed at all, and then let taxation increase as the scale went up, until the large landowners would find it unprofitable to hold land and be forced to sell. Whether the land was thus held in small farms by assignments for a period of years, or on a tenure or title that was exchangeable, the result would be that those who wished to cultivate the soil could do so on easy terms, without being burdened with an overwhelming debt, and placing themselves in the power of capital. Either system would multiply the opportunities, increase the earnings and cheapen the food of the working classes.

In the July number of the *North American Review*, 1885, there is a printed discussion between Cyrus Field and Henry George, from which we quote:

Mr. Field: "You propose for the present no change whatever in anything, except that the amount now raised by all methods of taxation should be imposed on real estate considered as vacant?"

Mr. George: "For a beginning, yes."

Mr. Field: "Well, what would you propose for the ending of such a scheme?"

Mr. George: "The taking of the full annual value of land for the benefit of the whole people. I hold that the land belongs equally to all, and that land values arise from the presence of all."

In the same discussion Mr. George states that he would not tax improvements, as that would be a tax on industry. The tax should be on the intrinsic value of land, that value being created by the population which makes this demand upon it. He holds that "in the complex civilization we have now attained, it would be impossible to secure equality by giving to each a separate piece of land, or to maintain that equality, even if once secured; but by treating all land as the property of the whole people we would make the whole people the landlords." Mr. Field then asks if it is his purpose that "the rate of taxation should equal the rate of annual rental, and that the proceeds of the tax should be applied, not only to the purposes of government, but to any other purposes that the legislature from time to time may think desirable, even to dividing them among the people at so much a head." In reply to this question Mr. George answers, "That is substantially correct." In a note to the writer, Mr. George says: "The conversation was correctly reported, and, as far as it goes, represents my views."

It is very evident that the interview quoted can only be taken as indicating the principles involved. It would be unfair to criticize a general plan by assailing some of the details. While, therefore, we cannot help considering details, we must accord to Mr. George the fullest credit for his suggestions as to taxation being one of the means, or, if he will, the chief means of remedying the defects arising from the mistake of giving a permanent monopoly of the land to a few individuals. The land, after all, as we have attempted to show, belongs to the whole people under the theory of eminent domain. All tenure under it is subordinate to that. This may be asserted in the broadest sense, and is always asserted in taxing it, and there is no limit to the authority of the state to tax. Whether the natural resources of land should bear all the tax is another question. Evidently Mr. George means that since all have a right to land, and yet as all do not desire to occupy land, therefore, taking the rent in tax and applying it to general purposes would be a simple and fair way of distributing it. This plan of Mr. George's necessarily involves taking the value of the land, which is what it will produce, from the present holders, and applying it in such a way as to equally distribute its benefits. Rent is to pay all public burdens. If that were done the rent tax would be merely an impost on production. Of course it will be said that where rent is paid now it creates such a tax on bread for *private emolument;* and so it does, and this is one of the most serious objections to it.

To give the city laborer a bonus from the rent of land and have that amount added to the price of his bread would hardly do. Any tax on land is necessarily a tax on bread. The policy we have suggested is to throw the land in small farms into the hands of cultivating holders, so that *every* agricultural laborer can become a holder. If this was accomplished it would be a grave question whether a heavy land tax would be wise. Land taxation, as a remedial measure against capitalist landlords, non-occupying holders, or holders of large farms, would be a wise measure. Where there exists a great class of cultivating owners, with small farms, who have none of these heavy burdens to pay, or but light burdens, the speculating holders could not enter into competition with them, and would not be able to charge the tax or rent levied by the government to the cost of production. In such a case this holding of land by capitalists and non-occupying landlords would cease to be profitable and the price of food be thus lessened. The reader will at once see the necessity of preventing an additional tax or rent from increasing the price of food. The people are deeply interested in being able to buy cheap food; that is, as cheap as is consistent with paying good wages to agricultural laborers. It is well enough to tax the interest that individual monopolists have in land, but it would be a doubtful policy to collect a rent which might add to the cost of producing bread and meat, even if the proceeds were applied to the support of government or distributed per capita to all the men and women of the country. Another objection is that by placing all public burdens on rent the rich men and millionaires in other business, would be tax free, and taxation would finally be a mere bread tax which the poor would have to pay equally with the rich.

Connected with the land question is the question of timber. The country of the United States has been largely denuded of its forests. Owners of land wasted it unnecessarily. Cutting timber on "Congress land" was at one time universal. Neither the statute nor the moral law seemed to lie against stealing timber. An effort has been made of late years to check the practice, but does not appear to have been very successful. Not only on the public lands, but on all lands a fair amount of the domain should be in forest. This is indispensable, as the wholesale and indiscriminate cutting of our forests is disastrous as affecting rainfalls, the volume of rivers, the crops and public health. Measures for the preservation of public timber are demanded, and should be enacted at once to compel planting of certain areas in new timber as the old timber is removed: to have the timbered areas of public land controlled by law, and held by public ownership.

The right to graze on the public domain free of charge is

one of the individual rights very freely asserted. If one or two sections had been reserved as commons in each township, where every man could graze his cow, and so held until denser population demanded other uses for it, it would in many respects have been a fortunate circumstance. The grazing lands, or, rather, lands only fit for grazing, are large tracts remote from settlement. Pasturage, especially in such regions, requires that the land be so divided as to have water fronts. Pasturage without water is worthless and the water must be so convenient that the cattle will not be kept poor by hours of driving to it each day. Any temporary lease of such lands would have to be made with these necessities in view. No title to these lands should be permitted to pass. Neither should they be leased in large tracts so that a few great monopolists could control our beef interests. Grazing tracts should not be large, but large enough to graze a herd from the care of which a family could derive a maintenance. The chief advantage of making these temporary grazing leases would be to utilize the lands in the public interest and reserve them for the period when wiser views on the land question will prevail. They ought to be withdrawn from sale at once.

No title or tenure to land should be held to convey mineral. Not only what are called the precious minerals, but coal, iron, petroleum or salt. No monopoly in either of these should ever be permitted. So far as mines or beds have been already opened and worked the remedies should be instituted in a careful way, recognizing only certain rights in the holders by way of indemnification, but slowly working to the logical end, the assertion of the rights of all the people. A law should at once be enacted to cover all cases of mines of any kind, or oil wells not opened and worked. These should be the property of the state. A royalty sufficient to assert and cover the public right should be exacted, and thus open the door to every man, rich and poor, who wished to develop them; this law should apply not only to public mineral lands but to all mineral lands, and the rights granted to prospectors ought to be carefully guarded to prevent monopoly. It would really be neither breach of faith nor breach of public obligation to assert the public ownership of minerals. All laws for the sale of mineral lands should be repealed. In point of fact the larger portion of public lands containing mineral, that have been sold, have been obtained by an evasion of the letter or spirit of the law.

The United States ought certainly to regulate the tenure of the railroad grants that have not yet passed from under the hands of the government. So far as the roads that received subsidies of bonds are concerned, it might be proper to resume the lands in lieu of the debt. At the time these roads thought they would be compelled to pay taxes on such lands, some of them proposed a similar measure, and as the public money really built many of these roads there would be neither injustice nor inconsistency in doing this, especially as the railroads for many years have failed to claim title. No lands should be deeded hereafter to any company. Where they may have been faithfully earned according to the terms of the agreement some adjustment should be made, but this open door to unrestricted speculation in lands should be closed immediately.

These suggestions touching the yet undisposed of public lands are made with a design of calling popular attention to the necessity of preventing another acre of them from going into the hands of capitalist speculators. The interest of land speculation is a very potent one, and will resist all attempts to curtail its emoluments. If arrested at this point the various necessary land reforms will be rendered much easier. In most of the Eastern and Central states, where the land has largely been monopolized, the landed interest already threatens to govern the country. Attempts to increase land tax have often been met by the defeat of the county or state officers who made them. One of the chief reasons why a landed aristocracy and great landed interests should not be permitted to grow stronger is that such a power will inevitably weaken and destroy a government of the people.

The evils of land monopoly have been discerned by thinking men at different periods of our history. Various remedies have been proposed for the individual monopolization of land. Among the experiments attempted were the formation of communistic societies. In many of them there has been a commingling of socialistic teachings with communal landholding. Not only the land but the interests of all industries were to be held in common. Some of the communistic societies have been to a large degree religious organizations. Attention was not only paid to industrial methods, but to the propagation of new moral and religious dogmas. Societies have been formed to propagate peculiar views as to marriage and all social relations, and these combinations of men and women have been of all kinds—Shakers, Amanist, Rappist, Oneida communists, Icarians, New Harmony settlers, and numberless others, down to Brook Farm.

The most wonderful of these organizations is the Mormon. They cannot correctly be called Socialists. They are in some degree land communists, as they endeavor to establish town communities. Their peculiar religious views, and, above all, their attempt to introduce polygamy into the United States, has largely given them the notoriety they enjoy, and has caused their other peculiarities to be overlooked. Driven from Nauvoo and from Missouri by violence, they finally took root in the great basin lying between the Rocky Mountains and the Sierra Nevadas. When they settled at Salt Lake, organization and concentration was a necessity. Agriculture without irrigation was impossible, and irrigation without combination equally impossible. They did not confine themselves to Salt Lake. Colonies were planted in all the Western territories. In Southern Utah, Arizona, and Western New Mexico, there is scarcely a valley with water that they have not traversed, and their colonies may be found everywhere. Along the Little Colorado they constitute the greater part of the population. The streams are dammed by the joint exertion of the colony. A large field of irrigated land is enclosed, in which each family has its portion of cultivated land. Great corrals are built for the stock, which is cared for in a common herd. The people live in villages. Their houses do not materially differ from those of other American settlers. The results of industry constitute individual property, and they are neither socialistic nor communistic, so far as that goes. They have a great deal of difficulty in reconciling their system with the land laws of the United States, but land speculation does not thrive among them in their new colonies. The writer has visited many of their villages, and found the people industrious, thrifty, and in comparatively comfortable circumstances for a new, wild country. Their polygamous practices have justly exposed them to the indignation of Christian people. Their hierarchy is inclined to be aristocratic, and assumes too many of the powers of government to be tolerated by Americans. If the settlements they have made were stripped of the last vestige of polygamy and the power of their church reduced to the proportions of other religious bodies, their improvements and industries in that arid region would be an interesting study.

Robert Owen's colonies were not societies of mere land reformers, but organizations of socialistic and communistic life. Individualism was sunk in the community. It was an attempt, not so much to give the individual fair play, as to merge the man in the group. These experiments failed. Many others grew up and perished like them. After the French revolution of 1848, Etienne Cabot, who had taken an active part in it, contemplated the founding of a colony on the idea of an equality of property. Taxation was to be removed from all articles of necessity, and a graduated income tax to supply all public wants. A colony was started in Texas under a grant to give the half of every alternate section of a certain locality for each settler, leaving the remainder to be sold by the state.* In a new country, wild and undeveloped, the colony weak and the population round it unsympathetic, its failure was a foregone conclusion. The colonists then rented the deserted Mormon town at Nauvoo. There they reorganized, but in a few years discord arose as to its management, a fate that seems to follow any communistic society. Another "Icaria" was founded in Iowa. For a time it was successful, and accumulated some property, but it possessed too many active thinkers to proceed permanently in harmony. The sacredness of the marriage tie was affirmed, but the children were under the care of the association. The social capital was common and indivisible. Article 18 of the constitution or contract may be quoted in full: "The principal object of this association in conducting the affairs described and considered in these articles being that of creating a fund which shall provide for the needs and comforts of the young, the old, the sick and the infirm, no dividend shall be paid to any member; but every accumulation of wealth shall be added to the common fund."† A member on withdrawing received $100 from this common fund, and the same amount was paid in some cases of expulsion. After the society had been organized an equal sum was required on admission. In many respects these social organizations resembled the House Communities of the Sclavonic races; only that the latter were often of one family stock.

The social and communistic organizations in the United States are interesting not only as experiments, but as evidences that those who felt the defects of the present forms of society were seeking a remedy. They were revolts against the extreme doctrine of selfishness and individualism, and although they did not prove to be practical ones, they still indicated the existing causes of dissatisfaction. The

* Icaria, page 34.

† Ibid., page 193.

North American Phalanx, of which Horace Greeley was vice president, was founded on the ideas of Fourier, and many local phalanxes were formed, none of them attaining practical or permanent success. The American public, outside of the persons connected with these organizations, but little understood them. Mormonism and the Oneida Perfectionists had made people suspicious of all new social combinations. In some cases these experimental communities were openly persecuted, but as a usual thing they had liberty to test their "experiment" under a general shade of suspicion. This prejudice is still used dexterously as a weapon against all new political ideas. Mr. Henry George, who is certainly neither socialistic nor communistic, has been pronounced to be both, by those who found it difficult to answer his arguments. Mr. Hyndman and Mr. Wallace have also, been called "communists" and "socialists," and even Mr. Chamberlain, a member of Mr. Gladstone's Cabinet, in making a speech in favor of a reform of the land system, and an increase of power for the people, was charged with communistic doctrine by the opposition papers. The epithets, "demagogue," "agrarian," "communist," are hurled at any man who advances new ideas, and, like the charge of witchcraft a century or two ago, only require vehemence, persistence and malice to give them force. Those who use them appeal to a somewhat strong element in society, intrenched ignorance. It is well to remember people who oppose large landed interests, and the profits of land speculation, encounter an opposition at once unscrupulous and formidable. It is also unhappily true that a strong gambling spirit has taken deep root with many of our people. By this is meant not ordinary gambling, but the spirit which deals in chances, and uncertain speculations. It arises from the disposition which makes haste to be rich. The avenues of industry and thrift are despised, and the sins of overreaching and commercial duplicity not sufficiently held up to reprobation.

I have referred to experiments, such as Icaria, chiefly to exhibit the conflicting ideas about social organization. On the one hand individualism with its extreme assumptions, on the other society as entirely submerging the individual. The faults in our form of social life do not arise from giving the individual full play in a field of exertion, but in allowing the individual too unlimited control over what affects others as well as himself. The civilization we are founding is based on the most absolute assertion of the independence of the individual. Our men brook no restraint. The family tie sits loosely, and the social tie if not overlooked altogether is considered merely as a means of amusement or gratification. To preserve the individual independence in a legitimate field of activity, repress its unjust and avaricious desires, and make it conform to the interests of all is the golden mean to be sought. In a community like Icaria men are supposed to be equally benevolent, working unselfishly for the common good. It is a noble conception, but, unhappily, all are not benevolent, all are not unselfish, all are not even honest. The individual, untrammeled by the views or whims of others, can best carve out his own fortune. It is this intense individualism that is the keystone in the arch of American society. It has its eminent advantages and marks the field of progress with monuments of human endurance and skill. It errs fatally when this individualism assumes to be supreme. There is a field for the individual and a field for the action of society. There is property for the individual, and wealth in the boundless stores of nature that is, and can only be, the property of *all* men. It is with the duties as well as the privileges of the individual we have to do. Let the individual work for his advancement, but there must be a perfect equity in all his transactions. The individual cannot be allowed a monopoly of any of the rights of nature. One family is no better than another family, one generation no better than another generation. When family ties are weak, where there is no moral or religious home instruction, where each member has not a tender solicitude for the welfare of others, then we may expect selfish adventurers to be let loose upon society. A father who has a child he loves, has a tender bond to bind him to the interests of society. Man owes his fellow man more than "civility." The men who framed this government, and who fought for years in its defense, uttered the doctrine, "We hold this truth to be self-evident that God created all men equal." It was the tears and prayers, agitation and perseverance of good men and women, that abolished American slavery, and made its crimes odious. It was such men as Howard who introduced prison reform. Able and self-sacrificing men have often arisen who have espoused the cause of the down trodden and the weak. The interests of mankind are indissolubly woven together.

Assuming an equitable system of land tenure to be possible, what are the remedies that will secure better pay for wage workers? How shall those who have been in the habit of selling their labor for money get a higher price for it? We have seen that the colossal fortunes, now threatening society with their overshadowing influence, have been chiefly made from the toil of artisans and laborers who have been kept in humble circumstances and comparative poverty. When we say there must be a fairer distribution of the proceeds of labor, the question occurs, Can it be brought about? It is evident that what modern political economists call "free competition" will not secure it. Capital has had the advantage, and has profited by it to obtain more than its share. Accumulated and organized capital has used its resources to speculate on the necessities of poor wage workers. To counterbalance this, labor must be thoroughly and intelligently organized. Each craft should be a unit. It has been said that manufacture and trade can only be carried on to the extent that capital is furnished to employ the workmen. Threats have been made that capital will withdraw from the alliance with labor if organized efforts are made largely to interfere with its profits. That is simply absurd. When capital is reduced to the necessity of taking two, or even one per cent., or being hid away uselessly in a stocking; it will take two, or even one per cent. With thorough intelligent organization labor is more potent than capital. One necessary step is to strip capital of all illegitimate sources of profitable investment, and chief among these is investment in land. The next would be to extinguish or change the character of public debts. No public debt ought to be permitted to extend beyond the generation that contracted it. Rulers have been in the habit of making too heavy drafts on posterity. Instead of the theory that public debts are a blessing, the doctrine must be maintained that perpetual debts are a curse. State, county or municipal debt should never be permitted to exceed a certain percentage on property and be payable in a limited period. All the enormous machinery of public debt is only an instrument for draining incomes from the work of laborers, with the additional drawback that raises the rate of interest and swells the inordinate profits of capital. Unfortunately the debts of great corporations and companies have almost the same effect, since the interest and principal are taken from the productive industry of the country, and the managers have really the power to add to the burdens of the people. When the corporations use the borrowed money with fidelity and economy in transportation lines, the objection to them is not so great, but when large portions of it go to swell private fortunes, it inflicts degradation as well as injury upon the workingman. There are no exactions so burdensome, and, no tyranny so remorseless as an inflated and dishonest credit system.

Public debts should be kept at the minimum, and never permitted to be indefinitely extended to burden one generation with the extravagance, wickedness or maintenance of another. It may sneeringly be said that this is impossible. Our war of the rebellion was one of the most expensive on record.

That debt is largely paid, and need not be extended beyond the generation that created it.

So far as debt may be necessary, it should be our sedulous desire to popularize our loans. It is better to borrow one dollar each from a million of people than a million dollars from one man. It is the better public policy, in placing a loan, to raise it from the dollar, the quarter, or even ten cent subscriptions of the people, than to appeal to a syndicate of bankers and millionaires. With a proper land system, and better security for the rights of labor, the government could borrow all it would ever properly need from the working people of these United States, as the French government does from the masses of her people. In that event it would be wise to encourage their moderate savings, and by such a safe institution as a postal savings bank, take up in small sums all the government needed to borrow. Each account should be limited, and if the certificates were made exchangeable, comparatively poor people would thus be enabled to invest small sums, knowing that when they were compelled to use the money it would be convertible. Giving it this quality could certainly be no worse than the system on which the national banks are based, which have their interest bearing bonds securely stored, and national bank notes issued to them for circulation. By the course here suggested the national bank notes would soon be superseded by these postal certificates. Above all we neither need nor want a large standing army to create a debt. Citizen soldiery are the safe and legitimate defenders of a republic.

One mode of helping wage workers would be by opening to them more freely other channels of enterprise and industry. Under a proper land system, with the country cut up into small farms of five, ten or twenty acres, such farms being purchasable or held only by actual cultivators a comparatively easy transition from one business to another could be had in case of necessity. When all mineral, coal, salt or petroleum belong to the whole people, and can only be worked on terms equal and fair to each individual, other fields of enterprise will thus open. If the laws were modified and perfected so that every unfair bargain, contract or transaction could be examined and set aside there would be a further security for poor laborers. All gambling, stock-jobbing or business conducted on the doctrines of chance or misrepresentation should be abolished. Law has made rapid progress in the past ten years; it must reach up to this standard. Precedents are on the statute book and human genius can compass the necessary results.

After all, the best help workmen can get must come from themselves. Capital is organized, labor must be completely organized. The laborers are the great majority and they by wisdom and determination can, under our form of government, have laws framed to secure and defend their rights. They can compel laws to be enacted in their interests, and make the instruments of justice the servants of the people, instead of the servants of rich corporations. It is true that it is always easier to discard a bad and unfaithful public servant than to get a good one, still, with perseverance it can be done. Every branch of labor should have complete organizations; these should be perfectly lawful in all their acts. Violence, terrorism, assassination, all these things are *suicide* to the interests of the laboring man. They are not needed. They are merely the wrathful outbursts of impotence. It has been said that strikes are a bad remedy; that they are wasteful and tend to lawlessness. People forget that employers have their strikes. Every time an employer reduces wages or increases the hours of service, or demands more work he *strikes for higher profits.* He uses the power of capital to coerce labor. In doing this he violates the most sacred laws of society. Capitalists have no right to say that labor shall not be organized. Bad though strikes may be, perhaps they are the only remedy. They will end when law enables arbitration to settle difficulties between capital and *organized* labor.

The workman is not strong enough to stand alone. Arbitration to have sufficient force to prevent revolution, must have law behind it, giving it power to enforce a fair share of products to working men.

Organized labor must control labor, instead of labor being controlled by accumulated wealth. How can this be done. Are the laborers poor? very well. Look at the millionaires of to-day. They were poor not long ago. They did nearly all their work on credit. Can organized labor, wisely managed, not do the same thing? If workingmen understand themselves thoroughly, and by organization make their trade a power, they can either get fair wages or carry on business themselves. The public requires that the laborer's work shall go on. Because there may be a certain need for accumulated wealth, the owners thereof have been able by organization into business companies, and by shrewd management, to control labor. Labor is a far more important factor than capital and ought to be able to wrest the management of business from its hands. Accumulated wealth, whether invested in machinery or other useful shape, should be satisfied with a small interest profit. Credit can keep any business running and organizations of workingmen must realize that in order to secure it their "yea, yea" and "nay, nay" must be as good as their bond. In associations of workingmen and co-operating societies their dependence to some extent rests. In these they are liable to have bad agents. So are railroad companies and stock-jobbing associations. Workingmen and artisans ought to comprehend their business sufficiently to *know when it is properly conducted.* It should be all carried on under their own eyes, while a capitalist often leaves his agent to manage without knowing what is being done. To confess that organized workingmen have not the brains and business capacity to manage their own work is an admission they cannot afford to make, and one which is not true as a question of fact.

There have been a good many theories about taxation.

One thing is certain: taxes have never been very popular with those who have to pay them. We witness to-day the greatest evasions of tax paying among the richest men of the country; men worth ten, twenty, fifty or one hundred millions, and who by a just public policy should carry taxation at a quadruple rate, sometimes do not pay taxes on a tenth part of their property, and none of them pay taxes on all their wealth. The science of keeping property off the tax roll does not seem to come into successful operation until the accumulation exceeds one hundred thousand dollars; this teaches us that in order to affect and reduce great accumulations of wealth, a more searching system of taxation must be adopted. There is with many of our people a deep-seated conviction against any taxation except for the payment of the simplest forms of government, honestly administered. The phrase often used "legitimate expenses of the government" is, however, rather vague. I hold that it is the legitimate business of government, local and general, to do or direct everything that concerns the common good, that cannot be safely left to individual enterprise, in order to insure perfectly equal dealing for all. Thus, for instance, it has been a very questionable policy that permits gas companies to usurp a public function, in tearing up the streets to furnish gas, and then allowing this monopoly, so created, to unmercifully fleece the people. Is there any reason why capital invested in a gas, railroad or insurance company should not have the percentage of its profits fixed by law? To prevent and correct abuses of management the percentage of official fees and salaries should also be fixed. Nor is it in the public interest or policy to permit the public highways, railroads or others, to be managed or controlled by monopolies. There are two ways this can be prevented. First the state could build, buy, own and operate them, or place these establishments completely under law and the superintendence of public officers. When stocks are subscribed, let it be done by public open subscription, let all contracts be on open competitive bids, and the most rigid inspections enforced on receiving work. The stockholders ought not to be allowed to control or abuse the patronage of the roads in any shape. Let the rates charged be fixed by law on the most economical basis, and let the dividends on stock be paid so as to certainly insure a small rate of interest. Whatever interest on investments was thus payed would at least be guaranteed and free from the robberies of stock jobbing companies, and would put an end to speculation in stocks. Even if part of the expenditure this system required had to be supported from taxes, it would be in the line of the public interests. Another just function for the public to perform is to take care of the helpless and to care for them well. The creation of a regular pauper system, the burden of which rests on the productive industry of the country is not desirable. The laborer in thus contributing largely from the proceeds of his labor, is incapacitated from saving, and discouraged from securing an independence of his own, and in old age naturally turns to the poorhouse he has supported. This pauperizing system multiplies a class that it is not the public interest to aid in increasing. On the contrary every encouragement and facility ought to be given to induce wage workers to save part of their earnings and so render them to some extent independent of every vicissitude. When want unavoidably comes, there must be suitable provision to relieve it, since there ought to be no actual suffering from such cause in a country possessing so much wealth. Hospitals, schools and asylums should be maintained. Temporary lodgings and a few meals to the destitute ought to be furnished in every town or city; this benevolence rigidly guarded to prevent idle dependence. All these should be established by the public, and the tax to support them charged *not to active producing industry,* but in all cases to *accumulated wealth.* Indeed, this ought to be the fundamental basis of all taxation, and would be a much needed and wise check to unnecessary accumulations.

Taxation should be graded, moreover, that it might not fall heavily on the needed competence that merely secures independence in old age. The mischievous accumulations of wealth are those devoted to maintaining a second or succeeding generation as a non-productive class. This the state has a right to prevent. A wise public policy should take means to prevent it, and one of the most efficient steps is to place the public burdens heavily on all such accumulations. There are other necessary public duties that would require the additional taxes thus raised. Our systems of sewerage in towns and cities are all more or less crude and defective. Neither the poor nor the rich should be exposed to the noxious gases or filth of our towns and cities. To place our streets, alleys and lots on a cleanly, healthy basis under the best scientific modes that have been or can be devised, would be a wise, and is really an indispensable measure. Closely connected with these should be a mode of furnishing pure, wholesome water for every community. From the water our people are now in the habit of drinking a large amount of the disease and death prevalent comes, and this can only be remedied by public effort. In case of a depression in our industries, labor would find employment on these public works. It is not the opinion of the writer that depressions in trade would exist if the ideas suggested were carried out. Instead of seeking a market for our manufactured articles in foreign countries where we have to compete with pauper labor, we would find buyers at home, the laboring classes would be enabled to purchase comforts, and even luxuries, and thus create all the market we want.

It will be seen that there are legitimate fields of expenditure that will consume all the taxes likely to be collected, without having recourse to the very questionable expedient of per capita distributions. It undoubtedly will be a wiser plan to aid and encourage the working poor to be independent and self-supporting than to subsidize them. Let the law rigidly see that they *get their own.* There are many other ways of aiding workingmen and building them up, besides paying an occasional small pittance from a fund outside of their earnings. From a careful observation of the subject it is the opinion of the writer that if the people of one of the most enterprising townships in New England had issued to them, say fifty dollars a year to every head of a family, for twenty or thirty years, it would ruin them. It may be as well to remember that Rome in the expiring days of the republic had distributions of money and corn.

As a means of producing and maintaining a greater equality of interests, one of the most potent levers is to be found in a just system of inheritance. In adopting the ordinance for the Northwest territory, the Continental Congress, in this its first opportunity, struck a blow at the law of primogeniture. As the colonies, and after them the states, claimed the power to regulate that matter, it was about the only opportunity afforded, in an aggregate way, to the active founders of the American republic. It is to be regretted that they did not go farther. What they did was merely to provide that in cases where there was no will, the family property should descend equally to all the heirs, and that the widow should have one-third of the personal property and life rent in one-third of the real estate. This was unfair to the wife, the equal member of the firm, and in cases where there was but little property, left her weak when she most needed assistance, and virtually broke up her household. It also contained another vice, which, like the foregoing, had crept in a limited way into the polity of Western Europe, that assertion of extreme individualism which finds its exercise in will making. The attempt to dispose of property by will is an attempt to dispose of a thing, after the title is void in the proprietor. This is a subject that has engaged the attention of the wisest men of ancient and modern times. There are a few cases where the disposition of property by will may be wise and permissible, but they are rare. The power of any man to make a disposition of any portion of the earth's surface after he has ceased to reside on the earth is a proposition which ought not to be tolerated. That a man should have power to make distinctions and classes in society, to create an aristocracy, to make some of his relatives rich and some poor, is a power, the justice of which may well be doubted.

It will be observed that under our system of inheritance the authority over the property of a decedent is divided. The law makes one disposition, and the man before he dies crystallizes his *will* on paper and makes another. Some things the law says he shall not devise. It is, then, competent for law to say he shall not bequeath anything. There is a growing disposition in our courts to set aside whimsical and unjust provisions of will. If a man with very considerable property decided at death that a great fortune should be left to one child, and a small amount to others, the general conviction would be that he had done wrong not only to his children but to society. In France, at the present day, a father can only will of his property what is equal to one child's share. Under the original Mahometan law no man was allowed to make a will. A just and intelligent law, fully considering the rights of the family and also the rights of society, is by far the best mode of determining the ownership of a dead man's property.

There is nothing about which people are more jealous than the rights of property. From this comes the extreme modern assertion of individual authority, to do what a man pleases with his own while living, and make any ridiculous or unjust disposition of it after he is dead. Of purely personal articles we can conceive how disposition by will may be properly made. Where property is limited in amount and not more than would constitute a modest competence, the law should determine the question of inheritance in the family. Where a large fortune is left the rights of society should be considered. These could be asserted in a tax on inheritance for beneficial objects and charities, and this tax ought to be graded according to the amount of property left. It should be one purpose of such a tax to prevent the creation of non-producing classes in the community, as no able-bodied man has a right to live without contributing by work to the interests of society. In wise laws of inheritance and taxation on inherited property, society has ample power to correct the wrongs and inequalities caused by avaricious men. If a man knew that his power over property would cease with his life, he would be apt to make a wise disposition of it while he lived; nor should he be permitted to evade the law of inheritance by *giving* great fortunes to his children just before his death, for such gifts ought to be subject to the same rate of tax as inheritance.

Whatever tenure or interest it is deemed best to give families in improvements, or use of lands, small holdings can be best maintained for the public interest by just and discriminating laws of inheritance. The evil of permitting long ground leases, the improvements erected thereon, and the increased value, to revert to descendants of the owners of the lands or lots, ought to be forbidden by law. The great fortune of the Duke of Westminster was created by leasing land in lots, near the suburbs of London, for one hundred years, the lessee to pay an annual rent, and the property, with the house that was on it, to revert at the expiration of the lease to the heir of the original owner. A grandson in this way inherited that which he never earned, and a great estate is thus built up by a contrivance which should never be tolerated.

One of the necessary remedies to advance the condition of wage workers in towns and cities, is to provide means to build houses for them. As matters stand, a considerable part of their earnings are expended upon rent, and they are not comfortably housed. During the first half century of the republic a large majority of even the working classes had houses of their own. At present the laborer, with nothing but his wages to depend on, can neither buy a lot nor build a house. Speculative prices and the inexorable demands of an artificial civilization have placed a home of his own beyond his reach. Some way must be found to furnish better houses to laboring men, and on terms they are able to pay. It is an unhappy circumstance when the laboring and producing masses cannot have some spot of earth, and some building, however humble, that they can call home, without sitting under the shadow of a landlord. What a volume of terror there is in the word "rent," when that word means that for failure to pay it a man's family may be turned into the street. No plan of human polity is perfect, and no system of distribution just, or can endure, that does not contemplate and carry the means with it to provide homesteads for workingmen. Unhappy he, who, without fault of his own, finds all the earth built up and fenced up against him, and even the rivers dammed back to grind the grist of the few millers who have preempted their banks. Cottage homes with a spot of garden, however small, are the best, where a man can spend a little of his time in healthy exercise. Long rows of dirty tenement houses, with few and small rooms, low ceilings, bad ventilation and dilapidation, make the heart ache. If small cottages are impossible in great towns and cities, a system must be devised to place within the reach of all, homes, with at least good ventilation, decency and comfort.

The question of homes for laboring men has for some time engaged the attention of British statesmen. It has become an important question in this country. The worst usurers and Shylock's of modern times may be found among the landlords of the tenement houses of the poor, who exact enormous rents for the most wretched accommodations. In this realm the doctrine of contracts rules supreme. Everything connected with tenements or lodgings for the working classes should be regulated by statutes that cannot be invaded. Steps must be taken to aid and encourage the poorer laborers and artisans to acquire independent and comfortable homes, as far as possible under their own control and management.

It has been the purpose of the writer to point out the two great causes of the impoverishment of the working classes, the monopoly of land, and the usurious profits of accumulated capital. In those two exhausting drains the workingman's share of the wealth of the world has been lost. Not until Christianity fully pervades our business and social system, and the doctrines of charity and brotherly love it preaches are accepted, can it overthrow the dominion of selfishness, avarice, and dishonest bargains. Until it does, law "by the people and for the people" can accomplish much. It is thus in the power of the people to correct the errors of the past, and shape the avenues to the great natural resources of our country, that they may be within the reach of all: giving an equality of privilege, and an equality of opportunity. It is the duty of "Law" to prevent a monopoly of "Land" as of all other monopolies, and thus afford just remuneration and a fair field to "Labor." Let it be our policy that the workers in the state shall be the first objects of its care, and should a dense population ever drive our rulers to encourage plans of emigration, let us see that the first emigrants are the non-producing classes.

INDEX OF AUTHORITIES QUOTED AND USED IN

LABOR, LAND AND LAW.

Federalist, The.
Ferguson's History of the Roman Republic.

Gallatin, Albert, Finances of the United States.
George, Henry, Progress and Poverty.
George, Henry, Our Land and Land Policy, State and National.
Giffen's Progress of the Working Classes.
Gray, John Henry, Laws, Manners and Customs of China.
Grote's History of Greece.
Guizot's History of Civilization.

Hall & Kinney, Indian Tribes.
Hallam, Middle Ages.
Hamilton's Hedaya, Compendium of Mahometan Law.
Hansard, British Parliamentary Debates.
Hanson, William, Fallacies in Progress and Poverty.
Hardwick, Christ and other Masters.
Haydn's Dictionary of Dates.
Heren's Ancient Nations of Africa.
Helprin's Reference Book.
Hellwald's Russia in Central Asia.
Herodotus, Carey's Translation.
Hobbes' Leviathan.
Holmes' American Annals.
Hoskyns, Sir Wren, Land in England, Land in Ireland, Land in Other Lands.
Hunter, Dr., Report to the British Privy Council.
Hutton's Central Asia.

Jefferson's Works.
Jennings' Antiquities of the Jews.
Jevon's Political Economy.
Jevon's State in Relation to Labor.
Johns Hopkins' University Series.

Kames, Lord, Antiquities.
Kelley's History of Russia.
Keltie, J. Scott, Statesman's Year Book 1885.

Laveleye, Political Economy.
Laveleye, Essays on the Land Systems of Belgium and Holland.
Lavergne, Rural Economy of Great Britain.
Lawson's History North Carolina.
Lecky's History of European Morals.
Lippincott's Gazetteer of the World.
Lowman's Civil Government of the Hebrews.

Macleod, H. D., Elements of Economics.
Madison's Works.
Maine, Sir Henry Sumner, History of Early Institutions.
Maine, Sir Henry Sumner, History Early Law and Custom.
Mallock's Property and Progress.
Malthus' Principles of Population.
Maryland Journal and Baltimore Advertiser, 1773.
Marco Polo. Wright's Edition Travels.
May, Sir H., Democracy in Europe.
McIntyre, Aristocracy.
Mill, John Stuart, Principles of Political Economy.
Moody, William Goodwin's Land and Labor.
Morse's Universal Gazetteer.
Mulhall's Dictionary of Statistics for 1884.
Müller, Max, Languages of the Seat of War.
Müller, Max, Chips from a German Workshop.

Nevius' China.

Ockley's History of the Saracens.

Paine, Thomas, Rights of Man.
Parsons' Remains of Japhet.
Plutarch's Lives.
Poor's Railroad Manual.
Prescott's Ferdinand and Isabella.

Raphael, History of the Jews.
Rawlinson, George, History of Ancient Egypt.
Rawlinson, George, Ancient Monarchies.
Rawlinson, George, Seventh Monarchy.
Rawlinson, George, Ancient Civilization.
Redpath's, James, Notes on Ireland.
Reports of Commissioner of General Land Office.
Ricardo, Political Economy.
Rogers, J. E. Thorold, Six Centuries of Work and Wages.
Rogers, J. E. Thorold, Social Economy.
Rollin's Ancient History.
Rubruquis' Travels.

Shaw, Albert Icaria, A study in Communistic History.
Sinding's History of Scandinavia.
Smith's Life of Lewis Cass.
Smith, Adam, Wealth of Nations.
Spofford's American Almanac, 1885.
Stepniak's Russia under the Tzars.
Stepniak's Underground Russia.
Stone's Life of Brant.
Strabo, Geographical and Historical Works.
St. Giles' Lectures. Faiths of the World.
Sumner, Prof. Wm. Graham, What Social Classes Owe Each Other.

Taine's French Revolution.
Tenant Farmer, Short Talks about Land Tenure.
Thiers' French Revolution,
Timayeins' History of Greece.

Vambery's History of Bokhara.
Von Ranke, Universal History.

Wallace, Alfred, Land Nationalization.
Washington's Works and Letters.
Williamson's History Tuscarora War.
Williams' S. W., Middle Kingdom.
Wine's Commentaries on the Ancient Laws of the Hebrews.

Young, Arthur, Travels in Ireland.
Young, Arthur, Travels in France.
Young, Edward, Labor in Europe and America.

TRIUMPHANT DEMOCRACY;

OR,

FIFTY YEARS' MARCH OF THE REPUBLIC.

BY ANDREW CARNEGIE.

---

1 volume, 8vo, - - - - - $2.00.

Mr. Carnegie, though born in Scotland, and a firm lover of the "old home," is a thorough republican in sympathy and in practice, and a radical of the radicals in his advocacy of a government of the people, by the people, and for the people. For royalty and its surroundings he has nothing but contempt, and his comparisons of monarchical forms and observances with republican simplicity and his scathing comments will be read with interest not only here but in England. Indeed, the work may be said to be intended primarily for British readers—to open the eyes of the masses in the United Kingdom to the wonderful advancement—physical, moral, political and intellectual—of the United States during the last half century, an advancement either little understood or wilfully misrepresented in Europe. Though various causes have contributed to this unexampled rate of progress, the principal one, in Mr. Carnegie's opinion, is the fundamental fact of the equality of the citizen in the Republic. To this grand principle all nations must eventually subscribe, he argues, and the sooner it is adopted by Great Britain the better for the country and the better for the people. Its author claims that it is pure missionary work on his part, and that his sole desire in its preparation has been to show his countrymen—and to prove by solid facts and figures—the superiority of republican over monarchical institutions. This is the true inwardness of his book and of its title—"Triumphant Democracy."

**** For sale by all booksellers, or sent, post-paid, on receipt of price by*

CHARLES SCRIBNER'S SONS,

PUBLISHERS,

743 & 745 Broadway, New York.

CONTEMPORARY SOCIALISM.

BY JOHN RAE, M. A.

One volume, crown 8vo, - - - - - - $2.00.

Such a book as this which Mr. Rae has written—a thorough history and analysis by a man of singularly candid and liberal mind, equally without prejudice and fanaticism—has long been needed and earnestly wished for by every student of socialism, and in all countries. The author writes with force and eloquence, but he looks at his subject in a clear, calm spirit, and penetrates it with greater subtility than any student or writer has done before. Among his chapters are admirably historical studies of the general subject and some vivid sketches of the leaders of the great movements. In short, Mr. Rae has given us a masterly book, and it will long be read after the present Socialistic movements have become matters of history.

"A useful and ably written book."—*London Saturday Review.*

"No subject more needs thorough and impartial discussion at present than this, and the work before us by John Rae is eminently able and helpful. It is distinguished in a remarkable degree by breadth of view and the grasp of underlying and widely reaching principles, and also by his minuteness of detail and the careful relation of facts and figures in support of its position."—*The Congregationalist.*

"He is very clear in his classification, distinguishing Socialism, on the one hand, from democracy, which is essentially political, while Socialism (as the existence of one section of Socialists prove), may be unpolitical or even anti-political, and, on the other hand, from Nihilism in its various forms. His general view by way of introduction is all that could be desired, and certainly his sketches of the leaders, especially of Lasselle and Karl Marx, are marked by knowledge, insight and considerable biographical tact."—*British Quarterly Review.*

*** *For sale by all booksellers, or sent, post-paid, on receipt of price by*

CHARLES SCRIBNER'S SONS,

PUBLISHERS,

743 & 745 Broadway, New York.

A New Edition, Library Style.

The History of Rome,

FROM THE EARLIEST TIME TO THE PERIOD OF ITS DECLINE.

By Dr. THEODOR MOMMSEN.

Translated, with the author's sanction and additions, by the Rev. W. P. Dickson, Regius Professor of Biblical Criticism in the University of Glasgow, late Classical Examiner of the University of St. Andrews. With an introduction by Dr. Leonhard Schmitz, and a copious Index of the whole four volumes, prepared especially for this edition.

REPRINTED FROM THE REVISED LONDON EDITION.

Four Volumes, crown 8vo, gilt top. Price per Set, $8.00.

Dr. Mommsen has long been known and appreciated through his researches into the languages, laws, and institutions of Ancient Rome and Italy, as the most thoroughly versed scholar now living in these departments of historical investigation. To a wonderfully exact and exhaustive knowledge of these subjects, he unites great powers of generalization, a vigorous, spirited, and exceedingly graphic style and keen analytical powers, which give this history a degree of interest and a permanent value possessed by no other record of the decline and fall of the Roman Commonwealth. "Dr. Mommsen's work," as Dr. Schmitz remarks in the introduction, "though the production of a man of most profound and extensive learning and knowledge of the world, is not as much designed for the professional scholar as for intelligent readers of all classes who take an interest in the history of by-gone ages, and are inclined there to seek information that may guide them safely through the perplexing mazes of modern history."

CRITICAL NOTICES.

"A work of the very highest merit; its learning is exact and profound; its narrative full of genius and skill; its descriptions of men are admirably vivid. We wish to place on record our opinion that Dr. Mommsen's is by far the best history of the Decline and Fall of the Roman Commonwealth." — *London Times.*

"This is the best history of the Roman Republic, taking the work on the whole — the author's complete mastery of his subject, the variety of his gifts and acquirements, his graphic power in the delineation of national and individual character, and the vivid interest which he inspires in every portion of his book. He is without an equal in his own sphere." — *Edinburgh Review.*

CHARLES SCRIBNER'S SONS, Publishers,

743 and 745 Broadway, New York.

www.ingramcontent.com/pod-product-compliance
Lightning Source LLC
Chambersburg PA
CBHW021842290326
41932CB00064B/349
* 9 7 8 3 7 4 4 6 6 6 3 4 3 *